RURAL HOUSES OF WEST YORKSHIRE, 1400–1830

Frontispiece [196] Wood Lane Hall, Sowerby, 1649; the open hall.

WEST YORKSHIRE METROPOLITAN COUNTY COUNCIL
ROYAL COMMISSION ON THE HISTORICAL MONUMENTS
OF ENGLAND

Supplementary Series: 8

Rural Houses of West Yorkshire, 1400-1830

LONDON · HER MAJESTY'S STATIONERY OFFICE

ISBN 0 11 701194 0

PUBLICATIONS IN THE SUPPLEMENTARY SERIES OF THE
ROYAL COMMISSION ON THE HISTORICAL MONUMENTS OF ENGLAND:

1. **Liverpool Road Station, Manchester: an historical and architectural survey**
(Manchester University Press, 1980)

2. **Northamptonshire: an archaeological atlas** (RCHM, 1980)

3. **Early Industrial Housing: the Trinity area of Frome** (HMSO, 1981)

4. **Beverley: an archaeological and architectural study** (HMSO, 1982)

5. **Pottery Kilns of Roman Britain** (HMSO, 1984)

6. **Danebury: An Iron Age Hill Fort** (RCHM, 1984)

7. **Liverpool's Historic Waterfront** (HMSO, 1984)

9. **Workers' Housing in West Yorkshire 1750–1920** (HMSO, 1985)

10. **Rural Houses of the Lancashire Pennines 1560–1760** (HMSO, 1985)

This publication has been assisted by a grant from West Yorkshire Metropolitan County Council.

Printed for Her Majesty's Stationery Office by Baker Bros (Litho) Ltd.
Dd 736279   C20   1/86

TABLE OF CONTENTS

LIST OF ILLUSTRATIONS

PLATES

PREFACE

The architectural wealth of West Yorkshire has long been recognized but is not fully reflected in published material. The threat to much of this wealth, as much from rapid development as from economic decline, has been keenly felt in this century, and many monuments have vanished with little record. When, therefore, the newly created Archaeology Unit of the West Yorkshire Metropolitan County Council approached the Royal Commission about possible co-operation between the two bodies, the idea of a joint survey of domestic building quickly developed. This publication is the fruit of a co-operation which has worked greatly to the advantage of both parties.

The joint approach to the subject and the resources for the survey – one investigator and a draughtsman working in the field for a period of three years – dictated that publication should not be in the form of a traditional Commission inventory. Instead, the aim has been to record a selection of houses illustrating the evolution of domestic architecture over a long period, and to present in published form a text explaining this development, together with appropriate illustrations and a select inventory. The houses are the source material for a discussion which brings out West Yorkshire's special character but also highlights the great variety of building to be found within the county. This variety is the product of important social and economic differences, differences still evident, albeit to a lesser degree, even today. The concern of the volume, therefore, is as much that of the development of society as it is that of architectural form, the assumption being that houses can tell us much of value about the process of social and economic change. Thus the work shares many of the themes of another publication in the Commission's Supplementary Series, *Rural Houses of the Lancashire Pennines*, by Sarah Pearson, which takes a smaller area for more detailed examination. Commissioners have been involved at all stages during the preparation of the volume but the views expressed are those of the author Colum Giles.

The Commissioners and the members of the County Council wish to express their thanks both to Mr. Giles and to all concerned in the production of this volume, in particular to the owners and occupiers of the houses recorded in the course of the survey. They are also appreciative of the experience and advice brought to bear by Mr. Eric Mercer, O.B.E., who has seen the project through to conclusion after his retirement from the Royal Commission. Finally, this volume bears witness to the value of co-operation; working together, the Royal Commission and the County Council have joined in a work which has offered both parties new opportunities and it is hoped that the public will benefit from this sharing of skills and resources.

JOHN M. SULLY
Chairman, Recreation and Arts Committee
West Yorkshire Metropolitan County Council

P.J. FOWLER
Secretary, Royal Commission on the Historical
Monuments of England

EDITORIAL NOTES

The figures in brackets which follow the names of buildings mentioned in the text refer to the numbering in the Inventory. Some buildings not mentioned in the Inventory, and which therefore lack a serial number, are either mentioned in the text or illustrated: some, like Ovenden Hall, Ovenden (Plate 45), were recorded in the course of the survey; others, like New Hall, Pontefract (Fig. 24), are known from other sources. Throughout the text, a building is identified by its ancient township; the modern civil parish in which it lies is noted in the Inventory.

All plans are at ground-floor level and are reproduced at the scale of 1:300; all sections and elevations, except that of Sharlston Hall, are at 1:150. Where phases are distinct and certain, they are indicated by hatching and outline, up to a maximum of three phases. Where they are more complex or uncertain, the plan may show a single phase, as on Fig. 141. On some plans and sections some later detail has been omitted. Room names are shown when their functions are clear. The names used are those employed in the probate inventories. In a few cases houses can be matched with inventories: the plans are then marked with the precise room names or with abbreviated versions of these; in the latter instance the full names are generally given in the Inventory description. The identification of some rooms, for example the many parlours and service rooms of a gentry house, can rarely be precise, and the plans show an interpretation of the evidence of house and document.

ABBREVIATIONS OF ROOM NAMES USED ON PLANS

B	Buttery	H	Hall	P	Parlour	Sc	Scullery
C	Cellar	Hb	Housebody	Pr	Privy	St	Stair
D	Dairy	K	Kitchen	R	Reception room		
DR	Dining Room	M	Milkhouse	S	Shop		

SOURCES

Probate inventories have a direct relevance to work of this nature, and the author was fortunate to be able to draw upon the sample selected by Dr. P. W. Lock and gathered for use in the Survey of West Yorkshire in the Post-medieval period. Modern West Yorkshire lay in the deaneries of Craven, Doncaster, Old and New Ainsty, and Pontefract, the last covering much the greatest part of the county, including the important textile-producing areas of Halifax and Bradford and a contrasting lowland area with the towns of Pontefract and Wakefield (for a map of the deanery, see Thornes 1981, 8). Inventories survive in bulk only for the period after 1688, and it was decided to concentrate on the deanery of Pontefract and to include all inventories from its West Yorkshire part from every fourth year in two periods. The years studied were 1689, 1693, 1697, 1701 and 1705 in the earlier period, and 1721, 1725, 1728, 1734 and 1738 in the later. This produced a sample of nearly 1100 inventories giving the data for the statistical analyses included both in the published survey (Thornes 1981) and in the present work. In addition, other inventories have been used where they relate to identifiable houses, but were not used in the statistical analyses. All the inventories, unless otherwise stated, are from the deanery of Pontefract and are held in the Exchequer Probate Records by the Borthwick Institute of Historical Research, University of York (henceforth referred to in notes as 'BIHR'). The date of an inventory given here is that of its proving in the ecclesiastical courts, not that of its compilation; this system preserves the means of identification employed by the Borthwick Institute. Many other documents used in this survey are held by the West Yorkshire Archives Service (WYAS).

ACKNOWLEDGEMENTS

It is a great pleasure to recognize the help which many people have given in the course of the West Yorkshire survey and in the production of this volume. Thanks must be recorded first to those responsible for the initiation of the survey, and especially to Philip Mayes, then County Archaeologist, whose brain-child it was, and to Robin McDowall and Eric Mercer, who recommended to the Commissioners participation in what was then a new venture for the Royal Commission and who were a constant support during the first years of the survey. Peter Fowler, Mr. McDowall's successor as Secretary, has maintained that support and has been a constructive critic throughout. The smooth running of the project was in large part due to the efforts of the administrative staff both of the Commission's London office and of the County Council's Division of Recreation and Arts; my thanks go to them for all their work.

No survey of this kind is possible without the help and advice of, and exchange of ideas with, a host of people, unfortunately too numerous to list. However, thanks must be recorded to Stephen Moorhouse and David Michelmore of the West Yorkshire Metropolitan County Council's Archaeology Unit; to Peter Lock and Robin Thornes, successive Post-medieval historians at that Unit; to Arthur Saul of the Bradford Metropolitan District Council Planning Department; to Val Hall and Stephen Whittle, who both gave a great deal of valued and voluntary assistance; to George Redmonds, Adrian Siswick, Peter Thornborow; and to Barry Harrison, who, through his own research and his work in organizing conferences, must take a great deal of credit for the awakening of historical interest in the vernacular buildings of Yorkshire. The staff of many archive offices and libraries have given much help; in particular I would like to thank Dr David Smith and the staff of the Borthwick Institute of Historical Research, University of York, Mrs Sylvia Thomas and the staff of the Yorkshire Archaeological Society, and the Director and staff of the Brotherton Library, University of Leeds.

The appearance of this volume is the responsibility of a number of people. I have been greatly helped by Philip Swann and Jon Prudhoe, draughtsmen at the Archaeology Unit; both have produced excellent work, often in difficult conditions. Jon Prudhoe prepared the final drawings, the merits of which are due entirely to him and any failings entirely to me. The photographs are the work of Terry Buchanan and his team of photographers (Tony Perry, Bob Skingle and Peter Williams) based at the Royal Commission office in York, and their quality adds much to the attractiveness of the volume. The organisation of the material into book form is the work of Ronald Butler, whom I would like to thank for guiding it through the editorial processes.

I owe a great debt to my colleagues on the Commission staff. Christopher Stell has allowed me to use his work on the upper Calder valley and has given much useful advice. Nicholas Cooper and Sylvia Collier have offered constructive criticism of the text and have shared their knowledge of buildings over a wide area of the country. Sarah Pearson's work on a similar project in Lancashire has meant that we have shared many of the same problems and preoccupations, and has allowed me to draw heavily on her for advice, ideas and criticism. She has never failed me, and her contribution to this volume through her constructive comments on my text is large indeed. Finally, it is very pleasing to record the debt of gratitude which I owe to Eric Mercer: he was instrumental in setting up the survey and in establishing what type of survey it was to be, and through discussion he has imparted something of his vision of the goal of studies of this kind. No author has been better served by a critic, for the content of the text and the arguments therein have benefited immeasurably from his unfailingly astute scrutiny and from his understanding of the development of domestic building. Any good things in this volume owe much to him.

In conclusion I must thank those but for whose help this work could not have been written, that is the owners and occupiers of the houses. People from all walks of life have welcomed me, have allowed me free access to their homes, and have shown a wide degree of awareness of the interest of the buildings in which they live. I hope that this volume is some return for all the time which they have given me and that it will contribute to a more general appreciation of the wealth of the county's architectural heritage.

COLUM GILES

RURAL HOUSES OF WEST YORKSHIRE, 1400–1830

INTRODUCTION

Houses have been studied for many purposes and their evidence has been used in different ways according to particular interests. This volume employs the house primarily as evidence for the evolution of rural society in the late and post-medieval periods, that is, as a valid historical source which can throw new light on old problems and suggest conclusions which more conventional documentary sources fail to illumine. The assumptions underlying this work are that the numbers of surviving historical houses in an area reflect the wealth of certain classes at the time of building, and that the size and form of a house often corresponds closely to the wealth and status of its builder. The presence or absence of historical houses in an area, or the presence there of an unusually high proportion of large or small houses, are, therefore, taken to be significant indicators of social and economic conditions, and the identification of major variations allows new questions to be formulated regarding the development of rural society.

Domestic building of the period 1400 to the early 19th century in West Yorkshire is the subject of this study. The earlier limit is determined by surviving remains, for little of pre-1400 date stands today. The later limit has less validity since it obviously marks no terminus in domestic building. However, by the early 19th century, the character of the county was changing rapidly; towns were growing quickly and industrial expansion was radically changing the economy. After 1830, much new housing was for emergent classes in newly-created urban centres, the outcome of forces that had scarcely existed in the earlier period. A rather different approach to the study of this later housing is required, and such a study has been made by Lucy Caffyn and will be published by the Royal Commission.

West Yorkshire is the product of the local government re-organisation of 1974, and its boundaries have no historical significance. It is not a large county, being some 40 miles from west to east and 25 from north to south. The modern county includes the major textile towns of Halifax, Huddersfield, Bradford and Leeds, and the county town of Wakefield (Map 1).

Its dominantly industrial and urban character is largely the product of the 19th century. Before c.1800, although the textile industry was of great significance in both the local and the national economy, the county had a rural character. The principal occupation over much of the county was agriculture, and industry was organised on a modest scale and generally in a rural setting. Agricultural conditions varied according to the terrain. The land is high in the west, where the gritstone hills form part of the Pennine chain. The central part of the county overlies the coal measures and provides good agricultural land, and the low-lying east, which includes the limestone belt, is used today for arable farming. The backcloth to this volume, therefore, is that of a rural area, in parts dependent on agriculture but in other parts practising a mixed economy in which industry played an important role.

This volume has two major but linked themes. The first, an indirect result of the variety of natural conditions within the county, is an investigation into the diversity of the building pattern in West Yorkshire. Different areas show very different patterns of building; no area of similar size in the north of England can rival the splendours of the upper Calder valley, but this wealth is not uniform throughout the county. Regional diversity is matched by social diversity, the second major theme. In some parts of the county, men of many different ranks were able to build permanently in our period, but in other areas and at certain times society was dominated by a particular group, either the gentry or the yeomanry. The identification of building zones and of who was building, and in what form, will, therefore, be the principal preoccupation of this study. Much is already known of the development of the county in the Middle Ages and the post-medieval period, for West Yorkshire has been well served by historians and antiquarians, but the study of surviving houses has the virtue of presenting this development on a broad canvas using, if certain assumptions regarding the reliability of the evidence are accepted, a single consistent source.

The method of investigation was not as scientifically sound as that permitted by some more conventional or statistical sources. First, houses surviving today are to some extent a random sample of those built in our period, and one may never be absolutely certain that important groups

Map 1 West Yorkshire; relief, drainage and principal towns.

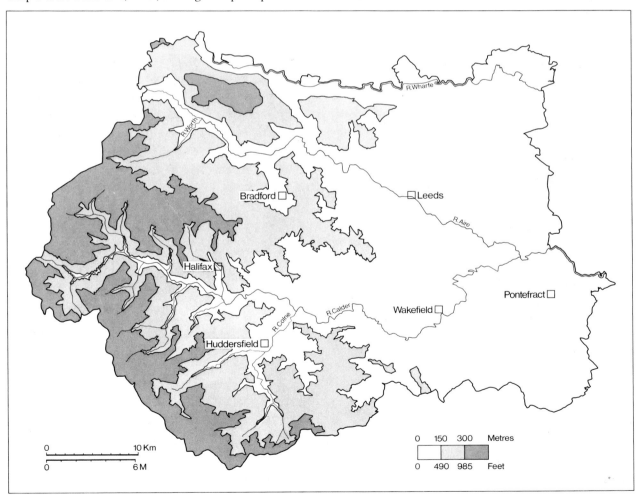

of houses have not been demolished with neither trace nor record. However, the likelihood is that, except in cases of wholesale destruction through special circumstances, like urban or industrial expansion, similar forces applied reasonably consistently throughout the area and that the present pattern of houses is a tolerably accurate reflection of building activity in an earlier period. This accepted, it remains to establish that the buildings recorded in the course of the survey are a representative sample, in terms of date, social status, area and so forth, of all surviving historical houses. In practice, of course, this is impossible to ascertain without a knowledge of the existence of all relevant buildings. Furthermore, different types of house merit different degrees of attention. Medieval houses, for example, figure far more prominently in this volume than their numbers alone warrant, but it is their historical importance which justifies the attention given both to recording and analysing them. If numbers alone were the criteria for inclusion in the sample, the study would be dominated by late and small houses, and the potential for historical investigation offered by earlier and larger ones would be largely neglected. The sample of houses recorded, therefore, was based not upon statistics, which were in any case lacking, but upon the need to take into account and illustrate the major developments in domestic building in a county of great diversity.

Many fine and important buildings were not recorded, and many subjective decisions were taken in the choice of which houses to record, but it is hoped that observation in the field allowed a reasonable assessment of the range of material to be covered. Recording was undertaken on a strictly selective basis except in a very few townships where efforts were made to note all relevant buildings. This quite deliberate approach is a departure from what has hitherto been usual Commission practice. Much work remains to be done before the development of housing and of the society which erected the houses is fully understood. Detailed local studies will complement and refine the general picture presented in this volume, and it is to be hoped that documentary historians take account of the evidence of the houses in their assessments of the forces producing change. The value of the house as a historical source lies not in a capacity to produce a precise and clear sequence of events but in the way that it illustrates broad social and economic changes, for buildings are the visible effect of developments which may move slowly but which determine the nature of society.

CHAPTER 1

THE HOUSES OF THE MEDIEVAL GENTRY, 1400–1550.

Within West Yorkshire, medieval houses of sufficient quality to permit survival into the 20th century were erected only by the upper strata of society, the nobility and gentry, whose houses are scattered thinly but widely over much of the county, and by small numbers of wealthy yeomen, whose houses are concentrated in one small area.[1] Many medieval houses have been demolished, and all the survivors have been subjected to later alterations and to the destruction of much of their original detail, but enough remains to demonstrate the evolution of the different types of house adopted by each social level.

The work of historians and antiquarians has established the distribution of noble and gentry families within West Yorkshire, and the survival of medieval houses in some of these locations allows the principal characteristics of the buildings of these classes to be identified. A combination of documentary research and fieldwork demonstrates that the gentry built houses of a certain type, but it is not clear that the 'gentry-type' house was built exclusively by families of gentry status. Some houses, for example, Lees Hall, Thornhill, may have been erected by families outside the ranks of the gentry, even though these families may later have achieved recognition. In the case of the Nettletons of Lees Hall, the construction of a gentry-type house was perhaps intended as a signal to the world that the family, clothiers from Huddersfield, considered that it had crossed the ill-defined boundary between classes, and certainly by the early 17th century the Nettletons were regarded as gentry. These possible exceptions, however, are not numerous enough to undermine the general correspondence between house-type and social status.

THE HOUSES OF THE MAJOR GENTRY AND THE NOBILITY IN THE EARLY MIDDLE AGES

Most of the medieval gentry houses which survive in West Yorkshire as standing structures date from after 1400, but enough is known of earlier houses to show that all the principal types of early-medieval gentry and aristocratic domestic buildings were present before then, albeit in small numbers. The scarcity is not simply a result of later destruction; doubtless some large and early houses have been destroyed without trace or record, but, since these houses were built by magnates and major gentry, it is likely that they were never as common as the later houses of the lesser gentry were to become.

Some documentary evidence suggests, but by no means proves, the existence in West Yorkshire of the type of complex which was a loose collection of buildings, many perhaps of different dates and added as new needs arose.[2] A document of 1341 describes the manorial residence in Rothwell as:

> . . . a certain manor house, hall, chapel, chambers, kitchen, bakehouse, brewery, barn, oxstalls, stables, and other houses necessary for the residence of the lord, built and enclosed within stone walls.

Another document, of 1358, listed a hall, diverse chambers, kitchen, barn and so forth, in the manorial complex at Calverley.[3] The documents are ambiguous, but their wording leaves open the possibility that within West Yorkshire in the 14th century there existed some manor houses which comprised discrete elements rather than a single dominant block supplemented by non-domestic detached buildings.

Pre-1400 secular buildings in West Yorkshire, either surviving as standing fragments or recovered by excavation, are of three types; the fortified house or tower house, the aisled hall, and the first-floor hall. The tower at Bolling Hall, Bowling, was part of the manor house of the Bolling family, which held land in five townships around Bradford by the end of the 14th century.[4] Harewood Castle, Harewood, hardly a house with serious defensive pretensions despite its tower-like form, was built by Sir William Aldburgh *c.*1366.[5] Aisled halls have been found at Kirkstall Abbey, at Sandal Castle, and at Old Hall, Elland; that at Kirkstall, dating from the early 13th century, was part of the guest house complex; that at Sandal, of the 12th century, was the main structure in the fortress of the earl of Warenne; and at Old Hall, Elland, where a 13th-century aisled hall overlay one of the 12th century, the house was the seat of the powerful Eland family.[6] The first-floor hall at the Moot Hall, Dewsbury, was part of the complex of buildings of the rectory manor, and the Old Hall, Thorpe Stapleton, possibly a first-floor hall with solar tower attached, was the seat of the Scargills, a prominent local family.[7]

These three types of early-medieval domestic building within West Yorkshire have, of course, a wide distribution outside the county. Tower houses are found in castles, and sometimes comprise castles in themselves, and both the aisled hall and the first-floor hall were the principal structures in royal and episcopal palaces and in the manor houses of the wealthy gentry.[8] West Yorkshire here follows the national trend because the people who caused the houses to be built belonged to classes which acted on a national or at least a regional stage. As a result, the buildings lack specifically local character. Such character begins to emerge only after 1400, when gentry of lesser rank, having little influence beyond their immediate neighbourhood, began to build houses of sufficient substance to last until the present day.

THE DEVELOPMENT OF THE GENTRY HOUSE IN THE LATER MIDDLE AGES

In the study of the later Middle Ages, the attention of the architectural historian shifts from the nobility and major gentry to the gentry of lesser means. This is partly due to the fact that few great houses were built within West Yorkshire in the period 1400 to 1550, for many of the most powerful families had already provided themselves with permanent seats before 1400. Largely, however, the change of focus is an acknowledgement of this first appearance of permanent building by a relatively numerous middling and lesser gentry. There are important differences between, on the one hand, the houses of these groups and, on the other hand, firstly, the earlier houses of the nobility and greater gentry, and, secondly, those few houses erected by the nobility and greater gentry in the same period. There is also, however, considerable diversity of size and form even within the group of lesser houses, and the architectural evidence emphasises that it would be a mistake to think of the gentry as a homogeneous class.

Quite when the lesser gentry began to build is a question which, in the present state of knowledge, can be answered only by hypothesis built upon slender evidence. Only two houses have yielded suitable timbers for dendrochronological testing, but these can be supplemented by documentary evidence relating to two further houses. Some houses, however, show a development towards a standard form, and the presumed sequence of building can help to illumine the question of dating. Lastly, enough is known of the economic conditions of the period to suggest which times were the most and the least propitious for building activity. The two houses dated by dendrochronology are not entirely typical of the fully-developed gentry house, and so it is not clear how closely the dates of Horbury Hall, Horbury (92), and Calverley Hall, Calverley with Farsley (41), represent the group as a whole. At both houses a hall range was added to an earlier wing in the last two decades of the 15th century to give a 'T' or 'L' plan. A similar date can be applied to New Hall, Elland cum Greetland (54), for a document implies that it was built *c.*1490; unlike Horbury Hall and Calverley Hall, New Hall was a fully developed hall-and-cross-wings house. The timber-framed part of Rothwell Manor can be dated with greater precision, for the manor was leased in 1487 on condition that major additions were made to the earlier house.[9] This evidence suggests that the late 15th century was a time of some building activity which, where entirely new houses were concerned, would result in an 'H' plan, and where earlier builds complicated the picture might produce something else. Given the clear development towards a standardised 'H' plan, houses which show an evolution towards that form may be regarded as earlier, at least typologically, than houses erected in a single build as a hall-and-cross-wings dwelling. A similar argument may be derived from the structural forms employed in the houses. The king-post truss was to supersede all other types of truss in most parts of the county to become the standard roof-type by the late Middle Ages. Even though all king-post trusses are not late, other forms, for example the crown-post, may be tentatively dated to a period before conformity to a single type had been established. Sharlston Hall, Sharlston (176) demonstrates both arguments; it became a hall-and-cross-wings house in three stages, and the king-post was first employed here only in a fourth phase of building. Thus on two counts, the house may be regarded as one of the earliest standing buildings in the county.

Other evidence lends weight to the thesis that most of the gentry houses under review were built between 1400 and 1550, and especially in the second half of that period. The rebuilding or remodelling of very many of the county's parish churches in the 15th century indicates that for the church at least this was a time of prosperity.[10] Recent historical research has demonstrated that the century after 1450 was marked by quickening economic activity, in which the gentry played an important part, and the establishment of the Tudor dynasty after 1485 brought more settled conditions to the area. Clearly the gentry invested some of their new wealth in building, but our lack of knowledge both of the short-term fluctuations of the late-medieval economy in this area and of the precise date of the houses makes it impossible to confirm or refute a close correspondence between building activity and the state of the economy.[11] General guidelines will serve for present purposes however, and it is enough to suggest that a pre-1400 economy recovering from depression was less likely to produce numbers of substantial gentry houses than a period of overall prosperity such as characterised the 15th and 16th centuries. The building of gentry houses continued after 1550, of course, but the form of those houses differed in many important respects from those houses which can be regarded as medieval.

THE EVOLUTION OF THE
HALL-AND-CROSS-WINGS PLAN

By the late 15th century, the lesser gentry of West Yorkshire had adopted a standard form of house which had a hall range flanked by storeyed cross-wings, giving an 'H' plan.[12] Some houses show stages in the evolution of this finished form, but the origins of the development lie with the earliest buildings within the county, those of the greater gentry and the aristocracy of the early Middle Ages, which, as is to be expected, have much in common with contemporary dwellings over a large part of England.

None of the structures discussed earlier is likely to have attained a full 'H' plan before 1400, but the guest house at Kirkstall Abbey gives the first known evidence of a departure from a simpler linear form. The 13th-century block had a double-aisled hall with a storeyed solar wing at one end and a service area at the other. The nature of the roofing at the service end cannot be established, but it is clear that, to give sufficient headroom, the solar end must have been roofed as a cross-wing even if it did not project on plan as later wings were commonly to do. The desire for expanded accommodation was expressed similarly at Old Hall, Elland, in the 13th century when a storeyed cross-wing, providing a first-floor solar decorated by a crown-post roof, was added at this time to the earlier aisled hall range.

Early houses of lesser status also show the use of a single cross-wing. At Calverley Hall (41; Plate 1), there survives, and at Horbury Hall (92; Fig. 1), there may be inferred, a wing, to which was added a later hall range whose form was in part dictated by the presence of the wing. At both houses the cross-wing was large, of four bays at Calverley

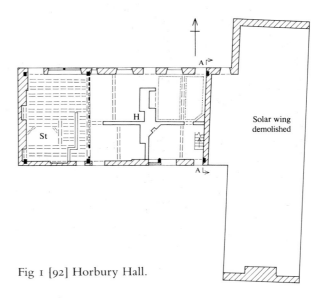

Fig 1 [92] Horbury Hall.

Plate 1 [41] Calverley Hall, from the SE, showing early solar, cased in stone in the 17th cent., flanked by hall and chapel wing, c.1485.

Plate 2 [176] Sharlston Hall, south front; the early hall lies to left of porch.

and possibly as many as five at Horbury. It is likely that the wings at these two houses were of such size because they were designed to provide at once superior rooms – solar and, at Calverley, parlour – and also service rooms, elements which were commonly separated to some extent in houses with two wings. The early 15th century form of the two houses, probably a hall range divided by a through-passage from a single large dual-purpose cross-wing, closely resembles earlier houses such as Chorley Hall, Cheshire, and the domestic block at Chepstow Castle, Monmouthshire, showing that the developments affecting the houses of the greater gentry and nobility in the 13th and 14th centuries over a wide area of the country were being paralled in the houses of West Yorkshire gentry of middling status in the later Middle Ages.[13]

It is not clear when the first 'H' plan house was built *ab novo* in West Yorkshire. This plan had become common in

superior houses of other parts of the country, perhaps by the 14th century but certainly by the 15th century.[14] Of the greater gentry houses of West Yorkshire, the 15th-century Thornhill Hall, seat of the powerful Savile family, was certainly built with one cross-wing, fragments of which remain today, and an early estate map shows that a second wing may have been an original feature.[15] At Methley Hall (128), built probably in the 1420s, later work and ultimate demolition make it impossible to be certain of the original plan, but it is conceivable that there were both upper and lower wings originally.

The houses of the lesser gentry show that at this social level the 'H' plan was developed in the course of the 15th century. Sharlston Hall (176) (Plate 2 and Fig. 2) was built in the first half of that century as a linear house, but by the end of the century both linear ends had been replaced by storeyed cross-wings. The same development is evident at

Fig 2 [176] Sharlston Hall, long section.

Plate 3 [26] Kiddal Hall, Barwick in Elmet; main front, with early hall flanked by later cross wings (*Copyright, Yorkshire Archaeological Society*).

Kiddal Hall, Barwick in Elmet (26; Plate 3) where the hall range, built of stone in the first half of the 15th century, was flanked by timber-framed cross-wings, probably of late 15th century date. These two houses show that the

Plate 4 [54] New Hall, Elland cum Greetland, the north front.

same evolution from a linear plan to one with two cross-wings because both originated early in the 15th century and because a linear plan was clearly felt to be inadequate after 1450. Later houses attained a fully-developed hall-and-cross-wings plan in a single build; New Hall, Elland (Plate 4 and Fig. 3) was built *c.*1490 in this form; Shibden Hall, Southowram, is of much the same date; and later examples include Rawthorpe Old Hall, Dalton (48) (Plate 5) of the early 16th century, and Chadwick Hall, Mirfield (139) of *c.*1550. Gentry houses of a slightly higher status which did not have a 'H' plan by the late-15th century owed their eccentricity to their earlier development. As we have seen, at both Calverley Hall and Horbury Hall the early phases of building included the provision of a large wing providing both services and solar, and when the houses were re-modelled in the late 15th century, the existence of this dual-purpose wing obviated the need for a second wing. Accommodation at the other end of the hall was restricted at Horbury to a linear bay, and it is possible that at Calverley there was nothing beyond the far end of the hall.

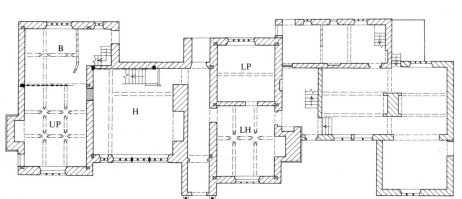

Fig 3 [54] New Hall, Elland cum Greetland.

Plate 5 [48] Rawthorpe Old Hall, Dalton.

The development of a standardised 'H' plan reflects two related currents in the society of the age, currents which affected the workings of the gentry household and which therefore had a direct bearing on the type of dwelling required at this social level. Mark Girouard expressed this idea succinctly when he described the late-medieval house as the result of two contrary forces, one centripetal, the other centrifugal.[16] Just at the time when the diverse elements of the earlier dwellings – hall, chambers, service rooms and so forth – were coalescing into a single block, the constituent parts of the household were drawing apart,

Plate 6 [207] Lees Hall, Thornhill; the hall.

each to be provided with more specialist accommodation according to status and function. The late Middle Ages saw subtle shifts in the role demanded of the rooms within the house, and the changing demands can be seen as the mainspring behind the evolution of plan.

The open hall was the hub of all the gentry houses under review. Usually the largest single room, and always the most impressive by virtue of its height, the open hall played a central role in the workings of the house. Its importance is demonstrated by a number of points. Firstly, it lay at the heart of the dwelling, and all visitors went directly to it either to be received there or to be taken on to more private apartments (Plates 6, 7). Secondly, its fittings reveal something of its role; it was a heated room, in some houses perhaps the only heated room.[17] Often, also, the open hall had a canopy over the dais end, emphasising the ceremonial nature of the room. Thirdly, the decoration of the hall, even if it might not be lavish in comparison with that in some of the splendid medieval halls in other parts of England, was generally the best in the house, showing that the room was designed to be an impressive area with a dominant role in the workings of the house. The nature of the hall will be examined in greater detail at a later point, but for present purposes it is sufficient to establish its importance as a reception area and as the place where the owner's status and wealth were publicly displayed.

Plate 7 [60] Woodsome Hall, Farnley Tyas; the hall.

By the 15th century, however, the hall was not, and had not been for centuries, the only superior room in the dwellings of the gentry. Langland complained that 'the rich (have) a rule to eat by themselves in a privy parlour, or in a chamber with a chimney, and leave the chief hall, that was made for meals, for men to eat in'.[18] This increased segregation within the household is expressed in the development of the two rooms named by Langland, that is, the parlour and the chamber, or solar, and the growth in their importance may be seen as one of the principal influences underlying the evolution of the gentry house from a linear plan to one with two cross-wings. Langland was writing of the nobility of the later 14th century, but the surviving houses of West Yorkshire reveal that similar changes were affecting the provincial gentry in the next century.

The solar occupied all or part of the first floor of one of the wings, usually that beyond the upper end of the hall. Some of the earliest houses within the county demonstrate the importance of the room in the Middle Ages. At Calverley Hall, the solar was heated and was of four bays, and at Sharlston Hall it was of three bays. The status of the room was sometimes emphasised by a decorative roof. In houses where the solar was large or elaborate, the room was clearly superior in its use, acting probably as a humbler version of the solar in a great house, that is, as a dining room for the head of the household and his chief guests, as a sitting and withdrawing room, and as the best bedchamber.[19]

There are signs that the importance of the solar or great chamber was not acknowledged in the late-15th century, at least in the houses of the minor gentry. Some, like New Hall, Elland (54), lack a single dominant chamber. Instead, the first floor of the wings is made up of a number of rooms of more equal status, undistinguished by any elaborate decorative work, although one room, usually the main chamber in the upper wing, might be heated. These chambers are likely to have had a less dominant role than the solar, probably lacking some of the ceremonial and public character of that room.

The restricted use of the solar in some of the late-medieval houses is partly a sign of the less sophisticated nature of the houses of the minor gentry and partly of the late date of many of these houses. It is conspicuous that the larger and earlier houses like Calverley Hall had a solar of high quality, and that smaller and later houses like New Hall might lack such a room. The diminished role of the solar in later houses is connected with the development of the parlour, a room which duplicated some of the functions and character of the solar but which lay on the ground floor beyond the upper end of the hall. Evidence for the use of the parlour in lesser gentry houses in the late Middle Ages is not abundant, but later documentary evidence and the fact that the main parlour was often heated, as at New Hall and Shibden Hall, Southowram, indicate that the room probably acted as the best bedroom, as a superior dining room, and as a withdrawing room; its functions, therefore were those of the solar in earlier and superior houses. Houses might, of course, have both solar and parlour; the early wing at Calverley Hall has, beneath the solar, a parlour decorated with richly-moulded ceiling beams, and Lees Hall, Thornhill (207), the upper wing gives a large

solar or great chamber over two ground-floor rooms, one of which is a parlour.

A house might only have one solar or great chamber, but it could have a number of parlours. At New Hall, Elland, the lower wing has two rooms, the larger of which, on the main front of the house, is too big for a service room and may have been heated from an early date; it is likely, therefore, that it is a lower parlour. The rebuilding of Chevet Hall in the first quarter of the 16th century provided four parlours, at least one of which was heated; one of these was used for dining and another as the private quarters of the son and heir.[20] At Woodsome Hall, Farnley Tyas (60), Arthur Kaye (d. 1574) had a heated low parlour, and there was a heated upper parlour as well, for Arthur's son John 'made new the pipe of the upp(er) p(ar)lour chymnay' in 1574. In 1569, John 'selyd his Dynyng p(ar)lar, cast out A Fayre wyndoo in yt, Bordyd yt', and ten years later made two further parlours out of another part of the house 'for lakk of Rowme'.[21] Not all of these parlours were high-quality rooms, but clearly some at least were heated and some had a superior function. The role of the parlour remained very general for a long time to come, but it was common to use the better rooms both as bedrooms and for eating and sitting.

The later Middle Ages was, therefore, a time of changing emphasis in the status and functions of the three main rooms – hall, solar, and parlour – within the gentry house. The problem for prospective builders was how to combine all three within a compact and workable plan. One constant was the position of the hall; this was always at the centre of the house, with other rooms grouped around it. The early open halls within West Yorkshire are very low; at Sharlston Hall (176), the walls of the room are only some 12 feet high (c. 4 metres), and at Kiddal Hall (26), the walls were only a little higher. There is no means of telling whether these two houses were representative of early, that is, pre-1450, open halls, but if they were it is clear that a simple linear arrangement of an open hall flanked by storeyed end-bays could not provide adequate space; the low eaves-line of the range would give rooms of extremely cramped proportions in those parts which were storeyed. If the solar was to have its status expressed visibly, a higher eaves line was required, and the best way of achieving this was to build a cross-wing. Thus at Sharlston and at Kiddal, the early low hall is flanked by later and higher cross-wings, the upper one of which provided a first-floor solar and a ground-floor parlour. Houses built in a single phase on an 'H' plan reveal the same difference between the height of the hall range and of the wings; at both New Hall (54) and Woodsome Hall (60; Fig. 4), the wall-plates of the wings are set some 2 feet higher than those of the hall range. Even though the hall at both these houses was higher than that at Sharlston and Kiddal, it was clearly still felt that justice could only be done to the parlour and solar by the provision of yet loftier wings able to give rooms of good proportions on two floors.

The desire to have an imposing solar and, later, the need to provide parlours may lie, therefore, at the root of the development of the cross-wing. The common provision of two cross-wings when a single wing could give a solar and a parlour is to be explained by the need for more than one parlour in the houses of the gentry in the late Middle Ages.

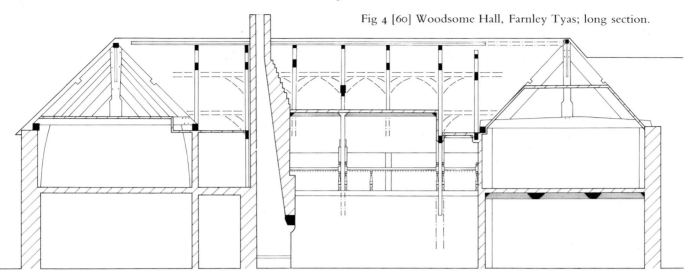

Fig 4 [60] Woodsome Hall, Farnley Tyas; long section.

The proliferation of parlours at Chevet and at Woodsome Hall in the 16th century has been noted, and even lesser families than the Neviles and the Kayes chose to have more than one parlour, as the plan of New Hall (54) indicates. The increasingly sophisticated demands of even quite modest gentry families meant that more parlours were needed as private rooms and bedrooms, and rather than set all these rooms in a single upper wing the common solution to problems of planning was to provide a lower wing. The result was a balanced plan which acknowledged a nice sense of priorities; the hall was in the centre, giving access directly or indirectly to all the main rooms of the house, the solar or great chamber was contained in a lofty wing, and the parlours opened off the hall to give private withdrawing rooms.

One result of this development of the plan is the creation of an elaborate elevation with gabled wings flanking the hall. It is difficult to assess the importance of aesthetic considerations to the builders of the houses, but the desire for a show front may have contributed in part as cause to the evolution of the 'H'-plan house. This type gave a sense of composition and display to the facade in a way that the linear plan could not match. The prestige of the cross-wing was to be cherished by the West Yorkshire gentry until late in the 17th century, when the form was to be expressed only in the gabled elevation of an otherwise flat facade. Something of the impression created by the use of gabled wings can still be seen at New Hall (54) and at Lees Hall (207; Plate 8); at the latter the framing of the wing, with its lozenge effect, may be termed decorative, even if it seems

Plate 8 [207] Lees Hall, Thornhill; decorative framing in upper wing.

erected by the Lancashire gentry of much the same period. The explanation advanced for the evolution of the 'H'-plan house, as originating in the need to provide a lofty solar and a number of parlours, has concentrated exclusively upon the evidence drawn from the houses of West Yorkshire. It would be a mistake, however, to suggest that the evolution of the plan in West Yorkshire was an entirely independent process, for it was to some extent at least a matter of imitation of a form already known elsewhere. The earlier development of the 'H'-plan house has been charted over a wide area of the country, and study of volumes published by the Royal Commission on Historical Monuments provides early examples of the type from many counties. Even a remote county like Westmorland shows 'a large number of 14th century and later manor houses, built on a normal medieval plan with a central hall and cross-wings at the two ends'.[22] Many of the Westmorland examples were the homes of very prominent families, and it would appear that the West Yorkshire gentry of the 15th century, including both major families like the Saviles of Thornhill and minor families like the Otes of Shibden, were imitating a form accepted among the major gentry of other areas.

Support for the idea that the 'H' plan was adopted as a matter of convention as well as because it provided the type of accommodation required is found in the West Yorkshire group of houses. It has been suggested that the cross-wing originated in the need to provide a generous and impressive solar, a linear extension of the low hall range precluding this. It has also been shown, however, that many of the later West Yorkshire houses of the minor gentry failed to exploit this capacity to provide a solar of high status. The minor gentry of the late-15th and early-16th centuries clearly felt that, while they may have needed comfortable heated chambers, the richly decorated and large solar, such as had been provided in the early houses of the wealthy gentry like Calverley Hall (41), did not meet their requirements. Nevertheless, the form of a house with cross-wings was retained and indeed the chambers in the wings are more commodious than would have been the case in a linear range. The lack of an elaborate solar in the late-medieval houses of the minor gentry in West Yorkshire suggests strongly that the 'H' plan, although originating in the need to provide a large solar, was adopted because it was accepted gentry form rather than just because it satisfied the demands of the builders with respect to the number and nature of the rooms contained within the dwelling.

Further evidence of the influence of fashionable ideas is found in a comparison of the houses of the minor gentry in West Yorkshire with those of the prosperous yeomanry of the south-east of England, where the Wealden type of house, built in much the same period as the gentry houses of West Yorkshire, provided the same type of accommodation as the local houses under review. They do this, however, in a linear form, an open hall and two-storeyed ends giving a simple rectangular block on plan, all under a single roof. It appears that the open hall of a Wealden house was commonly loftier than the hall in an early West Yorkshire gentry house like that at Sharlston; thus the storeyed ends of the Wealden type could provide better chambers, with no need of the extra height given by wings.[23] The Wealden house, it is true, could not provide an elaborate solar with its own decorative roof, but this was not of concern to the Kentish yeoman who did not require such a room.[24] Without implying that the example of the Kentish yeoman was known to the minor gentry of West Yorkshire, it may be suggested that the West Yorkshire gentry did have an element of choice in the planning of their dwelling. Had they wanted a linear plan, they could have raised the eaves of the hall to a higher level, thus providing what the Wealden type gave, an open hall flanked by storeyed ends with adequate, but not elaborate, chambers. They chose, however, the option of building higher wings because this gave a more impressive display front and because the chambers thus provided, which were in truth more elaborate than those of the Wealden house even if they did not approach the richness of the earlier solar, answered their need for more spacious accommodation on the first floor.

It appears likely, therefore, that the hall-and-cross-wings house adopted commonly by the minor gentry of West Yorkshire in the late-15th and early-16th centuries was the product of two forces, namely, the changing demands of the gentry which might by themselves have been sufficient to lead to an independent development of the type, and the influence of earlier architectural progress in other parts of the country. The houses of the county show some signs of having gone through an independent evolution from linear to 'H' plan, but the rapid acceptance of the latter form probably owed a great deal to its widespread use by the major gentry throughout much of England.

THE ELEMENTS
OF THE LATE-MEDIEVAL
GENTRY HOUSE

Hitherto the subject of discussion has been the evolution of the overall form of the gentry house in the later Middle Ages, and although rooms like the hall, solar and parlour have been brought into the discussion in order to show how their changing use determined to some extent the development of plan, little has been said of their particular character. Closer examination of the principal components of the house, however, may have the value of revealing a great deal about the status of the builders and of the way in which the house functioned as a dwelling.

THE HALL

The primacy of the hall has already been commented upon in general terms, and here one need simply repeat that in all the houses under review the hall was the single most important area for those public occasions which were part of the life of the gentry household, as well as being the room where much of its everyday activity was enacted. The nature of a hall in any one house depended very much upon the status of the builder, however, and the variety in the types of hall found in the houses of the West Yorkshire gentry is a sign that the class embraced considerable differences of wealth within its ranks.

All the late-medieval gentry houses of the county had a hall that was open from ground to roof. Only in the second half of the 16th century, did the single-storey hall form part of the dwelling, and houses with this type of hall will be considered in a later chapter. The open hall is the most characteristic room of the medieval house of all parts of the country and has an ancestry stretching back far beyond the scope of this volume.[25] The West Yorkshire gentry houses may be grouped into two classes according to the character of the open hall. In a small group of houses the hall is large and elaborate, in the remainder it is smaller and plainer, and it is suggested that the first group was built by men in the ranks of the major or middling gentry, and that the second was built by a newly-emerging minor gentry able to build for the first time in the late-15th century.

The size of the hall is a useful starting point in the examination of the houses of superior gentry. It may be inferred that the hall built probably in the 1420s by Robert Waterton at Methley (128) was very large by local standards, being at least 25 feet wide and probably as much as 50 feet long if the passage area is taken to lie within the hall.[26] Methley was a great house, and its possible 1200 square feet of floor area in the hall was not approached by the late-medieval houses of even the wealthiest gentry. Calverley Hall has a hall of some 875 square feet, Woodsome has a hall area of 700 square feet, Horbury has a hall area of 710 square feet, and Kiddal one of some 550 square feet. (*See* Table 1). These are the largest halls in the county, and from what is known of their builders they were the work of an upper band of the local gentry. The Calverley and Ellis families, of Calverley Hall and Kiddal Hall, were of knightly status, and the Kayes of Woodsome were rising quickly in the late Middle Ages to become one of the most powerful families in the county in the post-medieval period. Less is known of the Amyas family of Horbury, but the size of their hall and the other special features in their house suggests that in this case the building supplies a better idea of their prominence than do surviving documents.

As well as being large, these halls also displayed some features of plan and design which marked them out from the hall in the houses of the minor gentry. Firstly, they were heated by a lateral stack; lesser houses used a firehood. Secondly, they were entered by a through-passage rather than by the hearth-passage associated with the firehood. Finally, in these halls the roof was more richly decorated

TABLE 1. THE HALL IN THE MEDIEVAL GENTRY HOUSE

House, in order of hall size	Area of hall in sq. ft. (m²) excluding passage	Date of hall (approx.)	Features					Notes
			Through passage	Hearth passage	Decorative roof	Firehood	Dais canopy	
Methley (128)	1200 (111.8)	1420	★					Nobility
Calverley (41)	875 (81.5)	1485	★		★			False hammer-beam
Horbury (92)	710 (66.2)	1480	★		★		★	Arched-braced intermediate truss
Woodsome (60)	700 (65.2)	1520		★	★	★	?	Windbraces
Sharlston (176)	640 (59.6)	1400		★	★	★	★	Crown-post roofs over hall and wing
Lees Hall (207)	562 (52.3)	1500		★		★	★	
Rawthorpe (48)	561 (52.3)	1520		★		★		
Kiddal (26)	550 (51.2)	1400	★		★			Roof similar to Calverley?
New Hall (54)	505 (47.0)	1490		★		★	★	
Shibden Hall, Southowram	420 (39.1)	1490		★		★		
Brearley Hall, Midgley	420 (39.1)	1520		★	★	★		Deep arch-braced truss
Liley Hall (138)	399 (37.2)	1520		★	★	★		Deep arch-braced truss
Chadwick Hall (139)	387 (36.0)	1560		★		★		Gallery across hall
Fenay Hall, Almondbury	373 (34.7)	1550		★		★		Possibly yeoman status when built
Wheatley Hall, Woolley	342 (31.8)	1450	★					Crown-post in wing
Manor House, Havercroft with Cold Hiendley	324 (30.2)	1520		★		★		

A lateral stack is present or demonstrable at Calverley, Horbury and Wheatley; its presence is inferred at Methley and Kiddal. A spere truss existed at Calverley and Horbury.

than in minor gentry houses. These three elements are all linked, and it is impossible to isolate one as primary, with the other two following from it. It should also be pointed out that not all the halls in the superior group show all the features to an equal degree: one, indeed, shows only one of them. Furthermore, a decorative roof is present in some of the lesser houses too. Nevertheless, the general incidence of these aspects of plan and design serves to distinguish a small group of houses of men in the upper ranks of gentry society from a larger group of houses of the minor gentry.

Among the houses with a large hall considered earlier, Calverley and Horbury certainly heated the hall by means of a lateral stack on the rear wall, and the existence of a lateral stack may be inferred at Kiddal and Methley. Only Woodsome was not heated in this way. Outside this group, the lateral stack is found at Wheatley Hall, Woolley, and its presence may be inferred in the late-medieval hall at Baildon Hall, Baildon (17), and at the Manor House, Ilkley (99; Fig. 5).[27] There is little that unites all these houses apart from their status. Methley was the house of a major gentry family, and Calverley, Kiddal, Horbury, and Wheatley were all built by prominent or at least long-established families. The surviving fragments of medieval building at the Manor House and at Baildon Hall suggest a date early in the 15th century or possibly earlier and on the grounds that an early date is often an indication of higher status these houses may be considered to have belonged to the superior group at the time of their building even if they fell somewhat in status in succeeding ages. The Baildon family was certainly of ancient gentry origin, but nothing is known of the family responsible for the Manor House.

The association of the lateral stack with medieval buildings of high status is clear both within the county and in the country as a whole. Great houses and the houses of the major gentry all over the country display this feature, and as the open hearth fell out of use at this social level, the fireplace in the side wall became perhaps the most common means of heating the hall.[28] Its association with gentry houses is highlighted by its absence from the houses of the medieval yeomanry, and from the vast majority of post-medieval yeoman houses also.[29] Nor is the lateral stack to be explained as simply an early feature rather than a superior one. It is, indeed, found at early dates, even within West Yorkshire, for the late-13th-century Moot Hall, Dewsbury, was heated by a wall fireplace.[30] However, some of the West Yorkshire examples, such as Calverley and Horbury, were built at very much the same time as

houses without a lateral stack, and, furthermore, this means of heating the hall remained common in superior houses of later centuries too. It is clear that the medieval houses of West Yorkshire which have a lateral stack reflect the fashions current over much of the country among the nobility and greater gentry, and that these houses were built by a small elite of long-established or powerful county gentry.[31]

The use of the lateral stack goes hand in hand with the incidence of the through-passage plan. This plan has opposed doorways at one end of the hall, and the passage, whether screened or not from the body of the room, was an integral part of the hall. It is to be distinguished from the hearth-passage plan, where the reredos of the fire-area forms an effective division between passage and hall. Because the passage end of the hall was open to full view in houses with a lateral stack, more expense was lavished on making it an object of display in its own right. Grouped doorways through to the area below the passage were elaborated to give a decorative appearance; at Methley and at the Manor House, Ilkley, there is a pair of doorways in a stone wall (Plate 9) and at Baildon Hall are three grouped doorways with two-centred arches within a timber-framed

Plate 9 [99] Manor House, Ilkley; the through passage.

Fig 5 [99] Manor House, Ilkley.

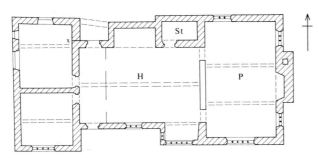

Plate 10 [17] Baildon Hall; grouped doorways leading from passage.

partition (Plate 10). At Calverley and Horbury, the entry bay was divided from the body of the hall by a spere truss (Fig. 6), a feature almost exclusively confined to the houses of the wealthiest gentry and of the nobility over much of the country. Its use at Calverley and Horbury is, perhaps, the strongest indication that these houses should be clearly distinguished from those of the lesser gentry.[32]

In houses with a large hall heated by a lateral stack, one further means of decoration was open to the builders; the roof, uncluttered by a bulky and unsightly firehood, called for emphasis in its treatment, and the superior group of houses supplied the need with unmatched splendour. Roof decoration, of course, had been a common means of expressing status since the 13th century in the houses of the great, and the open hall in particular had been singled out for elaboration. While decorative roofs are not confined to the houses of the superior gentry in West Yorkshire, certainly the most splendid treatment is found at this social level. Calverley Hall has a false hammer-beam roof (Fig. 7), and Horbury Hall has decorative king-post trusses with intermediate trusses of arch-braced collar form, the whole roof being enlivened with the only display of cusped

Fig 6 [92] Horbury Hall, spere truss.

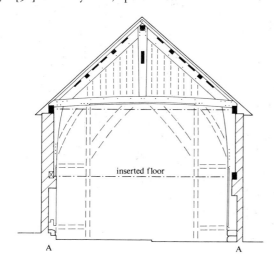

A   A

Fig 7 [41] Calverley Hall, Section through hall (after Sugden).

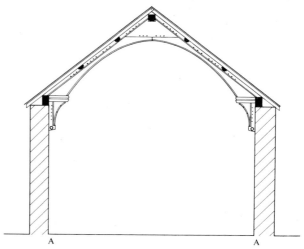

A   A

Plate 11 [92] Horbury Hall; hall roof.

windbraces yet found in the county (Plate 11). There is reason to think that Kiddal may have had a roof similar to that at Calverley, but later rebuilding at Methley deprived us of knowledge of the nature of the early roof there. Woodsome (60) with a large hall but a hearth-passage plan, has a central truss with deep arch-braces rising to a high collar, and there is evidence that the roof had two tiers of wind-braces; whether these were cusped or not cannot be established. (Fig. 8).[33]

One final aspect of the major gentry houses, one which does not concern the hall exclusively but which might appropriately be dealt with here as it serves further to differentiate the group from lesser houses, is the use of stone as the principal building material. Not all the houses mentioned above were of stone; Woodsome, Wheatley, and Baildon were timber-framed. However, the grandest houses were built in good quality masonry. At the pinnacle of county society, the Watertons used it at Methley and the Saviles at Thornhill, and their example was followed, whether consciously in imitation or not, by some of the substantial gentry. Stone was the principal building material at Calverley, in the hall range at Kiddal, on the ground floor of the display front at Horbury, and in the earliest phase at the Manor House, Ilkley. Fine masonry was always expensive and much prized in the Middle Ages;

Fig 8 [60] Woodsome Hall, Farnley Tyas; section through hall.

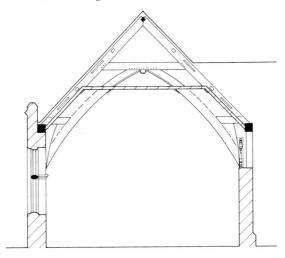

it is clear that a stone house was beyond the means of the minor gentry in the 15th century, for they built in timber. It is probable that stone was becoming more easily afforded by the middle decades of the 16th century, since one of the latest of the lesser gentry houses in the Middle Ages, Chadwick Hall, Mirfield (139), was built largely of stone, and certainly by the 17th century, stone had replaced timber as the commonest material for gentry and yeoman alike.

In contrast, the hall in the houses of the minor gentry was generally smaller, much plainer in its detail, and used elements which, unlike those of superior halls, have a distinctly local character. The hall had anything from 640 to 324 square feet of floor space, but both these extremes are exceptional, and more commonly it had an area of between 560 and 370 square feet. This is still a large range of size, and probably indicates significant differences of wealth even within this group of minor gentry.

In these smaller houses the hall was heated originally by a firehood and it will be suggested later that this choice was determined in part by the use to which the hall was put. Being of timber and plaster, the firehood was considerably cheaper than a stone chimney stack. Where the stone fireplace lent itself to decoration, the firehood was purely functional, the large and bulky flue rising from a bressumer spanning all or nearly all of the width of the hall. Its decorative potential was limited to some carving or moulding of the timbers of the surround. The firehood was built against a reredos wall at the lower end of the hall, the reredos forming a barrier between entry and hall; this association of entry and heating gave a hearth-passage plan, one which occurred in all the lesser gentry houses and distinguished them from most of the houses of the more substantial gentry. The use of the firehood deprived the builder of two means of decorating the hall. Firstly, any show of grouped doorways in the lower wall of the passage would not be visible from the hall, and there is little sign that expenditure was wasted on this form of elaboration. Secondly, the presence of a firehood ruled out the use of a spere truss. Only the roof was available as an object of display, but even here the small size of many halls and the existence of a bulky firehood tended to diminish the effect to be derived from ostentatious timberwork. In only three houses was there an attempt to enliven the hall by means of roof decoration. At Sharlston (176) a crown-post sat upon the head-beam of the dais canopy, and at Brearley Hall, Midgley, and Liley Hall (138), the central truss was of arch-brace form (Plate 12; Fig. 9). In other houses, the hall roof was unadorned; in the minor gentry houses of the Pennine west, for example, the roof was usually of king-post form.

Just as in the houses of the major gentry, therefore, the nature of the hall is determined by the means of heating, the degree of decoration, and the type of entry. Again it is difficult to isolate any one of these features as the cause of the others, but the method of heating calls for further comment. The origin of the firehood is obscure. It was not used in the houses of the great in the Middle Ages, either in West Yorkshire or in the rest of England, and makes its first appearance in a standing building in this county in the houses of the lesser gentry in the 15th century. Sharlston Hall, dating from the first half of that century, is the earliest

Plate 12 [138] Liley Hall, Mirfield; hall roof.

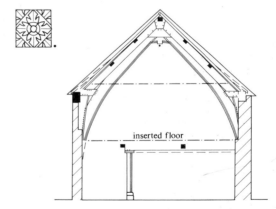

Fig 9 [138] Liley Hall, Mirfield; section through hall.

house to show signs of having had a firehood. For the following two centuries, it was to be the standard means of heating the principal room of houses of all ranks below that of the substantial gentry, and it continued to be used in very many yeoman's houses for much of the 17th century as well. It is not yet clear whether the firehood was devised as a suitable means of heating in buildings erected in permanent form for the first time in the 15th century, a case of necessity being the mother of invention, or whether these first permanent buildings merely continued the use of a means that had been present in earlier houses, whether of gentry or yeoman status, of impermanent form. To date, little is known of the plan of earlier houses in West Yorkshire, but it is to be hoped that future archaeological investigation of medieval habitation sites and the gathering of evidence from artefacts, such as the pottery curfews used to cover the hearth, will throw light on the antiquity of the firehood.[34]

In many respects the function of the hall in the houses of major and minor gentry was broadly similar, and its use as the main reception area has been noted. Clearly, the major gentry had a more impressive room, but that the hall, whether large or small, was intended to be more than just an all-purpose living area is shown by the common use of a canopy over the dais end of the room. The most splendid remains of a canopy are at Horbury, where, over the dais bench, curved ribs rose to a head-beam ornamented on its two visible faces with carved panels, one of which showed the Amyas arms (Fig. 10). Lesser houses, too, had a canopy; at New Hall, Elland (54) it sprang from a brattished beam on the side wall of the upper wing. The reconstruction at Lees Hall, Thornhill (207), gives a good idea of the impression created by the canopy (Plate 13). Sited at the upper end of the hall, which sometimes had a raised floor, the canopy emphasised the importance of

those privileged to sit on the dais bench beneath, setting them apart from the members of the household or visitors assembled in the body of the hall.[35]

It is extremely unlikely that the hall in the houses of the

It is extremely unlikely that the hall in the house of the major gentry was used for cooking, the wall fireplace being

Fig 10 [92] Horbury Hall; dais canopy beam, carved panel showing arms of Amyas family.

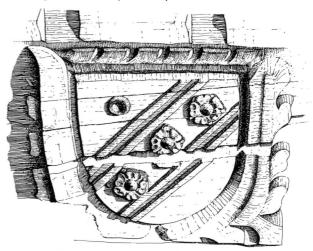

Plate 13 [207] Lees Hall, Thornhill; the dais canopy.

unsuited to the purpose unless very large and the high quality of the room's fittings and decoration suggesting that the main cooking hearth was more appropriately sited elsewhere. In the minor gentry houses, however, the main processes of cooking may have been done in the hall. The firehood was particularly suited to serve the main cooking hearth, for the area beneath it both gave plenty of room for movement around the fire, and, by means of hooks and cranes secured to the reredos and bressumer, made it easy to suspend cooking vessels over the fire itself. In post-medieval gentry houses, the hall was to be heated by a fireplace in a stone chimney stack, and it is known from documentary evidence that the cooking was not done here; instead, the main cooking hearth was in a kitchen which significantly was heated by a firehood in some houses.[36] The housebody in 17th-century yeoman's houses, commonly heated by a firehood, was certainly used for cooking, and it is very likely that in the late-medieval yeoman's houses, in which the housebody had a firehood, it was also the main cooking room. The many similarities between the hall in the house of a late-medieval gentleman of modest means and the housebody of a contemporary yeoman of high standing, the narrow social gap between the two, and the marked difference in the character of the hall of the major and minor gentleman, suggest that the hall in a minor gentry house may well have been used for cooking. If this was indeed the case, the importance of the hall within the house appears even greater, for at this less sophisticated level, where specialization in the functions of rooms was still poorly developed, the hall must have acted as a reception area on public occasions, as a general living area for much of the household, and as the principal cooking area. It may be that the all-purpose nature of the room explains why it should have lacked elaboration in its treatment.

The Parlour

The increasing importance of the parlour in the late Middle Ages was noted earlier, when the developing use of the room was seen as a contributory influence in the evolution of plan. Later alterations have made it difficult to discover how elaborate the best parlour was, but at Shibden Hall, Southowram, the ceiling of the room was brightly painted and had carved bosses.[37] That the best parlour here was intended to be a private room is shown by the indirect means used to reach it from the hall. The hall gave access to the rear area of the upper wing, and only through this did it connect with the parlour. The private room was not, therefore, a through route, for the plan deliberately set it apart from the household traffic. It is likely that both upper and lower parlours were provided in even the lesser gentry houses in West Yorkshire; it has been suggested that the main room in the lower wing at New Hall, Elland, for instance, was probably a parlour.

The Service Area

The lower wing of the standard late-medieval gentry house is generally thought to have been used, wholly or in part, as a service area, with rooms such as the buttery and milkhouse. Invariably, however, this wing has been the object of later alteration, and the nature and extent of the service rooms are difficult to recover.

It has been shown that the common medieval grouping of three doorways in the lower wall of the passage is found in only one house in West Yorkshire, Baildon Hall, Baildon (17). Here, the outer doorways probably led into buttery and pantry, with the central doorway opening into a passage leading through the wing to a detached building, possibly a kitchen. At Methley and the Manor House, Ilkley (99), there are two doorways in the lower wall of the passage, which probably led to service rooms at the lower end. The general absence of evidence for a passage to a detached kitchen might be thought to confirm the idea that, in the houses of the lesser gentry, the hall was used for cooking and that there was, therefore, no need for a distant cooking area. It should be pointed out, however, that such passages to a kitchen usually occur only in the houses of the great, and that in lesser houses it might well have been the through passage rather than a passage through the lower wing which was used to reach a detached kitchen. There is documentary evidence that in 1568 Horbury Hall had a detached kitchen, since removed. Only the great afforded themselves the luxury of a permanent detached kitchen, and it is possible that impermanent kitchens, easily and quickly replaced in case of accidental fire, were more common than surviving remains indicate. Other detached structures associated with the gentry house in this period, such as the bakehouse and brewhouse, have perished, and their presence may be assumed but not illustrated.

The incorporation of the kitchen into the main domestic block as a separate room will be discussed in the examination of the 17th-century gentry house, and represents a significant development in those houses. It is possible that the process by which the cooking hearth was either brought into the house or excluded from the hall had begun in the late Middle Ages. At Kiddal Hall (26), an immense stack was added to the lower wing (Plate 14), and at

Plate 14 [26] Kiddal Hall, Barwick in Elmet; the lower wing, with kitchen stack (*Copyright, Yorkshire Archaeological Society*).

Sharlston Hall (176), a timber-framed wing with an equally vast stack was added to the lower end of the house. In both cases, the siting and the size of the stack indicate that it was intended to serve the main cooking hearth. The date of these alterations cannot be established with any precision, but it is conceivable that in these houses the kitchen had come into the main block as a separate room before 1550.

Plate 15 The Old Rectory, Mirfield; decorative framing in cross-wing, with lean-to stair bay.

THE STAIR

The existence of an open hall between storeyed cross-wings necessitated the provision of two stairs, one serving each wing. The gallery across the open hall, designed to link the chambers in the two wings, is not found commonly in the gentry houses of the county in the late Middle Ages, since the presence of a dais canopy at the upper end of the hall precluded a gallery. In the 17th century it was clearly decided that the convenience of the gallery was more important than the outmoded ostentation of the canopy, and in a number of houses a gallery was inserted into the hall at the expense of the canopy, allowing one of the staircases to be removed. Of the late-medieval houses, only Chadwick Hall, Mirfield (139) had a gallery originally, and this is, perhaps, the latest house in the group. All the other houses must have been built with two stairs.

The site of the stair in the lower wing of the gentry house is not known; it is possible that the flight comprised a simple ladder set between the joists of the ceiling in the rear room of the wing. At the upper end of the house, however, there is evidence of a more imposing stair, usually housed in a bay set in the angle between the hall and the upper wing at the rear of the building. At New Hall, Elland, and at Lees Hall, Thornhill, the stair-bay is roofed by a continuation of the slope of the wing roof. It is likely that the stair opened out of the hall and, with a quarter-turn, rose to a chamber in the wing. Further examples of the lean-to stair-bay are found at Rawthorpe Old Hall, Dalton (48) and at the Old Rectory, Mirfield (Plate 15); at both the later stair-bay is sited on the main front rather than at the rear. The frequent occurrence of this stair position, whether at the front or the rear of the house, suggests that this was standard siting in gentry buildings.[38]

THE SOLAR AND OTHER CHAMBERS

The importance of the solar in early and superior houses was noted above. Houses like Calverley Hall and Sharlston

Hall had a large solar, and the importance of the room in both houses and in others is manifest in its decorative treatment. At Wheatley Hall, Woolley, West Royd, Hunsworth (98), Sharlston and possibly at Calverley too, the roof over the solar was of crown-post form. A degree of comfort was sometimes provided in the form of a fireplace, and that the room could have an enduring importance even in the houses of some of the minor gentry is indicated by the late-16th or early-17th-century alterations to Lees Hall, Thornhill, where the solar or great chamber, occupying the whole of the first floor of the upper wing, was embellished by the addition of a rich plaster ceiling. Clearly a large or decorative solar had a superior use, but many of the minor gentry felt no need for such a room. In many of their houses, the main chamber, hardly deserving the name of solar, was distinguished by being heated, though only slightly larger than other first-floor rooms. Its function in these lesser houses was probably that of a good-quality bedroom, with other chambers acting as lesser bedrooms for the household and as storerooms.

THE CHAPEL

The domestic chapel, never a common element of the late-medieval gentry house over the country as a whole and usually found at a high social level, formed a part of a number of gentry houses in West Yorkshire in the late Middle Ages. Burton Hall, Kirkburton, is said to have had a 'small domestic chapel of pointed gothic architecture', and there were chapels at Old Hall, Elland and, in later years, at Methley Hall, Methley.[39] Hawksworth Hall, Hawksworth (79), built after 1550 as the seat of the knightly Hawksworth family, had a chapel in the lower wing, but in 1580 Woodsome Hall (60) lost its chapel when it was 'devydid . . . into tow P(arl)lars for lakk of rowme.'[40] The best, indeed the only intact, chapel in West Yorkshire is that at Calverley Hall (41; Plate 16). The chapel wing here was built at the same time as the hall

Plate 16 [41] Calverley Hall; the chapel.

20

Plate 17 [60] Woodsome Hall, Farnley Tyas; main front, showing 17th–cent. stone casing and projecting outer wing.

range (c.1480), and the chapel roof is a miniature version of that in the hall. The wing is partly floored to give, on the first floor, a closet opening off the solar, and divided from the body of the chapel by a traceried screen. The magnificence of roof and screen is a sign of the high status of the Calverley family in the later Middle Ages.

The siting of the Calverley chapel is repeated in gentry houses over the whole country, and it is therefore possible to suggest that other chapels may be identified in surviving houses. The documents have shown that Woodsome Hall had a chapel in the 16th century, and the house has a block which projects forward from the upper parlour wing in just the way in which the chapel projects from the solar wing at Calverley (Plate 17). Similarly, at Sharlston Hall, a timber-framed wing was built in the 16th century against the earlier upper wing. At both houses, it is possible that these elements were built as domestic chapels.

THE ROOF

Roof construction in the gentry houses of the Middle Ages in West Yorkshire evolved slowly. Roof decoration was then a principal means of display, and its presence or absence was significant both within an individual house and as an indication of how far a builder was aware of fashions current nationally among men of this status.

Early Forms

Because most of the houses of the gentry date from late in the Middle Ages, the range of medieval roof types in West Yorkshire is more limited than in some other parts of the country. There is, however, evidence for the use of the crown-post at an early date. The solar wing at the Old Hall, Elland dating from c.1300, had crown-post trusses with parallel rafters, and the crown-post roof at Rectory Farm, South Kirkby, with its 'minimal passing-brace effect' has been dated to the 14th century.[41] Manston Old Hall, Austhorpe, had a crown-post roof, apparently over

the hall range rather than the solar wing (Fig. 11) and the form of the crown-posts, which were shaped and moulded, suggests a date earlier than the plank-like forms found in buildings thought to be 15th century.[42] Of this later date are the crown-post trusses in the roof at Sharlston, Wheatley Hall, Woolley and West Royd (98). Sharlston appears to have had a crown-post roof over both hall range and added solar wing, but in the other houses the crown-post was used only over the solar.

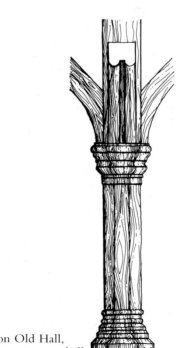

Fig 11 Manston Old Hall, detail of crown-post over hall.

That the crown-post, even in the plain forms employed in West Yorkshire, was intended as a prestigious and fashionable form is suggested by a number of points. First, the crown-post was used only in those areas of the house which had a superior use, that is, the solar and, in two instances, the hall. In areas where decorative forms were not required, the crown-post was absent. Secondly, the crown-post is never found in buildings known to have been of yeoman status; five of the six instances are from houses built by gentry, even major gentry in some cases, the one exception being West Royd, where nothing is yet known of the builder. Finally, the pattern of the use of the crown-post in the Middle Ages across the country shows that, before the 15th century at least, it was almost exclusively employed by men of high status.[43]

It is unlikely that the crown-post was used in West Yorkshire after 1450. The reasons for this are complex. In the first place, the lesser gentry houses dating from after 1450 placed less emphasis on the decoration of the solar and indeed on the solar itself; there was, therefore, little need for an elaborate roof over this room. Secondly, the crown-post was by this date falling out of use in gentry houses over much of the country, to be replaced as a prestige feature by newer forms of embellishment such as the hammer-beam or arch-braced roof. That it did not have a longer life in West Yorkshire is probably due in part to the infrequency with which it was employed even before 1450. It had never become part of the repertoire of the local carpenter, and fell out of fashion before there had developed either a lesser gentry or a prosperous yeomanry eager to take it up as a prestige feature.[44] When these classes did build, in the second half of the 15th century, they either did not require a decorative roof, or, in areas in the house where an elaborate roof was needed, they chose a more valued and current type such as the arch-braced truss.

In north-east England, possibly in northern England as a whole, it was only in towns that the crown-post was used in any numbers. Crown-post roofs have been recorded in Lincoln and Ripon and are known to have existed in Leeds.[45] The city of York provides the most abundant evidence, however, and the findings of the Royal Commission on Historical Monuments show that the crown-post was 'the most common type of roof truss used in York in the 14th and 15th centuries', the form having been recorded in perhaps as many as fifty buildings.[46] These range in date from the early-14th to the early-16th century, and in status from great public buildings such as the Merchant Adventurers' Hall to very small structures like a single-storey outbuilding behind the Shambles.[47] The inference is that in York the crown-post became a standard structural form because only here did a sufficiently numerous and prosperous class, presumably basing its wealth on commerce, develop in the period when the crown-post was still current as a fashionable feature of large houses and public buildings. This new urban merchant group perpetuated the use of the crown-post in such numbers that it became a structural norm, so much so that it could even be used in very humble and non-domestic buildings.[48] In the countryside, by contrast, smaller numbers and less continuity of building meant that the crown-post was confined to a few early buildings of high status.[49]

Later Roofs

After 1450, by far the most common form of roof in West Yorkshire is that employing king-post trusses. Within the county, there are no king-post roofs which are thought to pre-date 1450, but by the time that significant numbers of lesser gentry and wealthy yeomen began to build new houses in the late-15th century, the king-post had become very much the standard type. It was used in houses of both high and low status; the superior Calverley Hall and Horbury Hall, the less imposing New Hall, Elland, and many yeoman houses employed it. Fourteen gentry houses dating from the century after 1450 retain most of their roof intact; of these, half employed only king-post trusses, and the remainder used other forms in conjunction with the king-post.

That the king-post was used in these houses for its structural virtues rather than for its decorative qualities is clear from a study of the roofs in some of the superior buildings. The king-post was never used as the principal point of display, for although it formed part of the roof at Calverley and Horbury, at the first it was relegated to the end trusses of the hall, leaving the body of the room to be decorated by the false hammer-beam roof, and at Horbury the main work of decoration was by arch-braced intermediate trusses and by a show of cusped wind-braces. The large hall at Woodsome has principal-rafter trusses and a central truss of deep arch-braced collar form, and in this house the king-post was confined to use in the two wings where no decoration was required. Even in smaller houses, the king-post was rejected as a decorative form. At Liley Hall, Mirfield (138), the hall, so small that it is a surprise that any elaboration was lavished on the roof, has a decorative arch-braced central truss; at each end, however, closed king-post trusses were employed. At Brearley Hall, Midgley, the central truss in the hall is similar to that at Liley, and at Rawthorpe Old Hall, Dalton (48), both wings have a modest show of elaboration in the roof but again the king-post is relegated to the utilitarian areas of the house. Only one form of the king-post appears to have been considered as decorative in any degree, and this form employs a short king-post sitting on a collar and braced to the ridge. This type of truss is found at Rishworth Hall, Bingley, over the hall range (Plate 18), and at Rawthorpe

Plate 18 Rishworth Hall, Bingley; central truss in hall range.

Old Hall, in the solar wing. At a slightly later date, the short king-post was used over the great chamber at Hawksworth Hall (79), and in the 17th century the type continued in use both as a decorative form, as at Kershaw House, Midgley, and as a functional form in an attic, as at East Riddlesden Hall, Morton (140).

The decorative limitations of the king-post were, therefore, realised from the first in West Yorkshire.[50] Its popularity was due partly to its strength, the scantling of the timbers in a king-post truss being far heavier than in a crown-post roof. With the benefit of hindsight we know that other forms could serve as well, for the survival of the solar wing at Sharlston demonstrates that a crown-post roof was quite capable of supporting the weight of a heavy roof covering of stone flags. The lasting qualities of the crown-post truss may not have been evident to the builders of houses in the 15th century, however, and it may have been thought that the safety net offered by the massive king-post truss was justification enough for its widespread use. In houses or parts of houses where decoration was not required, therefore, the king-post, strong and structurally uncomplicated, was all but ubiquitous in the later Middle Ages.

STONE CONSTRUCTION

The use of good stonework in houses was confined in the Middle Ages to those of superior status. West Yorkshire has an abundance of good building stone, gritstones in the north and west, coal-measures sandstones in the centre and south-east, and limestone in the east. The prestige of masonry is seen most clearly at Horbury Hall, where the Amyas family, presumably unable to afford a house of stone throughout, built a hall range which had a half-height stone wall at the front but a timber-framed wall at the rear. Perhaps the finest example of the craft of the mason within the medieval houses of West Yorkshire was the oriel bay

added in 1501 to the hall at Kiddal Hall (26). Only in the mid 16th century, was stone used as the principal building material in a lesser house; Chadwick Hall, Mirfield, dates probably from *c.*1550, and is entirely of stone apart from the gables, which were timber-framed and had king-post trusses with herringbone braces. After 1550, stone was to become the standard building material for gentry houses.

Plate 19 [54] New Hall, Elland cum Greetland; close-studded partition.

TIMBER-FRAMED CONSTRUCTION

The alternative to stone as a building material in the late Middle Ages was timber, adopted widely by the lesser gentry and by the yeomanry.[51] Generous scantling and the common use of close-studding characterize the timber-framed houses of the gentry (Plate 19). In parts of the house which required decorative emphasis, large panels with

Plate 20 Wormalds Hall, Almondbury; jettied front range, with herring-bone framing.

diagonal braces were used; the wing at Lees Hall, Thornhill (207), is the best surviving example. Some houses are more elaborate; at the Old Rectory, Mirfield, the framing of the wing gable, the main display feature, is divided into small square or rectangular panels with an infill of herring-bone braces. A post-1539 date has been ascribed to this house on the evidence of the initials on the finial, and indeed this type of decoration appears to be generally later in date than the simpler and bolder style of Lees Hall.[52] It was used commonly in town houses in the second half of the 16th century, and in the jettied range at Wormalds Hall, Almondbury, probably similar in date (Plate 20).[53] Ornamental framing comparable to the style common in the Midlands and Lancashire is represented only by the porch at Sharlston Hall, erected in 1574; it has small square panels with quadrant braces, and the rail and jettied tie-beam were inscribed with a Latin text and the date.[54]

Other types of external decoration in timber-framed houses include carved barge-boards, finials, and tie-beams; at Fenay Hall, Almondbury, the barge boards survive, and the tie-beams are carved with tracery, lozenges, fruit and foliage motifs and the initials of the builders (Plates 21–2).

Plate 23 [48] Rawthorpe Old Hall, Dalton; stone casing of cross-wing, showing outline of jetty.

THE GEOGRAPHICAL DISTRIBUTION OF GENTRY HOUSES IN WEST YORKSHIRE IN THE MIDDLE AGES

Given the small number of surviving or recorded gentry houses, it is difficult to come to firm conclusions about the significance of their distribution in the Middle Ages. There is, however, one aspect of the distribution which merits comment. Most of the earliest houses, especially those with a crown-post roof, are concentrated in the eastern half of the county. These are also the houses of the major or middling gentry, and the implication is that these ranks became prominent first in the lower-lying parts of the county. Fourteenth-century tax returns have suggested a 'general pattern of increasing wealth from west to east' in the county and the contrast between the wealthy east and the 'smaller poorer settlements of the Pennine uplands' has been noted. The early houses of the east are important evidence that wealth here was largely confined to a few substantial gentry families. In the western half of the county a more numerous class of minor gentry developed only in the second half of the 15th century; their houses and those of the Pennine yeomanry suggest that in the western parts of the county in the late Middle Ages wealth was spread more evenly among more people. What the west lacked in extremes of wealth, it made up in the numbers of those able to express a moderate prosperity in building. This moderate but widespread wealth is reflected in contemporary taxation returns; these demonstrate that the shifting balance in the distribution of wealth had been so marked by the early 16th century that much of the west of the county bore a fiscal burden equal to that of the east. The evidence of the houses, however, indicates that this burden was spread through society in a rather different manner in the two areas.[55]

Plate 21 Fenay Hall, Almondbury; gable trusses.

Plate 22 Fenay Hall, Almondbury; detail of panel on tie-beam.

The jetty, although common in town houses, is rarely found in rural gentry houses. The best example of jettied construction is Wormalds Hall, Almondbury, but it is not clear that this was of gentry status or of medieval date. At Rawthorpe Old Hall (48), the confused masonry of the side walls of the east wing shows the successive phases of underbuilding an original double-jettied gable wall (Plate 23).

Notes to Chapter 1

[1] See Moorhouse 1981 for a discussion of the documentary evidence relating to the housing of the medieval peasantry in West Yorkshire.

[2] The supreme example of this type is the Bishop's Palace at Wells in Somerset; for an early view of it, see Girouard 1978, 67.

[3] For Rothwell, see Lister 1895; for Calverley, see YAS MD 130/3 and Moorhouse 1981a, 599.

[4] City of Bradford Art Galleries and Museums 1978. The tower was never a free-standing structure, and may be compared more closely with the type of solar tower found at Longthorpe, Northants, than with defensive tower houses; see Wood 1965, 166–7.

[5] Black 1968 and Pevsner 1967, 244–5. Sir William was the messenger of Edward Balliol, King of Scotland.

[6] The West Yorkshire County Archaeology Unit is preparing reports on excavations at Kirkstall and Elland; for Sandal Castle, see Michelmore 1983.

[7] For the Moot Hall, see Chadwick 1911, Wood-Jones 1961, and Pevsner 1967, 180. For the Old Hall, Thorpe Stapleton, see sketch by John Dixon in the library of the Thoresby Society, Claremont, Leeds, ref. 39C15, and photographs held by the Yorkshire Archaeological Society. The descent of the Scargill family is outlined in Michelmore 1981, 540. Doubt about the form of the house is because it is known only from the sketch and photographs.

[8] For examples of these types of building in the historic county of Yorkshire, see Ryder 1982, chs 7 and 8.

[9] I would like to thank Jennifer Hillam of the University of Sheffield for her work on the Horbury and Calverley timbers. For the date of New Hall, Elland, see Giles 1981, 1; for the date of Rothwell Manor, see Michelmore 1981, 488.

[10] See descriptions of numerous West Yorkshire churches, for example All Saints, Batley, and All Saints, Normanton, in Pevsner 1967, 96 and 379.

[11] See Jennings (forthcoming) for an account of the expansion of the economy in the upper Calder Valley in the late Middle Ages. The link between economic prosperity and building activity, put forward by Machin (1977, 44–8) has been questioned by Mercer (1980), who suggests that investment in building, an essentially un-remunerative expenditure, is more likely to have taken place after the close of a period of prosperity when there was less scope for more productive investment in a buoyant economy.

[12] For brevity the term 'H-plan' is used, even when the wings of a house fail to project at front and rear, for it is the separate roofing which gives the house its special form.

[13] For Chorley Hall, see Wood 1965, 74; for Chepstow Castle, see Faulkner 1958, esp. 175.

[14] For suggested 14th-century houses with two cross-wings, see many houses in Westmorland recorded and published in RCHM(E) 1936, for example Castle Dairy, Kendal, p 125. That the gentry house with two cross-wings was not the most common form throughout the country in the late Middle Ages is suggested by recent research in Lancashire and Northamptonshire; see RCHM(E), forthcoming (a), ch 1, and Woodfield, 1981, 156–7.

[15] The estate map of c.1600 shows the house with two wings; see Nuttall 1963, 17.

[16] Girouard 1978, 30.

[17] The use of braziers in other rooms cannot be ruled out. Documentary references to the use of portable fires in medieval houses in West Yorkshire are discussed in Moorhouse 1981, 812–3. There is no evidence in West Yorkshire of the type of house discovered recently in Wales which had a parlour open through two storeys heated by an open hearth; see Smith 1984, 144–7.

[18] Quoted in Wood 1965, 91.

[19] For the use of the solar or great chamber in medieval great houses, see Girouard 1978, 40–54.

[20] Preston 1935, 328–30.

[21] Huddersfield Central Library, Local Studies and Archives Dept, microfilm of Kaye Commonplace Book, 1560–1646. I am grateful to George Redmonds for making the results of his research available to me before publication. For more references to early alterations and improvements of Woodsome Hall, see Redmonds 1982, 7–10.

[22] RCHM(E) 1936, lx.

[23] Comparison of the two types of house is difficult given the paucity of published material; for an example of the Wealden house, see Mercer 1975, plates 6 and 7.

[24] When a better solar was required, it was necessary to re-roof the upper end of the Wealden house, as happened at the Pilgrims' Cafe, Battle, Sussex; see Mercer 1975, 13.

[25] See Mercer 1975, ch 1, for a discussion of the open hall in both superior and vernacular houses.

[26] Crump 1945; he gives a sketch plan and enough information to suggest that the 16th-century re-modelling of Methley Hall included a hall of the same size as its medieval predecessor.

[27] In both these and at Methley the medieval hall was replaced by later work, but the existence of grouped doorways to the service end, known in all three, implies a type of heating which left these doorways visible as a display feature. The firehood precludes this, and the presence in the later phases of all three houses of a lateral stack suggests that this was also the means of heating the earlier hall.

[28] Wood 1965, 58–9.

[29] It was used as a display feature on the front wall of some yeoman houses in the south-west of the country; see Mercer 1975, 54–5.

[30] Wood-Jones 1961.

[31] It is interesting to note, however, that in north-east Lancashire even minor gentry houses had a lateral stack; see RCHM(E), forthcoming (a), ch 1.

[32] For the use of the spere truss in England, see Mercer 1975, index entry for spere truss, and Wood 1965, 139–43.

[33] Liversedge Hall, Liversedge (111), seat of the Neville family in the Middle Ages, also had an elaborate roof: see inventory entry.

[34] Medieval curfews, either circular for an open hearth, or semi-circular for a wall fireplace, are discussed in Moorhouse 1981, 812, and in Moorhouse forthcoming.

[35] Something of the nature of the dais in medieval gentry houses is recorded by Watson, writing in the 18th century of the Savile house at Copley (Skircoat): 'the present hall is old and has the upper part of what is called the hall floor raised higher than the lower, as a mark how far the neighbours, tenants etc., were to approach when called in to entertainments: the owners of the house, with their family and chief friends, occupying the higher part' (Watson 1775, 287).

[36] See Marsh Hall, Northowram (128), of 1626.

[37] Brears 1982, 19. For an illustration of a richly decorated parlour in a great house, Haddon Hall, Derbyshire, see Girouard 1978, colour pl. II.

[38] This position of the solar wing stair is common in gentry houses in other parts of the country; see, for example, Lytes Cary, Somerset.

[39] Morehouse 1861, 79; Watson 1775, 557–8; Crump 1945, 318. For further documentary references to domestic chapels in West Yorkshire, see index entry, Faull and Moorhouse 1981, 994.

[40] For Hawksworth, see the evidence of the 1657 inventory and the early 18th-century sketch of the house by Buck, in Hall 1979, 204–5; for Woodsome, see Kaye Commonplace Book, microfilm, Huddersfield Library.

[41] For Old Hall, Elland, see Michelmore 1977; for Rectory Farm, South Kirkby, see Smith 1974, 258.

[42] The sketch of the crown-post at Manston Old Hall is redrawn from Platt and Morkill 1892, 69.

[43] For a discussion of the use of the crown-post roof in England, see Mercer 1975, 87–92.

[44] The longevity of the crown-post in the south-eastern counties of England has been explained as the result of its adoption in the late Middle Ages by a numerous section of the peasantry, the decorative and structural qualities of the roof type having been demonstrated in the earlier houses of the gentry and nobility; see Mercer 1975, 91-2.

[45] For Lincoln, see Jones 1974; a building in Kirkgate, Ripon, was recorded by Barbara Hutton (Harrison and Hutton 1984, 165); and an early sketch of Rockley Hall, Nether Headrow, Leeds, shows a timber-framed hall-and-cross-wings house with a crown-post roof in each wing (WYAS, Leeds, DB 204/2).

[46] RCHM(E) 1981, lxviii.

[47] For the latter, see RCHM(E) 1963, 72.

[48] The outbuilding in the Shambles has been mentioned, and an example of a domestic building of modest status is Church Cottage, for which, see RCHM(E) 1972, 98–9.

[49] That the position in Yorkshire was mirrored in Lincolnshire is suggested by recent research which showed that 'the towns . . . have a virtual monopoly of crown-post roofs, only the former parsonage at Coningsby . . . being a village outlier' (Roberts 1974, 299). Stanley Jones states (1974, 311) that the crown-post is the most common medieval roof-type in Lincoln.

[50] That the king-post need not be a severe form is shown by examples in other parts of the country; see, for instance, the roof of Framsden Hall, Suffolk, illustrated in Mercer 1975, pl. 66.

[51] One exception was Lord Darcy's great mansion at Temple Newsam, built probably in the late 15th and early 16th century in brick, perhaps the earliest use of this material in the county; see Fawcett 1972, 6–9.

[52] For evidence for the Old Rectory's date, see Walton 1955, 49.

[53] That the style of framing might well continue in towns into the second half of the 17th century is suggested by the evidence of the Woolshops, Halifax, where the timber-framed walls on two sides of the building were designed to be supported by stone walls on the other two sides, one of which bears a datestone of 1670. Such a late date was previously unsuspected, and it is not certain that the datestone refers to the original walling. The conspicuous lack of urban buildings of both stone and brick of 17th-century date, not only in Halifax but also in other West Yorkshire towns, may, however, be explained if, in fact, timber-framing remained the normal structural form up to 1670 and perhaps beyond. For evidence in Wakefield of rebuilding in timber-framing in the second half of the 16th century, see Walker 1939, 575ff. One of the most decorative of the Wakefield houses, Six Chimneys, is illustrated in Ambler 1913, 49–50.

[54] The full translation of the inscription is:

> In three things God and man is well pleased
> The good loving of brethren
> The love of neighbours
> Man and wife of one consent.
>
> In the name of the Lord this house was begun
> And by his provision finished and done
> By John Fleming, Cuthbert and Dorothy his wife
> Whose sons I wish to have an angelic life
> In the year of Our Lord 1574.

It has been assumed that the inscription records the construction of the porch rather than of the whole house, which appears to be one of the earliest of gentry houses in the county. For the text and other details of the Fleming family, see Hunter 1851, 77.

[55] For the 14th-century subsidies, see Yarwood 1981 and Forster 1967, 133–4. The 16th-century wealth distribution is mapped in Forster 1967, 137.

CHAPTER 2

THE HOUSES OF THE YEOMANRY IN THE LATE MIDDLE AGES

Contemporary with the houses of the gentry considered in the first chapter are dwellings which by their form, size and numbers suggest that they were the homes of families of a more numerous but poorer social group. It is unlikely that even a few of these were built by the gentry. Quite apart from the clear differences in size and plan between them and known gentry houses, it is improbable that considerable numbers of gentry families could have built houses and subsequently vanished without trace in the documentary record. The most likely builders were men at the pinnacle of 'peasant' society, describing themselves as yeomen.

In the 17th century non-gentry society had many gradations of status, including yeomen, husbandmen, labourers and others, though the probate inventories show that there was only a general correspondence between status and wealth. The yeomanry was especially diverse, some being as rich as many gentlemen, others being poorer than some husbandmen. The same blurring of social divisions was doubtless a feature of later medieval society, but the surviving non-gentry houses of the age were probably built by only the wealthiest section of the peasantry, that is, the yeomanry. It was in this period that this group began to assume a distinct identity in this area, rising out of the bulk of the peasantry, and the construction of substantial houses served to emphasize the change in their position. It was some time before lesser yeomen were able to build in permanent form, and centuries before the poorest ranks in society were to be provided with houses fit to survive into the modern age.

The late-medieval yeoman houses are as difficult to date as those of the gentry. However, the inclusion of a house in this chapter rather than one dealing with a later period supposes that some criteria have been applied. In no field of study is there an absolute break between medieval and modern, but in the study of vernacular building (which is by definition non-gentry building and which in practice in West Yorkshire during the late-medieval and early modern periods comprises the building of the yeomanry) the periods are divided by the nature of the main room of the dwelling, the housebody.[1] In medieval houses this room was open from ground to roof, and in post-medieval houses it was generally floored over to give a chamber on the first floor. The open room continued in use in some gentry houses and in many of low status well into the modern period, and it is found too, for reasons which will be examined later, in a very few yeoman houses. Despite the exceptions the distinction is a useful means of establishing the character of yeoman houses in two different periods, and this chapter will examine those houses not of gentry status and which are built with open housebody. The most common type of yeoman dwelling in this period in West Yorkshire is the aisled house, and there are also some unaisled houses, both of box-frame and of cruck construction. The different types will be studied in turn.

AISLED HOUSES OF THE LATE MIDDLE AGES

The first chapter involved some discussion of the aisled halls of the period before 1400, and it was noted that the West Yorkshire examples fit the national pattern closely, the halls at Kirkstall, Sandal, and Old Hall, Elland, having been built by major landholders. The later houses of the gentry in West Yorkshire were unaisled, and, as far as we are able to judge from standing structures, the aisle re-emerged in domestic buildings at yeoman level in the late Middle Ages.

Houses with an aisled construction are found widely throughout West Yorkshire. The greatest concentration is found in the Pennine west of the county, especially in the upper Calder valley, and there is no doubt that among these is a large group of medieval houses with an open housebody. Aisled houses are also found in the east of the county, but here there are suggestions that many may not be of medieval date. One can rarely prove the existence of an open housebody, and their plan is frequently of a type generally thought to be post-medieval in origin. There is

good reason to believe, therefore, that a significant number of the eastern houses may be post-1550 in date, floored to give a chamber over the housebody, and with an outshut rather than an aisle at the rear. The question will be discussed in greater detail later, and because of the significant differences between the houses of the two areas, the groups will be discussed separately.

THE AISLED HOUSES OF THE PENNINES

The existence of an important group of late-medieval aisled houses in the Pennine area of West Yorkshire has been recognized now for some years.[2] At the time of writing thirty-five certain or possible examples have been identified in the western half of the county, densely concentrated in the upper Calder valley, with outliers to north, south and east (Map 2).[3] The numbers there allow one to speak of the type as 'common' and thus, for the first time, of vernacular building. This concentration in the upper Calder valley, in the vicinity of Halifax, demands explanation, but first the general character of the buildings in the group should be discussed.

Map 2 Distribution of medieval aisled houses in West Yorkshire.

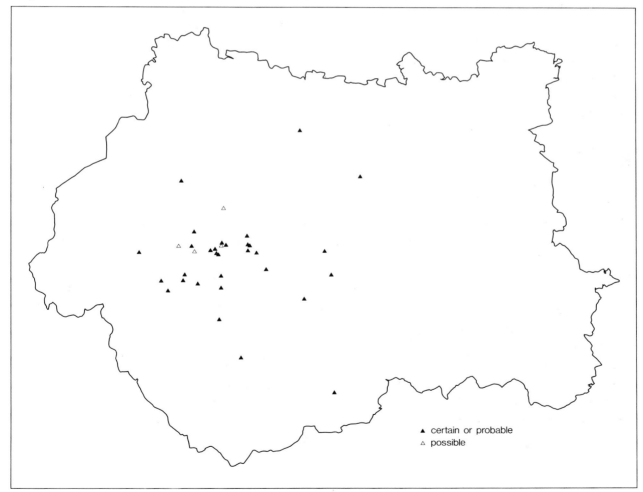

▲ certain or probable
△ possible

Plate 24 [166] Dam Head, Northowram, a house with a front aisle.

Plate 25 [143] Town House, Norland; the wall beneath the arcade plate is an insertion.

Fig 12 [184] Bankhouse, Skircoat.

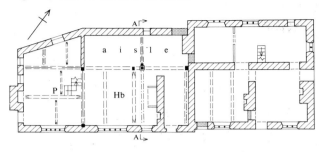

Fig 13 [184] Bankhouse, Skircoat; section through housebody, showing position of firehood.

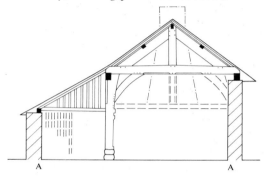

Plate 26 [184] Bankhouse, Skircoat; the arcade structure.

All but one of the aisled houses have or had evidence of timber-framing in their construction. The exception is White Hall, Ovenden, which appears to have been entirely of stone.[4] Other houses were of mixed construction: at Haigh's Farm, Sowerby, the outside walls were of stone except in the upper cross-wing, where the first-floor walls were timber-framed.[5] At the Old Hall, Heckmondwike (82), the cross-wing had ground-floor walls of stone and timber-framing above, and later casing has possibly obscured other instances of mixed construction. Where evidence for framing survives, the treatment of the walling was plain; close-studding is common in internal walls, and it is likely that the external framing was generally more modest than that of contemporary gentry houses. At Dam Head, Northowram (166), a rare piece of decorative herringbone framing survives, probably part of a bay added in the 16th century to give a cross-wing form to the upper end of the house (Plate 24).

The distinguishing feature of the houses in the group is a housebody open from ground to roof and given added width through the use of an aisle or aisles varying in extent and number. The houses always have one at the rear, but some have a front aisle as well: thus some are single-aisled and some double-aisled (Plates 25, 26; Figs 12–14).

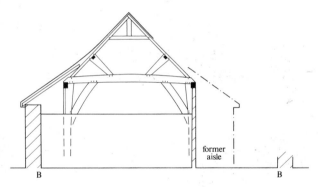

Fig 14 [143] Town House, Norland; section through passage area.

Probably because of the problems of lighting a double-aisled house with its wide span and low eaves, the former was the more common. In these houses the aisle might be confined to the area of the housebody, as appears to have been the case at Fur Street, Northowram, or might extend further along the rear. At High Bentley, Shelf (177), the house was aisled in the area of the housebody and the lower end, but the upper end took the form of a fully storeyed cross-wing. In linear houses the aisle might extend the length of the range, behind the housebody and both upper and lower ends: this was the case at Woodhouse Farm, Shelley.[6]

Not all the houses in this group had the aisle entirely open to the housebody. At High Bentley it is clear from the lack of mortices in the arcade plate that the aisle was not divided from the housebody, but in other houses, like Scout Hall Farm and Dam Head, both in Northowram, the arcade plate has mortices for a stud wall screening the open housebody from the rear aisle.[7] In houses with no division the aisle must have been regarded as an integral part of the housebody, but in those like Scout Hall Farm the two areas were probably functionally distinct. In the upper and lower ends of the aisled house, floored to give chambers, a screen beneath the arcade plate was necessary to close the chambers, off from the unfloored aisle; thus the lower bay at High Bentley has a close-studded wall on the line of the arcade plate.

The aisled houses of the Pennines are of two types, one linear in plan and the other built with a cross-wing at the upper end. In no case did a house have a cross-wing at both ends, in contrast to the late medieval houses of the gentry. The house with a cross-wing appears to have been the more common, slightly outnumbering linear houses where the nature of the original plan is known. The great size of the hall-and-cross-wing aisled house is significant, for it was a very substantial building, little smaller in terms of floor area than the unaisled 'H' plan houses of the contemporary lesser gentry. The extra space provided by the use of the aisle compensated for the absence of a second wing, although the first-floor accommodation was neces-

sarily more restricted. The small differences in the size of the house of the minor gentleman and of the wealthy yeoman suggests that, even if there was a social gap between the two, the differences of wealth might in some cases be narrow.

The aisled houses, both linear and hall-and-cross-wing, have a striking uniformity of plan, for they all adopted the hearth-passage entry. This was occasioned by the invariable use of a firehood to heat the housebody, for both the lateral stack and the upper-end fireplace are entirely absent from this group. In this aspect of their plan, therefore, the aisled houses are identical to the lesser gentry houses of the same period. All have a simple linear lower end, for in houses with a cross-wing, the wing always lay beyond the upper end of the housebody.

Despite the close proximity in terms of size between the larger aisled houses and the smaller gentry houses of the age, there were significant differences in the way the two types of dwelling functioned. The uses of the rooms in the gentry houses were changing constantly, but showed an increasing degree of specialization and sophistication. At

Plate 27 [184] Bankhouse, Skircoat; the dais canopy.

the level of the wealthy yeoman, there was also specialization, but of a kind which reveals the source of his wealth rather than his search for greater comfort. Little is known of room usage from documentary sources, for there are no probate inventories surviving from this period, and the main evidence for the way in which the house functioned lies in the buildings themselves. Despite fragmentary survival, the houses, when studied as a group, give occasional but significant clues about their internal workings.

The most important part of the house was the housebody, always the largest room in terms of floor area and, because open to the roof, of volume. It had many functions. It was the principal reception area, and the main room for dining and sitting. So much is suggested firstly by the frequent existence of a dais canopy over the upper end of the room (Plate 27), which, with the use of a well-worked plank screen behind the dais bench, as at Dam Head, Northowram, indicates an intention to emphasise the superior status of this area, and secondly, by the probable absence of permanent heating in other rooms. The firehood in the housebody commonly appears to have served the only hearth in the dwelling, and the housebody must have been the warmest and most comfortable room. If other rooms were heated, portable means such as braziers must have been used.[8] The hearth in the housebody had the further role, of providing the main fire for cooking. There is no evidence for the use of detached kitchens by the wealthy yeomanry of the later Middle Ages, and no sign of an internal kitchen in these aisled houses. Knowledge of the use of rooms in yeoman houses becomes more abundant for the late 17th century, many probate inventories surviving from after 1688. Even at that date, the housebody was frequently the site of the main cooking hearth, despite the many improvement which the general rebuilding of the age had brought. It is unlikely that the 17th century yeoman had brought the cooking from elsewhere into his living room, for much of the improvement in large yeoman houses in the 17th century lay in efforts to clear some at least of the cooking processes out of the housebody. The common use of the housebody for cooking in that century must be regarded therefore, as continuing the practice current in the late Middle Ages. Further, at a time when, as has been suggested earlier, the hall in some of the lesser gentry houses may still have been used for cooking, it is improbable that there was a more refined use for the housebody of even the wealthiest yeoman.

The function of the aisle to the housebody remains unclear. The question arises of why such a plan proved so suitable to the needs of the wealthy late-medieval yeoman in the upper Calder valley. It might be thought that the all-purpose nature of the housebody demanded a very large room, and that an aisle or aisles gave the additional space required to allow the room to function as a reception area, as a sitting and dining area, and as a kitchen, with all the storage needs following from this. This, however, ignores the fact that both within West Yorkshire and in other parts of the north of England there are yeoman houses, no more sophisticated in their use of the housebody, which are unaisled; some of the cruck houses in West and South Yorkshire, and some unaisled houses even within the upper Calder valley, show that not all yeomen felt the need for the added space provided by an aisle even though they used the housebody in much the same way as their prosperous cousins. Two theories may explain the use of aisled construction. The first is that the form had been current in impermanent houses of the yeomanry in the Middle Ages, and that the surviving aisled houses merely perpetuated a local tradition of building. The second is that the aisled house was adopted due to the special needs of the builders, which dictated that a more conventional unaisled form of house was inadequate in its accommodation and plan.

The first hypothesis will remain unproven until we know a great deal more about medieval peasant building in West Yorkshire.[9] There is, however, some support for the second theory, derived both from the form of the aisled houses and from the occupations of the builders. In all these houses, the lower end gives a single large room on two floors with, usually, an aisle at the rear. In the conventional interpretation of medieval houses, the area below the passage is generally said to have provided two service rooms on the ground floor.[10] The lower room in an aisled house seems, however, too large to have been a buttery or a pantry, and, because of the adoption of the hearth-passage plan with its reredos, did not communicate as closely with the housebody as the service rooms of, say, a Wealden house did with its hall. The hearth-passage plan isolates the lower end, perhaps deliberately due to the use of the area below the passage. It will be argued that the men who built the aisled houses were involved in the textile industry which developed markedly in the Halifax area in the 15th century, and it is suggested that the lower room of the aisled house was a workshop for the manufacture of cloth or, more likely perhaps, for the storage of raw materials and finished pieces. Such a use for the lower end is demonstrable in the yeoman-clothier houses of this area dating from the 17th century, and it is probable that in the late medieval aisled house, too, the area below the passage was non-domestic in function. If so, an explanation for the aisled form of the house may be found in the need to provide the service space which in some unaisled houses in other parts of the country was accommodated at the lower end. Because of the presence of the workshop, the storage functions of rooms like the buttery and pantry were transferred to the aisle behind the housebody, a site which was convenient, being in closer communication with the housebody than the lower end could be, given the use of the hearth-passage plan, and which was to be perpetuated in the 17th century, when local wealthy yeomen built houses with service rooms in precisely this relationship to the housebody either in an outshut or in a storeyed wing. Further, the aisle behind the housebody, open to the room or screened off from it, must have been dark even before the casing of these houses in stone in the 17th century, and probably could serve only as an area for cool storage, sited usually on the rear, north-facing side of the house.

Given the dominance of the housebody in the workings of the house, it is not surprising to find that the parlour and the solar, which in the houses of the contemporary gentry were taking on some of the functions of the hall, were less important at this social level. The main ground-floor room in the upper wing of a house like High Bentley (177) or at the upper end of a linear house like Woodhouse Farm, Shelley, was doubtless called a parlour, but it appears to have been unheated and to have lacked elaboration. If later inventories are any guide, the main parlour probably acted as the best bedroom and as a withdrawing area, with the chambers in the wing or at the upper end being used as bedrooms and storerooms. The household of even the wealthiest yeoman was unlikely to have been as large and diverse as that of a gentleman; in this more closely-knit yeoman household there was probably less need for 'family' to be distinguished from others and, therefore, less need for private rooms. Certainly the all-purpose use of the housebody suggests a life that was much more communal than that being increasingly developed by the gentry, even if the provision of a cross-wing, with room for more than one parlour, is perhaps the first sign of changing social relationships within the ranks of the yeomanry. Just two houses, Lower Hollins, Warley (218) and Dam Head, Northowram (166) show an evolution which demonstrates a need for an expanded upper end: in these houses, the original single-bay linear end was later enlarged to give a wing with, presumably, a new parlour on the ground floor and a chamber on the first floor.

In some gentry houses, the nature of the roof gave an indication of the uses of some parts of the house, decorative trusses appearing over the rooms with a superior function and plain trusses elsewhere. In yeoman aisled houses, however, the roof was not used as a means of display. In many houses the housebody was open to the roof in only a single bay and was closed at one end by a firehood and at the other by a dais canopy which tended to cut off the room at wall-plate level, and thus there was little scope for an elaborate roof. The upper chamber was less developed in its use than the solar or great chamber of a gentry house, and again, therefore, it lacked special treatment in its roof construction.

The most common roof-type in these aisled houses, is the king-post truss. In closed trusses, the apex might have upright braces, as at High Bentley (177), or 'A' braces, as at Lower Hollins (218). Open internal trusses usually lack braces entirely, like that over the housebody at Bankhouse, Skircoat (184). At Town House, Norland (143), the central truss of the cross-wing has a king-post with a pair of 'V' braces, a type which occurs frequently in the 17th century but which here appears to be contemporary with the aisled main range of the mid-16th-century (Fig. 15). Roofs usually terminate in full gables, but the lower end at High Bentley and the upper end at Lower Hollins had a hip. Four

aisled houses do not have a king-post roof. Lower Bentley Royd, Sowerby, had a collar-rafter roof, probably of a date earlier than any of the houses with a king-post. The other three also have collar-rafter roofs, but two-Town House and Town Street, Bramley (39) – have bay divisions marked by angled queen posts rising to clasp side-purlins; the precise nature of the roof in the third house – Yew Tree, Mirfield – cannot be determined.[11] There is little certainty at present about the implications for dating of the different types of roof, but the fact that all are found in association with the open housebody demonstrates that all may be regarded as medieval.

DATING

Hitherto, little reference has been made to the date of particular aisled houses. The one general assumption has been that all are medieval because built with an open housebody, and it is necessary to give as close an idea as possible of what is meant by this in order that the economic and social implications suggested by the houses may be related to developments in other fields.

There is, unhappily, very little that may be adduced from the buildings themselves, to give a reliable idea of when the aisled houses were built, for variety of type and of style is very limited. However, the group as a whole may be compared with the gentry houses thought to date largely from the last decades of the 15th and the first half of the 16th century, and including some in the same area as those presently under consideration. There are many points of similarity between the two groups, both in terms of plan, where the hearth-passage is the standard form, and of structure, the same techniques of timber-framing and roof construction being employed in many gentry and yeoman houses alike, with the exception of the aisled technique which is restricted to the latter type. On these grounds, the yeoman houses may be thought to date from much the same period. The lack of early roof types in the yeoman houses suggests that they are not earlier than the gentry houses, and the presence in Town House, Norland (143) of a type of king-post truss normally associated with a 17th century date but which here must be earlier because contemporary with a range giving an open housebody, indicates that some of the aisled houses may have been built nearer 1550 than 1500, and even after 1550.

The length of the period during which such houses were

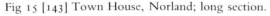

Fig 15 [143] Town House, Norland; long section.

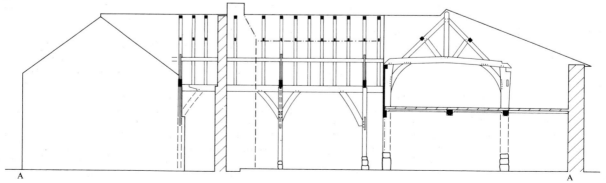

A   A

built may be judged from a study of the evolution of the type. There is little indication of an early groping towards an optimum form, for some which have a claim on admittedly uncertain structural grounds to be amongst the earliest in the group, like High Bentley (177) attained this in a single build. There are, however, a few signs of change: Lower Hollins (218), and Dam Head (166), were built as linear houses but later had a timber-framed wing added to the upper end, converting them to the superior plan type. Structural changes may be noted also: in what may be regarded as early examples of houses with a cross-wing, the wing is framed independently of the main range, sometimes because a part-bay was being left at the upper end of the housebody to give a dais area with a canopy. This is the case at High Bentley. This independent framing of the two parts of the house is not exclusively an early feature, however, for Town House also shows this technique. Integrated framing, in which the side wall of the wing and the end truss of the housebody were combined in the same structure, must have been more complex for the carpenter and for this reason its appearance at Haigh's Farm, Sowerby and at Lower Field Farm, Shelf (178) may be regarded as an advance in technique and probably as a sign that these are later in date than many houses with independent framing. If so, the implication is that the aisled house with an open housebody continued in use for a sufficient length of time for improvements to be conceived of and implemented. The century 1475 to 1575 probably covers the period in which the majority of yeoman aisled houses were built. Yeoman houses of a very different form, with a floored-over housebody and built of stone rather than of timber, began to appear in the upper Calder valley in the last decades of the 16th century, and although there may have been some overlap between medieval and post-medieval forms, it is likely that the appearance of the new type of dwelling marks the end of the aisled house's period of currency.

The Builders Of The Aisled Houses Of The Upper Calder Valley

The appearance of a numerous group of houses of substantial form, showing a large degree of uniformity in plan and structural technique, is strong evidence for a significant social development. That significance is enhanced when it is remembered that the concentration found in the upper Calder valley is unique within West Yorkshire and, in the present state of knowledge, in the whole of the north of England. Important questions are raised concerning the social and economic background to the houses, the identity and occupations of the builders, and the reasons why the houses should be built in one part of the county and in no other part, at least in such numbers.

Certain knowledge of who built any aisled house is lacking but in no case can a gentry family be associated with this type of dwelling. Even the Old Hall at Shelf, the manor house of one of the two manors within the township, belonged to a yeoman family after 1488, when the manor was conveyed to Richard Fourness, yeoman.[12] The Stancliffe and Benteley families, long resident at Scout Hall Farm, and High Bentley respectively, were prominent in local affairs, representatives being listed among the list of township constables.[13] The Fold, Ovenden was prob-

ably the home of the Illingworths in the late Middle Ages, but neither here nor among the Bothes of Fur Street, Northowram, and the Haighs of Haigh's Farm, Sowerby, is there evidence of any claim to gentry status.[14] Positive evidence of status and occupation is found in connection with two other houses. Bankhouse (184) was probably built by the Waterhouse family, possibly after 1534 when Robert Waterhouse, yeoman, is recorded as purchasing the half of the Bankhouse estate not already in his hands. When he died in 1553, Robert was said to posses one messuage called Bankhouse, a barn, a fulling mill, and some other property.[15] The Draper family held Broadbottom, Wadsworth, from the 14th century, and in 1517 Henry Draper negotiated to buy a fulling mill. When he died in 1536, administration of the goods of Henry Draper, "late of Brodbothome, clothier" was entrusted to his wife Elizabeth.[16]

The picture is far from complete, but the evidence relating to the probable builders of the aisled houses shows that the families concerned were not of gentry status. The number of houses, although large in terms of surviving medieval buildings, does not suggest that they were ever as common as large yeoman houses were to become in this area in the 17th century. The future discovery of further examples in the upper Calder valley will not alter the impression that these late medieval yeoman dwellings were exceptional in their time, standing out as distinct from the mass of peasant houses. The inference to be drawn from their numbers and from their size is that the aisled houses were built by men at the pinnacle of peasant society, always a small minority within the rural community.

Why a class of prosperous yeomen developed in the upper Calder valley and not elsewhere in this period has as yet no simple and unequivocal answer, and the explanation is likely to lie in a complex combination of circumstances. Two aspects appear to be of primary importance, however: first, the terms by which men held their lands, and, second, the development of a profitable system of dual occupation.

The territory covered by the modern county of West Yorkshire was dominated in the late Middle Ages by two great estates, both in royal hands. The honour of Pontefract and the manor of Wakefield were vast, stretching from east to west of the county and including within them many sub-manors.[17] Almost all the area distinguished by the concentration of late medieval aisled houses, that is, the upper Calder valley, lies within the manor of Wakefield, forming perhaps half its total area.[18] Just two townships in the upper Calder valley lie in a detached part of the honour of Pontefract. In neither of these two townships, Elland-cum-Greetland and Southowram, have aisled houses yet been recorded, but they occur in townships adjacent to them, Norland, Skircoat, Northowram and Hipperholme-cum-Brighouse, as well as in some others besides. On these grounds, it might be thought that the substantial differences between the tenurial conditions in the two manors were a determining influence in the development of a prosperous yeomanry. The manor of Wakefield owed the service of a single knight, but the honour of Pontefract was held for sixty knights' fees, and this early discrepancy had led to different charges in the two institutions.[19] The manor of Wakefield had developed a system of copyhold tenure which in practice allowed land to be held on generous terms and with a high degree of security, conditions which were highly favourable to the tenantry and which were doubtless helpful in the rise to fortune of a powerful yeomanry. However, the differences in tenure between the manor of Wakefield and the honour of Pontefract cannot be the complete explanation for why a number of large yeoman houses appeared in the late Middle Ages in one and not the other, for it fails to explain why it is only one part of the manor of Wakefield which is distinguished by these houses. Neither in the eastern part of the manor, in the low-lying area around Wakefield itself, nor in other upland parts, like the graveship of Holme in the south-west of the county, nor, indeed, uniformly throughout the upper Calder valley, are concentrations of medieval yeoman houses found. The circumstances which permitted the construction of the aisled houses were not, therefore, common to the whole manor, but were peculiar to one part of it. Favourable tenure, found throughout the manor may have been a prerequisite of the development of an upper yeomanry, but by itself is insufficient as an explanation of this phenomenon.

The growth of the textile industry in the late Middle Ages is the second aspect of this discussion. The rapid expansion of the industry in the West Riding of Yorkshire in the 15th and 16th centuries has been charted, and there is a great deal of contemporary evidence for the importance of cloth production in the regional economy.[20] Even though the industry was found over a very wide area, both in the Pennines and in the lowlands to the east, it appears that it was concentrated most intensely in the hinterland served by Halifax, that is, in the upper Calder valley. The aulnage rolls show the growing importance of Halifax in the 15th century, and the industry had become so vital to the fortunes of its hinterland by the mid 16th century that its special structure was protected from provisions applied elsewhere. This protection entered the Statute Book in the form of the Halifax Act of 1555, which permitted the operation of wooldrivers (middlemen) serving in the Halifax market. The wording of the preamble to the Act, even allowing for the conventional hyperbole of such pleas, makes clear the dependence of the population on the textile industry, for it asserts that the inhabitants of the parish of Halifax, which includes virtually the whole of the upper Calder valley, 'altogether do lyve by cloth making'.[21] The growth of the industry had greatly affected the valley, for the same Act claimed that there were 'above fyve hundrethe households there newly increased within this fourtye years past', and Camden, writing in 1586, observed that;

> . . . the inhabitants are wont to give out, that this parish of theirs maintaineth more men and women, than other living creatures of what kind soever. . . . Moreover, the industrie of the inhabitants heere is admirable, who in a barraine soile, wherein there is no commodious, nay scarce any dwelling or living at all, have so come up and flourished by clothing (a trade which they took to not above three score and tenne years agoe at the farthest) that they greatly enrich their own estates, and winne the praise from all their neighbours; yea, and have proved the saying to bee true 'that barrain places give a good edge to industry'.[22]

Camden may have been wrong about the date of the establishment of the industry in the upper Calder valley, indeed he may have drawn upon the Halifax Act for this information, but he is an important witness of the effects it had had on the local economy by the second half of the 16th century.

There are other indications that industrial activity was causing significant social and economic changes. In his study of the Lay Subsidy of 1546, R. B. Smith observed that the wapentakes of Agbrigg and Morley, of which the upper Calder valley formed a part, showed certain peculiarities. The high percentage of men in these wapentakes paying tax on goods of more than £20 value was, he believed, a reflection of the fact that Agbrigg and Morley 'were the centres of cloth production where the "Halifax system" is found, and where the opportunities for middlemen were probably greatest', and his conclusion is that it was textiles which 'made Agbrigg and Morley the richest area in the Riding in terms of taxable wealth'.[23] It is not possible from Dr Smith's evidence to isolate the upper Calder valley from the other parts of the wapentakes in order to assess to what extent the wealth of this one part accounted for the peculiar riches of the whole, but if textiles were indeed the source of local wealth, and if the upper Calder valley was the most important cloth-producing region, where large profits were to be made by middlemen and manufacturers, then the concentration of many of the most lucrative aspects of the industry in the Halifax area might be thought to have played a large part in producing the remarkable taxation returns of 1546. Further work on the returns, with a view to establishing the distribution of taxable wealth within the wapentakes of Agbrigg and Morley, would allow this hypothesis to be tested.

The precise sequence of events and the respective weight to be accorded to a number of different influences are still unclear, but it is suggested that easy tenurial conditions in the manor of Wakefield aided the accumulation of wealth needed to initiate a significant expansion of an established textile industry, but that, for reasons beyond the scope of this volume to explore, it was in the upper Calder valley, rather than in other areas similar in geographical character and tenurial customs, that the industry came to be most heavily concentrated, especially those aspects of the industry which yielded the greatest profits. The dependence of the upper Calder valley on a system of dual occupation is well-attested by 16th century commentators, but in contrast to some other areas, where dual occupation is thought to have been a forced result of population pressure on a hard-pressed peasantry and to have provided little more than a subsistence economy, the Halifax region grew famously wealthy through its successful blend of involvement in both agriculture and industry.[24] The relationship of the late medieval houses to this economic prosperity is a matter of debate. There is documentary evidence that some at least of the aisled houses were occupied by yeomen engaged on a large scale in textiles, and it has been suggested that the very form of their houses may reflect their need for a workshop to be incorporated within the main dwelling block. Whether all the aisled houses were built by yeoman-clothiers is beyond proof. It is probable that the buoyant economy generated by the profits of

MEDIEVAL AISLED HOUSES

Broadbothom, Wadsworth (SE 007266)
Stell 1960; Stell 1965, 6, 7, 9.★

Mare Hill, Warley (SE 049272)

Lower Hollins, Warley (SE 057238)

Fold Farm, Ovenden (SE 067288)

White Hall, Ovenden (SE 083268)
Mercer 1975, 222–3

Long Can, Ovenden (SE 068264)
RCHM Threatened Buildings Records

Haighs Farm, Sowerby (SE 030232)
Atkinson and McDowall 1967, 79–82.

Lower Bentley Royd, Sowerby (SE 053233)
Atkinson and McDowall 1967, 86–8.

Deerstones, Sowerby (SE 038221)

Town House, Norland (SE 070229)

Bankhouse, Skircoat (SE 096225)

Fur Street, Northowram (SE 088269)
Mercer 1975, 221–2.

Dam Head, Northowram (SE 100274)

Sladden Street, Northowram (SE 090265 approx)
Mercer 1975, 222.

Scout Hall Farm, Northowram (SE 096276)
Mercer 1975, 222.

House in Northowram
Mercer 1975, 16.

High Bentley, Shelf (SE 123274)
Atkinson and McDowall 1967, 81, 83–5.

Old Hall, Shelf (SE 122284)
Mercer 1975, 225.

Lower Field Bottom, Shelf (SE 124273)

Smith House, Hipperholme with Brighouse (SE 143246)

Prior's Mead, Hipperholme with Brighouse (SE 132264)

Cinderhills, Hipperholme with Brighouse (SE 123268)

Old Lindley, Stainland (SE 093190)
Pacey 1964, 201–4.

Manor House, South Crosland (SE 117148)

Woodhouse Farm, Shelley (SE 217148)
Mercer 1975, 223–4.

Old Hall, Heckmondwike (SE 214239)

112 Town Street, Bramley (SE 247350)

Yew Tree, Mirfield (SE 185213)
Record held by West Yorkshire Unit

Hagstocks, Northowram (SE 096272)
Ambler 1913.

Ridings, Ovenden (SE 062271)
Westerdale 1983.

Peel House, Gomersal (SE 207267)

Middle Hall, Liversedge (SE 195238)

Manor House, Manningham (SE 151345 approx.)

West Scholes, Thornton (SE 098314)

Old Hall, Esholt (SE 181401)

★ *Reference (if not recorded by survey)*

---

industry created as well a prosperous group engaged in supplying both the necessities of life and luxury commodities, but it will be argued later than men of this type found the unaisled house more suited to their needs.[25] A number of points combine, therefore, to suggest that it was the textile industry which, in all likelihood, was responsible for the erection of the group of aisled houses found scattered over a wide area in West Yorkshire but overwhelmingly concentrated in the upper Calder valley.

The probable association of the houses with the textile industry has important implications for the dating of the buildings. The short-term fluctuations in the fortunes of the industry in the later Middle Ages have not been studied, and there is, indeed, even conflicting evidence for the date at which it first began to grow significantly. The aulnage rolls suggest that Halifax was of great importance in the last third of the 15th century, but both Camden and the Halifax Act of 1555 suggest that the period of greatest expansion may have been the first half of the 16th century.[26] On this evidence, it seems unlikely that any of the aisled houses date from before 1475, and probable that most of them are 16th rather than 15th century in date.

This tends to confirm the conclusion drawn from the buildings themselves that the majority of the aisled houses were built in the century 1475–1575.

UNAISLED HOUSES IN THE PENNINES

As well as the group of aisled houses considered above, there are a few buildings both in the upper Calder valley and in other parts of the Pennine belt which today show no sign of aisled construction but which are of medieval date. They are characterised by fragmentary survival, and it is impossible in many cases to be certain of their original form. Because of this uncertainty, it is difficult to assess their significance and the relationship between aisled and unaisled houses in the area.

It is not even certain that many of the unaisled structures did not originally form part of dwellings which were aisled in another part. Three houses in the upper Calder valley – New Heath Head, Midgley; Lower High Sunderland, Northowram; and Shibden Fold, Northowram – contain remains of a cross-wing which might well have been attached to an aisled main range originally, but in every case the main range has been replaced by later work. Two other houses in the upper Calder valley – Binroyd (145) and Old Hall (144), both in Norland, – have been demolished, and although some records exist, they demonstrate only that the houses were timber-framed. It is possible, perhaps even probable given their high yeoman status, that both were aisled. These buildings, therefore, suggest that the concentration of aisled houses in the upper Calder valley may have been even denser than indicated by the evidence of houses whose form is known more certainly.[27]

Perhaps the clearest example of an unaisled medieval yeoman house in the Pennines is Fletcher House, Almondbury, in the Holme valley south of Huddersfield. It appears to have had a linear plan of three cells, an open housebody and a hearth-passage entry.[28] The importance of this house lies in the way that it shows unaisled building to have been known among the yeomen in the Pennines in the late Middle Ages. It makes it more likely that some less certain examples, with more fragmentary remains, such as Throstle Nest (220) and Westfield (219) both in Warley, were also unaisled, and this in turn has some highly significant implications. If unaisled yeoman houses were present in the Pennines in the late Middle Ages, even if they were not as common as aisled houses, it becomes clear that the yeoman about to build had options open to him. That the majority of substantial yeomen in the upper Calder valley opted for the aisled house must be regarded as the result of a deliberate choice. It may still have had an ancient ancestry among local peasant houses, although this remains to be proved, but it seems more likely that it became common not, or not just, because it was a traditional structural form but rather because it met the requirements of a yeomanry which demanded what amounted to a special-purpose building, part dwelling and part workshop. If the aisled houses were the homes of prosperous yeoman-clothiers, the unaisled houses may have been built by yeomen who did not require a workshop. In these houses the lower end could be turned to service use, and there was therefore, no need for an aisle. The occasional yeoman rising to prominence solely or mainly on the profits of agriculture, perhaps because the size of his holding was particularly large, or the middleman supplying the food and luxury markets, may well have been the type of man who found the unaisled house more suited to his requirements.

CRUCK CONSTRUCTION IN WEST YORKSHIRE

Within the Pennine west of the county, one further group of buildings requires consideration at this point. All these either use, or show evidence for the earlier use of, cruck construction. The controversy surrounding the subject of crucks demands that the issues raised by the buildings should be treated together, although since crucks appear in both the medieval and post-medieval periods this involves a disruption of the chronological approach hitherto adopted in this work.

The origin of cruck construction is beyond the scope of the present survey, and has been dealt with in a recent work.[29] Moreover, there is no reason to think that the West Yorkshire evidence would help in the search for origins, for none of the surviving buildings is of a date earlier than many surviving non-cruck structures. The important questions here concern the numbers of cruck buildings, their functions, their distribution within the county, and their relationship to non-cruck buildings. To answer these questions, it is necessary to consider domestic and non-domestic buildings, for this highlights significant aspects of the problems.

To date, sixty-one buildings with crucks in them have been noted in West Yorkshire. Some crucks survive in standing structures, others have been demolished but are known from earlier records, and others remain only as timbers re-used in later buildings. This number will grow with more detailed local research, but, even allowing for the selective nature of the present survey, it is not large. There are perhaps twice that number of surviving box-framed structures of various types and dates within the county, and in South Yorkshire, a county of smaller size but with a similar variety of terrain, there are over three times as many cruck buildings.[30] However, this number gives little idea of how common cruck buildings may once have been in the western part of the county. There are reasons why box-framed buildings survive in circumstances which involve the demolition of cruck buildings. The low nature of most of the surviving crucks meant that such buildings were less adaptable and less susceptible to improvement, and would, therefore, be more likely to be demolished, leaving no trace unless some of the timbers were re-used in successors on the site. In the manor of Cracoe, which included the township of Silsden, in the north-west of the county, cruck construction appears to have been the norm in the second half of the 16th century, for the surveys of the manor contain many references to buildings, non-domestic as well as domestic, of this type. In 1556, for instance, William Davye possessed '1 house of 3 payre of crockes lately erected', and 1586 Stephen Kytchen had a 'firehouse of four paire of Crokes of Ashe Tymbre one Barne of five paire of Croks of Ocke Tymbre latelye buylded one other howse for hay of three paire of

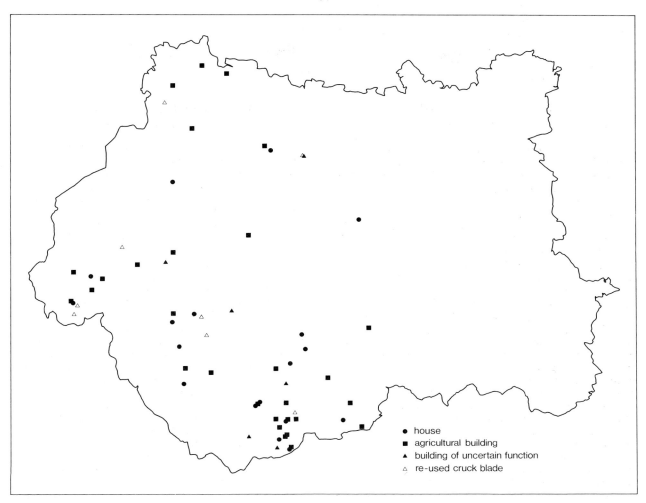

Map 3 Distribution of cruck buildings in West Yorkshire.

Croks latelye buylded of Ocke Tymbre, two other houses the one whereof is of three paire of Croks and Thother of two paire Ashe tymbre'.[31] Elsewhere, there are earlier evidences of the use of crucks. A 'grangiam de sex postes vel sex crokkes' was to be built in Yeadon in 1380; in 1432 a house in Ovenden was to be 'de octo laquearibus – Anglice, 8 crukkes', and in 1537 in Greetland there was a 'domum sex cruckes'.[32] From the surviving buildings and from the documentary evidence, it is clear that crucks were in widespread use over much of the Pennines.

The distribution of cruck buildings within West York-shire has a striking pattern (Map 3). All are located in the western, upland, half of the county apart from two outliers in the central area. The same picture is to be found in South Yorkshire where 'all but a dozen of the 150 known cruck buildings . . . are confined to its western third'.[33] This total has since grown, but J. T. Smith's observation on the 'astonishing sharp division on the eastern boundary be-tween cruck and non-cruck areas' still applies.[34] Even within the western half of West Yorkshire, there is a particular concentration in the valleys of the Colne and

Holme. Roughly half the total is located here, and it will be argued later that this emphasis is an accurate indication of the importance of cruck building in this part of the county and that there are good reasons for it.

The sixty-one examples of cruck building can be divided into three groups according to their function. Eighteen were houses, another group, of twenty-nine, were agri-cultural buildings, usually barns, and in the rest – fourteen in all – the crucks survive only as re-used timbers and the function of the building from which they came cannot be determined. The houses are not an impressive group, at least in comparison with the medieval aisled houses of the upper Calder valley. A very few approach the size of the lesser aisled houses in plan, but the use of crucks in West Yorkshire brought with it low side walls giving cramped accommodation on upper floors. Nevertheless, some of these cruck houses must have started life as the biggest yeoman dwellings in their immediate vicinity, for the large examples are found where aisled houses are least densely concentrated or non-existent. In Honley, for example, the earliest yeoman house recorded is the cruck-built Upper

Plate 28 [89] Upper Oldfield, Honley; crucks survive in the housebody.

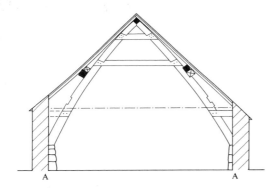

Fig 16 [89] Upper Oldfield, Honley; section through housebody.

Plate 29 [90] House at Upper Oldfield, Honley.

Oldfield (89), built probably in the mid 16th century on a linear plan of four bays, with an open housebody of one-and-a-half bays (Plate 28; Fig. 16). A smaller house nearby is also of cruck construction (Plate 29). In Slaithwaite, there are two cruck houses – Birks (185) and the Old Hall (186) – of similar form and size to Upper Oldfield, and they probably remained the largest yeoman dwellings in the township until the rebuilding of Hill Top Fold (187) in the late 17th century (Plates 30, 31).

Most of the other houses were much smaller. Mr. Walton claims that a few were of a single bay only, but his evidence suggests that some were once larger; at Carr House Farm Cottage, Hepworth, for instance, both the

Plate 30 [185] Birks, Slaithwaite.

Plate 31 [185] Birks, Slaithwaite; interior of housebody.

plan, with a central entry in the gable wall, and the nature of the walling, insubstantial enough to have belonged to an internal division rather than to a wall exposed to the Pennine weather, are unlike anything recorded elsewhere.[35] Perhaps the most that can be said is that many of the houses were small and low, probably giving a single-storey range of two or three rooms. The details of plan are frequently obscured, for in cruck buildings the walls, free from the task of carrying the roof, were very liable to be altered and even replaced wholesale, thus obliterating the original arrangement of doors and windows.

The agricultural buildings are equally varied. Some of the cruck barns are very substantial, fit almost to compare with those of Lancashire. At Thorpe House Farm, Almondbury, the barn measures some 24 feet from ground to apex, and the trusses of the barn at Linthwaite Hall are of very heavy scantling and well-finished form. The function of some of the smaller agricultural buildings is not certain; at Upper Fold Farm, Thurstonland (209), for instance, a cruck truss is used in a small outbuilding of indeterminate function (Plate 32; Fig. 17). Most of the smaller buildings employ crucks of poor finish and slight scantling.[36]

The problems involved in dating cruck buildings have assailed students for many years, and opinions vary widely. In West Yorkshire, there is little upon which to base firm judgements. Documents have demonstrated the use of crucks in the late Middle Ages and have suggested that they were standard in new peasant houses and outbuildings, in Silsden at least, in the second half of the 16th century. The frequency of the references to the use of crucks there, indicates that they were far from obsolete, and it is likely that they continued in use for some time afterwards, in houses and other structures.

The buildings in which crucks are found varied in size and function, and the explanation for their use lies in a consideration both of the buildings' status and of their relationship to other contemporary buildings. The picture is one of the progressive abandonment of cruck construction, with the wealthy choosing other forms at an early date and, after a lengthy period when crucks were rejected by intermediate levels, a final appearance of the form in the dwellings of the poorer members of rural society and in the non-domestic buildings of these and higher levels. The date at which cruck construction was abandoned in any one area depended on the wealth of important sections of its society. In areas with an early development of a prosperous yeomanry, and where wealth percolated also to the lower peasantry, crucks fell out of use at an early date because all men able to build a durable house could afford something better than that offered by cruck construction. Where large parts of the peasantry were poorer, however, cruck building continued to offer many men an improvement on houses of impermanent construction, and in these areas cruck construction persisted until yeomen and lesser men were able to emulate their counterparts elsewhere and build superior houses in non-cruck form.

In West Yorkshire, as far back as the record can take us, the cruck was used in dwellings only when other types of permanent structures were beyond reach. In the Middle Ages, a cruck house might give an open room of fair size, but had only very restricted storeyed accommodation at either end; it was, therefore, never able to rival the capacity of the aisled and unaisled box-framed houses of the upper yeomanry and the gentry. In the post medieval period, the fully-storeyed house became the norm for the yeomanry, and again the cruck house was at a disadvantage. Only those who could not afford a fully-storeyed house erected low cruck houses which were probably rather better versions of the type of house in which their ancestors had lived. Thus when it first emerged into the record the cruck in West Yorkshire was not superior and ancient, but rather inferior and, it will be argued, much later in date than has been thought hitherto. It was cheaper to erect and simpler in its carpentry than a box-framed structure, and the external walls, to judge from the poor survival rate and from the one house in which the nature of the original walling is known, were less integral to the structure as a whole, therefore requiring less sophisticated prefabrication, and apparently of poor quality.[37]

The low regard in which the cruck was held in West Yorkshire is clear even in the earliest instance of its use. At Sandal Castle, the domestic and service buildings dating from the mid 13th century and later included a hall built to replace the wooden aisled hall and a detached kitchen, both

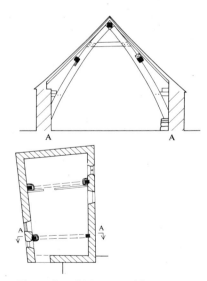

Plate 32 [209] Upper Fold Farm, Thurstonland; small outbuilding of cruck construction.

Fig 17 [209] Upper Fold Farm, Thurstonland; plan and section.

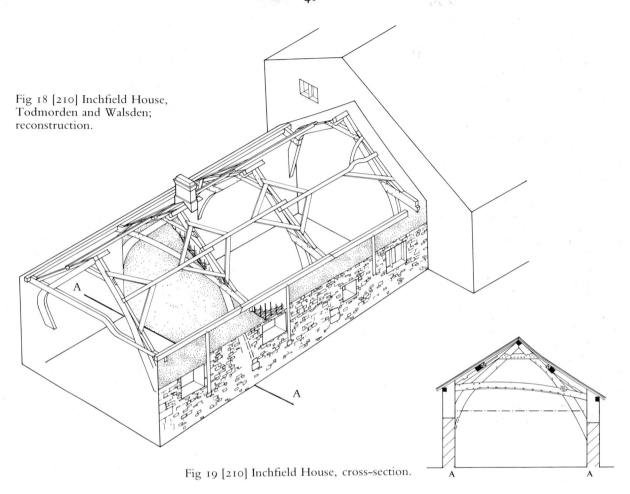

Fig 18 [210] Inchfield House, Todmorden and Walsden; reconstruction.

Fig 19 [210] Inchfield House, cross-section.

built of stone, and a timber-framed brewhouse of cruck construction. In a great house of medieval date, therefore, the cruck was restricted to a service outbuilding of subordinate status.[38] None of the gentry houses of the late Middle Ages used crucks, all being either of stone or box-framed. The large barn at Linthwaite Hall, Linthwaite, an early 17th century gentry house, may date from the 16th century, but is more likely to be broadly contemporary with the house.[39] After the appearance of a very few barns like this, the gentry ceased using crucks in any type of structure capable of surviving into the modern age.

The use of crucks by the rest of the rural population presents a more complex picture, and has to be considered area by area within the Pennine part of West Yorkshire. Easily the wealthiest part, in terms of buildings, is the upper Calder valley, and it has been shown that a significant number of prosperous yeomen were able to build permanent houses here in the late Middle Ages. None, however, employed crucks in his house, for the aisled and un-aisled box-framed dwelling offered superior accommodation. In this period, crucks were certainly in use here in houses, as the documentary references reveal, but at a lower social level. In the post medieval period, the

upper Calder valley continued to be the wealthiest part of the Pennine belt, and as a direct result crucks are little in evidence in either houses or barns. When the lesser ranks of the yeomanry came to rebuild in vast numbers in the 17th century, they were able to provide themselves with fully-storeyed dwellings, and the re-use of cruck timbers in some of these indicates that these new houses may well have replaced cruck houses of earlier generations. Crucks are found in the upper Calder valley only in very small houses, like Inchfield House, Todmorden (210) (Figs 18, 19), and in small outbuildings. The major agricultural buildings were of non-cruck form, most of the larger houses having a sizeable aisled barn nearby. The last use of crucks here is in mean structures like that at Bullace Trees, Warley (243), where a single low cruck truss of inferior workmanship supports the roof of a building of uncertain use and possibly mid 17th century date. Thus, surviving crucks are comparatively rare in the upper Calder valley because each level of society, rebuilding at different times from the late Middle Ages to the 18th century, was wealthy enough to erect superior non-cruck dwellings and barns. Crucks are found in the dwellings of the poorest levels at a late date, for the cruck was the lowest common denominator in the dwellings of different parts of the Pennines, and the upper Calder valley, peculiar in the wealth of many ranks of its society, like all other parts of the Pennines had its share of the poor.

In the north-west of the Pennines in West Yorkshire, the picture is much the same. There is a growing body of evidence for building by a small upper yeomanry in the late Middle Ages, but the houses of this building period and of the 17th century rebuilding by such men were of non-cruck form. Again, crucks were used here not by these wealthiest yeomen, but by a more numerous body of lesser men. If the Silsden evidence can be applied to a wider area, it suggests that significant numbers were engaged in a rebuilding in the second half of the 16th century, taking the form of the cruck houses which distinguished this middling section of the peasantry from the poorest levels of rural society, to whom the cruck house was still an unattainable goal. The houses of this rebuilding do not appear to have been large, and those of which some record survives are low and of simple plan. Dwellings like the cottage at Bracken Hall, Baildon (19) are probably of the type which represented an improvement for this middling band of rural society in the early modern period (Fig. 20). The scarcity of these houses is probably due to the fact that later rebuilding has replaced them with more spacious dwellings, rather than because only a few were ever built.

The fullest evidence of the progressive abandonment of crucks comes from the south-west of the county, from the valleys of the Colne and Holme. Here is concentrated the bulk of the West Yorkshire cruck buildings, and the variety of type and date is probably greatest. Of all the Pennine areas within the county, this is the poorest in its buildings; timber-framed houses are few and the yeoman rebuilding of the post-medieval period produced a poorer crop than elsewhere. The impression that levels of wealth among the peasantry were lower here than elsewhere is confirmed by the documents, for the Hearth Tax of 1672 shows that many townships had a very large proportion of people taxed at a minimum rate.[40] It is no coincidence that cruck houses are most common here, an inferior type of house being more likely to appear in an area of lesser overall wealth.

Even in the late Middle Ages, the cruck house here was not for the very few wealthiest yeomen, for these built aisled and unaisled houses.[41] These non-cruck houses represent the rare emergence of men comparable in status to the wealthy yeomen of the upper Calder valley. Below them, it is suggested there was a small number of yeomen who were indeed able to build in the late Middle Ages, but could not afford houses of great size. Instead, they built cruck houses, linear in plan and much more restricted in accommodation than the yeoman houses of the upper Calder valley. The larger of the two houses at Upper Oldfield, Honley (89), with its accompanying cruck barn, is the best surviving example, and Old Hall (186) and Birks (185), both in Slaithwaite, probably belong to this group.[42]

The smaller cruck houses of this area, such as those recorded by Mr. Walton, are of uncertain date.[43] If they are medieval, as he believed, they represent the unique survival from that age of permanent dwellings of a lower peasantry. This seems unlikely, however, for it is clear that this area was consistently poor in its peasant society in this and later periods; areas which had a much wealthier society in the

Fig 20 [19] Cottage at Bracken Hall, Baildon; 19th-century sketch of interior.

late Middle Ages show permanent building only by a small upper section of the peasantry. It is more likely, therefore, that the small cruck houses of the south-western part of the county are the post-medieval dwellings of a level of rural society which, in more favoured parts, was able to afford to erect fully-storeyed, non-cruck stone houses. Because the poorer yeomanry or husbandmen here could not afford such substantial houses, but were able to invest in a rebuilding of sorts, they turned to the cruck house which, however mean in comparison with the storeyed stone houses of the better-off yeomen of this and other areas, nevertheless represented for them at that time an improvement in living conditions and was far superior to the impermanent houses of the mass of the rural population. The survival of some numbers of these small cruck houses is due to the continuing poverty of the levels of society which built them; unlike the situation in the upper Calder valley, where the re-use of cruck blades in the house of the lesser yeomanry in the 17th century reveals the ability of large numbers of men to replace cruck houses with something better, the cruck houses in the south-west continued in use because funds were more rarely available to finance this process of replacement. How late the cruck continued to be used in new building is not clear, but the farm complex at Upper Fold Farm, Thurstonland (209), possibly reflects its last fling; here a large yeoman house of the late 17th century has probably contemporary agricultural buildings which include two large barns, neither of cruck construction, and a very small outbuilding which uses crucks of rough workmanship; the inference is clear that the cruck, unfit to provide adequate accommodation in either house or barns, was relegated to a minor building.

The broadest contrast in the distribution of crucks in West Yorkshire is not, however, between parts of the Pennine west, but between their once common use over all that half of the county and their virtually complete absence from the eastern half. In the west the existence of cruck building reflects the emergence of an intermediate level of the peasantry, much poorer than the wealthy yeoman with his box-framed or fully-storeyed stone house, but nevertheless sharply distinct from the mass of the poor who remained unable to afford the comfort of a cruck house.

What is noticeable about the east of the county in the late Middle Ages and early modern period is the absence not merely of cruck houses but of any number of houses of comparable status, unless some of the small aisled and unaisled eastern houses may be considered as such.[44] If the cruck houses of the west were the products of a rise of a lesser yeomanry, the dearth of evidence in the east for houses of similar status suggests strongly that this social phenomenon did not affect that part of the county in the same degree. The post-medieval houses of the area indicate that peasant society was generally poorer here than in parts of the Pennine west and that a rebuilding in stone occurred at a later date. Most important to the present discussion is the possibility that the section of the peasantry which in the west built cruck houses was retarded in its development in the east until such a late date that it enjoyed its rebuilding in the period when crucks were an obsolete form in new houses, however humble. Cruck houses fail to appear in the east, therefore, not because an alternative carpentry tradition was entrenched and produced houses of a like status, but because the rebuilding by poorer men which produced cruck houses in the west did not occur there at a time when cruck building had advantages.

In general, therefore, the use of crucks in West Yorkshire depended on a combination of circumstances. Firstly, a moderately wealthy section of the peasantry had to emerge for whom cruck building represented an improvement in living conditions. If the levels of wealth were too high, as in the upper Calder valley among the upper yeomanry in the late Middle Ages and among the lesser yeomanry there in the 17th century, crucks would not be used, for superior forms could be afforded. If, however, the emergent section was somewhat poorer, larger numbers of cruck houses could be built, as was clearly the case in Silsden in the second half of the 16th century. Secondly, timing was important, for if the development of these sections of the peasantry occurred at a late date, as in the east of the county, crucks would not be used because they were by then an obsolete form. A true understanding of the significance of the distribution of cruck building awaits much future research, but the study of its incidence as a social phenomenon can add significantly to an appreciation of how rural society developed.

LATE MEDIEVAL YEOMAN HOUSES IN THE EAST OF THE COUNTY

The western boundary of West Yorkshire follows a natural division along the line of the Pennine watershed, but there is no such clear boundary in the east. The low-lying, arable-dominated east of the county runs imperceptibly into the Vale of York, an area of nucleated villages clustered around church and gentleman's residence, very different in character to the Pennines with its dispersed settlement. The buildings of the eastern part of the county show much closer affinities with those of the Vale than with Pennine houses, and it is to the Vale that one looks to set the rather scanty West Yorkshire material in its context.[45]

The persistence of timber-framing in this area well into the 17th century frequently makes it very difficult to determine whether a particular building is of medieval or later date, for it is not enough to demonstrate simply that a house is timber-framed for it to be considered medieval, as was very frequently the case in the Pennines. The proof of a medieval date lies in the evidence for the existence of an open hall or housebody, but it is precisely this sort of detailed structural evidence that is so often missing or hidden in the eastern houses. Even when it is clear that a house had an open main room, and thus that it qualifies as medieval in this study, it is far from obvious that it was erected before many other local timber-framed houses which show evidence of having had a floored-over housebody. Some of the houses with an open main room are small and some with a floored-over housebody are large, and it is possible that the two types were broadly contemporary, the latter being the post-medieval houses of the most prosperous yeomanry and the former being the houses of poorer men unable to build a fully-storeyed dwelling.

Until more certain evidence of dating is gathered through the application of dendrochronology the question of when many of these eastern houses were erected is best treated with caution.

Whether medieval or not, houses with an open housebody are few in the east. As in the west, there are two types, aisled and unaisled, but the character of the buildings is very different in this area. Of the aisled houses, those two which certainly had an open housebody are small; Cheesecake Hall, Oulton with Woodlesford (169) had a linear plan, was low in height and was aisled only in the area of the housebody, although here there were front and rear aisles, and Crag House, Adel cum Eccup (11) is of similar height but had only a rear aisle. Less certain examples of the type are larger: Earlsheaton Hall, Soothill, was four bays long and appears to have had a rear aisle and end-aisles similar to those of some Vale of York houses, but it is not proven that this house had an open housebody; the height of the range certainly allows room for two storeys throughout.[46] Other eastern timber-framed houses (for example, Old Manor House, Thorner (205); Hill House Farm, Normanton (164); and the Old Malt Kiln, Bramham cum Oglethorpe (33)) are of two storeys today and probably always were, for none shows any trace of medieval character. The open housebody of the Pennine aisled house usually survived the casing of the timber-framed structure in stone, but in no instance do these eastern houses show in their stonework a suggestion that their timber-framed predecessor had an open main room. Furthermore, in none was there a dais canopy in the area of the housebody. The surviving timberwork in the eastern houses is of a much poorer quality than that of the Pennine aisled houses, and roof structures, where they survive, lack early character; at Croft Holding, Walton in Ainsty (217) and the Old Malt Kiln, the roof is of simple paired rafters, some pairs having collars, and is made up of timbers of slight scantling and poor finish. In plan, too, these houses indicate a post-medieval date; in none is there clear evidence for the common medieval hearth-passage and through-passage plans, and the most common type is the lobby-entry, a plan usually associated with a post-1550 date in yeoman houses.

The strongest evidence that many eastern timber-framed

Plate 33 [175] Hazelwood Cottages, Rothwell.

Fig 21 [175] Hazelwood Cottages, Rothwell; section through parlour end.

houses are post medieval with a floored-over housebody and a continuous outshut, rather than medieval, with an open housebody and an aisle, is provided by the nature of the arcade structure. In the eastern houses, the bay lengths vary much more markedly than in the Pennine aisled houses, one short bay usually providing the main stack or firehood. More important is the absence of evidence in the arcade-plate for a distinction between a central area open to the roof and storeyed end-bays. In the Pennine aisled house, such a distinction obtained; the arcade-plate in the area of the housebody usually lacked a framed wall beneath it, but in the end-bays such walls existed, and either survive today as close-studded partitions or are revealed by mortices and peg-holes in the arcade plate. This demonstrates the existence of storeyed end-bays flanking an open housebody; in the area of the housebody, the aisle was undivided from the main span but where the house was storeyed, fully-framed walls divided the chambers from the open aisle. In the eastern houses, the arcade structure is very different. Only the principal posts and the braces up from those posts are morticed and pegged into the arcade-plate and for the rest the plate is entirely blank throughout the length of the house. Instead of fully-framed walls beneath the plate, the eastern houses have screens of unpegged studs and lath and plaster, fixed to, rather than jointed into, the arcade-plate. These screens, of simpler workmanship and cheaper than the fully-framed divisions within the Pennine aisled house, are possibly original.

Significantly, such screens exist not only in the undoubtedly storeyed ends of the house, but also in the area of the housebody, and suggests that the houses were storeyed throughout, having, therefore, a continuous outshut rather than an aisle. If so, these houses may be seen as roughly contemporary with some larger eastern houses of certain post-medieval date. Such is No.176 Leeds Road, Lofthouse with Carlton (123), a hall-and-cross-wing house of the early 17th century, of two storeys throughout and with an outshut behind the hall range divided from the main span by a partition of unpegged studs beneath the arcade plate.

Also in the eastern part of the county is a group of unaisled houses, whose numbers, fewer than ten, and generally fragmentary survival make their significance difficult to assess. There is, however, reason to think that some at least were built with an open housebody. Hazelwood Cottages, Rothwell (175), has walls only a little over 10 feet high, and an early ceiling only in the parlour; it is likely, therefore, that the housebody, and perhaps the lower room as well, were unceiled originally (Plate 33; Fig. 21). A house in Main Street, Mickletown, Methley (132), is of hall-and-cross-wing form, and the fact that the cross-wing is much higher and of two full storeys suggests that the main range was capable of giving only a low open housebody. At Stoney Lane, Nos 2 and 4, Crigglestone (44), the early timber-framed range is low, but it is not clear whether the housebody was open to the roof (Fig. 22).

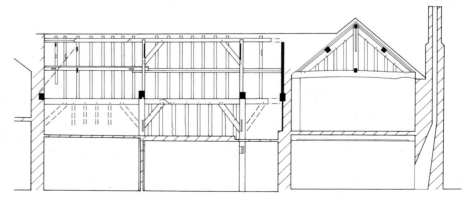

Fig 22 [44] Stoney Lane, Nos. 2 and 4, Crigglestone; long section.

Plate 34 [22] Oak Tree Cottage, Bardsey cum Rigton.

An open room is certainly present in two further houses, but in neither is this the housebody. At Oak Tree Cottage, Bardsey cum Rigton (22), and at Hanson House, Normanton (163), the room at the end of the range was originally open from ground to roof, and in both houses the adjacent

Fig 23 [163] Hanson House, Normanton; north elevation.

bay was floored to give two full storeys (Plate 34; Fig. 23). It is highy unlikely that the end room of a house of at least three rooms was the housebody, and these two houses appear to represent an intermediate stage in the transition from medieval houses with an open housebody to post-medieval houses of two storeys throughout.[47] In these houses the housebody was ceiled, but the open end room was a service area or kitchen. The heavy joists in the floored bay at Hanson House suggest a date not later than the mid 16th century, but Oak Tree Cottage is possibly later.

Whether these timber-framed houses with an open room – either housebody or kitchen – are medieval and earlier than other timber-framed houses in the area built with two storeys throughout is still not clear. Because some are low, the relationship between the open housebody and storeyed end-bays will not be the same as that found in the medieval yeoman houses of the Pennines, and it is possible that the open room was adopted of necessity rather than because it had a particular function which could only be expressed by its lofty proportions. If so, many of the eastern houses may be the post-medieval dwellings of men who could not afford or who did not require a fully-storeyed house such as was being erected by their wealthier contemporaries.

The consideration of the houses, both aisled and unaisled, of the eastern part of the county has encroached upon the post-medieval period, but this has been necessary in order to demonstrate the differences between the eastern houses and the apparently similar houses of the Pennines. Much doubt still surrounds the eastern buildings, and among them there are perhaps more medieval houses than has been admitted. Even so, however, the general argument remains unaltered; the eastern part of West Yorkshire shows a poorer pattern of medieval yeoman houses than does the Pennine area as a whole and the upper Calder valley in particular. In both numbers and the size of houses, the east is inferior, and nowhere is there as dense a concentration of substantial houses as is found in the upper Calder valley.

The conclusion to be drawn from this is that a prosperous yeomanry able to express in building its elevation from the mass of the peasantry, failed to develop in the east of the county in the later Middle Ages, at least to the extent that it did in part of the Pennine west. The reasons for this are not clearly understood. It was argued that the existence of a profitable system of dual occupation permitted the rise of the yeomanry in the upper Calder valley, with involvement in textiles being of crucial importance. The textile industry was present in the east of the county as well; Leeds, Wakefield and Pontefract were all important centres in the late 15th century.[48] However, there is little to suggest that the industry was as deeply-entrenched in the rural areas in the east as it was near Halifax. Certainly the later probate inventories show progressively less involvement with textiles as one moves east through the county, and it appears that, although the industry brought great wealth to an urban merchant group, it did not enrich the rural peasantry. A simpler economy, dominated by communal arable husbandry, offered advancement only to the few yeomen who farmed exceptionally large holdings, and permitted closer control by the gentry who drew off the major profits both of the exploitation of the land and of the mineral resources underlying it.[49] In these circumstances, no powerful and numerous yeomanry emerged in the east in the Middle Ages, and the few men who were able to build never approached the wealth of the prosperous yeoman-clothiers of the Pennine dales.

Notes to Chapter 2

[1] The term 'housebody' was generally applied to the main room of a yeoman house in 17th-century documents and is deliberately distinct from the 'hall' commonly found in gentry houses. Because the distinction had important social considerations the terminology will be retained as far as possible in this volume. A gentry house might, therefore, have an open hall and a yeoman house an open housebody, even though the latter's plan might be described in this chapter as a 'hall-and-cross-wing' type.

[2] See Stell 1960, 15–22; Stell 1965, 6, 7, 9; and Atkinson and McDowall 1967.

[3] It is interesting that no medieval aisled houses were found during a survey of domestic building in an area to the west of the upper Calder valley, on the western slopes of the Pennines in north-east Lancashire. See RCHM(E), forthcoming (a).

[4] Mercer 1975, 222.

[5] Atkinson and McDowall, 79–81.

[6] For Fur Street, Northowram, see Mercer 1975, 221–2; for Woodhouse Farm, see Mercer 1975, 223–4.

[7] For Scout Hall Farm, see Mercer 1975, 222.

[8] There is some documentary evidence for the use of braziers in 14th-century peasant houses; see Moorhouse 1981, 813.

[9] Excavations in the north of England, for example at Wharram Percy and West Whelpington, have hitherto failed to unearth anything to suggest that aisled houses of impermanent form commonly sheltered the peasantry in the Middle Ages. An aisled building was excavated at Colton, Temple Newsam, in West Yorkshire, but its use and status are far from clear. See Andrews and Milne 1979; Jarrett and Wrathmell 1977; Yarwood 1981a.

[10] See, for example, Mercer 1975, monuments 212, 231, both Wealden houses in Kent and therefore close in status to the aisled houses in the upper Calder valley.

[11] For Lower Bentley Royd, see Atkinson and MacDowall 1967, 86–8. Photographs of Yew Tree are deposited in the Sites and Monuments Record of the West Yorkshire Archaeology Unit.

[12] Lister 1905, 234–9; Lister traced the site's history and quoted a deed of sale of 1627 which provided for a division of the house on the line of the 'bench wall or wogh (murus sedilis sive partitio)', rare documentary evidence for the existence of a dais bench at the upper end of the housebody.

[13] Pearson 1898, 236–9; Trigg 1946, 37; Lister 1905, 241–2.

[14] Ogden 1905; Gilks 1974, 54–5; Atkinson and McDowall 1967, 79.

[15] Kendall 1914, 101–6.

[16] Ogden 1903.

[17] For a study of tenure in the two manors, see Michelmore 1981c, 248–51.

[18] For a map of the two great manors, see Faull and Moorhouse 1981, map 25.

[19] Michelmore 1981c, 249, 254.

[20] Heaton 1920.

[21] The aulnage rolls are today regarded more sceptically than when Maud Sellers used them in 1912, but the figures still serve to show the expansion of the Halifax trade in the 15th century; see Sellers 1912, 410. The Halifax Act is discussed in greater detail in Bowden 1962, 120; he points out that, following the great complaints against the effects of legislation, 'in parliamentary eyes, only the parish of Halifax vindicated its claims for special consideration'.

[22] Camden 1610, 692. This is supported by James Ryther of Harewood, writing to Burghley in 1589, who attributed the prosperity of the Halifax clothiers to their enterprize: 'no parte of the countrie yealdith so many rich men as the most barren, no parte so many poore as the most fertill' (*Yorks Archaeol. J.* 56, 111).

[23] Smith 1962, 236, 251.

[24] See Thirsk 1961 for a discussion of rural industry in other parts of the country. In a lecture to the Yorkshire Archaeological Society on 15 Oct. 1980, Professor Bernard Jennings suggested that the upper Calder valley took the lead in the development of a large-scale textile industry because the effects of population pressure on agricultural resources manifested themselves there first. The evidence will be presented in Jennings, forthcoming.

[25] It was noted in 1639 how the wapentakes of Agbrigg and Morley were dependent on other areas of agricultural produce; see Cliffe 1969, 2.

[26] Sellers 1912, 410; Thornes 1981, 8–9; Camden 1610, 692, quoted above, p. 34.

[27] For New Heath Head, Midgley, see Stell 1960, 23–7; he suggests that the wing was, in fact, a free-standing house, but its siting across the contours and its relationship to the 17th-century main range make it more likely that it formed the upper cross-wing of the medieval house. For Lower High Sunderland, see Gilks 1972a; for Shibden Fold, see Gilks 1977.

[28] For a record of the building, see Manby 1964; he suggests that the house had an open housebody of three bays heated by an open hearth under a louvre. Recent work has suggested, however, that the room may have been heated by a firehood, the site of which leaves room for a passage next to the service bay. It seems unlikely that the housebody was of three bays, for no house apart from those of the superior gentry had a room of this size. Possibly the open truss at the west end of the present house was sited next to the wall of a cross-wing which acted as the end wall of the housebody; this method of division is common in houses with independent framing of main range and cross-wing.

[29] Alcock 1981.

[30] Alcock 1981, 152–4. Five examples should be added to Alcock's list and three deleted from it. The additions are: Lower Folds, Stainland (SE 080183); Lower Allerscholes, Todmorden (SD 936207); North Hollingworth, Todmorden (SD 939217), all re-used crucks; and Lower Stub, Erringden (SE 004261) an agricultural building. Those to be deleted are Great Mitton (SD 715389), in Lancs; Crock House, Keighley (SE 042357) and Upper Fold Farm, Thurstonland (SE 162103), both duplicated entries.

[31] WYAS, Yorkshire Archaeol. Soc., DD 121/31/1, 10. The reference to a firehouse probably indicates a domestic building, but the other 'houses' appear to have been non-domestic.

[32] WYAS, Leeds, ST 778(3), Esholt Court Rolls, 6 Jan. 1380; Moorhouse 1981, 807; Walton 1948, 66. I am grateful to Mr. Stephen Whittle for bringing the Yeadon reference to my attention.

[33] Ryder 1979, 12.

[34] Smith 1975, 3.

[35] Walton 1955, 13–16. Dean Head Farm, Hepworth, another house noted by Walton (1955, 16) as a one-bay structure, has been demonstrated by Mr. D. J. H. Michelmore to have been larger originally; see report by him held by West Yorkshire Metropolitan County Council's Archaeology Unit.

[36] For the large barns at Thorpe House and Linthwaite Hall, see Walton 1955, 29–35.

[37] See Inchfield House, Todmorden (210), for a house which retains evidence for original walling.

[38] The inference that the brewhouse was cruck-built is drawn from the discovery of a collar which can only have come from a cruck building; see Michelmore 1983b. A similar case of the use of crucks in an inferior building in a complex of high status is suggested by the reference in c.1258 to the 'boveria cum postibus qui conveniunt in sumitate domus' on the lands of St. Paul's at Sandon, Herts. Extract of survey in VAG Newsletter, No. 4, Jan. 1983, 3.

[39] For a record of the barn, see Walton 1955, 29–33.

[40] The 17th-century rebuilding and the documentary evidence are discussed in detail in Chapter 4.

[41] See Manor House, South Crosland (191); Woodhouse Farm, Shelley (Mercer 1975, 223–4); and Fletcher House, Almondbury (Manby 1964).

[42] For a record of the cruck barn at Upper Oldfield, see Walton 1955, 20–4. The doubt surrounding the two Slaithwaite houses lies in their date, for there is nothing to prove that they are not post-medieval and therefore the dwellings of a level of the yeomanry inferior to that which invested in this age in fully-storeyed, but still small, stone houses of non-cruck form. See inventory entries for details. That crucks were the poor relations elsewhere is suggested by the 1635 survey of Ripley (North Yorkshire) which shows that cruck buildings were generally small, larger houses being timber-framed but of non-cruck form. See Harrison and Hutton 1984, 8.

[43] Walton 1955, 13–35.

[44] It is perilous to attempt a close comparison between the size and status of houses in different areas, for both the medieval and post-medieval periods show that houses were consistently smaller in the east of the county than in, especially, the upper Calder valley. A yeoman of a certain amount of wealth might, therefore, build a house of six rooms in the west, but in the east a house of four rooms would suffice for a man of similar status. Whether these few small timber-framed houses of the eastern area are the direct equivalent in terms of status of the Pennine cruck houses remains very uncertain; despite their broadly similar size, it is possible that they were built by men of higher relative status than the occupants of the western cruck houses. Another matter of uncertainty bearing on this question is whether the two groups of houses are similar in date.

[45] The researcher is fortunate that the Vale has received the thorough attention of the North Yorkshire and Cleveland Vernacular Buildings Study Group. The results of their research over the whole area, of which the Vale forms only a part, are in Harrison and Hutton 1984.

[46] Wrathmell 1972.

[47] Another house of this type, but with an outshut along the rear, was Dungeon Royds Farm, Rothwell, recorded by the Medieval Section of the Yorkshire Archaeological Society.

[48] Sellers 1912, 410.

[49] The regional agricultural differences within the county in the Middle Ages are discussed by Moorhouse 1981b.

CHAPTER 3

THE HOUSES OF THE NOBILITY AND GENTRY, 1550–1800.

The purpose of this chapter is to trace the evolution of the largest houses in the post-medieval period. At the beginning of this period a gentleman of moderate means might erect a house that differed little from the standard form developed in the late Middle Ages and which displayed features of a strong local character, but at its end such a man could build himself a house designed by an architect and showing all the latest ideas on planning current over a wide area of the country. The two types of house are very different, and the explanation for the evolution will be sought in the changing needs of gentry society.

The sources for this study are much more plentiful than those for the examination of earlier or smaller houses. Many houses survive or were recorded before demolition, and their architectural qualities have long attracted the attention of historians. The story of individual houses is in some cases well documented in the papers of this increasingly literate class.[1] Estate records, correspondence, diaries and so forth reveal much not only about the building of houses but also about the life of the age, and the development of gentry society, both over the whole country and in West Yorkshire, is one of the more certain areas of historical study of the period.[2]

In the period before the Civil War, the gentry were drawn into the structure of government to the extent that their co-operation became vital to the workings of state. An incipient sense of national identity was created through the influence of education and through the attraction of London, the seat of the court and of parliament, and the commercial, professional and social capital. Fashionable ideas spread from this centre, and current trends in architecture were not the least influential in giving identity to the nobility and gentry. The impact of new forms on the provincial gentry is illustrated by the experience of Sir Henry Slingsby, who in 1640 left his North Yorkshire estate for the London season and was 'invited to supper at my Ld. Hollands at Kinsington. . . .'

> Here, besides the entertainment wch we had, I was much taken with the curiosity of the house; & from that house I took a conceite of making a thorough house in part of Red House [*his Yorkshire home*] wch now I build; & that by placing the Dores so one against another & making at each end a Balcony that one may see cleare thro' the house.[3]

The percolation of such ideas – however imperfectly understood and executed in the provinces – may have been slow, but it contributed to the adoption in the late 17th century of a type of house that would not look out of place in distant parts of the country.

The life of most gentry families, however, revolved not around the capital but around the county. Local government was county-based and depended heavily upon the gentry's active participation. The formal occasions of assizes and elections created networks of political and commercial alliances, frequently cemented by marriage, and a busy social life.[4] The administrative duties and social life of a prominent Yorkshire squire in the late 17th and early 18th centuries can be traced in Sir Walter Calverley's diary.[5] Sir Walter visited London occasionally, attended the assizes at York and the sessions at Leeds, and travelled around the county visiting his fellow gentry, in return entertaining them at his seat and trailing them around the polite society of his own area. He attended cock fights in Leeds and horse races at Bramham; when life became too hectic he repaired to the fast-growing spas of Scarborough and Harrogate, where in all probability he found other gentry families seeking respite. It is clear from the diary that Sir Walter felt that he belonged to an identifiable group united by personal acquaintance and family ties, even if it was divided in its political affiliations. Sir Walter was one of the major gentry of the West Riding, but even gentry of more modest means had a part to play in county life, and through the medium of local administration and more parochial social gatherings they too were drawn into an awareness of their social identity within the shire.

The number of gentry families in Yorkshire increased significantly in the late 16th and 17th centuries. Between 1558 and 1642 the ranks of the gentry in the county as a whole swelled by over a fifth, primarily due to the elevation of yeoman families, and West Yorkshire supplies many examples of this change of status in this period.[6] The Holdsworths of Southowram, the Deardens of Sowerby, and the Otes family of Northowram all rose from the yeomanry, and the last two marked their promotion by the construction of a new house.[7] The gentry, therefore, included new and long-established families, and among both there could be a great variety of wealth. At one end of the scale were a few families like the Saviles of Thornhill, with an income of £7000 a year in the mid 17th century, and its middle ranks were made up of families like the Tempests of Tong, who lived on an annual income of £600. Nearly one third of the gentry families, however, had estates worth less than £100 a year, and clearly these extremes make it impossible to talk of the gentry as if it were a homogeneous group.[8] The surviving houses are among the best illustration of this, for the residences of great families like the Saviles differed widely from the homes of minor gentlemen living on a fraction of the Saviles' income.[9]

The houses of the nobility and gentry will be divided for study by period and by status. There are two small groups of great houses: the first comprises the 'prodigy' houses of the Elizabethan and early Stuart period; the second, after a long gap in which the development of the great house is not represented by outstanding monuments in West Yorkshire, starts with Bramham Park in the early 18th century and reveals the adoption of new ideas on country house design. Both groups will be touched upon only briefly, for the evolution of the great house is seen more clearly when studied over a much wider area; in fact, the nobility had achieved a national style by the beginning of this period, if not before. Furthermore, most of the houses in the two groups have received the attention of earlier architectural historians, and the reader is referred elsewhere for a fuller discussion of their character and evolution.[10] The main subject of this chapter is the houses of the gentry as distinct from those of the nobility. The latter may serve as the standard against which the more numerous lesser houses can be judged; in some aspects the great houses proved influential, in others their example was not followed. The gentry houses had their own independent evolution, however, especially in the period before 1680. After this date the distinction between them and the great houses is less clear, in all but size, and 1680 marks a convenient division for the study of early and late groups of gentry houses.

THE PRODIGY HOUSES, 1580–1640

It is unfortunate that none of the late medieval houses of the nobility and greater gentry survives in West Yorkshire to show how different from them were the great houses of the late 16th and early 17th centuries. That these were indeed a significant departure from late-medieval building practice is suggested by the fact that three of the prodigy houses – Methley, Temple Newsam and Ledston – while incorporating some earlier work, swept much away in a thorough remodelling in a new style and form, and it is clear that the innovation and experimentation characteristic of Elizabethan and early Stuart architecture over much of the realm was also present in West Yorkshire. The seven houses of that period can be divided according to size into two groups: Kippax Park, Old Hall, Warmfield cum Heath, and New Hall, Pontefract, were all large, but were dwarfed by the four great houses of Howley, Ledston, Methley and Temple Newsam. The survival rate of these has not been good: Howley was demolished in the 18th century, and the very size of the others has posed such a threat to their existence in modern times that only Ledston and Temple Newsam stand today, both much altered from their original state.

The four great houses were all built on an open courtyard plan. Howley, dated 1590, was probably the most impressive (Plate 35), in its heyday being compared with Theobalds and Audley End.[11] Unlike earlier courtyard houses it was designed to face outwards and to present a symmetrical elevation to the world on its entrance front. Methley (128), dated 1588, Ledston and Temple Newsam, both remodelled in the two decades before the Civil War, all had long wings flanking a central range containing the

hall, and in all three symmetry played an important part in the external design (Plates 36, 37). All the architectural conceits of the period were present in these houses: receding and projecting planes, an elaborate storeyed porch, a skyline varied through the use of higher towers, angle turrets, and even, at Temple Newsam, of a balustrade in the form of an inscription of silhouetted letters. All the houses, too, were multi-storeyed, either in the main ranges themselves, as at Ledston and Temple Newsam, or through the use of towers rising above a two-storey principal block, as at Howley and Methley.

The size of these houses was vast. The smallest, Methley, had main elevations of about 100 feet (30 m) in length; the principal front at Temple Newsam is 190 feet (58 m) long; and Howley is said to have been 60 yards square. With their size and height they had a huge capacity: in the 1672 Hearth Tax returns, which may include later additions and some outbuildings in the assessments for these houses but which nevertheless clearly reveal the gulf between them and the homes of the rest of the population, Ledston had twenty-five hearths, Methley forty-three, Howley forty-four, and Temple Newsam forty-five.[12] Built with an eye on the court and with the need in mind to accommodate an itinerant monarch or peers with their still large households, these houses could provide suites of private apartments as well as an impressive public area. At Temple Newsam in 1565, that is, in the great house which existed before Ingram's reconstruction, chambers were set aside for the ladies, the gentlewomen, the Earl of Lennox, and for Lord Darnley, and there were many good quality chambers at Methley in 1657.[13] Furthermore, all four houses had a long gallery for the use of the gentle-born. The principal public room was the hall: that at Methley was

Plate 35 Howley Hall, Morley (from Whitaker 1816).

Plate 36 Ledston Hall.

Plate 37 Temple Newsam House; a mid 18th-century view (*reproduced by permission of Leeds Art Galleries*).

Plate 38 Kirklees Hall, Clifton; the hall screen, smaller than that at Methley, but of similar date.

Plate 39 Old Hall, Warmfield cum Heath.

lavish in its treatment, with large windows and a splendid screen (cf Plate 38).[14] In 1657, however, this room was sparsely furnished, with only two tables and four forms; the display of armour there suggests that its primary function was that of a reception room, decorated to display the power of the Savile family. In houses of this size, the great chamber, often set over the hall, might be the most important room for public occasions. The household regulations of Thomas, Lord Fairfax of Denton (1560–1640), just outside West Yorkshire, show that the hall might be used for dining, since gentlemen were instructed to take breakfast either there or in a parlour (the ladies were waited upon in their chambers), but that on occasions of dining in state the head of the household and his chief guests sat at the table in the great chamber, leaving the hall to the superior servants and any gentlemen who had been unable to find a place above.[15] The hall, therefore, might be large and magnificent, as at Methley, but it was by no means the only public reception room in the houses of the nobility.

The great size and sophistication of the four great houses reflects the status of their builders. The Savile family of Howley and Methley, Sir Arthur Ingram of Temple Newsam, and Thomas Wentworth, Earl of Strafford, who started to rebuild Ledston, all played a part in affairs of state and reaped the rewards or paid the penalties which went with their position. The houses show a growing gulf at this social level between family and servants, and demonstrate the slow process of dissolution which the united medieval household was undergoing in this period. When the nobility were next to build in West Yorkshire, after a gap of over half a century dominated by the buildings of lesser men, its houses had perfected a design which allowed two different societies to co-habit under the same expansive roof.

Smaller than these great houses, but very much larger than the residences of the middling and minor gentry, are three houses of advanced design: Kippax Park has been demolished with little record, but much is known of the New Hall, Pontefract, and of the Old Hall, Warmfield cum Heath. The builders were men of lesser status than those responsible for the great houses, but were nevertheless major figures. The Blands of Kippax and the Kayes of Heath both had more than local influence, and Pontefract was built for the third son of the Earl of Shrewsbury. The houses were built in the last two decades of the 16th century and show the adventurous spirit of the age. Symmetry dominates the main front at Heath, and only the off-centre doorway ruins the balance of the principal elevation at Pontefract, where the lavish use of glass recalls Hardwick (Plates 39, 40). The houses were multi-storeyed with, at Pontefract three, and at Heath two floors above a service basement. Turrets rose above the skyline to give belvederes or banqueting rooms, and at Heath these were crenellated in imitation of a fortified dwelling.

Perhaps the most important aspects of Pontefract and Heath concern their plans and internal arrangements. Both approached, but did not achieve, the form of a double-pile

Plate 40 New Hall, Pontefract (*reproduced by permission of J.E. Holmes*).

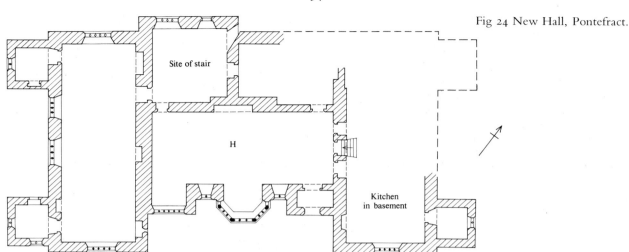

Fig 24 New Hall, Pontefract.

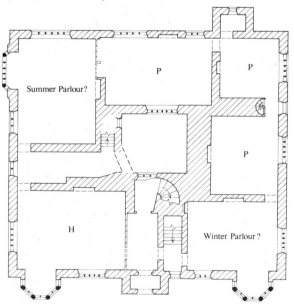

Fig 25 Old Hall, Warmfield cum Heath; principal floor plan (after Weaver).

block (Figs 24, 25). Pontefract had a room and a staircase behind the hall giving added depth in the central area, which in the medieval house was occupied by the hall alone. At Heath, the courtyard of a large house was shrunk to the size of a small well in the centre of the block, designed merely to give light. In their internal arrangements the houses showed significant departures from the layout of the late medieval gentry house. Both had a single-storey hall, a large room but in neither case the largest or grandest in the house. That at Pontefract was the more traditional in plan, being entered at its lower end and having service doorways grouped in its lower wall. At Heath, the hall is placed in one corner of the block, and the central entry to the house opens into a passage to one side of the hall. The hall's diminished status is shown by the

extra attention lavished on other rooms. In both houses the most splendid room was the great chamber on the first floor, and both had a long gallery. At Heath there were five heated parlours on the main floor, four with plaster ceilings, and heated chambers on the top floor. It is clear that in these houses the provision of private apartments was a priority in the design, and the use of more than one storey for this involved the incorporation of a spacious stair at Pontefract. The siting of service rooms, including the kitchen, in a basement was another departure from late medieval practice. It represented a much more convenient arrangement than that offered by a distant, detached kitchen, and gave a very compact plan. In addition, the use of a service basement allowed the main floor to be raised above ground level and gave it the added dignity of an approach up a perron.

Heath and Pontefract belong to a group of houses in the north and midlands of England built in the late 16th century and associated with the name of Robert Smythson.[16] Thorpe Salvin in South Yorkshire, Barlborough in Derbyshire, and Wootton in Staffordshire show many similarities which cannot be explored here but which serve to reveal that the builders of the West Yorkshire houses were fully abreast of the fashions of the age, and were taking little if anything from the traditional forms of the area. These houses were new departures in West Yorkshire, and so great was the difference in size and sophistication between them and the houses of the middling and minor gentry that many of their most advanced features – a service basement, compact planning and symmetry – either remained inappropriate to smaller houses or could not be reconciled with the sometimes conflicting demands of lesser men.

THE HOUSES OF THE MIDDLING AND MINOR GENTRY, 1550–1680

Unlike the largest houses of the late 16th and early 17th centuries, which departed radically from the form of earlier buildings of similar status, the houses of the bulk of the gentry retained strong links with the type of dwelling developed in the late Middle Ages. Innovation there certainly was, however, for no house of this status was built along exactly the same lines as its medieval predecessor. The story of the gentry house in this period reveals a conflict between the slowly evolving way of life of the class, which created the need for a particular type of dwelling, and new Renaissance ideas of house planning. Before 1680 the two were not entirely compatible, and it is the shifting balance accorded to these two considerations which resulted in a period of great experimentation.

The essential form of the gentry house in West Yorkshire in the period 1550–1680 was the 'H' plan or hall-and-cross-wings house developed in the late Middle Ages. The form proved capable of great variety, both of appearance and of size, this variety being determined partly by the passage of time and partly by the requirements of individual builders. When a large house was needed by a man of commensurable wealth, it could take the form of a multi-storeyed block with boldly projecting wings, seen at Kildwick Hall, Kildwick (107; Plate 41). At Barkisland Hall, Barkisland (24), the lower wing does not project, but the three storeys and the depth of the block make the house a large one (Plate 42). At a more modest level, the top storey was not required and the hall range was flanked by two-storey

Plate 41 [107] Kildwick Hall.

Below: Plate 42 [24] Barkisland Hall, 1638.

Plate 43 [66] Oakwell Hall, Gomersal, 1583.

Plate 44 [25] Howroyd, Barkisland, 1642.

Plate 45 Ovenden Hall, c.1662.

Plate 46 [30] New Hall, Bowling, 1672.

wings: examples of different dates include Oakwell Hall, Gomersal (66), of 1583; Marsh Hall, Northowram (167), of 1626; Howroyd, Barkisland (25), of 1642; and New Hall, Bowling (30), of 1672 (Plates 43–6).

This hall-and-cross-wings house was, however, very different from its medieval predecessor, both in its overall form and in its internal arrangements. As gentry society slowly changed, so it demanded a different type of dwelling, with more rooms and increased specialization. Because internal changes and the growing complexity of

the dwelling had a direct effect on overall planning and external appearance, these aspects will be examined first.

THE HALL

Occupying a central position in the gentry house was the hall, the largest single room in most houses. The majority of gentry houses of this period were built with a single-storey hall, but a significant minority had a hall open through two storeys (Plate 47). The function of the hall depended in part on the status of the builder and on the

Plate 47 [196] Wood Lane Hall, Sowerby, 1649; the open hall is lit by a large window.

complexity of the house which he erected. In houses with a number of private rooms, comfort was not a prime requirement in the hall, and the room retained the nature of a public area which acted also as the centre of distribution within the house. To this end, many houses had an entry directly into the hall without the intermediate stage of a passage or a lobby. In a house like Marsh Hall (167) or Old Hall, East Ardsley (152), the visitor went straight into the hall, to be directed from there to the private reception rooms such as parlours and chambers (Fig. 26). Especially

Plate 48 [25] Howroyd, Barkisland; detail of painted glass in hall.

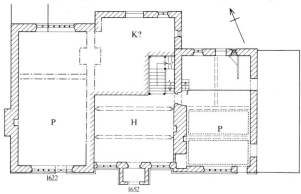

Fig 26 [52] Old Hall, East Ardsley.

in houses which had dispensed with the passage entry, the hall communicated directly with the principal rooms on the ground floor and, by means of the stair which generally opened out of one corner, with the best rooms on the first floor.

In all houses, however, the hall was much more than a means of reaching other rooms. Above all, it was a reception area in its own right, used for many of the public

occasions and household gatherings which were a feature of gentry life. To impress both the visitor *en route* to private reception rooms and at assemblies gathered in the hall itself, the room received some of the most elaborate decoration in the house. This is where the open hall came into its own, for although some single-storey halls might have, for instance, a plaster overmantel, as at Old Hall, East Ardsley, or a good fireplace, as at Lumb Hall (51), the potential for display was greatest in a lofty room. Plasterwork was frequently lavished on the ceiling and on the overmantel, a gallery commonly ran around two or three sides of the hall, and heating was by a large and elaborate fireplace. In some houses there is evidence that painted glass was used in the windows, as at Howroyd (25), but this form of decoration was not necessarily confined to houses with an open hall (Plates 48, 49).

Plate 49 [25] Howroyd, Barkisland; the hall.

Perhaps the best example of a hall which acted both as a means of communication within the house and as a display area is that at Wood Lane Hall, Sowerby (196): open through two storeys, it gives access to parlours, to service rooms and, by means of the gallery which runs around three walls, to most of the chambers as well; it is decorated with a fireplace, a plaster ceiling, and woodwork, in the form of panelling and an arcaded frieze over the fireplace (Plate 50; Fig. 27).

In two houses there is evidence that the advantages of an open hall were realized, for both show a rejection of the single-storey hall. At Oakwell (66) the house was built in 1583 with a single-storey hall, as the inventory of 1611 demonstrates, but by the middle of the century that had been swept away in favour of the open room which survives today, transforming a room which in 1611 was probably used mainly for dining into a richly-decorated

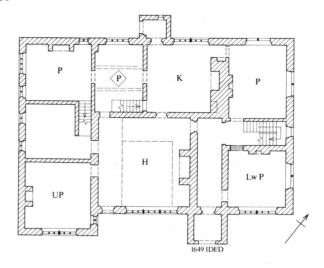

Plate 50 [196] Wood Lane Hall, Sowerby; the hall gives access to all the main rooms on two floors.

Fig 27 [196] Wood Lane Hall, Sowerby.

Plate 51 [66] Oakwell Hall, Gomersal; the remodelled hall of the mid 17th century.

Plate 52 [66] Oakwell
Hall; detail of screen
in hall.

entrance and reception area (Plates 51, 52).[17] East Riddlesden Hall (140) shows a similar change of heart, but here the single-storey hall was never built: the rebuilding in 1648 of the lower wing of the medieval house provided fireplaces both for a single-storey hall and for a chamber over it, but when the hall range itself came to be rebuilt the open hall was retained, and the chamber fireplace survives incongruously above the magnificent fireplace of the hall (Plate 53). The preference for the open hall is seen also in houses of medieval date which were altered in the 17th century; many improvements were made to these houses at the later date, but in some the open hall remained, with the addition of contemporary embellishments. At New Hall, Elland (54), for example, the new chimney stack which replaced the firehood received a plaster overmantel, and at Fenay Hall, Almondbury, the hall was ceiled at tie-beam level with decorative plasterwork.

The last of the open-hall houses, Wood Lane Hall, was built in 1649, although some of the alterations to medieval houses date from the second half of the 17th century. The option of the single-storey or the open hall was available to the gentry, but it is not clear why some chose one and some the other. There is little difference in status between men like John Dearden of Wood Lane and James Oates of Marsh Hall (167) on the one hand, and Robert Shaw of Old Hall, East Ardsley (52), and Francis Baildon of Baildon Hall (17) on the other; although the builders of some open halls were relatively new to the gentry ranks, other equally recent arrivals built houses with a single-storey hall. The open hall had an aura of antiquity and of status at this time, and it is possible therefore that some new men chose it to bolster their claims to gentility and as a means of associating their families with a respectably ancient origin.

The use of the open hall involved the sacrifice of a chamber, and though this was of little consequence to many of the minor gentry, some more prominent men with different requirements clearly felt the loss too great. For instance, Hawksworth Hall (79), built c.1600, had a single-storey hall, probably because at this high social level greater value was attached to the prestige of a great chamber set over the hall. This great chamber is a splendid room with an oriel bay at the upper end and a plaster ceiling (Plate 59); in 1657 it was furnished more richly than the hall, which only had four tables and two forms. In many smaller houses with a single-storey hall, the chamber over the hall is not distinguished from other chambers in its decoration, and the inventories suggest that in fact this room might have had an inferior use. In these cases the choice of a single-storey hall, such as that at Lumb Hall, Drighlington (51), owed less to the desire to create an impressive first-floor room than to the need to provide greater comfort and convenience than was given by a lofty open room, for the hall might still have an important role in the daily routine of domestic life. Although never used for cooking, as it probably had been in medieval houses, the hall in some houses was as much a living area as a public and ceremonial room: at Shibden Hall in 1677 it appears to have been used as a secondary dining room, as it was at New Hall, Bowling (30), in 1699, and at Murgatroyd, Warley, in 1695 it was decorated with pictures and a show of weaponry, being used for sitting and the reception of visitors. There is no absolute correlation between the nature of the hall and its function, but clearly the open hall was more appropriate when an impressive entrance and reception room was the principal requirement, and the single-storey hall more fitting when either a great chamber or a more comfortable living area was needed.

Parlours and Chambers

The degree to which the hall might have a specialized public use depended on the sophistication of the private rooms within the house, and many of the gentry houses of

Plate 53 [140] East Riddlesden Hall, Morton; the hall fireplace, with fireplace above for intended chamber.

this period show an increasing emphasis on comfort and privacy, expressed most markedly in the evolution of the parlour and of the best chambers. In the medieval gentry house the role of the parlour is obscure, although a few houses appear to have had heated rooms and even some modest decoration. Inventories show that in the period 1550–1680 the number of parlours in gentry houses was high: the very large Bretton Hall, a major gentry house, had eight parlours in 1675, and the smaller Wood Lane Hall (196) had five (Fig. 27), but most had two or three.[18] Some parlours were given specialist and superior functions; a dining parlour was commonly provided, and many houses contained one or more parlours used as private apartments by the leading members of the household, where guests might be received and entertained.[19] The bigger the house and the wealthier the family the more elaborate this provision of private rooms became. At Bretton several parlours were well appointed: the King Henry Parlour, for example, had tables, four chairs, a bed and a truckle bed, valued, with some other furniture, at £66. The names applied to some of these rooms reveal their private nature: at Woolley in 1660 Mr. Michaell had his own parlour, as did John Murgatroyd of East Riddlesden in 1662, and in 1667 William Richardson had his 'owne lodging Roome', containing a bed, a little table, six chairs, two stools and a few other items. The withdrawing room which was not also a bedroom is uncommon in this period; only Murgatroyd in 1695 had a withdrawing room named as such, and its contents – tables, a carpet, nine leather chairs and so forth – show that it was a cosy sitting room.

The treatment of the best parlours in the gentry houses reflects their superior use. Dining parlours and the best private parlours were heated by small but well-worked fireplaces: at least three of the five parlours at Wood Lane Hall (196) were heated, and at Oakwell Hall (66) the Great Parlour, the Little Parlour and the New Parlour all have fireplaces (Plates 54, 55). Large windows made the parlours airy, pleasant and sunny living areas, and the use of plaster ceilings emphasized their importance: at Baildon Hall (17)

Plate 55 [51] Lumb Hall, Drighlington; fireplace and overmantel in main parlour.

and at Woodsome Hall (60) only the best parlour is so decorated, but at Marsh Hall (167) both principal parlours have richly worked ceilings, and at East Riddlesden Hall the dining parlour and John Murgatroyd's private parlour received rich ornament (Plates 56–8).

Plate 54 [196] Wood Lane Hall, Sowerby; fireplace in back parlour.

Plate 56 [17] Baildon Hall; ceiling in main parlour.

Plate 57 [140] East Riddlesden Hall, Morton; the dining parlour.

Plate 58 [140] East Riddlesden Hall; John Murgatroyd's 'owne Parlour'.

Plate 59 [79] Hawksworth Hall; the great chamber, with plasterwork dated 1611.

Only a minority of the parlours in a house had this superior nature, however. The inventories show that many were sparsely furnished bedrooms, often for servants or lesser members of the household. These rooms could be used for storage as well as for sleeping. The occupier of Atkinson's parlour at Calverley in 1651 shared the room with the household store of butter and with forty-three cheeses, and at Fixby (1567) the unfortunate occupant of the parlour slept alongside a vat of swine grease. Many of these parlours are set at the back of the house and, in

Plate 60 [207] Lees Hall, Thornhill; plaster ceiling added to medieval solar.

contrast to the best parlours facing south, must have been cheerless rooms.

Some of the best private and even public rooms in the gentry houses of this period were located on the first floor. The great chamber, whether set over a single-storey hall, as at Woolley and Hawksworth, or in a wing, was clearly of prime importance: at Hawksworth in 1657 it was used as the main dining and sitting room, probably for public occasions, and its status is attested by the sumptuous plaster ceiling of 1611 (Plate 59). At Bretton in 1675 the Great Chamber was the most expensively furnished room in the house and, despite the presence of a dining parlour on the ground floor, may have been used for dining in state. Most of the inventories naming a Great Chamber describe the dwellings of families of more than local influence, for Calverley (1651), Hawksworth, Woolley (1660), Barnbow (1672) and Bretton were all the seats of knightly families. At this social level the imitation of the practices of the nobility was not extravagant and far-fetched; these houses reflect something of the way of life that, among the nobility and richer gentry, produced houses like Hardwick Hall and Gilling Castle with their spectacular Great Chambers.[20]

Even at the level of the middling and minor gentry some of the chambers could have a superior use. The Best Chamber at Newhall, Bowling in 1699, for instance, contained the most expensive bed in the house, and the ten chairs of different kinds there indicate that, as well as being the bedroom of the head of the household, it was one of the main sitting rooms. More often, however, the better chambers were private apartments: at Hawksworth in 1657 rooms were set aside for individual members of the household, for Sir Richard himself, Mr. Bayldon, the Young Mr., and Mr. Parkinson. The better chambers were often well-lit rooms: at Crawstone Hall, Elland-cum-Greetland (55), they were lit by mullioned and transomed windows, and even though there is a progressive reduction in the size of windows on each of the floors at Barkisland Hall (24), the upper rooms are still generously provided with light, suggesting that some at least were private chambers. The plasterwork in the two best chambers at Marsh Hall (167) shows their superior use, and at Lees Hall, Thornhill, alterations and additions to the late medieval house provided a plaster ceiling in the solar and a new lower wing with a large and decorated chamber (Plate 60). The best chambers were usually heated: the great chamber at Hawksworth Hall has a large fireplace, and one of the chambers at Barkisland Hall has a fireplace which is particularly rich in carved work (Plate 61). Lumb Hall (51) has three heated chambers, two with plaster ornament (Plates 62, 63), and at East Riddlesden Hall even the small porch chamber has its own miniature but still well-worked

Plate 61 [24] Barkisland Hall; fireplace in chamber.

Plate 62 [51] Lumb Hall; fireplace and overmantel.

Plate 63 [51] Lumb Hall; detail of plaster in chamber.

Plate 64 [140] East Riddlesden Hall, Morton; heated chamber.

Far left:
Plate 65 [140] East Riddlesden Hall; fireplace in porch chamber.

Left: Plate 66 [99] Manor House, Ilkley; best chamber, with fireplace and garderobe.

fireplace (Plates 64, 65). At Oakwell Hall (66) and Manor House, Ilkley (99), the best chamber is not only heated but also has a garderobe sharing the stack with the fireplace (Plate 66).

By no means all the chambers of the gentry house were decked out with plasterwork and fireplaces to act as superior rooms. The inventories show that some were assigned to the use of servants as bedrooms, and many others appear to have been unheated and poorly furnished, often acting both as store rooms and as lesser bedrooms. Not all servants' chambers were entirely devoid of comfort, however, for the attic rooms at East Riddlesden Hall (140), although squeezed into the roof space, were provided with fireplaces (Plate 67).[21]

Because some of the chambers had a superior use, the stair connecting them with the better rooms on the ground floor was given new emphasis in this period. The standard position for the stair in the medieval house, in a bay at the rear of the house at the upper end of the hall, was continued in houses like Manor House, Ilkley, and Baildon Hall. In houses with a range of rooms behind the hall the same position is found: at Lumb Hall (51) and at Old Hall, East Ardsley (52), the stair functions in just the same way, rising out of one corner of the hall (Fig. 28). At Kildwick Hall (107) the stair occupies the rear of the upper wing but still opens directly out of the hall, stressing its role as a channel of communication. The stair commonly rose to a landing

Plate 67 [140] East Riddlesden Hall; heated attic.

giving access to the principal chambers: at the Old Hall, for example, the landing opens into the best chamber over the hall and into a panelled chamber in the east wing, and at Lumb Hall it communicates closely with the two better chambers. At other houses the stair rises to the gallery which gives access to the chambers, an arrangement seen at Oakwell Hall (Plate 68). Because the route to the best chambers was an important one, the stair area was

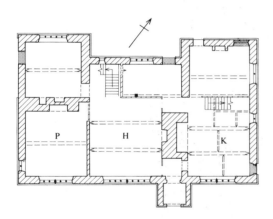

Fig 28 [51] Lumb Hall, Drighlington.

Plate 68 [66] Oakwell Hall, Gomersal; stair rising out of corner of hall.

frequently made impressive through the use of well-carpentered stairs, not a common feature of either medieval gentry houses or the post-medieval houses of the yeomanry. Good staircases survive at Baildon Hall, Oakwell Hall, and at East Ardsley; at Kildwick the stairwell is decorated with plasterwork (Plate 69).

One of the reasons why the private rooms of the gentry house multiplied and became more elaborate in the 17th century lay in the need not only to accommodate a large resident household, but also to lodge visiting gentry and their households. The frequent exchange of visits among the major and middling gentry, recorded vividly by Sir Walter Calverley, was of course a continuation of medieval practice and part of the same custom which led the nobility into ruinous expenditure on the palaces of the Elizabethan and Jacobean age.[22] But where amongst the nobility this custom could produce specially built suites of rooms reserved exclusively for guests of great importance, at the level of the county and parish gentry more modest provision was made. Possibly some of the named chambers in the inventories were lodgings, perhaps used by the household when not occupied by a visitor, in the same way that Lord Salisbury used the royal lodgings at Hatfield in the king's absence. Only at Woodsome Hall (60) is there a suggestion that special provision was made for visiting households: here was built in the early 17th century a large two-and-a-half storey block connecting with the rear of the house (Plate 70). The three chimney stacks show that at least six fireplaces were provided, and there are remains of decorative plasterwork on both ground and first floors. This block was possibly built to house visitors in some style and comfort with the minimum of disruption to the residents' domestic arrangements.[23]

Above: Plate 69 [17] Baildon Hall; stair.

Plate 70 [60] Woodsome Hall, Farnley Tyas; block at rear, possibly for lodgings.

SERVICE ROOMS

Along with the development of the public areas of the house and of the private rooms, the 17th-century gentry house also shows important changes in the service rooms, as the inventories demonstrate. At Lazencroft in 1557, for instance, there were nine rooms set aside for domestic work or for storage, including a kitchen, a bakehouse, a milkhouse, two larders and a buttery. Subsequent changes in the service area make it difficult to discover how the various rooms were arranged, and what survives in many houses today is generally a series of rooms undistinguished by any structural clue to their original use. Cellars, however, became more common in this period. Some were only half-sunk, causing the floors of the rooms over them

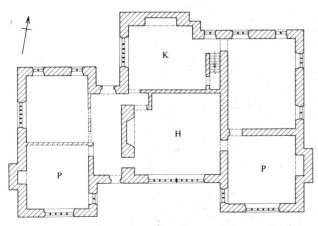

Fig 29 [12] Shuttleworth Hall, Allerton (after Walker).

to be raised above the level of the rest of the house, as at Old Hall, East Ardsley (52), and Baildon Hall (17). At East Riddlesden Hall (140) there is a range of fully sunk cellars under one side of the main block, and here and elsewhere these subterranean areas were used for the storage of drink.

Of the ground-floor rooms, only the kitchen can be identified with confidence, and its incorporation into the house is one of the most important developments of the period. In the late Middle Ages the major gentry appear to have used a detached kitchen, but at the level of the lesser gentry there are indications that the hall was the site of the cooking hearth (see above, p. 31). In post-medieval gentry houses the hall was never used for cooking; it was not heated by a firehood, and its decorative nature and its other functions preclude this use, a conclusion confirmed by the inventories. Kitchens had been created in medieval houses by the addition of a large stack to the lower wing, as at Kiddal Hall (26) and Sharlston Hall (176), but whether these alterations date from the medieval period or later is not clear. The rejection both of the cooking hearth in the hall by the lesser gentry and of the distant detached kitchen by the major gentry and by some of the nobility led to the same end, the integration of the kitchen into the main block, although the means of attaining this differed according to status. The prodigy houses, we have seen, commonly employed a service basement, but this was not a solution preferred by the minor gentry. The convenience of having a purpose-built, internal kitchen communicating closely with the rooms it was designed to serve led to its siting on the ground floor, at the rear and usually close to the hall and the dining parlour. At Marsh Hall (167) the kitchen was sited in an outshut behind the hall (Plate 71), and at Shuttleworth Hall, Allerton (12; Fig. 29), and Howroyd, Barkisland (25; Fig. 30), it is in the same

Plate 72 [140] East Riddlesden Hall, Morton; the kitchen.

position but in a two-storey wing projecting at the rear. The kitchen at Wood Lane Hall (196) is behind the hall, and instead of projecting it is completely contained within the main double-pile block. The same is true of East Riddlesden Hall, where the kitchen communicates closely with the Dining Parlour (Plate 72). Another common site for the kitchen was at the rear of one of the wings: at New Hall, Bowling (30), and at Oakwell Hall (66), it is sited here (Fig. 31), and the 17th-century alterations to the lower wing of Shibden Hall created a kitchen in this position. Lumb Hall

(51) is unique in siting the kitchen at the front of the house, where it shares the main stack with the hall (Plate 73). Even in this period, however, some gentry found it preferable to build a detached kitchen, presumably because the advantages of close proximity were outweighed by the desire to reduce cooking smells and possibly the risk of fire within the main block. Coley Hall (86) appears to have had a detached kitchen in the 17th century (Plate 74), and at Kildwick Hall (107) the kitchen block, dated 1673, is set away from the house at the rear (Plate 75). At Chapel Fold,

Fig 30 [25] Howroyd, Barkisland.

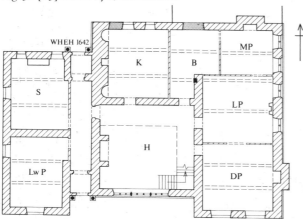

Plate 73 [51] Lumb Hall, Drighlington; the kitchen.

Plate 74 [86] Coley Hall, Hipperholme with Brighouse; block to right, formerly detached, probably provided cooking hearth.

Plate 75 [107] Kildwick Hall; kitchen block of 1673 to left, behind main block.

Plate 76 Chapel Fold, North Bierley; kitchen block to extreme right, just touching hall range.

North Bierley (Plate 76), the kitchen is contained in a wing built onto one corner at the rear of the house.[24]

The importance of the kitchen is reflected both in its position within the house and in its large size. The kitchen at Lumb Hall and at East Riddlesden is a spacious room, large enough to permit the free movement of many people all busy with the different tasks associated with the preparation and serving of food. In both houses the kitchen was heated by a large fireplace, but in others, such as Marsh Hall and New Hall, Bowling (Fig. 31), a firehood was used. The size of some of the kitchens, their constant warmth and the furniture revealed in some of the inventories suggest strongly that the rooms may also have been used as a servants' hall: at East Riddlesden in 1662 the kitchen contained a table, a form, and seven chairs, enough to provide a dining and sitting area for some of the household servants and estate workers. The link between the outside world and the kitchen is emphasized by a further feature, for very often the room was provided with its own external doorway, allowing its users to come and go out of sight of, and unhindered by, the family and distinguished visitors. This segregation of the menials had important implications for the hall and for the principal

Fig 31 [30] New Hall, Bowling.

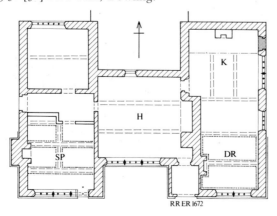

entry at the front of the house: these could be seen more and more not as common ground for all members of the household, as in the medieval house, but as the preserve of the quality, underlining the growing gulf within the gentry house at this period.

PLANNING AND DESIGN

The increased complexity of the internal arrangements of the post-medieval gentry house had far-reaching effects on its planning and external appearance. When combined with changing ideas on the aesthetics of design, this led ultimately to a new type of house, but in this period progress was made in a number of stages as essentially medieval forms were adapted to a changing way of life.

The development of double-pile planning was the most significant change in this period. The medieval hall-and-cross-wings house had severe limitations, for the fact that the hall range was only a single room deep meant that, when a large number of rooms was required, one or both of the cross-wings had to be of great length. The result, as at Horbury Hall (92), was a plan that lacked balance and convenience. The hall-and-cross-wings plan was retained in one form or another until 1680, but in its medieval form it was not capable of satisfying the more complex demands of the contemporary gentry. Oakwell Hall (66) shows the result of combining the medieval plan with post-medieval advances: the house has four parlours, an internal kitchen, and a number of service rooms, but because the hall range is only a single room deep the result is a straggling plan that lacked easy and convenient circulation (Fig. 32). Similarly at Hawksworth Hall (79) the 1664 additions to the early 17th-century hall-and-cross-wings house were built not around the core of the dwelling but as an extension to one side, giving an impressive elevation of great length but a plan in which the hall was deprived of one of its principal functions, that of acting as the hub of the house (Plate 77).

The solution to the problem of combining the 'H' plan with the demand for more rooms lay in setting a room or range of rooms behind the hall. This had the virtue both of keeping the plan compact and of emphasizing the hall's

Plate 77 [79] Hawksworth Hall; early house to left, with additions to right.

central position. Because the 'H' plan was still the dominant form, the result could not be called a double-pile plan, for with its projections at front or rear, or both, the house lacked the economy of construction and unity of design that were the principal advantages of the true double-pile. Crawstone Hall (55), of 1631, was built as a simple rectangle, but most houses, while achieving the character of the double-pile in so far as they were built two rooms deep throughout, were in fact only a step in that direction. At best they can be said to have an informal double-pile plan.

In the medieval gentry house, at least in origin, the most important division was a lateral one between the best rooms – hall, parlour, solar – and the service rooms. These were often confined to the lower wing, with a passage marking the boundary between the two areas. There is,

however, reason to believe that this division was breaking down even in the lesser gentry houses of the late Middle Ages, for at New Hall, Elland (54), the lower wing may have been built with a parlour. After 1550 the increase in the number of parlours and the need to retain a compact plan necessitated the siting of one or more in the lower wing. When this was combined with the siting of superior chambers over the parlours flanking the hall, the result was a main elevation lined with the principal rooms of the house – hall in the centre and parlours and chambers in the wings. Many houses show this composition, including the Old Hall, East Ardsley (52), and Shuttleworth Hall, Allerton (12; Fig. 29), but perhaps the best example is Marsh Hall (167) of 1626: here the main front is made up of an open hall flanked by parlours and chambers, all four with lavish plaster decoration (Plates 78–83; Figs. 33, 34).

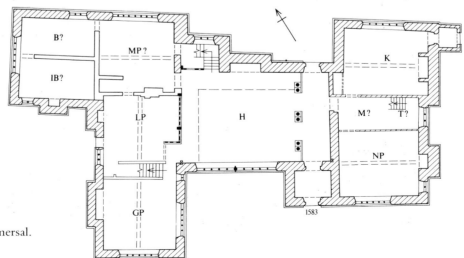

Fig 32 [66] Oakwell Hall, Gomersal.

MARSH HALL

Fig 33 [167] Marsh Hall, Northowram.

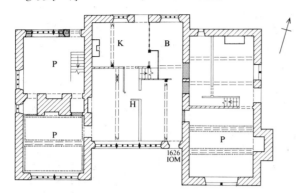

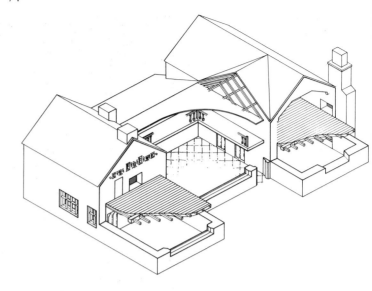

Fig 34 [167] Marsh Hall, Northowram; reconstruction.

Plate 78 [167] Marsh Hall, Northowram, 1626; the front.

Plate 79 [167] Marsh Hall; the rear.

Plate 80. [167] Marsh
Hall; the upper parlour.

Plate 81 [167] Marsh
Hall; the lower parlour.

Plate 82 [167] Marsh Hall; the upper chamber.

Plate 83 [167] Marsh Hall; the lower chamber.

In this and other houses the functional axis lay not on the line of a passage, as in medieval houses, but between the front and rear, for the service rooms, displaced from their traditional position at the lower end and now including a kitchen, were placed at the rear. In its contrast between the main elevation, balanced although still assymetrical, and the back, where convenience rather than display was the main consideration, Marsh Hall clearly reveals the changed axis of the post-medieval gentry house.

The new importance of the display front is evident in the treatment of the wings of the house. The 'H' plan gave a balanced elevation, with wings flanking the hall range, and even in houses without projecting wings the gabled form of the ends of the building was retained: at the Rectory, Guiseley (77), of 1601 (Plate 84), and at Woodthorpe Hall, Sandal Magna, built probably in 1677 in the last years of the hall-and-cross-wings tradition, the gables are purely decorative (Plate 85). At Wood Lane Hall (196), the upper end is in the form of a projecting wing, but the lower end, despite simply continuing the line of the central part of the house, is given its own gable. At other houses there were gables not only at the ends of the elevation but also over the central area, as at Holdsworth House, Ovenden (Plate 86) and Baildon Hall (17; Plate 87). In houses without

Above: Plate 84 [77] The Rectory, Guiseley, 1601.   *Below:* Plate 85 Woodthorpe Hall, Sandal Magna, c.1677.

Plate 86 Holdsworth House, Ovenden, 1633.

Plate 87 [17] Baildon Hall.

Plate 88 [55] Crawstone Hall, Elland cum Greetland, 1631; wing of *c.*1700 in foreground.

Plate 89 [51] Lumb Hall, Drighlington.

Plate 90 [140] East Riddlesden Hall, Morton; block of 1648 to left, Starkie wing of 1692 to right, open hall in centre.

projecting wings the result was a flat elevation with gables over each of the three elements, as at Crawstone Hall (55; Plate 88) and Lumb Hall (51; Plate 89). The most extravagant use of the gable as a decorative form is at East Riddlesden Hall (140), where the 1648 block is triple-gabled on three sides (Plate 90).

Another aspect of design which shows the increasing attention paid to the appearance of the house, at least on its main elevation, is the experimentation with the nature and position of the entry. Unlike the use of the gable, this was permitted by changes within the house. As long as one end of the house was occupied by inferior service rooms, there was a clear need to divide it from the hall by means of a passage (Plates 91, 92), and medieval gentry houses invariably had either a hearth-passage or a through-passage plan. Both continued in use in the new type of house in

Plate 91 [66] Oakwell Hall, Gomersal;
the passage.

Plate 92 [25] Howroyd, Barkisland;
the passage.

which the lower wing contained a parlour, examples being Oakwell Hall, Shuttleworth Hall, and East Riddlesden Hall. The persistence of these plans is evidence that the hall, even the open hall, was still a living area rather than an entrance vestibule, for it was insulated from the external doorway by the passage or screens. The passage plan, however, had lost much of its utility in the post-medieval house, for it served to isolate the lower parlour rather than to integrate it into the rest of the living area. Furthermore, it was not susceptible to incorporation into a balanced facade, for only when there were four rooms instead of three on the main front could the passage be sited centrally; a rare instance of this successful combination is seen at the Rectory, Guiseley (77).

A number of alternatives were explored by the gentry in the 17th century. The off-centre entry was retained in many houses, in the form either of a doorway opening into the hall at one corner, as at Marsh Hall and Ovenden Hall, or of a lobby entry, found at Lumb Hall and at New Hall, Bowling (30), of 1672. Neither, however, was an improvement to the external appearance of the house. Like the entry into the passage, the lobby entry could be part of a symmetrical facade only when the tripartite form of the house was abandoned; this was done at Horton Hall (93), where the doorway, sheltered by a porch, opens against the side of the stack heating hall and parlour (Fig. 35). In the tripartite house only one entry position could satisfy the desire for symmetry and so allow the gentry to imitate the example of the prodigy houses, the central entry opening directly into the middle of the hall. Although possibly employed at Woolley Hall, a major gentry house, as early as 1635, the first and only occasion this solution was adopted in a minor gentry house before 1680 was in the rebuilding in 1652 of Old Hall, East Ardsley (52). This example (Fig. 36) remains isolated because, although the central entry allowed a symmetrical elevation (not in fact attained at the Old Hall because it is the product of more than one building phase), this advantage was outweighed by other considerations. The central entry opening directly into the middle of the hall changed that room into little more than an entrance vestibule. In the period before 1680 this was not contemplated by the bulk of the gentry, who,

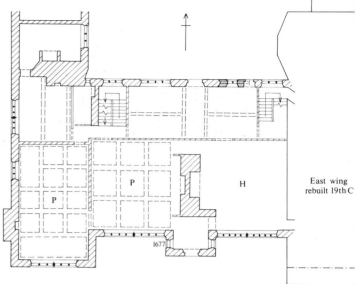

Fig 35 [93] Horton Hall.

despite drawing off some of its former functions to other rooms, still demanded at least something of the form of the medieval hall. The off-centre doorway, often into a passage, allowed entry into one end of the hall, in the style of medieval houses, and the siting of the best rooms and the stair at the opposite end consolidated the role of the hall as the ceremonial centre of the house. Not until this lingering notion of the role of the hall had weakened could the central entry gain popularity, and this was achieved only when the design of the house had changed in other important respects.

THE 18th-CENTURY COUNTRY HOUSE

The development and perfection of a type of house which was able to satisfy the demands of men of widely differing fortunes over much of the land is, arguably, the greatest

Fig 36 [52] Old Hall, East Ardsley; principal elevation.

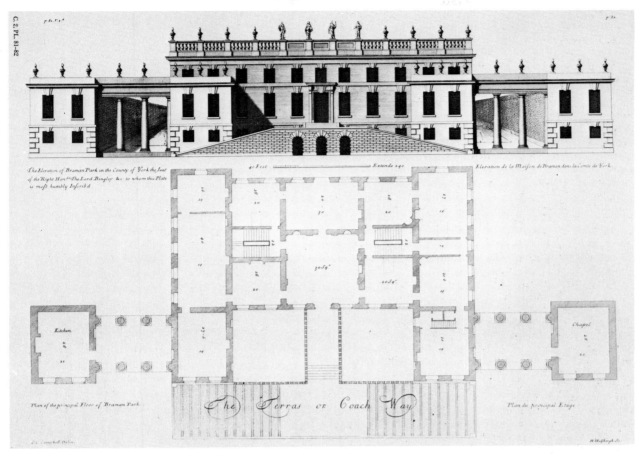

Plate 93 [31] Bramham Park. Colen Campbell's drawings of main elevation and principal floor.

achievement of English architecture in the post-medieval period. The acceptance of this new type of house in West Yorkshire in the late 17th and early 18th centuries represents the application by the local gentry of national styles or ornament and design to the idiosyncratic type of house, so different from contemporary gentry houses in other parts of the country, which it had evolved in the previous century. The newness of the gentleman's residence should not be exaggerated, for much of the rationale for the new type of house was present in the old, albeit in a form influenced still by the vestiges of medieval notions of planning. In West Yorkshire, as elsewhere, it was a fusion of independently attained needs and imported Renaissance ideas on design, disseminated through the rise of the architectural profession, which produced what is instantly recognizable throughout the length and breadth of the country as the classical English gentleman's residence.

The needs of the gentry did not change suddenly in the late 17th century, and the gentleman's residence preserved the functional axis of the pre-1680 house and the relationship between the rooms. What the gentry wanted was, essentially, the same house as they had developed over the previous century, but with two improvements – a greater sense of overall design, and an enhanced economy and convenience in the plan. The double-pile rectangular block answered the first need, and the second improvement involved the perfection of a system of circulation within the house. The changes are seen not only in the houses of the gentry, but also in the residences of the nobility, and it is perhaps these largest houses which changed the most under the impact of the new ideas.

The gap of three-quarters of a century between the latest of the prodigy houses in West Yorkshire – Temple Newsam and Strafford's work at Ledston – and Bramham Park, the first of the county's great houses to be designed along the new lines, makes it impossible to trace from local examples the stages of evolution which houses of this status underwent. This was the age of May, Mills, Talman, and, above all, Sir Roger Pratt, who is generally credited with the application of double-pile planning to the largest houses.[25] This was also the period in which a stricter, classical style of ornament was widely adopted, free of the extravagance of Elizabethan and Jacobean taste. By the time that Bramham Park (31) was completed in 1710 the new principles had been thoroughly absorbed. Colen Campbell's drawings show the original character of the house better than the surviving building and reveal the gulf between it and the earlier group of great houses (Plate 93).

Plate 94 Heath House, Warmfield cum Heath. James Paine's remodelling of an earlier house, 1744.

Dominating the composition is a central block of eleven bays, symmetrically disposed and with a uniform skyline. The symmetry is emphasized by low wings projecting from the main block and by pavilions linked by colonnades. The principal floor, raised to the level of a piano nobile above a service basement, is entirely occupied by the best public rooms and private apartments. Occupying the central area are the hall and the saloon. The hall, a magnificent 30-foot cube, is very much an entrance and reception area, for the doorway opens straight into the middle of it without the intermediary stage of a screens passage. Grouped around these public rooms are the private apartments, which at this level of society could include withdrawing rooms, a dining room, and sitting rooms, as well as the usual bedrooms and dressing rooms.

The system of apartments and common rooms is seen more clearly at another country house, Nostell Priory (61), where the principal floor provided three apartments as well as a Common Setting Room, a Drawing Room, a Dining Room, servants' bedrooms, and, of course, the public area of Hall and Saloon.[26] Because much of the life of the great house was still conducted on the first floor, an impressive stair was an important part of the design: at both Bramham and Nostell two staircases link the hall closely with the first-floor rooms. The increased compartmentalisation of the plan and the growing gulf between master and servant produced in the great house a secluded service area and an intricate system of internal communiation. At Bramham and Nostell, as was common in the country houses of the period, services were confined to the basement, and the kitchen is in one of the detached pavilions. At Nostell, but apparently not at Bramham, the internal segregation was extended to the communication between the floors, for in addition to the main staircases linking the best rooms on the principal and chamber floors, the plan provided two smaller stairs for the use of servants moving between the basement and the rest of the house.

THE GENTLEMAN'S RESIDENCE, 1680–1800

Bramham, Nostell, and Carr's Harewood (built 1759–71) are all country houses which, by virtue of the elaborate demands of great families, followed and developed Pratt's model of the double-pile. They had their imitators among slightly smaller houses, for Paine at Heath House (Plate 94) and Carr at Heath Hall both incorporated some of the elements of the country house on a reduced scale.[27] The greater part of gentry building activity after 1680, however, was undertaken by gentlemen of lesser means, and for them many of the features of the country house were not appropriate. The piano nobile, for instance, was rarely so emphatically expressed in their houses, and the basement often contained little more than a few cellars. The association of hall and saloon and the elaborate system of apartments were not required by most gentry families, and the distant, detached kitchen was more retrogressive than advantageous at this social level. The picture of the development of the gentry house after 1680 is one of great variety, for as well as being diverse in terms of wealth, the gentry included men of very different degrees of aspiration and taste.

Yorkshire shared the north of England's somewhat delayed acceptance of the double-pile house. The earliest perfect example of the style in the county is Bell Hall, Naburn (North Yorkshire), built in 1680 on a regular plan of a single block five bays by three, with a symmetrical

facade, a main floor raised above a basement, and a hipped roof with dormer windows lighting attics. Despite the late arrival of the type, however, its convenience and fashionable qualities were quickly appreciated, and a flood of building activity by the Yorkshire gentry followed. The success of the new type is seen in the fact that, when Samuel Buck came to sketch the houses of the Yorkshire gentry in 1719–20, one third of the buildings which he recorded show the influence of the recently received ideas. Clearly the period after 1680 had been marked both by a rapid replacement of older, possibly medieval, houses, and by the construction of new houses by recently emerged gentry families.[28]

Within West Yorkshire the picture is similar. Some houses achieved something of the character of the new type at an early date: Clarke Hall, Stanley cum Wrenthorpe (201), for instance, was built with a symmetrical front in 1680 but lacked a double-pile plan (Plate 95), and High Fearnley, Wyke (251), was built as late as 1698 with a double-pile plan but with no attempt at symmetry on the main front. Perhaps the first house to approach closely the form and style of the new residence was Scout Hall, Northowram (168), built in 1681 by John Mitchell, a

Plate 95 [201] Clarke Hall, Stanley cum Wrenthorpe; the symmetrical front of 1680.

first-generation gentleman (Plates 96, 97).[29] The house is not perfectly symmetrical, but its chief significance lies in its simple plan, in which all the elements of the dwelling are contained within a rectangular block (Fig. 37). Soon after Scout Hall was built other houses appeared: Eshald Hall at Heath, Kippax Hall, Horsforth Hall and the vicarage at Leeds all had a symmetrical design and a double-pile plan, and from 1680 until the middle of the next century and beyond there was a steady stream of gentry building activity, overwhelmingly dominated by the idea of a formally designed house.[30]

The range in size of gentry houses after 1680 was as wide as the range of wealth within the class. Most were designed with a five or seven-bay frontage: typical examples of five-bay houses, of various dates, are Newstead Hall (78) and the Old Rectory, Methley (130), both early 18th-century, Kettlethorpe Hall (43), of 1727, Burley House (40) and Haugh End, Sowerby (198), both of the late 18th century (Plates 98–102). Austhorpe Hall (15) is an early example of a seven-bay house (1694), followed by Esholt

Plate 96 [168] Scout Hall, Northowram, 1681; the house reroofed in 19th century.

Plate 97 John Mitchell, gentleman, of Scout Hall; artist's impression of house in background (*reproduced by permission of Calderdale Museums Service*).

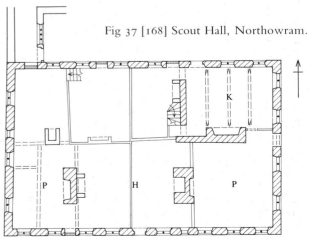

Fig 37 [168] Scout Hall, Northowram.

Plate 98 [78] Newstead Hall, Havercroft with Cold Hiendley, 1708.

Plate 99 [130] Old Rectory, Mickletown, Methley, *c.*1700.

Plate 100 [43]
Kettlethorpe Hall,
Crigglestone, 1727.

Plate 101 [40]
Burley House, 1783.

Plate 102 [198]
Haugh End, Sowerby,
*c.*1770.

Hall (59) of *c*.1706, Lupset Hall (14) of 1716, and Farfield Hall, Addingham (2) of *c*.1728 (Plates 103–6). Some houses were larger: Bretton Hall was of nine bays, and at Walton Hall, Walton, a frontage of eight bays was contrived (Plate 107).[31] Height also varied: most houses were of two storeys above a basement, but at Scout Hall and at Heath House extra rooms were accommodated in a third storey. Further expansion could be achieved in a number of ways. Detached pavilions of the type used in great houses were not common, but John Carr used them at Heath Hall and at Pye Nest, Skircoat; and at Armley House (*c*.1818) Robert Smirke employed balancing wings joined to the main block by single-storey links.[32] The use of low attached wings, seen at Kettlethorpe Hall (43) and at Netherton Hall,

Plate 103 [15] Austhorpe Hall, 1694.

Plate 104 [59] Esholt Hall, *c*.1706.

Plate 105 [14] Lupset Hall, Alverthorpe with Thornes, 1716.

Plate 106 [2] Farfield Hall, Addingham, 1728.

Plate 107 Walton Hall.

Plate 108 [181] Netherton Hall, Shitlington.

Plate 109 [212] Tong Hall, 1702, heightened in late 18th century.

Plate 110 [62] Butterley Hall, Fulstone, 1742.

Plate 111 Old Hall, Silsden, 1682.

Shitlington (181), extended the facade (Plate 108). A modest gain in internal area could be contrived by the shallow projection of the end bays from the central part of the block: this device, representing perhaps the last vestige of the medieval hall-and-cross-wings tradition, is seen at Tong Hall (212; Plate 109) and at Lupset Hall (14).

Smaller houses, too, adopted something of the form and style of the new type of dwelling; indeed, as far as plan is concerned, it was at the level of the smaller gentry house that the double-pile had first become common. Butterley Hall, Fulstone (62), not even a full double-pile, is of just three bays and two-and-a-half storeys (Plate 110), and the unusual Netherton Hall (181) is compressed into a main block of three bays and three lofty storeys. Houses of just three bays are not common, however, and were probaby either the seats of minor branches of families or the residences of men hovering on the indefinable boundary between the lesser gentry and the wealthy yeoman or professional classes.

The dominating characteristic of the exterior of the post-1680 gentry house is symmetry. The exceptions were either built soon after 1680 and therefore show the continued influence of older ideas, or incorporated earlier remains in a remodelled facade. The former is the case at Old Hall, Silsden, of 1682 (Plate 111) and at High Fearnley, Wyke (251), of 1698, and perfect symmetry was precluded

Plate 112 [86] Coley Hall, Hipperholme with Brighouse; the remodelled main front.

at Shann House, Methley (129), by the inclusion of earlier work in the scheme. Where the builder was free from these restrictions the rule of symmetry predominates. Some houses have a very simple facade with regularly spaced windows on either side of a central doorway, as at Newstead Hall (78) and at the refronted Coley Hall (86; Plate 112). Emphasis of the central bay was used to reinforce symmetry: at the Old Rectory, Methley (130), the central bay projects slightly, and at Austhorpe Hall (15; Fig. 38) the projecting bay is capped by a small pediment. The balance of the principal front at Lupset Hall was emphasized by an especially elaborate frontispiece, contain-

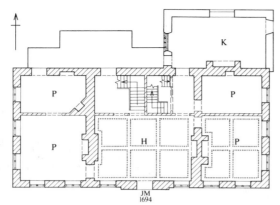

Fig 38 [15] Austhorpe Hall.

ing an ornate doorway and first-floor window, and, rising above the parapet, a miniature pediment framing an oculus. Larger pediments were used to express the importance of the rooms in the central area – hall and best chamber – and in the first half of the 18th century the extent of the pediment corresponded to the size of those rooms. At Esholt Hall (59) and at Farfield Hall (2), for instance, the pediment, like the hall, is of three bays, Later, the pediment became simply a decorative feature, disassociated from the plan: at Burley House (40) and at Haugh End, Sowerby (198) it is of three bays but the hall is of one, and at Netherton Hall (181) a giant pediment extends the entire length of the three-bay main block.[33] Projecting wings, as well as being a means of gaining more space, also contributed to symmetry, shown by the elevations of Tong Hall (212) and Lupset Hall. Bay windows, too, emphasized the symmetry of an elevation and were used at an early date at Clarke Hall (201) and in the second half of the 18th century at Gledhow Hall, Potter Newton (173), at Netherton Hall, and at the remodelled north front at Tong.

The new formality of the entrance front, and at some houses of more than one front, is matched by the introduction of an urbane style of ornament. The mullioned window was replaced by the cross-window with a casement, and the richly moulded doorways of the earlier age gave way to more severely classical styles. The ornament of the main front was usually restrained, but at Kettlethorpe Hall (43) the windows have rich carvings incorporated into their surrounds, and at Farfield Hall the main elevation has a full array of classical ornament, with fluted giant pilasters supporting a pediment with escutcheon, and a vermiculated parapet originally crowned by vases. Earlier styles might co-exist with the new ornament where display was not a consideration: at Tong Hall, for example, the status of the basement is marked by the use of mullioned windows, and the treatment of the back of many houses is very much inferior to that of the main front.

The interior of the double-pile residence was initially designed to provide the same type of accommodation as had been contained within the pre-1680 house. A hall was flanked by parlours, and the rear was occupied by further parlours, the stair, and by service rooms (Fig. 38). Although the majority of gentry houses after 1680 have three rooms on the main front, some have only two, the hall and a parlour. There are perhaps two reasons for the abandonment of the tripartite arrangement of the front. Gentry of small fortune might require a less extensive house but wish to retain the appearance of the standard residence, achieved by abandoning one of the parlours and siting the hall in one corner of the block. In a house like Butterley Hall (62), therefore, the doorway, central in the elevation, opens into one end of the hall, which is necessarily larger than the adjacent parlour because it includes the entrance bay (Fig. 39). In other houses the expense of building does not appear to have been an influence, and the choice seems to have been made to restrict the ground-floor accommodation because superior rooms were provided on the upper floors. This certainly is the case at Thorpe Hall (209), a large house of three storeys but with only two reception rooms on the ground floor. The inadequacies of that floor, however, are redeemed by the magnificence of the chambers, which are richly

Fig 39 [62] Butterley Hall, Fulstone.

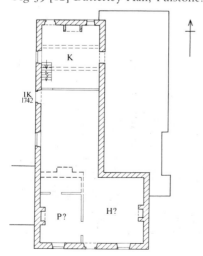

Plate 113 [201] Clarke Hall, Stanley cum Wrenthorpe; the hall.

Above: Plate 114 [97] Newhouse Hall, Huddersfield; the hall.

Below: Plate 115 [129] Shann House, Methley; the hall.

decorated and of lofty proportions. That smaller houses, too, might turn the chambers to superior use is demonstrated by Arthur Jessop's account of a visit to Butterley Hall in 1744. He describes how he 'went up into the Room to dinner', revealing that the best dining room was on the first floor.[34]

Unlike the majority of pre-1680 gentry houses, all but a very few double-pile residences have an entry opening directly into the hall. Its use as an entrance hall, one of its functions in the earlier period, is confirmed by this aspect of plan, for the direct entry, whether in the centre of the hall or, more rarely, at one end, excluded the comfort required in a room used for much of the everyday life of the household. The magnificence of the open hall was rejected after 1680 in favour of a more modest single-storey room, but its decoration with plasterwork shows that it was intended to impress visitors en route to the reception rooms (Plates 113–16). The inventories suggest that not all the life was taken out of the hall in this period, however, for the chairs, tables, clock and birdcage in the hall at Whitley Beaumont in 1704, and the chairs, tea table, pictures and looking glass in that of Samuel Stocks of Methley in 1738 demonstrate that it still had a role as an important part of the living area. The clearest indication that it was regarded as a place in which to while away time in comfort is given in the inventory of Thomas Ramsden of High Fearnley, dated 1727: here the hall had a clock, numerous chairs, a collection of tables, maps and pictures decorating the walls, chessmen and dice.

From an early date the hall's primary function as an entrance area and channel of distribution was reflected in the plan of some of the smaller houses. In these the

Plate 116 [15] Austhorpe Hall; the hall.

extravagance of a large hall, used only rarely either as a private sitting room or for public occasions, was repudiated and the hall was reduced to a single bay. This deprived it of the capacity to act as a living room, but did not impair its most important function, to serve as the centre of distribution within the house. It is not clear precisely when the single-bay hall made its first appearance in West Yorkshire, but Newstead Hall (78) of 1708, and the Old Rectory, Methley (130), dating probably from the first decade of the 18th century, both appear to have been built with this plan (Fig. 40). Later examples include Kettlethorpe Hall (43) of 1727, and by the second half of the century many houses, among them Burley House (40), White Windows, Sowerby (197) of 1768, and Netherton Hall (181) adopted the more compact hall (Plate 117, Fig. 41). The fact that the single-bay hall, lit by a fanlight over the doorway, proved so popular in smaller houses is symptomatic of the changing way of life of the gentry. Unlike his medieval ancestor, who required a large open hall for the public entertainment of households made up of many different ranks, the 18th-century gentleman increasingly removed much of the public life into suites of rooms which, among the very wealthy, might include a ballroom. The nature of the occasions, too, was different, for the later age tended much more to segregate by status. Gatherings were largely meetings of equals and more private events than the assemblies common in an earlier age. There was, therefore, less need to provide a large hall for communal occasions, and the reduction of the hall to the status of a vestibule is an aspect of social segregation which is reflected elsewhere in the plan of the gentry house.

The assumption by the hall of a single primary function is part of the development of a centralized system of circulation, the most significant advance permitted by the plan of the double-pile house. The hall might have a number of other functions according to its size and elaboration, but after 1680 it always acted as an entrance area. Its chief role now was to give convenient access to as many of the ground and first-floor rooms as possible. To do this, size was not important, and in the houses of the minor gentry and professional men the hall could be reduced to a single bay. Siting, however, was vital, and the hall retained its position in the centre of the main front to allow it to open into the flanking parlours. In the pre-1680 gentry house the stair had usually opened out of one corner

Plate 117 [181] Netherton Hall, Shitlington; the single-bay hall.

of the hall, but this relationship was improved after 1680 by balancing the hall on the main front with the staircase hall at the rear. This change also improved the convenience of the first floor, for the stair in the double-pile house rose to a landing at the centre of the block. Through the additional improvement of a transverse corridor dividing front from rear rooms, a complete system of circulation was developed which gave convenient and independent access to a large number of the best rooms on both ground and first floors.

Fig 40 [130] Old Rectory, Mickletown, Methley.

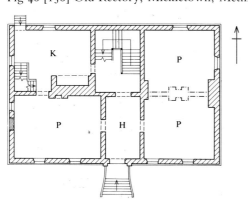

Fig 41 [181] Netherton Hall, Shitlington.

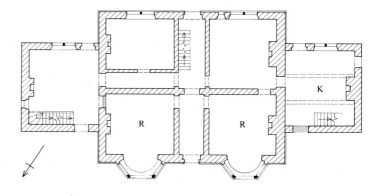

Plate 118 [130] Old Rectory, Mickletown, Methley; the stair hall.

Plate 119 [129] Shann House, Methley; the stair hall.

The close link between entry and stair is a feature of some of the first houses to be built after 1680. At Austhorpe Hall (15) the three-bay hall leads directly to the stair hall, and at the Old Rectory, Methley, and Newstead Hall the hall is reduced to a vestibule giving access to flanking parlours and to the rear of the house with its balancing stair hall (Plates 118–19). Transverse corridors increased the sophistication of the circulation at Farfield Hall (2; Fig. 42) and at two of the later houses, White Windows and Netherton Hall. Because the stair was a vital

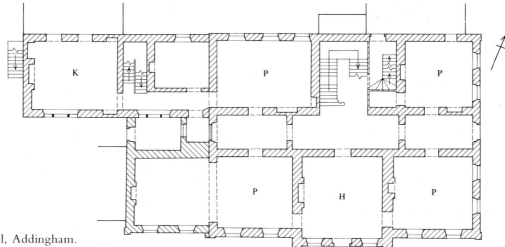

Fig 42 [2] Farfield Hall, Addingham.

Plate 120 [2] Farfield Hall, Addingham; the secondary stair is visible through the open door.

Plate 120 [2] Farfield Hall, Addingham; the secondary stair is visible through the open door.

link in the system it was given a new prominence in the design, and the stair hall is frequently one of the most impressive areas of a house. At houses like Farfield Hall and Lupset Hall (14) it rises through two storeys and is fitted out with a well-worked staircase (Plates 120, 123). The stair hall at Newstead Hall was lit by a Venetian window and decorated with panelling and plasterwork (Plate 122), and the remodelling of Newhouse Hall, Huddersfield (197), in the late 17th century, although retaining the older plan of a stair rising out of one corner of the hall, emphasized the importance of the stair area by a lavish plaster ceiling (Plate 121).

The link between hall and stair is shown very clearly by the alterations made to earlier houses in the course of the

Plate 121 [97] Newhouse Hall, Huddersfield; ceiling over stair hall.

Plate 122 [78] Newstead Hall, Havercroft with Cold Hiendley; the stair hall.

Plate 123 [14] Lupset Hall, Alverthorpe with Thornes; the staircase rises to a landing.

Plate 124 [40] Burley House; the stair hall.

Plate 125 [197] White Windows, Sowerby; the stair hall.

Plate 126 Bramham Biggin; the combined entrance and stair hall.

18th and early 19th centuries. At Bramham Biggin (Plate 126) the 1756 refitting of the interior acknowledged the superfluity of a large hall and compressed two rooms into a single one which acted both as an impressive entrance area and as a stair hall. This new type of entrance/stair hall was

also contrived at Hawksworth Hall (79; Plate 127) and, in the early 19th century, at Woolley Hall, where the stair rises out of one end of the hall behind a colonnade. Kirklees Hall, Clifton, received equally drastic remodelling in the 18th century, and here a new entrance front was created with a doorway opening into the same type of combined entrance/stair hall.

The demise of the hall as a living area was complemented by a growing specialization in the rest of the house. Much of the life, both public and private, of the inner family was conducted in the best parlours and chambers. The number of parlours varied with the size of house, from perhaps just two at small houses like Butterley Hall (62) and the Old Rectory, Methley (130), to as many as three or four in large houses like Farfield Hall. The post-1680 gentry inventories have an average of two-and-a-half parlours and show that in this age it was very unusual not to set one aside as a dining room. Two inventories list two such rooms, a low and a great dining room at Farfield Hall in 1714, and a large and a little dining room in Edward Allot's house at Crigglestone in 1721. The use of a second dining room confirms that the hall, which in an earlier period would have included this function, now often lacked the character of a living room.

Parlours were frequently furnished as comfortable rooms: in 1715 John Empson had, as well as a dining room, a great and a little parlour, both of which were sitting rooms. Rarely is a withdrawing room named as such in the pre-1740 inventories, but the furniture of many parlours shows that they had this function. Even as late as the 1730s it was still common to use one parlour as a bedroom as well as a sitting room, and very few inventories suggest that bedrooms were confined to the first floor. The surviving houses show that the best parlours were invariably heated in the new double-pile house and that frequently they were decorated with plasterwork and panelling. Some of the best decorative work at Austhorpe Hall (15) is in the parlours flanking the hall (Plates 128–9), and at Clarke Hall (201) the main parlour has a sumptuous plaster ceiling (Plate 130). In the houses of the very wealthy, the best rooms could be magnificent, and at Farfield Hall one splendid parlour

Plate 127 [79] Hawksworth Hall; the entrance and stair hall.

Plate 128 [15] Austhorpe Hall; plaster decoration of the parlour.

Plate 129 [15] Austhorpe Hall; fireplace and panelling in the parlour.

Plate 130 [201] Clarke Hall, Stanley cum Wrenthorpe; the dining room.

Plate 131 [2] Farfield Hall, Addingham; the best parlour.

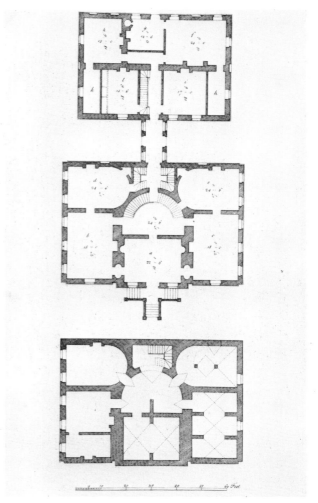

Plate 132 [27] St Ives, Bingley; plan of the principal floor.

survives, fitted out with a marble fireplace, panelling with pilasters, and a plaster ceiling (Plate 131).

By the second half of the 18th century the increasingly specialized and public uses of the parlours is reflected in the names by which rooms were known. The term 'parlour' is somewhat anachronistic when applied to houses of this date, and more usual descriptions of ground-floor rooms are as drawing room, dining room, library, study, and, occasionally, sitting room. Burley House (40), built in 1783, was described as having a Dining Room, a Breakfast Room, a Drawing Room, a Study, and a Parlour.[35] The ground floor of the gentleman's residence was no longer made up of a number of private parlours; instead the plan gave a sequence of reception rooms, sometimes grouped in a circuit around a top-lit staircase hall. St Ives, Bingley (27), built in 1759, is a good example of the type (Plate 132). Entry was into a hall of no great size or pretention, opening in turn into the staircase hall. Grouped around are the reception rooms, varied in shape to give interest to the circuit followed by the guests at entertainments.[36] The type of assembly staged by the major gentry at the end of the period is illustrated by an account of a ball given in 1818 at Woolley Hall: 500 invitations were issued, and on the night the guests, merely passing through the hall, were entertained in one wing, where 'the drawing room, library and anteroom, decorated in a splendid manner, formed a promenade for the company', the main action taking place in a specially constructed temporary ballroom leading out of the anteroom.[37] The same rooms, when not in use on public occasions, acted as comfortable sitting rooms, and in this respect the 18th-century residence proved to be very adaptable.

Before the ground floor came to be dominated by public reception rooms and special-purpose rooms like the library, some at least of the public rooms of the gentry house were on the first floor, approached by the main stair. The chambers at Thorpe Hall (208), for instance, are the most impressive rooms in the house (Plate 133), and the decoration of the best chamber in some houses suggest that it was intended to serve as more than simply a bedroom (Plate 134). The inventories confirm this, and show that some chambers acted also as reception rooms. At Whitley in 1704, for example, the best chamber had a scrutore, a screen, three Japan tables, eleven chairs, and a cabinet with china and plate, as well as a silk bed. As the public life of

Plate 133 [208] Thorpe Hall; large windows light the chambers.

the house became concentrated on the ground floor, however, the chambers assumed the character of bedrooms and sitting rooms for the informal reception of visitors. The best chambers were, of course, outnumbered by bedrooms occupied by the lesser members of the household and by living-in servants, and these were more utilitarian in character.

Much of the success of the double-pile house lay in the way it permitted two entirely separate systems of circulation to operate in complete independence. The hall and main staircase were the pivots in the system which served

the polite society within the house, but the house also sheltered another world, that of the servants operating in their own domain. The problems of design were considerable: it was necessary to take into account the growing need to segregate the two societies and yet to maintain a close and convenient relationship between them. The servants must be distant and inconspicuous, but at the same time able to respond quickly to their masters' demands. To this end the kitchen, the most important service room, was usually set at a remove from the best rooms of the house (Plate 135). Only Tong Hall (212) employed a service

Plate 134 [129] Shann House, Bingley; panelling in main chamber.

Plate 135 [201] Clarke Hall, Stanley cum Wrenthorpe; the kitchen.

Plate 136 [181] Netherton Hall, Shitlington; service wings overlooking the rear.

basement with a kitchen, and more common sites for the kitchen were in a wing at the side or the rear of the main block. At Austhorpe Hall (15) there is a low kitchen wing at the rear, and at Farfield Hall (2) a long wing at one side. Netherton Hall (181) employs balancing service wings on either side of the main block, their status and function revealed by the way in which they present a blank wall to the principal front (Plate 136). The detached kitchen, still used in great houses, was not a feature of smaller ones, although James Paine designed St Ives, Bingley (27) with a service building behind the principal block and linked to it by a single-storey corridor (Plate 137). Only in the smaller

Plate 137 [27] St Ives, Bingley; side view, showing service block at rear.

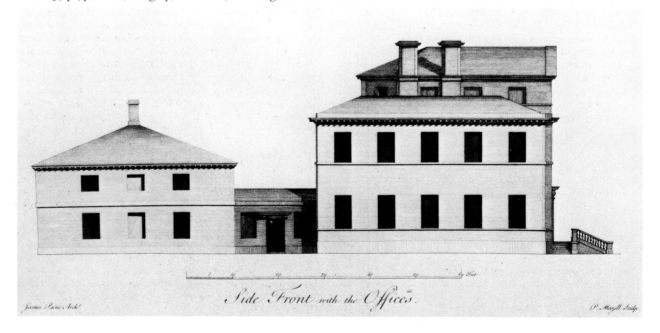

Side Front with the Offices.

James Paine Archt.

P. Mazell Sculp.

Plate 138 [78] Newstead Hall, Havercroft with Cold Hiendley; the backstairs.

Plate 139 [197] White Windows, Sowerby; the backstairs.

houses, like the Old Rectory, Methley (130), was the kitchen in the main block, where it was confined to one corner at the back. All these devices were intended as a compromise between the convenience of having a kitchen close to the rooms which it served and the desire to hide it away from the living area of the house.

The servants had a perpetual need to come and go between the service area and the family rooms, for their work – the serving of meals, cleaning, the lighting of fires, attendance on the family, and business matters – involved a close link between the two worlds. The main staircase in the 18th-century residence generally rose only between the ground and first floors, serving the best family rooms. The servants, however, had a much larger orbit, frequently spending some of their time in the basement, some in the attics, and some on the main floors, both in the service area and in the better rooms. For them to be able to serve the family with the minimum of disturbance two improvements were incorporated. The first was the system of corridors permitting independent access to a large number of rooms on the ground and first floors. The transverse corridor, used by Pratt at Coleshill, was of less use in smaller houses, where a central hall on the ground floor and a landing on the first floor might do the job just as well. Some houses, however, did use it, with the result that at Farfield Hall and at White Windows (177) the best rooms

open not into each other but into a corridor. The more informal plan of the post-1750 residence, in which rooms were regarded as part of a circuit, lessened the value of the transverse corridor, but served to increase the importance of the second device used in the double-pile house from its first appearance. This was the backstairs, a secondary staircase which linked all floors and which was generally sited to connect with the stair hall on the ground floor and with the landing or corridor on the first floor (Plates 138, 139). The servants could go from basement to attic without disturbing the life of the family and they could attend to their tasks in the best rooms without using the main staircase. At Farfield Hall the backstairs, linking closely with the stair hall and the transverse corridors on the main floors, descends to the basement and rises to the attics, as it does at Tong Hall after the remodelling of the second half of the 18th century. The close link between the service rooms and the second stair is attested by the inventory of goods at High Fearnley in 1721: it lists goods 'under Kitchen Staires', the name showing both the position of the staircase and its status.

The success of the double-pile house depended initially on its systematization of the existing needs of gentry society and on its ability to meet the requirements both of the builder of a country house and of the minor gentry with more modest ambitions. Its continued success is due to a

Plate 140 [197] White Windows, Sowerby.

further quality, its capacity to incorporate changes within the overall scheme. The house of 1800 was very different from that of a century earlier, the differences lying mainly in the increased sophistication of the systems of circulation and in the changes in the nature of the best rooms brought about by the evolution of gentry society, but both houses were based on the same concept of the double-pile residence. The enduring prestige of the type is attested by the way in which it was adopted in the second half of the 18th century, not only by men intent on building a country seat at the centre of an agricultural estate, but also by an increasingly wealthy and influential merchant class eager to move out of the towns and set themselves up on a suburban estate. There is a large number of such residences around Halifax and Leeds; White Windows, Sowerby (177), is one (Plate 140), Gledhow Hall (173) built for a merchant by John Carr in 1764 is another, and Leventhorpe Hall

provided ideal for another merchant because it was 'happily situated in one of the richest vales of a fruitful country, too distant to be annoyed by the Nuisances and yet near enough to share the important advantages of a Manufacturing District'.[38]

The archetypal residence, the preferred home of great and lesser gentry and of the new professional and merchant classes, is the direct descendant of the double-pile house developed in the 17th century, subtly adjusted to meet the changing and often specialized needs of an evolving society. By adopting this type, wealthy men of both new and old families were so thoroughly absorbed into the mainstream of national architectural development that, when J. P. Neale came to depict the country seats of the land in the early 19th century, his West Yorkshire examples were in no way distinguishable from the houses of distant parts of England.[39]

APPENDIX

GENTRY INVENTORIES USED IN ANALYSIS OF HOUSES

DATE OF INVENTORY (and will if significantly different)	NAME OF TESTATOR	REFERENCE
1557–1680 (Total 18)		
1557	John Gascoygne of Lazencroft	(Gascoigne Papers GC/F4/1, Leeds City Archives)
May 1567	John Thornhill of Fixby	(Brears 1972, 13–19)
1611	Robert Batt of *Oakwell*	(Foster 1954)
1638	George Wentworth of Bretton	(Brears 1972, 83–6)
October 1646	William Franck of Cottingley	(Preston 1929, 132)
1650	Thomas Wentworth of North Elmsall	(Bright Papers, AR B 4937, Sheffield City Libraries)
February 1651	Henry Calverley of *Calverley*	(British Library, Add. Ms. 27411)
January 1655	William Horton of *Barkisland*	(D225, Horton Mss., Bradford City Library Archives)
February 1657	Sir Richard Hawksworth of *Hawksworth*	(Bright Papers, Br.P.89/a/1, Sheffield City Libraries)
October 1660	Sir George Wentworth of *Woolley*	(WWB Box 16, Brotherton Library, University of Leeds)
July 1662	John Murgatroyd of *Riddlesden*	(HAS/B:13/42, Calderdale Metropolitan Borough Archives)
July 1667	William Richardson of North Bierley	(Brears 1972, 124–31)
March 1672	Sir Stephen Tempest of Barnbow	(Gascoigne Papers, Leeds City Archives)
December 1675	Sir Thomas Wentworth of Bretton Hall	(Brears 1972, 145–53)
February 1678	Thomas Lister of *Shibden Hall*	(Lister 1926)
August 1696 (proved Nov.)	James Oates of Murgatroyd, Warley	(BIHR)
March 1696 (proved Nov.)	Joshua Dearden of *Woodlane*, Sowerby	(BIHR)
June 1699 (proved Sept.)	Richard Richardson of *Newhall*, Bowling	(BIHR)
1689–1740 (Total 26; all in BIHR and Pontefract Deanery except that of 1714)		
February 1689 (proved March)	Edward Hippon of Featherstone	
May 1689	Joseph Armitage of Dudmanstone	
May 1689	Stephen Ellis of Hipperholme	
October 1696 (proved Feb. 1697)	Isaac Naylor of Halifax	
July 1697 (proved Aug.)	John Whittell of Marshall Hall, Elland	
February 1700 (proved Aug. 1701)	Timothy Brooke of Birstall	
May 1700 (proved April 1701)	George Power of *New Hall* in Elland	
April 1701 (proved Dec.)	John Marshall of Sharlston	
May 1701 (proved Sept.)	William Midgley of Halifax	
August 1704	Richard Beaumont of Whitley	
June 1714 (proved July)	George Myers of Farfield, Addingham	(Craven Deanery)
November 1715	John Empson of *Wyke*	*(continued overleaf)*

DATE OF INVENTORY (and will if significantly different)	NAME OF TESTATOR	REFERENCE
November 1718 (proved Dec.)	Elkanah Hoyle of *Swift Place*, Soyland	
December 1719 (proved Jan. 1721)	Jeremiah Batley of Lightcliffe	
March 1721 (proved April)	John Newson of Gaubert Hall, Hipperholme	
April 1721	Edward Allott of Crigglestone	
May 1721 (proved June)	Thomas Wheatley of White Cross, Emley	
July 1721 (proved Aug.)	William Clifton of Houghton	
September 1724 (proved Jan. 1725)	Thomas Hanson of Bothroyd in Rastrick	
December 1724 (proved Feb. 1725)	William Wager of Ackton	
August 1727 (proved Oct.)	Thomas Ramsden of *High Fearnley*	
May 1734 (proved July)	John Atkinson of Methley	
May 1734 (proved Aug.)	Ely Dyson of *Clayhouse*, Greetland	
September 1737 (proved June 1738)	John Oates of Thornhill	
June 1738 (proved July)	Francis Ramsbotham of Birks Hall, Ovenden	
July 1738	Samuel Stocks of Methley	

Houses italicised are known to survive. The inventories of both 1696 and 1699 list the goods within houses built before 1680 and, as the form of a house places some limitations upon the way in which different rooms may be used, the functions of rooms which they reveal are taken to be a tolerably close reflection of their original uses.

Notes to Chapter 3

[1] For a recent study of a West Yorkshire gentry house, see Markham 1979.

[2] For studies relating to the Yorkshire gentry, see Cliffe 1969; Roebuck 1980; and Forster 1973, 1975, 1976, 1976a.

[3] Parsons 1836, 51–2. The dissemination of ideas on house building among the gentry of East Anglia in the 16th and 17th centuries has been explored in Airs 1978.

[4] For the development of a county society in England in the period leading up to the Civil War, see Everitt 1969; 'though the sense of national identity had been increasing since the early Tudors, so too had the sense of county identity, and the latter was normally, I believe, the more powerful sentiment in 1640–60' (Everitt 1969, 5). For the marriage alliances of the Yorkshire gentry in the 17th century, see Roebuck 1980, 54.

[5] Margerison 1886.

[6] Cliffe 1969, 16–18.

[7] For the Holdsworths, Deardens and Otes, see respectively Bretton 1942, 85–7; Kendall 1906, 126–8 and Anon. 1902, 26; Kendall 1912, 375.

[8] Cliffe 1969, 28–32.

[9] The belief that a gentleman's status should be reflected in the size and splendour of his house was well expressed by Lord Wentworth, who in 1633 advised Sir William Savile of Thornhill: 'Considering That your Houses in my Judgement are not suitable to your Quality, nor yet your Plate and Furniture, I conceive your Expense ought to be reduced to two Thirds of your Estate, the rest saved to the accommodating of you in that kind' (quoted in Cliffe 1969, 103).

[10] For Ledston, see Oswald 1938; for Temple Newsam, Kitson and Pawson 1927 and Gilbert 1963; for Pontefract New Hall, Girouard 1966, 137–8; for Heath, see Weaver 1977. For a brief general survey of these and later large houses, see Linstrum 1978, ch. 2.

[11] Parsons 1836, 52. The date of Howley is not entirely certain; see Linstrum 1978, 51.

[12] Purdy 1975, 666, 669, 670, 679.

[13] Crossley 1920a.

[14] See Crump 1945, plates IX and XIIb for illustrations of the hall and screen. The screen was saved when Methley was demolished and is in store at Temple Newsam.

[15] Quoted in Markham 1979, 14.

[16] For other Smythson houses, see Girouard 1966 and 1983. The plan and historical significance of houses of this status are discussed in Mercer 1954; he compares these 'gentry' houses with the palaces of the courtier class.

[17] Full references to the inventories are given in the appendix to this chapter.

[18] The average number of parlours in the gentry inventories of this period is a little over three.

[19] The custom of receiving a guest in a bedchamber continued in the 17th century, even in the royal household; see Girouard 1978, 130–1.

[20] Both are illustrated in Girouard 1978, plates 49, 51 and colour plate X.

[21] The number of servants in the gentry household of this period is discussed in Cliffe 1969, 111–14. Although not all servants lived within the house, it was not uncommon for the gentry household to include a score or more: there were twenty-five at Hawksworth in 1658 and twenty at Sharlston in 1640.

[22] For Sir Walter Calverley's diary, see Margerison 1886. For the frequent visits which the Wentworths of Woolley could expect from branches of the family, see Markham 1979, 11–12.

[23] For Hatfield, see Girouard 1978, 115. There is evidence that some of the houses of the major gentry in Lancashire at this period provided lodgings permanently set aside for the use of visiting households; see RCHM(E) forthcoming (a), ch. 2. Not all visits were welcome, however, for Sir Thomas Hoby played reluctant host to a band of revellers at his house in Hackness (North Yorkshire) in 1600; seven young gentlemen demanded lodgings after a hunting party and disgraced themselves by gaming, drinking and disrupting devotions. The incident suggests that requests for lodging by fellow gentry were met without question, even when, as in this case, some of the visitors were from rival families; see Meads 1930, 269–72. The rivalry between Hoby and his neighbours is explored in Forster 1976.

[24] It is not clear that Chapel Fold is a gentry house, for it has not been possible to trace the family responsible for its construction. The detached kitchen continued in use in great houses long after this period; examples will be noted at Bramham Park and Nostell Priory later in this chapter.

[25] Pratt wrote that 'as to the double-pile, it seems of all others to be the most useful, first for that we have there much room in a little compass, next that the chambers may there be so laid out, as to be only of use to each other, but nothing of restraint, item great convenience there for

backstairs, item that it is warm, and affords variety of places to be made use of both according to the diverse times of the day, and year also, as shall be most requisite, besides that herein a little ground is sufficient to build upon and there may be a great spare of walling, and of other materials for the roof' (quoted in Gunther 1928, 24).

[26] See Hussey 1955, 14–15, for the provision of apartments in the baroque and Palladian county house. The system of apartments at Nostell is shown in Woolfe and Gandon 1967, plate 71.

[27] For details of Heath House, see Hall and Hall 1975, 13–18.

[28] Samuel Buck's sketchbook has been published; see Hall 1979.

[29] Oliver Heywood recorded the completion of the house in his diary:
Mr Jo. Mitchell of Scout the last week in Christmas (as they call it) to season his new house, kept open house, entertained all comers, had fearful ranting work, drinking healths freely, had 43 dishes at once. I have scarce heard the like in our parts, his wife was the musitian. Lord put a stop. (Turner 1881–5, vol. 2, 287.)

If Heywood is to be trusted, Mitchell was a wastrel, spending his time in hunting and feasting. His hunting activities were recorded both in the carved lintel of the main doorway at Scout Hall, which shows a hunting scene with a fox, four hounds, and a figure possibly intended to represent Mitchell himself (Fig. 138), and in his portrait, in which the parvenu gentleman stands proudly in front of his new house with his favourite bratchet gazing up at him (Pl. 63). This painting, removed from Scout Hall, is kept at Bankfield Museum, Halifax.

[30] Kippax, Horsforth and Leeds vicarage have perished, and Eshald has been swallowed within what is now Heath Hall, but the appearance of all four was recorded by Buck; see Hall 1979.

[31] For an illustration of Bretton Hall, see Linstrum 1978, 66.

[32] For Heath, see Hall and Hall 1975, 14; for Pye Nest, Kendall 1925, pl. facing 13; for Armley, see Linstrum 1978, 82.

[33] In this Netherton Hall was similar to Milnes Bridge House, Longwood, although there the pediment and main block were of five bays; see Neale 1818–23, vol. 5 (no pl. nos), and Ahier 1933, 28–37.

[34] Whiting 1952, 94.

[35] For the description of Burley, see WYAS, Bradford, Hailstone collection, Deed Box 1, case 5, Item 50. Leeds town houses certainly had drawing rooms, dining rooms, breakfast rooms, libraries and so forth rather than parlours by the second half of the 18th century; see Wilson 1971, 198.

[36] The design of the small country house in the middle decades of the 18th century is discussed in Girouard 1979, ch. 7, in which changes in plan are linked with the evolving social life of the urban and rural gentry.

[37] The contemporary newspaper description of the occasion is quoted in Markham 1979, 41.

[38] Advertisement in the *Leeds Intelligencer*, 15 July 1815, quoted in Wilson 1971, 206. Wilson discusses the expansion of Leeds in the second half of the 18th century and the merchants' dilemma, unsure whether to maintain close contacts with their trade in the town or to move out to more pleasant surroundings (1971, 194–206).

[39] Neale 1818–23.

CHAPTER 4

THE YEOMAN REBUILDING OF THE 17th AND 18th CENTURIES

Local peculiarities of building within West Yorkshire have been evident in the discussion of medieval housing and to some extent in the study of the post-medieval houses of the gentry, but have hitherto comprised only a minor theme. The examination of the buildings of the yeomanry in the post-medieval period, however, emphasises this regional diversity, showing it to be a theme of major importance, in which the differences in the evolution of various areas within the county become apparent. Its boundaries include areas which display a tremendous variety of building, and the purpose of this chapter is to demonstrate that the differences are the product of historical forces which affected the social and economic development of the region. This development can be studied through a number of sources, but it will here be argued that the evidence of the houses of the period adds valuable support to the conclusions to be drawn from documents and suggests conclusions and questions which the documents fail to reveal.

It is impossible to deal in equal detail with all areas within the county. Destruction connected with urban growth or industrial expansion has removed much evidence, now lost to the record, and historical enquiry has focussed on some areas and not on others. Thus, while much may be learned about the yeomanry of the upper Calder valley, little or nothing is known of their counterparts in, say, the north-eastern part of the county. Certain areas, however, will here be studied so that the vast amount of evidence from this period may be reduced to manageable proportions. The Pennines west of the county can be divided into three parts, with the upper Calder valley dividing north-western and south-western areas. Outside the Pennines a group of townships in the central part of the county merits study, and finally, the eastern lowlands, although showing much variety, can be taken as a unit to present a contrast with the upland areas.

Not all the houses considered in this chapter were certainly built by yeomen. A very few may have been built by minor gentry families, perhaps newly elevated and soon to fall again leaving little trace in the documentary record. Others may well have been built by men in lower social groups: probate inventories of the period show how some husbandmen could be as wealthy as many yeomen. The likelihood is, however, that the vast majority of the dwellings under review housed men below the level of the gentry and above that of the mass of the rural poor (made up of husbandmen, wage earners and the destitute), and the probate inventories reveal a sufficient range of wealth within the yeomanry to account for the wide variety of their houses. A further complication is the status of the clothiers, a numerous group in this period, especially in the Pennines. The inventories show that in the late 17th and early 18th centuries clothiers might be men of some substance, but they fail to reveal why one man should be called a clothier and his neighbour a yeoman when both were heavily involved in the textile industry. In part it was doubtless a matter of prestige, yeoman being a very loose social description and clothier a well-defined occupational label. Contemporary confusion is evident in the way the probate records differ in their descriptions, for there are many cases where a man is called a yeoman in his inventory but a clothier in his will, and even more cases when the opposite is true. It is certain that many houses of the age were built by such men. No attempt has therefore been made to exclude clothiers' houses from consideration here. Any attempt would be impossible given the available knowledge, but even if possible would be misleading, for in many parts of the county the clothiers formed a significant section of non-gentry society, perhaps less wealthy in the main than the yeoman-clothiers but still sharply distinct from the ranks of the poor below them.

Throughout this work the assumption is made that the variety and distribution of building within the county is the result partly of differences in the wealth and status of individuals within specific areas and partly of differences in social structure between those areas. This assumption is of particular importance in the present chapter, and fortunately it is possible to illustrate the truth of one of its foundations: that construction of a new house or modification of an old one required a significant amount of capital. A house built for a minister in Rawdon in 1674–5 cost some £88, including the carriage of materials but possibly not their cost.[1] Less expensive, and probably more representative of the cost of building for many of the county's yeomen, were the alterations and additions made to a house in Ovenden in 1648–9: for £11 a builder contracted to rebuild part of an old house, inserting fireplaces in the hitherto unheated parlour and chamber; to build an extension providing a new parlour and chamber; and to set stones for ranges in the kitchen, the house, the parlour and the chamber. All this, and a few other jobs besides, was to be completed within just over a year, on pain of forfeiting 40s.[2] To the labour charges outlined in the building contract must be added the costs of materials and of bringing them to the site, and it is likely that in this period the accumulation of enough capital to finance large-scale building operations took a considerable time. Profit from the sale of a piece of cloth was measured in pence or shillings rather than in pounds, and capital accumulation in agriculture could be equally slow and more uncertain.[3] Building operations could also be lengthy, for Jonathan Priestley, a prosperous yeoman, appears to have taken three years to finish his house in Northowram.[4] For most yeomen, therefore, the task of building a new house was not to be undertaken lightly; it was certain to be expensive and might also involve prolonged disruption.

HOUSES OF THE UPPER CALDER VALLEY

The upper Calder valley, which encompasses great expanses of high moorland as well as some more productive land on the lower slopes, and which includes the town of Halifax, is the best starting point for the study of yeoman housing. Its buildings are by far the richest in the county, and have been the subject of some pioneering studies.[5] Despite this attention, however, the number of surviving 17th-century houses there is still unknown, and even if it were, there would remain uncounted many houses demolished before adequate records could be made. There may well have been over 500, perhaps as many as 1000, substantial stone houses of 17th-century date, as well as many barns of impressive size. Together these demonstrate a high level of investment in building.

A very large number of 17th-century houses remain, with a wide range of sizes among them. The range may be illustrated by houses from different townships. Flailcroft, Todmorden (211), is a two-cell house of the mid-17th century, to which was added, probably shortly afterwards, an outshut (Plate 141). Everill Shaw, Heptonstall has a simple linear plan of three cells (Plate 142) and Upper Foot, Midgley (136), supplements this by a rear kitchen wing and an upper cross-wing (Plate 143). At the top of the scale are houses like Great House, Soyland (199) which has a block of three cells in line and two rooms deep, with, on the other side of a passage, a lower end of a single cell (Plate 144). These larger houses are not uncommon, and although it is now impossible to assess the proportion of large houses to the whole body of building, the impression is that they formed a significant part of the rebuilding in the upper Calder valley. More detailed study of individual townships will bring out this point more clearly.[6]

Yeoman rebuilding was spread over a long period, embracing the last decades of the 16th century and the whole of the 17th and 18th centuries. Some idea of the timing of the rebuilding in the upper Calder valley and of its intensity here compared to other parts of West

Plate 141 [211] Flailcroft, Todmorden.

Plate 142 Everill Shaw, Heptonstall.

Plate 143 [136] Upper Foot Farm, Midgley.

Plate 144 [199] Great House, Soyland.

Yorkshire may be gained by an examination of the datestones which adorn so many of the houses of the age.[7] Mrs Barbara Hutton found that the most intense cluster of datestones is in the area around Halifax, and when her material is supplemented by later work and by other sources the dominance of the upper Calder valley is striking. In the period 1600–1749, the twenty-two townships of the valley, comprising about a sixth of the area of the modern county, have just less than half the total of recorded datestones. In the first fifty-year period,

1600–49, 55 per cent of the datestones come from the upper Calder valley; in the period 1650–99, its share is 43 per cent; and in the period 1700–49 it has 44 per cent of the total. (For a full breakdown, see Table 2). Not only was the rebuilding most intense in the upper Calder valley, it also started earlier there than in other areas, for in the first half of the 17th century its share of datestones falls below half in only one decade, the 1640s; in two, the 1610s and the 1630s, the proportion rises to 60 per cent and over. Building activity in the rest of the county is more marked

TABLE 2: DATESTONES 1600–1749

Date	Numbers		
	i. All West Yorkshire	ii. Upper Calder valley only	Upper Calder Valley as percentage of total
1600–09	25	13	52
1610–19	36	23	64
1620–29	40	21	52
1630–39	63	38	60
1640–49	44	21	47
	208	116	55
1650–59	39	18	46
1660–69	54	25	46
1670–79	74	36	48
1680–89	63	27	42
1690–99	69	25	36
	299	131	43
1700–09	54	32	59
1710–19	46	24	52
1720–29	39	15	40
1730–39	26	8	34
1740–49	23	4	17
	188	83	44
1600–1749 (total)	715	338	47

Area of West Yorkshire = 797 square miles
Area of upper Calder valley = 136 square miles = 17 per cent of area of West Yorkshire

NOTES:
Post-1750 datestones exist in some numbers, but because interest has focussed on the earlier period, knowledge of them is too inconsistent to allow useful analysis. As was the case with Mrs Barbara Hutton's statement in 1977, this table is a summary of the state of knowledge at the time of compilation; current re-listing by the local authorities and the Department of the Environment will soon allow an assessment of a much larger body of material.

SOURCES:
Hutton   1977. (I would like to thank Mrs Hutton for allowing me to examine her records; her help represented a great saving of time. Fieldwork has permitted some amendment to her material, but these changes and further material have served to confirm Mrs Hutton's conclusions).
Secondary sources; printed works such as Heape 1926 and articles in the *Transactions of the Halifax Antiquarian Society*.
Fieldwork, both undertaken in the course of this survey and undertaken by other parties. (I would like to thank Mr. Adrian Siswick and the Planning Department of Kirklees Metropolitan District Council for giving me access to records gathered in the course of a re-listing project).

in the second half of the 17th century and in the 18th century. In the upper Calder valley, therefore, the evidence of the datestones suggests that the yeoman rebuilding was intense, early and prolonged.

A more detailed impression of the rebuilding in this area may be gained through a closer study of two townships, Warley and Norland. Both have an abundance of houses of 17th and early18th-century date. Warley is fairly large, of 4025 acres, and Norland is small, being of only 1273 acres. A large part of both townships comprises high moorland, and Norland in particular is inhospitable, lying largely on the north-facing, steeply-inclined slopes of the hills descending to the rivers Calder and Ryburn. Despite these natural disadvantages, the existence of sixty-two houses, ranging in date from the late 16th century to the mid 18th century, can be demonstrated in Warley, and in Norland the figure is twenty-eight; in both these figures represent the minimum, for there may well have been other houses of the era which have been demolished without trace.[8] The rebuilding in these townships, therefore, involved very large numbers, and while there are some poorer townships, in terms of building, in the upper Calder valley, there is no reason to believe that Warley and Norland are at all exceptional. The intensity of rebuilding found here is likely to have been characteristic of very many more townships within the upper Calder valley.

It is perilous to draw conclusions concerning the timing of the rebuilding in these two townships from their small number of datestones, but some significant points emerge from their examination. The rebuilding started early in Warley, and there is a marked quickening of activity in both townships in the 1630s, Warley having six datestones and Norland three from this decade. The Warley datestones are divided equally between the first and the second halves of the 17th century, with eleven from each, but in Norland the second half of the century was by far the busier, with datestones outnumbering those of the first half by twelve to six. The local variations within the upper Calder valley were marked, therefore, and for reasons not yet fathomed one township might enjoy an early rebuilding and a near neighbour a rebuilding that was late in the context of the valley but quite normal elsewhere.

Many of the early dated houses in Warley and Norland are large, and a picture emerges of successive phases of rebuilding, the first affecting the wealthiest levels of yeomanry and succeeding waves reflecting the building activity of poorer but still substantial yeomen. In Warley, for example, the earliest dated house, Peel House (228), of 1598, has a hall-and-cross-wing plan supplemented by a rear kitchen wing. Murgatroyd, built by the gentry Murgatroyd family, has a fireplace dated 1632, and Roebucks (227), of 1633, is of similar size to Peel House. It is likely that the decorative porch, dated 1633, at Stock Lane House was originally attached to a substantial dwelling, and Haigh House (232), of 1631, is of three cells with a continuous outshut along the rear. Not until the second half of the 17th century were small houses built; White Birch (239) with two cells and further rooms in an outshut, is dated 1654, and Butterworth End, Norland (154) of similar size and plan, is thought to date from 1663. Outside these two townships, the earliest reliably-dated small house, that is, one with two main rooms, is Lower Birks, Stansfield, of 1664, and there are many later dated houses of this size.[9] On the other hand, some simple linear houses of three cells were built at an early date; Mr. Stell recorded two built in the late 16th century, Croft Gate, Langfield, of 1598, and Lower Crimsworth, Wadsworth, possibly of 1599.[10] These offer no more, perhaps even less, accommodation than the two-cell house with an outshut, and it is possible that the gap between the simple linear three-cell houses like Croft Gate and the larger versions of the same plan, with a rear wing and/or an outshut, was regarded as less significant than that between all these essentially three-cell houses on the one hand and houses with just two main rooms on the other. While some small versions of the former might have been built in the early

Plate 145 [232] Haigh House, Warley, 1631.

Plate 146 [228] Peel
House, Warley, 1598.

Plate 147
[219] Westfield,
Warley.

17th century or even in the late 16th century, the abandonment of one of the units was not acceptable or appropriate until a new level of the yeomanry, with different requirements, came to build after 1650.

Perhaps the most important aspect of the rebuilding in the upper Calder valley is the high proportion of large houses. The rebuilding produced not, as one might have expected, a few big houses among many smaller ones, but very many houses far in excess of the minimum standard of accommodation, that is, the two-cell house with an outshut which was the smallest dwelling deemed worthy of investment. Warley and Norland both have examples of the two-cell house, but in both townships there are many more larger buildings. Warley in particular shows every gradation up from the smallest house, to dwellings like Roebucks (227) and Westfield (219; Plates 145–7). In Norland, the largest houses were Old Hall (144) and Binroyd (145) but not much smaller than these were Town

Plate 148 [145] Binroyd, Norland (*reproduced by permission of Halifax Antiquarian Society and of Calderdale District Archives*).

House (143) and Lower Old Hall (146; Plates 148–50). If it is accepted that the size of a house corresponds approximately to the wealth of the builder, then these townships, and many more in the upper Calder valley, had a remarkable social structure in the 17th century. Warley had its resident gentry family, the Murgatroyds, but Norland is said to have lacked such adornment, and in both the dominant social group was the yeomanry.[11] The houses show that this group was numerous and, that it contained many levels of wealth, with a significant bias towards men of substantial fortunes. The dominance of the yeomanry may be expressed numerically, even if only approximately. Most of the houses in both townships were built before 1700, and if it is accepted that the population at that date was little different to that recorded in the Hearth Tax of 1672, the proportion of men able to build substantial dwellings may be calculated. In 1672 there were 188 households in Warley and 58 in Norland, and by the end of the century the vast majority of the surviving houses (62 in Warley and 28 in Norland) had been erected. By 1700, therefore, about a third of the households had been able to rebuild in Warley, and in Norland nearly a half. All but a very few of these households were headed by a man of yeoman status, and the position of the yeomanry is reflected clearly both in their numbers and in the size of their houses.

Plate 149 [143] Town House, Norland.

Plate 150 [146] Lower Old Hall, Norland, 1634.

Plate 151 [68] Peel House, Gomersal.

OTHER AREAS OF WEST YORKSHIRE

No area of any size can match the upper Calder valley in the intensity and early date of its rebuilding, nor in the proportion of large houses. There are some small pockets elsewhere which show evidence for a prolonged rebuilding affecting many yeomen of widely differing fortunes; the townships surrounding Bradford, for example, had a great wealth of building of this age and class, but the growth of the city has obliterated much fine housing in townships like Horton and North Bierley.[12] Two townships in the centre of the county, Gomersal and Liversedge, preserve a large number of houses. The numbers are smaller than those encountered in the upper Calder valley, and the gentry are more strongly represented, but it is clear that, in a very local context, these townshps too were rich in yeoman building, both having had at least thirteen yeoman houses built or added to in the 17th and early 18th centuries.[13] The rebuilding appears to have been concentrated in the second half of the 17th century, later than in parts of the upper Calder valley, but the preponderance of large houses found there is also found here; another Peel House (68; Plate 151) and Highfield House (69) in Gomersal, and Haigh Hall (114) and Syke Fold (120) in Liversedge are all large even by the standards of the upper Calder valley. The evidence of the houses suggests that yeoman society in these townships by the end of the 17th century was similar to that of the upper Calder valley in its bias towards wealth at the upper end of the scale, but that it differed in other respects; absolute numbers are smaller, and the rise of the yeomanry was a more recent phenomenon and narrowly confined to a smaller area. Furthermore, the proportion of men able to rebuild was significantly lower than in the upper Calder valley, where a third and even a half of the households had substantial dwellings by 1700. Here the number of yeoman houses built by the early 18th century is as low as one-ninth of the total of the households recorded in the 1672 Hearth Tax.

In the Pennine west of the county outside the upper Calder valley, the yeoman rebuilding is concentrated in the second half of the 17th century and in the first part of the 18th century, and is dominated by smaller houses. In the north-western part of the county, an area largely made up of the upper valleys of the Wharfe and the Aire and the tributary valley of the Worth, the number of houses in some townships is high, even approaching that in the upper Calder valley; Bingley and Addingham, for example, both have a great wealth of yeoman building.[14] Overall, however, numbers are smaller. The area is certainly not without large houses; the township of Keighley, for example, has a hall-and-cross-wings house in Laverock Hall (100), a house with a single cross-wing in No. 124, Ingrow Lane (102), a three-cell double-pile house in Manor Farm, High Utley (104) and a number of three-cell houses

Plate 152 [100] Laverock Hall, Keighley, 1641.

with continuous or partial outshuts (Plates 152–3).[15] Notably dominant in the area, however, is the two-cell or simple three-cell house; Keighley has at least eight two-cell buildings, and in Addingham very few houses have more than two rooms on the main front, even though the accommodation provided by this type of house could vary from the fully double-pile High House Moorside (7) (1697?), to the simple two-cell Gildersber Cottage (4) of 1717 (Plates 154–5).

The timing of the rebuilding in stone in this north-western area (a rebuilding which must have replaced many of the cruck houses considered in Chapter 2) is shown by the evidence of datestones to have been concentrated in the second half of the 17th century; of the datestones from the period 1600–1749, 51 per cent record building activity in the period 1650–1699, 26 per cent are from the first half of the 18th century and only 23 per cent date from the first half of the 17th century. This delayed rebuilding, compared to that of the upper Calder valley, must in part explain why the range of buildings here is biased towards the smaller house, for by the time that many of them were built ideas of compact planning were well established among the yeomanry, and even wealthy men, like the builders of Trench Farm, Baildon (20; 1697), and Hill End

Plate 153 [104] Manor Farm, Utley, Keighley, 1677.

Plate 154 [7] High House Moorside, Addingham, 1697.

Plate 155 [4] Gildersber Cottage, Addingham, 1717.

House, Horton (95; 1714), planned their houses with just two rooms on the main front. The small size of so many houses, however, and especially of those earlier ones dating from the age when large houses were still being built in the upper Calder valley in some numbers, is also a reflection of the lower levels of wealth found in this north-western area. The conclusion to be drawn from the smaller numbers of generally late and small houses is that the yeomanry here developed at a later date in the 17th century, were less numerous, and were, with some notable exceptions, rather poorer than their cousins to the south.

Similar conclusions, although with far fewer reservations, emerge from a study of the buildings of the south-western area, made up largely of the valleys of the Colne and Holme rivers. The picture of rebuilding here is distorted to an unknown extent by the uncertainty surrounding the incidence and persistence of cruck building (see Chapter 2). Conceivably many yeomen, not wealthy enough to afford a fully-storeyed stone house, were engaged, even in the 17th century, in a rebuilding which produced some numbers of smaller houses of cruck construction. Later destruction makes it impossible to determine how common these may have been, but such a disguised rebuilding must be borne in mind when the more obvious houses of the rebuilding in stone are considered. Of these, there is a very thin scatter of large houses among small and late ones. In the township of Slaithwaite, the largest surviving yeoman house is Hill Top Fold (187), built on a hall-and-cross-wing plan in a number of phases. The rest of the houses in Slaithwaite are either much smaller, such as the single-storey Woolroyd (188) of the late 17th century, and the cruck-built, Birks (185), built possibly at the same time or perhaps merely cased in stone at that date (Plates 179, 30), or much later, such as the small laithe house (189), dated 1736, a few yards from Birks. In Wooldale, Totties Hall (249), of 1684, is the largest yeoman house, built with two cross-wings by the wealthy Jackson family (Plate 156). It dwarfs other yeoman houses in the

Plate 156 [249] Totties Hall, Wooldale, 1684.

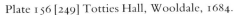

Plate 157 [250] Longdene, Wooldale, 1696.

Plate 158 [126] Green Top, Marsden, 1671.

township, which has a very few three-cell houses and rather more two-cell ones; Longdene (250), of 1696, is characteristic of the type of house commonly found in the area, having two rooms at the front and further rooms in an outshut (Plates 157–8). The datestones repeat the pattern of the north-western area, with half coming from the second half of the 17th century, with peaks in the last decades, and the other half divided roughly equally between the first half of the 17th century and the first half of the 18th century. In terms of numbers, this south-western area is easily the poorest in the Pennines, for there are fewer datestones, and fewer houses on the ground, than in the north-western area. Even when the possibility of a cruck rebuilding is remembered, it is clear that the yeoman rebuilding here was later, meaner and involved smaller numbers of men than elsewhere in the upland west of the county. Houses like Hill Top Fold and Totties Hall testify to the occasional emergence of men of great wealth, who dominated yeoman society to a much greater extent than did their counterparts in the multi-tiered society of the upper Calder valley and of parts of the north-western area.

THE REBUILDING IN THE EAST
OF THE COUNTY

Investigation of the yeoman rebuilding of the eastern part of the county is hampered by the nature of that rebuilding and by later developments. There is strong evidence that timber-framing continued in use in parts of the east of the county well into the post-medieval period, that is, into the era characterized by the fully-floored dwelling. This timber-framed rebuilding has been disguised by later casing in brick and stone, and the lack of easily visible evidence of early work is a severe handicap in a survey as selective as this has had to be. The extent of this early rebuilding may only be assessed on the completion of exhaustive research into the buildings of a large part of the eastern area. Even then, the later developments mentioned above will play their part in distorting the picture, for the east of the county has been most seriously affected by the destruction of early housing which accompanied the growth of towns and of large-scale industrial enterprises. The expansion of Bradford in the west, it is true, caused the destruction of much fine building, but in the east the massive growth of Leeds and the development of coal mining have also left large areas devoid of early housing.[16] It is now impossible to determine whether these areas had a great wealth of yeoman houses, or whether the existing buildings replaced a poor pattern of earlier housing. The most that the researcher can do is to hope that the least-altered townships are more or less representative of the nature of the yeoman rebuilding in a wider area, using as a check documentary sources to discover the distribution of taxable wealth in both denuded and unscarred townships.

Despite the difficulties, it is important to attempt an assessment of how widespread was the rebuilding in timber-framing in the eastern half of the county and of its probable date. The Pennine west of the county has many timber-framed houses, but the vast majority of these are medieval in date, being built with an open housebody. The post-medieval rebuilding was carried out almost entirely in stone, as we have seen. In the east, however, many of the timber-framed houses appear to have been built with a floored-over housebody, a point discussed in Chapter 2, and it is significant that these are among the larger timber-framed houses of the area. Smaller than them are some of the houses with an open main room, and it was argued that both types may belong to the period after 1550, the larger houses being the homes of the wealthier yeoman, building houses of modern form but in traditional materials, and the smaller ones representing the poorer yeoman's rebuilding in more durable form of a type of house that was still medieval in concept. The yeoman rebuilding of the east may, therefore, be complicated by this diversity, but if it has this dual character one significant point emerges concerning the levels of wealth involved. The larger timber-framed houses like Leeds Road, No. 176, Lofthouse with Carlton (123) are smaller than the largest post-medieval houses of the upper Calder valley, and the smallest timber-framed houses like Cheesecake Hall, Oulton (169) and Lanes farm, Methley (131) are less substantial and have less accommodation than the smaller two-storeyed yeoman houses of that area. Both wealthy and lesser yeomen in the east, therefore, built smaller houses than their counterparts in the upper Calder valley, and the inference that the class as a whole was less wealthy is unavoidable.

It is not clear how large a proportion of the population was affected by the post-medieval timber-framed rebuilding, for the limited accommodation of some of the timber-framed houses in the east must have led to their rapid replacement when funds were available for further improvement. The detailed investigation of one eastern township, Bramham cum Oglethorpe, brought to light one certain timber-framed house and two probable examples, but it is likely that there were once many more. A map of Alwoodley, a township to the north of Leeds, drawn up in 1682, shows houses pictorially, and every one is represented as a timber-framed building, from the large Hall down through many degrees to small houses and even outbuildings.[17] There is no means of knowing, of course, how many of the houses shown were built in the post-medieval period and how many had survived from the Middle Ages, but if the evidence of the map may be relied upon it is clear that virtually all the population of Alwoodley – husbandmen, yeomen, even perhaps, gentry – were housed in timber-framed buildings well into the second half of the 17th century.

The date of the yeoman rebuilding in timber-framing is shrouded in doubt. The number of dated stone houses in this eastern area begins to grow in the late 17th century, suggesting that this was the period when timber went out of use as the principal building material for the yeomanry, and it seems likely that the map of Alwoodley records the aspect of the township at the very end of the timber-framed period. The timber-framed front range of the Nook Inn, Oulton (Fig. 43) is dated 1611, and the heavy scantling of the framing does not suggest that the date records the

Fig 43 Nook Inn, Oulton with Woodlesford; timber-framed gable.

last fling of a debased method of construction. Until dendrochronology has provided reliable data, perhaps the most that can be said is that good quality timber-framing probably continued in use well into the 17th century.

The later stone houses of the eastern yeomanry are more easily compared with the yeoman rebuilding in the Pennines. Few houses in the east of the county show datestones, but the recorded examples suggest that the last three decades of the 17th century were marked by quickening building activity here, activity which continued well into the next century. The results of this rebuilding were a great deal less spectacular than that of the Pennine west. By the standards of its area, Bramham cum Oglethorpe displays a wealth of yeoman houses, and can be used to compare the relative riches of the east and west of the county. Seven houses in the village centre deserve attention. The most imposing of the yeoman houses, as distinct from those like the Old Hall which were in all probability of gentry status, is the Manor House (32), a name which suggests something more than a yeoman

Plate 159 [32] Manor House, Bramham.

Plate 160 [33] Old Malt Kiln, Bramham.

Plate 161 [34] Heygate Farm, Bramham, 1682.

Plate 162 [35] Hillside, Bramham.

house (Plate 159). No gentry family can be associated with it, however, and if it was indeed the home of a gentry family the generally low level of wealth found amongst the eastern yeomanry must also have been characteristic of the local minor gentry, for the house is of two storeys and of two rooms in the main range, supplemented by a two-and-a-half storey rear wing and an outshut. By the standards of the upper Calder valley, it is a medium-sized house; in Bramham, it is a large one. The Old Malt Kiln (33), a timber-framed house cased in stone in the 18th century, has a similar number of ground-floor rooms, but is smaller both on plan and in height (Plate 160). Smaller in turn than this are simple linear houses like Heygate Farm

(34), of two full storeys, and Hillside (35) of one-and-a-half storeys (Plates 161–2) and the township also has examples of two-cell houses.[18]

Bramham is not exactly representative of yeoman building in the whole of the east of the county, for there other townships which show not this range of houses of many different sizes but, instead, a concentration of fewer and larger houses. In Lofthouse-with-Carlton, for instance, the only clear examples of yeoman houses of the rebuilding are the timber-framed Leeds Road, No. 176, built on a hall-and-cross-wing plan, and the brick Pyemont House (Plate 163), which probably had two cross-wings originally. In South Elmsall, Broad Lane Farm East (192),

Plate 163 [124] Pyemont House, Lofthouse with Carlton.

Above: Plate 164 [192] Broad Lane Farm East, South Elmsall.   *Below:* Plate 165 [1] Old Hall, Ackworth.

dating probably from the last quarter of the 17th century (Plate 164), is not only by far the largest yeoman house of the township but also the only one of its date. The house, like many in the eastern part, and especially the south-eastern part, of the county, has a third storey: its size therefore is difficult to judge from its plan alone. Some of the eastern houses – for instance, Old Hall, Ackworth (1); Kirkbank, Badsworth (16); Common Farm, South Kirkby (193); and Pear Tree Farm, Wintersett (248) – are, therefore, much larger than their simple plans suggest, and a house of just three main ground-floor rooms, such as Old Hall, Ackworth, is the equivalent in accommodation of a much more complex Pennine house with only two storeys (Plate 165).

When the diverse results of the yeoman rebuilding of the east of the county are considered together, taking into account the early rebuilding in timber and the late one in stone and, more rarely, in brick, the pattern revealed is very irregular, some townships showing much building and others very little, and poor in comparison with much of the Pennine west of the county. Numbers are smaller in the east, and the houses, despite the existence of some large three-storey dwellings, are in the main very much more modest than those of, especially, the upper Calder valley. Building activity in the east suggests that the 17th century was a time of steady gain for the yeomanry, but that few were able to build at any one time. An early rebuilding in timber-framing probably affected a few both of wealthy and poorer yeomen, this difference in wealth being expressed in the nature of their dwellings. The later rebuilding produced some fine and large houses, but these tended to be isolated within their township and represent the occasional rise to prominence of exceptionally wealthy yeomen. In addition, a small number of men were able to build, notably in the late 17th century, but the size of their houses indicated that they rarely approached the wealth of the greatest Pennine yeomen.

In summary, this general survey has shown that the rebuilding was most intense in the upper Calder valley, where it started early and resulted in a very high proportion of large houses but also included the smaller dwellings of a yeomanry that had many gradations in wealth. A small central area has a lesser density of houses but a similar proportion of large ones, though here the rebuilding appears to be slightly later in date. The north-western area also has large numbers of houses, generally later in date and rarely so big. The east of the county has a disguised rebuilding in timber-framing that is difficult to assess, but the impression is that the varied yeoman rebuilding here was much less intense than in larger parts of the Pennine belt and somewhat delayed in date. The conclusion is that a numerous and wealthy yeomanry developed first and most spectacularly in the upper Calder valley and that only parts of the rest of the county were able to match this at later dates.

DOCUMENTARY EVIDENCE

A number of documentary sources may be used to throw light on this conclusion. The County Rate, raised c.1600, provides evidence for the distribution of taxable wealth, and although the part played by yeomen wealth in the pattern of the whole is not distinguishable, the Rate has some bearing on the respective wealth of different parts of the county. The analysis of the returns, arranged according to the sum paid by each township per 1000 acres, is useful in revealing that there had been some redistribution of taxable wealth between the mid 14th century and 1600; in 1334, there was a 'general pattern of increasing wealth from west to east', but by 1600 the townships with the heaviest burden of tax were concentrated in the centre of the county.[19] This method of analysing the returns, that is, by computing the tax paid per 1000 acres in each township, tends to obscure some significant aspects of the figures, however. If the townships are graded simply by the amount of tax paid a rather different pattern of distribution results. The upper Calder valley, with an average charge of 11.5d per township and including some townships like Sowerby (37d) and Northowram (19d) with much higher assessments, then appears to have been a particularly heavily-burdened area, for the average charge per township in the county as a whole was only 6.3d. The high charges are not simply due to the large size of many of the townships, for townships of comparable size in other parts of the county show lower assessments; Barwick-in-Elmet, much the same size as Sowerby, paid only 9d, and the charges on Temple Newsam (6d), Harewood (6d), Shitlington (9.5d), and Methley (13.5d), were all lower than that on the approximately equal-sized Northowram. The contrast is not only one between the upper Calder valley and the east of the county, for other parts of the Pennines failed to match the former's high assessments. In the north-west of the county, where townships were similar in size and where a few of them are very heavily rated, the average charge on each was 9.6d (or just over 8d per township if Keighley, whose assessment of 44d probably reflects urban rather than rural wealth, is omitted) and in the south-west, the figure fell to a poor 4.7d per township.[20] The County Rate suggests that the upper Calder valley townships were highly assessed because they had greater concentrations of wealth in the early 17th century, and it is safe to assume that much of that wealth was in the hands of the yeomanry. To this extent, the County Rate may be taken as support for the pattern of yeoman houses in West Yorkshire; though levied before all but a few of those houses were erected, it is useful in setting the scene for the developments of the 17th century.[21]

Later and better-known taxation returns indicate a similar concentration of wealth in the upper Calder valley. The Hearth Tax returns of the late 17th century allow an insight into the structure of local society, and the 1672 figures for the area of modern West Yorkshire reveal striking local differences even within the building zones. This is a timely corrective to the tendency to think of one area as uniformly wealthy and another as uniformly poor. Within the upper Calder valley, some townships had a very small proportion of large houses: in Stainland, for instance 3 per cent of houses had three or more hearths, and in Stansfield the figure was only 6 per cent. Despite these local differences, regional comparison is illuminating, and three areas of approximately equal size were chosen for study, to compare the distribution of wealth revealed in the Hearth Tax with the pattern suggested by the yeoman houses (Map 4). The houses suggest that the clearest contrast within the Pennines was that between a wealthy upper

Calder valley and a poor south-western area, and therefore both these areas were selected for study, along with those of a south-eastern area chosen to coincide broadly with the region covered by the probate inventories. The assumption underlying the analysis of the Hearth Tax Returns is that, despite evasion and omission, the source reflects reasonably accurately the distribution of wealth at the time of assessment.[22] Table 3 summarises the social composition in the three areas

TABLE 3: DISTRIBUTION OF WEALTH, 1672

Area	% of households			
	exempt from tax	paying tax on		
		1–2 hearths	3–4 hearths	5–5+ hearths
Upper Calder valley 79230 acres	8	67.5	18.1	6.4
South-west 70461 acres	4.4	83.6	9.2	2.8
South-east 76722 acres	10.2	65.5	17.1	7.2

The most striking contrast revealed by both the table and the distribution of larger houses is that between the poverty of the south-western area, where only 12 per cent of householders paid tax on three or more hearths, and the wealth of the other areas, where overall nearly 25 per cent were subject to such charges. If wealthy yeomen are most likely to have built houses of three or more hearths, the low proportion of such houses in the south-west can fairly be taken to reflect the absence of such a class from the area in 1672. This conclusion is certainly that suggested by the yeoman houses, for the rebuilding here occurred mainly after this date and resulted largely in a pattern of small houses. The map shows the surprisingly uniform character of the area, with only three townships having more than a fifth of their houses assessed at three or more hearths; of these, Rastrick, can be considered as part of the hinterland of Halifax, Almondbury has some urban characteristics, and Denby reflects a pocket of yeomen wealth running away to the south and expressed in some fine building by

the class. For the rest, the picture is one of low levels of wealth, and the Hearth Tax gives a strong confirmation of the pattern suggested by the surviving houses.

The evidence of the Hearth Tax appears at first sight to contradict that of the yeoman houses in one very important respect. The houses indicated that a numerous and very wealthy yeomanry was present in the upper Calder valley in the 17th century but that the south-eastern area lacked such a class. The table, however, suggests that the contrast was by no means so extreme, for the south-east has quite as high a proportion of large houses.

What the table obscures, however, Map 4 clarifies; whereas the south-east shows a similar structure of wealth to that of the upper Calder valley as a whole, nowhere can it match the extraordinary concentration of wealth found in the immediate vicinity of Halifax. The townships ringing this town all have a very high proportion of large houses, and particularly remarkable are Skircoat and Hipperholme with Brighouse, where over half the houses had three or more hearths. It is the poverty of some of the outlying townships within the upper Calder valley, a poverty matching that of the south-west, which reduces the picture of overall wealth in the area. The south-east does, indeed, have its wealthy townships (although the two wealthiest – Chevet and Nostell – are statistical freaks, having between them just four houses, two of which are the residences of great gentry families), but these tend to be scattered throughout the area with none of the concentration of wealth seen in the hinterland of Halifax, and, with the exception of Chevet and Nostell, never rise to the heights found in that zone, even close to the urban centres of Wakefield and Pontefract.

The reason for the similarity in the pattern of overall wealth in the two areas is of the greatest significance, for it reveals societies with very different structures. The Hearth Tax Returns include the gentry, the nobility, and professional classes such as the clergy, distinguished from the bulk of society by a title, most commonly 'Master'.[23] These titled people are included in the figures showing the overall wealth of the various areas. The vast majority of them paid tax on a large number of hearths; 24 per cent on three or four hearths, 44 per cent on five to eight hearths, and 24 per cent on nine or more hearths; Table 4a shows the proportions and numbers in each of the three areas chosen for study. When the titled people are segregated from the untitled, a picture emerges of a south-eastern area in which society is dominated by titled people and an upper Calder valley society in which the dominating class was the

TABLE 4a: HOUSES OF TITLED PEOPLE

Area	Exempt from tax		1–2 hearths		3–4 hearths		5–8 hearths		9–9+ hearths		Total
	No.	%	No.	%	No.	%	No.	%	No.	%	
Upper Calder valley	0	0	7	14	10	21	22	46	9	19	48
South-west	0	0	2	7	9	32	12	43	5	18	28
South-east	0	0	9	7	32	24	60	44	35	25	136
Totals	0	0	18	8	51	24	94	44	49	24	212

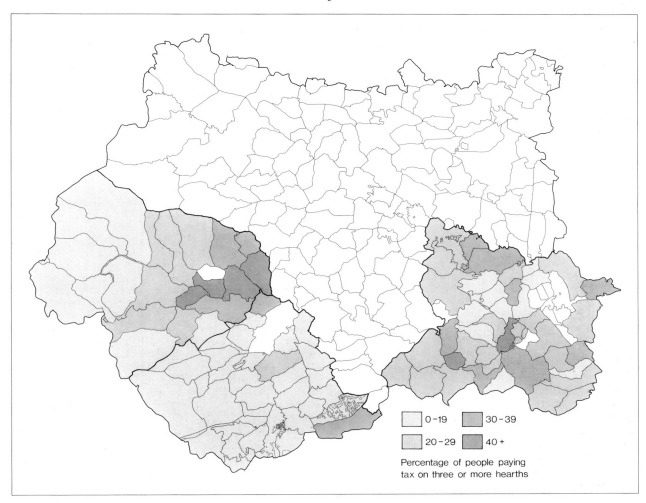

Map 4 Distribution of wealth in selected areas of West Yorkshire, taken from 1672 Hearth Tax Returns.

yeomanry. Tables 4b and 4c summarize the figures, the south-western area being included as an interesting comparison to both areas. The significant points in the tables concern the varying densities of titled and non-titled people paying tax on large houses in the two areas of present interest. Title-holders were very much more prominent in the south-east than in the upper Calder valley, being approximately three times more common and three times more thickly concentrated there (Table 4b). When title-holders are excluded from the Returns of people paying tax on a large number of hearths (Table 4c) leaving therefore just the non-gentry, predominantly yeoman, taxpayers, the society of the upper Calder valley emerges as the wealthier; non-titled people paying tax on three or more hearths were numerically more common and more densely distributed in the upper Calder valley than in the south-

TABLE 4b: TITLE HOLDERS

Area	Number	Average per township	Average density 1 title per	Titles as % of total households
Upper Calder valley	48	2.4	1650 acres	2
South-west	28	0.8	2516 acres	1.6
South-east	136	3	564 acres	6.4

TABLE 4c: ANALYSIS OF HOUSES OF THREE OR MORE HEARTHS

Area	Number	No. occupied by title-holder	Remainder	Average No. of remainder per township	Average density of remainder; 1 per
Upper Calder valley	601	41 (7%)	560	28	142 acres
South-west	215	26 (12%)	189	5.4	372 acres
South-east	521	127 (24%)	394	8.5	194 acres

Analysis of houses of five or more hearths

Area	Number	No. occupied by title-holder	Remainder	Average No. of remainder per township	Average density of remainder; 1 per
Upper Calder valley	157	31 (20%)	126	6.3	628 acres
South-west	50	17 (34%)	33	0.9	2135 acres
South-east	155	95 (61%)	60	1.3	1278 acres

east, and when those paying tax on five or more hearths are isolated for study, the wealth of yeoman society in the upper Calder valley is even more striking, with twice as many taxpayers of this category. The conclusions are that while the south-east might appear to be as wealthy as the upper Calder valley, a large part of its wealth lay in the hands of the gentry, and the yeomanry of the area were, if not entirely absent, then far less numerous than in the upper Calder valley. There the position was reversed; where two thirds of the largest houses were occupied by the gentry in the south-east and only one third by the yeomanry, in the upper Calder valley wealthy yeomen occupied four out of every five of the largest houses. When the Hearth Tax Returns are examined in detail, therefore, they bear out the conclusions permitted by the buildings alone. The value of the houses as a historical source goes beyond that of a mere complement to the documentary sources, for without the insight into the structure of society given by the surviving buildings, there is a danger that the documentary records might give a misleading impression of the nature and wealth of society in different areas.

Probate inventories are another source which may be used to check the conclusions suggested by the houses of the yeoman rebuilding. The inventories of yeomen, (either so styled in their inventories or calling themselves 'yeoman' in their wills), survive in some numbers from the late 17th century and first half of the 18th century, allowing a comparison of the numbers and wealth of the class in different parts of the county.[24] The upper Calder valley (except the township of Todmorden and Walsden, which remained part of Lancashire until 1888 and which, therefore, figures in none of the documentary sources used here) lies in the western part of the deanery of Pontefract, and its yeoman inventories were compared with those of a group of townships in the east of the county, this eastern area covering about two-thirds of that studied in the analysis of the Hearth Tax Returns. The yeoman inventories from every fourth year in the period 1689 to 1705 numbered forty-one in the upper Calder valley, but only twelve in the eastern area. If the production of these documents is taken as significant in itself, it is clear that yeomen wealthy enough to have their goods inventoried were much more common in the upper Calder valley, there being one inventory for every 1956 acres there and one for every 4665 acres in the east.

The small numbers of yeoman inventories from the eastern area make conclusions about the wealth of the class less certain than when dealing with the more numerous

TABLE 5: AVERAGE AND MEDIAN VALUES OF YEOMAN INVENTORIES FROM THE UPPER CALDER VALLEY AND THE EASTERN PART OF THE DEANERY OF PONTEFRACT.

	Upper Calder valley (80228a)		Eastern area (55986a)	
	1689–1705 (41 invs)	1721–1738 (46 invs)	1689–1705 (12 invs)	1721–1738 (24 invs)
	£	£	£	£
Average excluding debts	79	46	77	102
Median excluding debts	51	32,34	54,79	73,91
Average including debts	171	81	70	130
Median including debts	70	29	49,54	91,113
Average density, 1 inv per	1956acres	1744 acres	4665 acres	2233acres

documents from the upper Calder valley. Nevertheless, comparisons are worthwhile, and the results taken from all yeoman inventories from the two areas are set out in Table 5. One of the problems of analysing inventories is whether or not to include the value of the balance of debts as part of a yeoman's estate. If debts, both inward and outward, are omitted from the reckoning, the eastern yeoman appears to have been only very slightly poorer on average, and markedly wealthier when median values are considered, than his upper Calder valley counterpart in the period 1689–1705. If this is an accurate reflection of the standing of the yeoman in the two areas, the most significant aspect of the documents is that yeomen appear to have been far more numerous in the upper Calder valley but no more wealthy. This conclusion conflicts with the evidence of fieldwork which has suggested that the eastern yeomanry was both poorer and smaller in numbers than that of the upper Calder valley.

If, however, the calculations are based on the standards of the appraisers of the inventories, who clearly believed that debts were an important consideration in the valuation of a man's property, a rather different pattern emerges. By including the value of the balance of debts, adding the appropriate amount in cases where the value of inward debts was greater than that of outward debts, and subtracting in cases where the balance was a negative figure, the yeoman of the upper Calder valley in the period 1689 to 1705 appears to have been far wealthier on average than the eastern yeoman, and, also, noticeably richer when median values are taken. The upper Calder valley yeoman frequently had sums, both great and small, out on loan, something which suggests both confidence in the system of debt and the ability to take money out of circulation with a view to its increase through investment.[25] When debts are included, therefore, the inventories suggest the existence in the upper Calder valley in the late 17th century of a yeomanry engaged in a profitable economy. Much of the surplus of that economy was put into a system of loans, but the houses of the area indicate that the same profits lay behind the vast numbers and large size of the yeoman dwellings of the period.

The inventories of a later period, that from 1721 to 1738, present a different picture and indicate that the eastern yeoman had made considerable progress. Yeomen wealthy enough to have their goods inventoried were still less common than in the upper Calder valley but the difference in density between the two areas was much less pronounced than in the late 17th century. Furthermore, and much more significant, the eastern yeoman now appears to have enjoyed far higher levels of wealth, both including and excluding debts, than his counterpart in the upper Calder valley, who while becoming no less numerous, shows a very sharp fall in both average and median wealth. It will be argued later that the wealth of the eastern yeoman is to some extent illusory, much of it being invested in less remunerative directions than was the case in the upper Calder valley, but inventories nonetheless suggest a dramatic flowering of the eastern yeomanry in the first half of the 18th century. Why this did not produce a rebuilding as widespread as in the upper Calder valley at an earlier period, and with as many large houses, is not immediately apparent. The eastern area certainly shows some large

yeoman houses of the late 17th century and of the first half of the 18th century, but the rebuilding here never matched that of the upper Calder valley. The inference is that, despite apparent wealth, the funds which financed the rebuilding in the upper Calder valley could not be spared in the east for investment in building; although levels of wealth may have been high, the rate of return on capital investment was low here, and a simpler economy produced less of the easy profits which there could be released for the ostentation of building houses.

These documentary sources extend our knowledge of the yeomanry in the 17th and 18th centuries, but their interpretation has been helped considerably by conclusions suggested by the houses. The consideration of both documentary and monumental evidence has built up a picture of a yeoman society which varied in numbers, wealth, and stage of development area by area within the county. The documentary sources indicate that, within tolerable limits, the pattern of houses is a reliable guide to the development of yeomanry, and the question to be addressed next is that most important one of what explains the distribution of wealth suggested by both sources.

THE SOURCE OF THE WEALTH OF THE UPPER CALDER VALLEY

A very large part of the answer lies in an explanation for the extraordinary wealth of the upper Calder valley. Deprived of this area, the pattern of housing in West Yorkshire would appear much like that across wide stretches of the north of England. The immediate question is why a numerous and unprecedentedly wealthy yeomanry developed in that area. The valley's unique character in the post-medieval period was nothing new, for exactly the same concentration of substantial yeoman houses there was noted for the medieval period. The concentration there of medieval yeoman houses was explained by reference to favourable tenure and, especially, to the early developments of a profitable system of dual occupation based upon the textile industry and agriculture, and the same combination of influences were clearly at work in the post-medieval period as well.

The 17th century saw great changes in the land-holding patterns in the valley. The townships within the manor of Wakefield, of which all but three in the upper Calder valley formed a part, were of two sorts; those within a graveship (a group of townships separately administered and electing a grave who was responsible for the collection of rents) were dominated by copyhold tenure; the rest enjoyed freehold tenure. This theoretical division was fast breaking down in the 17th century, and the Manor Book of 1709 reveals the extent to which freehold tenure had encroached upon the copyhold areas.[26] Copyhold tenants within the manor of Wakefield were still present in great numbers, but just as in the earlier period the terms upon which they held their land were far from punitive; entry fines were reasonable and succession secure. Moreover, progress had been made by the copyholders, for in 1608 the tenants of the graveships were given the chance to compound their entry fines in return for a payment of thirty-five years' rent, and very many of them throughout the manor obliged a hard-pressed monarch and paid for the added degree of legal security.[27] As well as an improvement in the terms of copyhold tenure in the manor, there was also a move towards enfranchisement, the conversion of copyhold to freehold. The numbers involved are not known, but probably many chose to pay the heavy charges for the privilege of freehold tenure. In 1607, fourteen men from Sowerby and Hipperholme paid a total of £545 for their enfranchisement, and in the period 1609 to 1641 eighty-five tenants in the manor of Halifax and Heptonstall (a rectory manor within the manor of Wakefield) paid to convert their tenure from copyhold.[28] It is difficult to assess quite how far-reaching the process of conversion became, but some idea of its scope may be gained from the 1709 Manor Book. In Warley, a township within the graveship of Sowerby and originally, therefore, dominated by copyhold tenure, no less than fifty tenants held freehold land, and in Sowerby itself the number of freehold tenants was sixty-two.[29]

An improvement in tenurial conditions cannot, however, be solely responsible for the great wealth of the upper Calder valley (which indeed may have been the cause of the improvement), for both better copyhold conditions and enfranchisement were common to other parts of the manor of Wakefield. The copyhold tenants of the graveship of Holme in the south-west of the county and of the eastern graveships around Wakefield shared in the composition of 1608 and in the conversion of copyhold to freehold tenure; there were, for instance, thirty-seven freehold tenants in the graveship of Holme in 1709 and thirty-nine in the graveship of Horbury.[30] Some idea of the proportion of freeholders within graveships in different parts of the manor can be obtained by comparing the list of freeholders given in the 1709 Manor Book with the number of householders in the same area listed in the 1672 Hearth Tax. The validity of the comparison is open to question, for the sources are separated by nearly forty years and by the different purposes for which each was compiled. However, the results are worth considering, for they show that the number of freeholders listed in 1709 comprises 21 per cent of the households in the graveship of Sowerby (the townships of Sowerby, Soyland, and Warley), but only 11 per cent in the graveship of Holme (a group of seven townships). This suggests that the process of enfranchisement may have gone further in the upper Calder valley than in the south-west of the county, although to substantiate this a great deal more work needs to be done.[31]

The importance of tenure in determining the distribution of yeoman wealth should not be exaggerated, for it is equally valid to maintain that pre-existing wealth determined the pattern of land-holding. The high proportion of freeholders and the large number of copyholders who compounded in 1608 in the area of the upper Calder valley, instead of being the cause of greater wealth in that area, may be interpreted as a sure sign that wealth already existed and was, in fact, the one thing that enabled the upper Calder valley yeomen to improve their legal status. It cost much to alter tenure in this period. The payment for composition in 1608 of thirty-five years' rent proved to be no obstacle to nearly 400 men in the graveships of Sowerby and Hipperholme. Similarly, the price of converting copyhold to freehold, a price which, under the avaricious Sir Arthur Ingram, could rise as high as £200 but which generally came at more reasonable rates, was well within the reach of the ambitious yeoman.[32] The yeomen of the upper Calder valley had prospered as copyholders, and many would continue to do so. Others, however, found

Plate 166 Fleece Inn, Elland cum Greetland.

themselves in a position where they could easily afford to alter the nature of their tenure. Composition and enfranchisement gave an added measure of security to the tenant, but they did not create wealth; this was probably the product both of earlier favourable tenure and of aspects of the economy which that tenure had encouraged.

A demonstration of the influence of tenure in this period is offered by an examination of the houses of the two townships within the upper Calder valley which lay in the honour of Pontefract. Elland-cum-Greetland and Southowram provide no examples of the late-medieval aisled houses common in neighbouring townships, a strong indication that, in the late Middle Ages, tenure was indeed a pre-condition for yeoman prosperity. It was suggested that land-holding conditions in the honour of Pontefract at that time inhibited the development of a yeoman class which in the neighbouring townships of the manor of Wakefield, where land was held under more favourable terms, was rising through following a profitable system of dual occupation. In the 17th century, the yeoman houses of the two areas present much less of a contrast. Elland-cum-Greetland and Southowram may not show the wealth of some of the other Calder valley townships, but a yeomanry had clearly developed sufficiently to permit the erection of many houses, some of which, like the Fleece Inn (56) and Backhold Hall (195), could be very large (Plate 166).[33] The datestones on the houses of these townships indicate that the main building period was especially the 1670s and 1680s. The suggestion, therefore, is that unfavourable tenure might retard economic development, and delay rebuilding; in some circumstances, its influence might be so strong as to prevent development, but in this period and in this area, other, stronger forces were at work to overcome the obstacle of more severe tenurial conditions.

Tenure is at its most cogent as an influence in social development when land is the chief resource upon which members of society depend. The argument that tenure had less importance in the development of the yeomanry in the upper Calder valley in the post-medieval period than it did in the same area at an earlier period and still had in other areas in the 17th century depends upon the demonstration that an alternative resource had replaced, or at least begun to rival, land as the principal source of wealth, In West Yorkshire the alternative was, of course, the textile industry, and although industry and agriculture were very often combined elsewhere in a system of dual occupation, it was the unique concentration of industrial wealth which distinguished the upper Calder valley from the rest of the county in this period.

The textile industry of West Yorkshire in the post-medieval era may be studied mainly through sources dating from the last part of the 17th century and the early 18th century. Although it is not certain that the organisation of the textile industry as described in probate inventories and the observations of Daniel Defoe characterized the 17th century as a whole,[34] it is clear that by then the textile industry was an essential element in the economy of the valley, and its earlier importance was seen as the principal reason for the appearance of significant numbers of yeoman houses there in the late Middle Ages (see Chapter 2). Different aspects of the industry were pursued throughout much of the county; in Pennine dales to the north and south of the upper Calder valley, in the central area to the south-west of Leeds, and in the east, where Leeds and Wakefield were important marketing centres. It was, however, in the Halifax area that the industry was most heavily concentrated and had made the deepest impression on yeoman society. The special protection of the Halifax Act of 1555 and Camden's observations were cited earlier as evidence for the predominance of the valley's textile industry in the 16th century, and in the post-medieval period there are strong indications that it continued to elevate the yeomanry to a position unrivalled elsewhere.

The upper Calder valley impressed Defoe so forcibly that he was impelled to describe the unique effect that the textile industry had wrought upon the landscape and economy of the area by the early 1720s; he noted the dense population in the townships around Halifax, where the country was 'infinitely full of people; these people all full of business; not a beggar, not an idle person to be seen . . . . This business is the clothing trade', without which, he said, not a fifth of the inhabitants could be supported on the strength of the quality of the land. The people 'scarce sow corn enough for their cocks and hens' and the area was reliant upon food supplies brought from other parts of the county. Defoe had no doubt about which part of the system of dual occupation was dominant, describing how 'all can gain their bread, even from the youngest to the ancient', by means of employment in some stage of the textile industry. In a lyrical passage, he conjured up a picture of the dramatic effect created by the industry in its rural setting;

> hardly a house standing out of a speaking distance from another, and (which soon told us their business) the day clearing up, and the sun shining, we could see that almost at every house there was a tenter, and almost on every tenter a piece of cloth, or kersey, or shalloon, for they are the three articles of that country's labour; from which the sun glancing, and, as I may say, shining (the white reflecting its rays) to us, I thought it was the most agreeable sight that I ever saw . . . we could see through the glades almost every way round us, yet look which way we would, high to the tops, and low to the bottoms, it was all the same; innumerable houses and tenters, and a white piece upon every tenter.

Defoe stressed that what he described was 'all belonging to and in the parish of Halifax', and although he went on to describe the 'noble scene of industry' in adjoining parts of the county, and especially the approaches to Leeds, he clearly regarded the upper Calder valley as a unique phenomenon which required special report and explanation.[35]

The importance of the textile industry in the economy of the valley is brought out by the probate inventories of the late 17th and early 18th centuries. Yeomen with an interest in textiles (usually dubbed yeoman-clothiers by historians) were consistently wealthier than those who engaged in agriculture alone or in agriculture combined with some other industrial activity. The yeoman-clothier was in general, over twice as wealthy, for in addition to his investment in the textile industry, he had a larger stake in agriculture than a simple yeoman; he was, therefore,

Fig 44 Average wealth of yeoman-clothiers and yeomen in the parish of Halifax, 1689–1738, as expressed in the value of probate inventories.

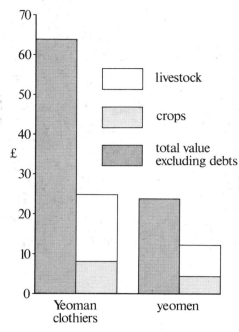

in the textile industry; the shop was full of trade tools and he had a stock of eighty-six kerseys valued at £151. John Fielding of Hartley Royd in Stansfield died in 1698 with goods to the value of £147, and the most valuable item in the inventory was his stock of wool and yarn, priced at £17 10s. Even poor yeomen depended upon the income derived from the industry; John Cockcroft of Bellhouse in Erringden died in 1691 apparently owing more than he was worth in worldly goods but with the ubiquitous pair of looms and a supply of wool, yarn, and oil among his meagre possessions.[37] The equipment needed to set up as a small manufacturer was within the reach of very many people. The average price of a loom in this period was less than £1, and the outlay could easily be recouped once cloth was flowing from it.[38] It was noted earlier that the western yeoman was wealthier than the eastern if debts were taken into account, but the gap between the two was probably much greater than is immediately apparent. While a loom might cost £1, it could very quickly pay for itself and continue to produce profit and provide a livelihood, but the eastern yeoman, participating in an economy dominated by agriculture, was involved in costlier investments in agricultural gear and livestock (£4 5s for an ox, £2 16s for a cow, 12s for a pig, and so on) which, as well as being expensive, produced less profit and were a great deal slower to repay their value.[39] The difference between the two economies, the one dominated by industry and the other by agriculture, was, therefore, in part in the rate of capital turnover; rapid in the textile industry, slow in agriculture.

That the upper Calder valley's economy was based on dual occupation and not entirely dominated by textiles is disclosed by the high level of investment in agricultural buildings there, the most prominent of which are the many substantial aisled barns of the post-medieval period (Plates 167–8). The special connection between the textile industry and the men of greatest wealth is, however, capable of one final demonstration. A number of standing houses can be

wealthier on both counts (see Fig. 44).[36] At the top of the social scale were men like Robert Sutcliffe of Greenwood Lee in Heptonstall (83) who died in 1718 possessed of a sumptuous house, the furnishings of which describe a refined way of life, and goods to the value of £679. Sutcliffe combined an interest in agriculture, represented both in the large barn beside the house and in the stock, crops and husbandry gear listed in the inventory, with involvement

Plate 167 Ellistones, Stainland; large barn next to house.

Plate 168 [147] Lower
Wat Ing, Norland;
aisled barn next to
house.

linked with yeomen engaged in textiles. Greenwood Lee (83), Hartley Royd and Bellhouse have all been shown to be the houses of yeomen-clothiers (Plate 169), and significantly many of the largest houses were built by men involved in the most lucrative aspects of the industry.[40] Samuel Wade of High Bentley (177) was a large manufacturer dealing with the London cloth market through an agent, and died with a great deal of money owed to him for cloth in London and with a stock of finished kerseys and cloth still in the loom. William Thomas of Broadbottom in Wadsworth was clearly a middleman and merchant of

some standing, for as well as the usual looms, he had large stocks of wool, a great deal of wool 'at spinning in Lankashire', '32 peecwools out at Making', a large number of fine and coarse kerseys, and a long list of debts, including £147 due 'from James Maude of Rochdale in Lancashire Mercht. against whom a statute of Bankrupt was lately Sued out'.[41] The builder of Lower Old Hall, Norland (146), was a dyer, and we have seen how some of the gentry houses of the area were built by men whose fathers had been yeomen-clothiers.[42] Defoe is a contemporary witness to the association of large houses and the

Plate 169 [83] Greenwood Lee, Heptonstall, home of the Sutcliffe family.

textile industry: seeking to explain the deserted countryside of the valley, he remarks significantly that 'if we knocked at the door of any of the master manufacturers, we presently saw a house full of lusty fellows, some at the dye-fat, some dressing the cloths, some in the loom, some one thing, some another, all hard at work, and full employed upon the manufacture'.[43] He thus reveals the nature of the largest houses in the upper Calder valley; not all, but certainly very many, were the houses of these 'master manufacturers', men like William Thomas who might combine supervision of manufacture with both supplying materials and marketing the finished cloth. These men were frequently farmers on a large scale as well, but undoubtedly they owed their wealth and large houses primarily to their control of key aspects of the textile industry. Working at the loom was the lot of the poorer yeomen, building smaller and less elaborate houses, and of the outworkers, unable to build in permanent form in this period. Where these last lived was observed by Defoe's sharp eye, for 'among the manufacturers' houses are likewise scattered an infinite number of cottages or small dwellings, in which dwell the workmen which are employed'.[44]

THE INFLUENCE OF TEXTILES AND AGRICULTURE ELSEWHERE IN WEST YORKSHIRE

The importance of a textile industry in the rise of a prosperous and numerous yeomanry helps to explain concentrations of yeoman houses elsewhere in West Yorkshire, although the influence of tenure in determining where the industry might flourish remains a matter for further enquiry. A small central area of the county, producing white cloths, has a large number of sizeable yeoman houses, especially in the townships of Gomersal and Liversedge. Some of the biggest of these were built by yeoman-clothiers. Peel House, Gomersal (68), was erected by Richard Peel, whose inventory of 1699 shows him to have been heavily involved in textiles as well as in agriculture, and in Liversedge the scene was dominated by the several branches of the Greene family: the main branch rose from clothier to gentry status in the 17th century and erected the very substantial Lower Hall, and junior branches, variously described as yeoman, clothier and merchant, were responsible for the construction of the Old Hall, Haigh Hall and other sizeable houses in the township.[45] The townships near Bradford once showed a great wealth of large yeoman houses; that these were the homes of men engaged in the textile industry is suggested by a number of probate inventories of yeoman-clothiers wealthy enough to rival those of the Halifax area. William Hodgsons of Bowling had over £200 worth of wool and cloth and was worth £768 at his death in 1693, while Thomas Hodgson of Horton died in 1697 with a wool chamber and shop packed with large stocks of wool and cloth and with goods and debts to the value of £226.[46] It is likely that the townships surrounding Bradford had much the same relationship to the town as did the upper Calder valley townships to Halifax, for in the 17th century Bradford was a fast-growing centre for the marketing of

cloth and doubtless provided wealth for many a yeoman-clothier dealing in the trade.[47] That the houses of Bradford appear to have been less opulent than those of the Halifax area is probably a reflection of the later development of the town, but may also be connected with the greater rate of subsequent destruction there, for it was Bradford, or 'Worstedopolis', which enjoyed the greatest expansion in the 19th century and which has suffered heavily from modern clearance.

The houses of West Yorkshire demonstrate that, wherever the textile trade flourished as a rural industry in the early modern period, it produced wealth for many yeomen. Of course, not all large houses were built by yeomen-clothiers, for the concentration by large parts of the population on industry opened the door for others to accumulate riches through supplying specialist markets. Thus the builder of Royds Hall, Heaton (81), a large house even by upper Calder valley standards, was a maltster, and Henry Jackson, who probably built Totties Hall, Wooldale (249), appears to have lived entirely on rents and the profits of agriculture.[48] The industry produced profits for the gentry mainly through its control of certain processes, such as fulling, but gentry inventories indicate that, in the main, there was little involvement in the actual production and marketing of the cloth, even though it was precisely these activities which had brought about the rise of some former yeoman families to gentry status.[49] It was clearly the yeomen who benefited most from the textile industry, and the lucrative aspects of supply, production and marketing were controlled by them and provided the foundation of very many substantial fortunes.

If the great wealth of yeoman housing in the upper Calder valley and, to a lesser extent, in the Bradford and white cloth producing areas is to be explained by the concentration there of the yeomen engaged in the most rewarding aspects of the textile industry, the poorer houses of outlying Pennine areas can be seen more clearly as the product of an economy dependent on the biggest market centres but disadvantaged by its distance from them and by its inability to compete on equal terms with a long-established industry. The yeomen of the upland townships like Keighley and Haworth to the north of the upper Calder valley and of the Colne and Holme valleys to the south were certainly engaged in the industry, but they were apparently left with the crumbs from the rich man's table: for only a very few were there openings in the most profitable processes, and the inventories of the Haworth area, for instance, suggest that yeomen here were far more often occupied in the physical processes of making up the cloth.[50] This manual work, of course, yielded smaller profits than did control of supply and marketing, and these areas formed dependencies or colonies of the wealthy market centres. The dominance of Halifax was not threatened until, in the 18th century, the clothing industry began to diversify, allowing newer centres like Huddersfield to corner the market in more specialized products.

The inventories show that there was progressively less involvement in industry the further east one travelled in the county. There was a great deal of merchant wealth concentrated in the towns of Leeds and Wakefield, but to the east of these rural industry was less prominent. Of yeoman inventories from the western uplands of the county 60 per cent show a connection with industry; this falls to 35 per cent in the central part of the deanery of Pontefract, and to just 20 per cent in the east of the county. This pattern of diminishing involvement in industry helps to explain why there should be fewer yeoman houses of the rebuilding outside the textile-producing parts of the county. An agricultural economy produced wealthy yeomen, but these were few in number because they owed their status to their unequal share of a much more limited commodity, land. Furthermore, the creation of a large fortune was a slower process in an agricultural economy. At harvest time, it is true, the profits to be made were very much larger than the weekly return from industry, but this one return had to see the yeoman who was solely engaged in agriculture through a good part of the year. The vagaries of each harvest and of the market for agricultural produce also made his life very uncertain: one year he might not be able to sell the produce of a bumper harvest, and the next his crops might fall well below expectation. Above all, however, the farmer pure and simple had no protection against slump, for he was entirely dependent on the agricultural market. By contrast, the yeoman practising a system of dual occupation could ride out a depression in textiles by falling back on farming, and survive an agricultural depression through concentration on trade. It was only when an agricultural slump coincided with a depression in trade that the Pennine yeomen were in serious difficulty; just such a conjunction appears to have come about in the 1690s, for the Reverend Robert Meeke, writing in 1693, commented that 'many are in hopes of a fruitful spring. Lord, grant it, and afford seasonable weather for corn. Every(thing) is very dear, and poor people's labour is cheap, for our trade of cloth here is much down, money is scarce. I have lent to several who are now indebted to me, and yet I am forced to borrow myself, because I cannot get in my own'.[51]

The effect of agricultural depression on an area where few people were engaged in the production of cloth was seen in mid-Wharfedale in the late 17th and early 18th centuries: here 'farming activity drastically declined in the rural regions, emigration tended always to be high, and real incomes fell to a very low level indeed'.[52] The evidence

for this decline, based on documentary sources, is in conflict with the picture suggested by the yeoman houses, for it was in precisely this period that townships such as Addingham enjoyed their yeoman rebuilding. The discrepancy can be reconciled by one of two hypotheses. Either the picture of decline embracing the majority of the rural population may disguise the rise of one small part of society, the yeomanry, who expressed their riches in building, or alternatively the yeomanry, suffering alike from depression, turned the profits made in earlier good years to rebuilding when investment in agriculture offered little apparent certainty of return. In either case the main point remains unchanged, that the West Yorkshire yeomanry operating in a simple agricultural economy were even more vulnerable to depression, and the fewer, generally smaller, and later houses of the yeoman rebuilding in purely agricultural regions are a reflection of the more restricted opportunities these offered the yeomanry for the steady accumulation of profit.

The yeoman rebuilding in West Yorkshire was diverse in its nature and reflected differences of economy within the area during the early modern period. Tenure probably created the conditions in which a textile industry could develop in the upper Calder valley in the late Middle Ages, and by the 17th century a large and wealthy yeomanry had emerged there as a result of the exploitation of a profitable system of dual occupation. The degree of prosperity and the timing of the rebuilding, even within upper Calderdale, depended on the combined influence of tenure and industry, but the yeomanry's position is clearly reflected in the construction of an extraordinary number and range of houses. Outside this most favoured area small regions enjoyed localized prosperity, but elsewhere the smaller numbers of houses, the generally later date of the rebuilding, and the more restricted range of size are to be explained differently. In other parts of the clothing belt the cause was perhaps harsher tenure, distance from the main centres of the industry, and exclusion from the most remunerative aspects of the trade; in the lowland east of the county and in the farming dales to the north the explanation may be the general absence of a system of dual occupation which offered similar returns and security.

Notes to Chapter 4

[1] WYAS, Leeds, Badgery Collection, 1056/132. I am grateful to Mr. George Sheeran for bringing this to my attention.

[2] Lister and Brown 1902.

[3] The debt structure revealed in the inventories is generally taken to show the system by which money was saved and invested in interest-earning loans. The specific link between this system of loans and building activity is discussed in Machin 1978, 139–42.

[4] Heywood tells us that Priestley started work in 1688, but the datestone on the house reads 1691 (Turner 1881–5, vol. 4, 131).

[5] See Stell 1960 and 1965, and Pacey 1964.

[6] The inventories of the late 17th and early 18th centuries show the same wide range in house size, some listing just one or two rooms and others ten or more. Even taking into account the source's vagaries, the inventories clearly describe yeoman houses of very different sizes.

[7] The assumptions that datestones record the erection of the houses in the vast majority of cases and that the proportion of dated to undated houses remains fairly constant so that the pattern revealed by the datestones is representative of all houses, not only those dated, have

been discussed in Machin 1977, 40–7. Two caveats may be entered in relation to the West Yorkshire evidence, however. First, the figures represent datestones from all types of building and some will therefore record building activity by other classes, principally the gentry. Secondly and more seriously, it is not clear that different areas showed the same predilection for datestones. If they did not, datestones may falsely suggest that in the same period one area was very active but that in another little building was taking place. Further, differences as obvious as the predominant building materials can materially affect the result. For example, timber-framed buildings rarely have, or at least rarely retain, datestones, and later casing disguises not only datestones but also the existence of these timber-framed buildings. Hence, the degree of building activity in the east of the county in the early 17th century, when timber-framing was still the rule, remains largely unknown, evidenced by a single surviving dated structure, the Nook Inn, Oulton, of 1611; the same period was clearly a time of great activity in parts of the Pennines where stone was the principal building material and where datestones, therefore, survive. For this reason comparison between dissimilar areas is dangerous, and although broad comparisons have been made in this study, it is important to realize the pitfalls of this approach. Such comparisons are much more valuable in areas of uniform character, and in this respect differences in time within the Pennine western half of the county form a much more reliable subject for study.

[8] Brief details of some of these houses and a list of the others are given in the Inventory.

[9] Stell 1960, 73–4.

[10] Stell 1960, 62–3, 69–70.

[11] Watson 1775, 258, says of Norland that 'there has no Gentleman's family settled in this township', and research has failed to unearth evidence for long-established gentry families. The Taylors, responsible for the construction of a number of Norland houses, appear to have risen to gentry status by the early 18th century, for John Taylor, gentleman, was listed as a freeholder within Rishworth-cum-Norland in 1709 (Charlesworth 1939, 12).

[12] The Bradford area has been studied in detail by George Sheeran: his results will be presented in a M.Phil. thesis, University of Bradford. He also proposes to publish a shorter account of the vernacular houses of the area; see Sheeran, forthcoming.

[13] Details given in the Inventory.

[14] See Inventory under Addingham.

[15] See Inventory under Keighley.

[16] The change brought about by urban growth was commented upon by Whitaker: he remarked of Hunslet that 'a greater change can scarcely be conceived of in the character and apprarance of a place now and of old. Under the Gascoignes and Neviles, the features of Hunslet were a great manor house and park, a slender and obsequious population, a feeble and unskilful husbandry; but quiet, cleanliness and repose. I need not expose the contrast' (Whitaker 1816, 98).

[17] WYAS, Leeds, LF/M53.

[18] The Inventory contains details of eastern houses similar to those found in Bramham: see entries for Bardsey-cum-Rigton, Thorner, Walton and Crigglestone.

[19] Yarwood 1981, 292–3.

[20] The figures omit urban townships. The returns apparently omit some rural townships, but some or all of these were probably included in the returns for neighbouring townships; Soyland, for instance, is not mentioned, but the particularly high return from the adjacent Sowerby is probably a combined assessment for both. In these cases, the averages for the area have been worked out by dividing the total tax paid in each area by the number of townships, including those for which no returns are distinguished. Of the areas mentioned, the upper Calder valley and the south-west are as shown on Map 4, which deals with the 1672 Hearth Tax returns, and the north-west is a group of twenty-four townships (including Keighley) to the north and west of Bradford.

[21] The detailed figures are taken from the returns published in Barber 1870. The original returns have not been consulted and there is much to be learnt regarding the nature of the wealth taxed and the basis of the assessments. The Rate appears to have been designed to help in the maintenance of bridges, and there is evidence that, with periodic minor adjustments in the assessments of some townships, the proportion of taxation established continued to be the basis of county levies until the 19th century.

[22] Data for the analysis is taken from Purdy 1975. Towns have been omitted. Some townships are not separately listed in the returns, but were included in the figures of a neighbouring township. Where it is known that a township was so included, it is taken to be represented in the analysis. Map 4 shows parent and daughter townships with the same pattern of wealth; thus Soyland, included in the returns of Sowerby, is shown on the map as having the same proportion of larger houses, for it is now impossible to segregate the returns of the two townships.

[23] An absolute division between gentry and non-gentry society cannot be maintained on the evidence of titles, for some yeomen may have been included as 'Masters'. This does not affect the main point of the argument, however. For the distinction between a 'Master' and a 'Yeoman', see Campbell 1967, 52.

[24] The basis of the sample from which the yeoman inventories were taken is explained in the Note on Sources.

[25] The question whether to include debts in calculations afflicts all students of the source. In this study of the textile industries of the West Riding in this period Dickenson chose to include inward debts but to ignore outgoing debts, as the latter would tend to obscure the true scale of the operations of some of the yeomen and clothiers (Dickenson 1974, ch. 1). In the present study, however, outward debts have been

regarded as important in determining the testators' wealth, and their consideration certainly leads to conclusions in conformity with those suggested by the evidence of fieldwork. The value of the house as a historical source is very clear in this matter, for it has suggested which of a number of approaches to the documents will yield the most faithful results.

[26] The Manor Book was compiled in 1709 as a sort of Domesday Survey for an incoming lord, the Duke of Leeds; see Charlesworth 1939.

[27] Ellis 1962, 260–1. The Manor Book indicates that by 1709 the majority of the copyhold tenants had compounded (Charlesworth 1939, 17).

[28] Ellis 1962, 263.

[29] Charlesworth 1939, 11–12.

[30] Charlesworth 1939, 8–9, 15, 16.

[31] A similar quick comparison between the upper Calder valley and the eastern graveships is not permitted by the evidence, for it is not clear that the two sources consistently refer to the same geographical areas.

[32] Ellis 1962, 263–4.

[33] For the houses of the Elland area, see Pacey 1964. Southowram houses have been studied by Mr. Wyn Westerdale, who revealed fascinating differences between the form and date of houses here and in other parts of the upper Calder valley; especially interesting has been the discovery of small numbers of timber-framed houses, probably of late 16th or early 17th-century date, with a floored-over housebody; see Westerdale 1983. The re-listing of the Elland Urban District in 1982–3 recorded the existence of thirty houses certainly or probably of 17th-century date. I am grateful to Mr. Peter Thornborrow for this information.

[34] It is significant that the historian of the West Riding woollen and worsted industry starts his story in 1689, the earliest date for which probate inventories survive in some numbers; see Dickenson 1974. Earlier sources in Lancashire suggest that the textile industry there underwent very important changes, particularly concerning the rise of the master-manufacturer employing wage-earning outworkers, in the course of the 17th century; see RCHM(E), forthcoming (a).

[35] For his description of the Halifax area, see Defoe 1971, 490–7.

[36] Fig. 44 is reproduced by permission of West Yorkshire Metropolitan County Council and originally appeared in Thomas 1981, 9. The calculations which formed the basis of the table differ from those undertaken for the present survey in their exclusion of debts.

[37] BIHR, May 1698, July 1691.

[38] Thornes 1981, 8.

[39] Ibid.

[40] For Greenwood Lee, Hartley Royd and Bellhouse, see Stell 1960.

[41] BIHR, May 1714.

[42] See, for instance, Wood Lane Hall, Sowerby (196), built by John Dearden, a first-generation gentleman; John's father, Richard, was a yeoman who, dying in 1626, left sixty kerseys and trade tools. See Kendall 1906, 126–7.

[43] Defoe 1971, 493.

[44] Ibid.

[45] For the rise of the Greene family in the 17th century, see Peel 1893, 150–65. Thomas Greene of Liversedge described himself as 'Merchant' in his will, and Joseph Greene of Hightown called himself 'Yeoman' in his: see BIHR, Aug. 1714 and July 1724.

[46] BIHR, April 1693 and Dec. 1697.

[47] In a memorable passage Joseph Lister described how, during the siege of Bradford in the Civil War, the town's inhabitants, under fire from royalist artillery, protected the church tower by hanging wool sacks over the sides (Wright 1842, 21-2).

[48] Inventories of Timothy Rhodes and Henry Jackson, BIHR, May 1722 and Feb. 1728.

[49] There are certain exceptions: the Murgatroyds are reckoned to have been wealthy merchants in the Halifax market; and a shop and shop chamber are listed in William Horton's house at Howroyd, Barkisland, and in Thomas Lister's Shibden Hall, although the contents of these rooms do not point to an active role in the industry. In the shop at Shibden Hall, for instance, the strongest link with the textile industry is the mention of six pairs of old walker shears. For the Murgatroyds, see Hussey 1943, 440; for Horton's and Lister's inventories, see appendix to Chapter 3.

[50] See Baumber, 34–42.

[51] In 1694 Meeke reported that a poor man said 'that he had been four days at market with a piece, and could yet receive no money; that he was forced to buy bean meal to make bread. Oatmeal being dear; and nothing almost got for work' (Morehouse 1874, 61, 75).

[52] Pickles 1981, 64.

CHAPTER 5

THE ELEMENTS OF THE YEOMAN HOUSE AND THE EVOLUTION OF ITS PLAN, 1600–1800.

In the field of architectural studies, the early modern period is characterized by great change and experimentation, and nowhere is this more evident than in the domestic building of the yeomanry. We have already seen how the West Yorkshire gentry adapted medieval practice to meet new needs until the point was reached when this process of modification gave way to a thorough rethinking of house design. The same period was equally eventful for the yeomanry, perhaps more so, because in most parts of the county this class was first able to build permanently at this time. The 17th and 18th centuries witnessed the slow working out of ideas on house planning and the progressive erosion of the intensely local character of yeoman building. By the end of the period essentially the same type of house could be found over a wide area of the county and beyond; building materials varied, of course, and no two houses were ever exactly the same, but the principal development in this period was the growing uniformity of yeoman dwellings.

The most important sources for the study of what yeomen of widely differing fortunes demanded of their dwellings in terms of elaboration and decoration are the houses themselves and probate inventories. The houses have been subjected to ceaseless modification over the centuries, a process which has obscured much original detail but which is itself eloquent of their occupants' changing requirements. The inventories have well-known deficiencies as a source but, nevertheless, provide a most valuable insight into the way in which the yeoman house functioned. It is unfortunate that those for the West Yorkshire area survive only in large numbers for the period after 1688, for the absence of earlier documents denies the student the chance to assess to what extent room uses and so forth changed during the course of the 17th century. Despite the weaknesses in each source, however, the study of large numbers of both buildings and inventories reveals a fair picture of what was common and what exceptional.

The purpose of the present chapter is to examine the nature and functions of the rooms within the yeoman house, and then to study how its plan evolved during this period. There is, perhaps, a bias in favour of the larger houses, for these tend to reveal a clearer distinction in the functions of rooms and, furthermore, have a wealth of associated documentary material. Smaller houses of necessity had more general uses for rooms, and it is less easy to discern when the inventories relating to them are affected by the omission or compression of important detail.

ROOM FUNCTIONS

THE HOUSEBODY

Central to the working of all yeoman houses was a principal room, the housebody. In medieval houses this had been open to the roof, but in the post-medieval period it most commonly took the form of a single-storeyed room with a chamber over it. A few yeomen, however, clung to medieval forms, although why they did so varied according to their position. The largest group of yeoman houses which had an open housebody in the post-medieval period is made up of the survivors from the late Middle Ages, the aisled houses of the upper Calder valley, updated to meet new needs. These had been built a century or more before by men at the pinnacle of yeoman society, and although their 17th-century occupiers may have been matched in wealth by yeomen who chose to build houses with a single-storey housebody, families like the Wades of High Bentley and the Thomases of Broadbottom were nevertheless still amongst the most prominent of their area. It might be thought that the retention of the open housebody was simply the inevitable consequence of the decision to case the medieval house in stone rather than to demolish and build afresh, the existence of earlier work precluding the modern form of a chamber over the housebody. This does not appear to be an adequate explanation, however, for many large yeoman houses built with a single-storey housebody replaced medieval houses on the same site; some, indeed, show the reuse of timbers which may well have come from those earlier dwellings. When new forms were required, therefore, the old was commonly swept away without compunction. Nor can the retention of the open housebody be the result of limited funds, for it is commonly found in houses with a great deal of 17th-century work: at High Bentley (177), for example, it is clear that, had Richard Wade required a single-storey housebody, he certainly possessed the means to satisfy his wishes, for he expanded and improved the medieval house in a number of ways (Plates 170, 171).

The decision on the part of the wealthy yeomen who occupied medieval aisled houses, firstly, not to insert a floor over the housebody when those houses were still in their timber-framed state, and, secondly and more significantly, to retain the open room even when they were casing the houses in stone and expanding and improving them, must be seen as a very deliberate choice. These men may not have been the only wealthy yeomen in the upper Calder valley, nor necessarily the richest, but they were very substantial. Furthermore, even if they were not the direct descendants of the families which originally built the houses, they may have felt themselves associated with a long tradition of superior yeoman status. It cannot now be established how many yeomen chose to replace medieval houses with an entirely new dwelling, but possibly for some major yeoman families the retention of the open housebody was a means of establishing a sort of yeoman 'pedigree' and of distinguishing themselves from the bulk of newer families. Above all, however, the open housebody was a demonstration to the world that they were in many respects not far removed from the status of the neighbouring minor gentry families, such as the Deardens of Wood Lane (196) and the Hortons of Howroyd (25), who also, against the drift of the age, retained the open room.

Like the gentry houses, these yeomen houses were complex and specialized in their domestic arrangements, and the open housebody had a function, permitted by this specialization, which was designed to display the status of the resident family. It functioned, in fact, in much the same way as did the open hall of the gentry house. It was a living room and a room used for the public occasions which were clearly part of the way of life of the wealthy yeomanry, for the alterations commonly made to it in the 17th century reveal the desire to create an impressive area for the reception of guests. It was no longer open to the roof, for it was usually ceiled at tie-beam level to give a room rising instead through two storeys, but its decorative qualities were enhanced by the insertion of rich plasterwork, both on the ceiling and on the walls and chimney breast. In some houses, a gallery was inserted to run around one or more of the walls, and in most the firehood which had heated the room was replaced with a well-carved fireplace in a stone chimney stack. High Bentley (177) shows most of these changes, Old Hall, Heckmondwike (82; Plate 172), retains its plaster ceiling of *c.*1640, and at Lower Hollins (218) the firehood was replaced in 1688 by an elaborate fireplace (Fig. 45). The replacement of the firehood indicates an important change in the function of the housebody, for it signals the removal of the cooking hearth from the room.

Fig 45 [218] Lower Hollins, Warley; detail of fireplace in housebody.

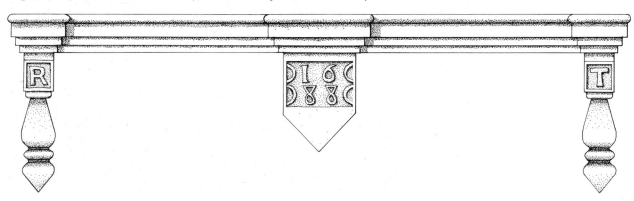

Plate 170 Fold Farm, Ovenden.

Plate 171 [177] High Bentley, Shelf.

Plate 172 [82] Old Hall, Heckmondwike; the housebody, with inserted ceiling of *c*.1640.

Plate 173 [82] Old Hall, Heckmondwike; the added kitchen wing.

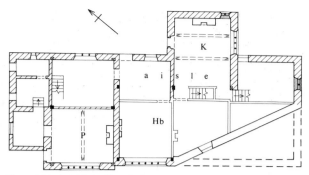

Fig 46 [82] Old Hall, Heckmondwike.

These alterations to the housebody were frequently accompanied by the addition of a heated kitchen wing (Plate 173; Fig. 46), changes which emphasize that these wealthy yeomen, like their minor gentry neighbours, saw their main room, not as a general living room also used for cooking, as it had been in the late Middle Ages, but as a more specialized, formal room for the reception and entertainment of guests.

The inventory of the goods of Samuel Wade of High Bentley shows the increased sophistication in the domestic arrangements among these yeomen: the open housebody was furnished with thirteen chairs, tables, and a form, indicating that it was used for sitting and dining, but there is no sign of the cooking gear which encumbered the housebody of lesser men. The open housebody persisted in these houses, therefore, both because it expressed high status and implied ancient origin, and because it answered the needs of the occupiers by providing an impressive room with a superior function. It continued in fashion for these few yeoman families into the 1670s and beyond: Smith House (87) was cased in stone in 1672, and Town House (143) in 1677; these and the other houses in the group continued to use the open housebody perhaps into the 19th century.

If the open housebody was a conspicuous badge of status, as has been suggested, it is perhaps surprising that more men did not adopt this form when building from new in the 17th century. Very few wealthy yeomen appear to have taken this option, and the example of Christopher

Nettleton of Ryecroft, Tong (213), stands almost alone. Nettleton, a prosperous farmer and tanner, built a house of only modest size but of high quality, dominated by the open housebody (Plates 174, 175). In 1693 this was furnished as a sitting and dining room, as was the heated Great Parlour, but also in the housebody, gathered in the fire area below the firehood, were a number of cooking implements – a dripping pan, a toasting jack, a bill, some knives and a ladle – which suggest that the room had not been entirely cleared of cooking duties. Certainly the main business of cooking was done in the kitchen, for all the spits, pots, pans and so forth necessary for the preparation of food were there, and it is possible that the housebody was used only for warming food and for the cleaner and more immediate processes involved in the serving of meals. Nettleton, perhaps, valued the prestige conferred by the open housebody, but at the same time failed to realize its full potential, something which is reflected both in his use of the room and in the absence of elaborate decoration such as is found in the upper Calder valley houses. Perhaps, too, the use of a firehood rather than of a carved stone fireplace in a chimney stack reveals that the housebody of Ryecroft was always intended to have a more workaday function than was the case in the upper Calder valley dwellings.

Not all yeomen who wanted their housebody to act as a reception and superior living area chose the open room, for a few wealthy men, of similar standing to those who retained the medieval form, built houses which were

Plate 174 [213] Ryecroft, Tong, 1669.

Plate 175 [213] Ryecroft; the housebody open through two storeys.

Plate 176 [146] Lower Old Hall, Norland; the single-storey housebody.

storeyed throughout. The best evidence for the superior single-storey housebody again comes from the upper Calder valley, and the finest example of the type is Lower Old Hall, Norland (146), of 1634 (Plate 176). The house is large, with an original kitchen wing, and throughout the living area there is a wealth of decorative detail. The presence of a heated kitchen relieved the housebody of the need to provide a cooking hearth, and instead the room could be turned over exclusively to the reception and entertainment of guests. Its importance is evident in its sumptuous treatment, for it is decorated with an intricately carved fireplace, a plaster overmantel and frieze, moulded beam and joists. In other houses, too, the single-storey housebody received special treatment: at High Hirst, Wadsworth, and at Bean Hole Head, Stansfield, for example, it is decorated with plasterwork, and at Pyemont House, Lofthouse (124), the room, significantly called the hall in the 1722 inventory, was large and impressive (Plates 177, 178).[1] These few houses suggest that the single-storey housebody was not incompatible with a superior use;

Plate 177 [124] Pyemont House, Lofthouse with Carlton; the housebody.

Plate 178 [68] Peel House, Gomersal; the fireplace in the housebody.

although less impressive by its very nature than an open room, it could, when required, have much the same function.

Before we leave the subject of the open housebody, one further group of houses with this feature should be noted. Unlike the former aisled houses, these are small, none being larger than three cells originally. Different types are discernible within the group. Cruck houses, such as Birks (185) and Upper Oldfield (89), were cased in the post-medieval period retaining the open housebody, and it is possible that other cruck houses were built from new in the course of the 17th century (see Chapter 2). The cruck houses are concentrated in the west of the county, and in the same area are a small number of stone houses giving just a single storey, as at Woolroyd, Slaithwaite (188; Plate 179), or an open housebody with storeyed end-bays, as at Frost Hole, Erringden (58; Fig. 47).[2] These western houses

Plate 180 [11] Crag House, Adel cum Eccup.

clad in stone to give a very cramped loft above the housebody (Plate 180).

The size of all these houses demonstrates that the open room was not chosen because the sophistication of the dwelling permitted it a superior role, as in the houses of some of the wealthiest yeomen. It is likely that these small houses represent the lower threshold of yeoman building, and that they were rather better, because permanent, versions of the type of dwelling inhabited by much of rural society below the level of the yeomanry. Small, single-storey or partially floored houses are known to have sheltered the poorer levels of rural society in West Yorkshire at a later period, and in other areas in earlier times.[3] The yeomen, if yeomen they were, who built these houses in the 17th century were able to afford a permanent version of the type of house they had always lived in; for them, modest prosperity resulted not in a more complex, storeyed dwelling, but merely in one in which the improvement lay largely in the durability of its construction. In these houses, the housebody continued to be an all-purpose room, used for cooking, sitting and eating, and it dominated the dwelling far more completely than did the floored-over housebody in a fully storeyed building.

At the two extremes of yeoman society, therefore, and for entirely different reasons, some men retained the open housebody until its final appearance, at least at this social level, perhaps in the last decades of the 17th century. The

Plate 179 [188] Woolroyd, Slaithwaite; a single-storey house.

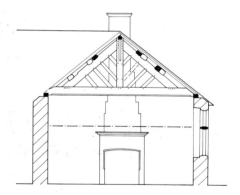

Fig 47 [58] Frost Hole, Erringden; section through open housebody (after Stell).

may be seen as the counterparts of the small timber-framed houses of the east of the county which were noted in Chapter 2; some of these eastern houses, for example Hazelwood Cottages, Rothwell (175), may well be post-medieval, with the housebody remaining open until a late date or, as appears to have been the case at Crag House, Adel cum Eccup (11), floored-over when the house was

Plate 181 [200] Great Greave, Soyland.

attention devoted here to the open housebody is, however, entirely out of proportion to its numbers, for the vast majority of yeoman houses in this period were built with a single-storey room. There is no sign of a slow change from open housebody to floored-over room; from the very beginning of the rebuilding the latter type was overwhelmingly dominant. Clearly for the bulk of the yeomanry there was no question of which provided the most suitable dwelling, and houses like Peel House, Warley (228), of 1598, Great House (199) of 1624, and Great Greave (200), both in Soyland (Plate 181), express the preference of men who approached or matched in wealth the occupiers of houses with an open housebody but who, given the opportunity of building from new, chose a different type, also adopted by hundreds of yeomen of lesser means. For all but a very few yeomen, therefore, the rebuilding in stone was the occasion of abandoning the form of the medieval house, whether of permanent or impermanent nature.

The floored-over housebody was adopted by the bulk of the yeomanry after 1600 for no more complex reason than because it corresponded most closely to their requirements. The inventories usually reveal it as an all-purpose room for cooking, sitting and dining. Fifty-eight per cent of yeoman inventories from the deanery of Pontefract sample describe a housebody used for cooking; very often it was the principal cooking area. The room's importance is revealed by the fact that nearly a quarter of the inventories mention no heating in the house apart from the range in the housebody; the fire here, therefore, provided heat for the preparation of food and warmth for the household. The all-purpose housebody is well illustrated by the 1689 inventory of the goods of Samuel Swaine of Horsforth: pots, pans, spits, fire tools and other equipment show that it was the main cooking area, despite the presence of a back kitchen, apparently unheated and used for storage and possibly for dairying. Tables and forms indicate that the housebody was used for dining, and the presence of six chairs suggest that it was also the most comfortable sitting area.[4] In this house, therefore, the housebody had a dominant role, despite the existence of two heated parlours which were used as bedrooms of some quality and possibly also as private sitting rooms. In houses without such rooms, the housebody was still more central to the workings of the dwelling. In the house of Christopher Holmes of Haworth, for example, the housebody was used for cooking, sitting and dining, but was supplemented only by an unheated parlour used as a bedroom, an unheated kitchen used for storage, and chambers for sleeping and storage.[5]

The principal requirement for most yeomen, therefore, was a housebody which could most easily act as a comfortable living and working area. Considerations of display were of small importance to these men, who had little need to maintain themselves in the style of more dignified yeomen. Consequently, the open housebody, a room designed to impress, had no value, and was both a wasteful extravagance and a room unsuited to everyday living. The floored-over housebody had many advantages: it was less draughty, easier to heat, and its use created a chamber giving added space on the first floor. Furthermore, as we have seen, it was not incapable of elaboration

and could, when required, have something of the splendour of the large open housebody (Plates 182–4).

The means of heating the housebody changed within this period. By far the most common method in houses of the first half of the 17th century was the firehood; its former presence is frequently revealed externally by the fire-window, generally of two lights, which lit the fire area, and internally by the scarf joints in the spine beams, which

Plate 182 [215] Rose Farm, Walton; the single-storey housebody.

Plate 183 [111] Kilnhurst, Langfield; the housebody.

Plate 184 [246] Mytholme, Wilsden; the housebody.

Plate 185 Carlton Husthwaite, North Yorkshire; firehood structure, tapering to apex of roof.

Plate 186 [85] Barrack Fold, Hepworth; heck-post and bressumer of firehood, and later fireplace.

Plate 187 [227] Roebucks, Warley; firehood replaced by fireplace.

were extended when the firehood was replaced by a smaller stone stack (Plates 185, 186). The firehood continued in use for much of the century, but began to be rejected in new houses of its later decades in favour of a stone chimney stack. The firehood had advantages, in that it allowed a great deal of room to move and work around the cooking hearth, but it also had its drawbacks. It was very bulky, it may not have been very efficient at removing smoke, and it must have acted as a funnel causing draughts. Furthermore, it was difficult to heat the chamber over the housebody if the room below had a firehood. These disadvantages were clearly keenly felt, for not only did the firehood fall out of use in new houses during the 18th century, but it was also replaced in already old houses at the same period. The housebody of Roebucks, Warley (227), shows the change: originally heated by a firehood in a large fire area, it received a new, much smaller, stone stack in the early 18th century (Plate 187). Such stacks could provide very large fireplaces. At Glenesk Farm, Morton (141), for example, the fireplace was certainly large enough to have served as the main cooking hearth (Plate 188). Most however, were smaller and that in the housebody at Mould Greave, Haworth (80) of 1742, for example, was possibly never intended to serve as the principal cooking hearth (Plate 189). In some houses a small and well-worked fireplace in the housebody signals the removal of cooking to the kitchen, but in others there is no alternative site for the cooking hearth, and small fireplaces like that in the housebody at Cherry Tree Farm, Eccleshill (53), of 1754, must have been considered adequate for a small yeoman household of limited means (Plate 190).

The degree to which the functions of the housebody changed in the course of this period is difficult to assess. The inventories of the 1730s, the latest in the sample, describe much the same type of room as do those of the late 1680s, but this span includes only a small part of our period. The housebody in a house of c.1800 was clearly very different from that in a house of the early 17th century, if for no other reasons than because changes in the rest of the house affected its role, and because the design of the yeoman house had altered so much over the period. In the course of the 18th century the concept of the housebody as a useful, general-purpose room tended to be confined to small and simple houses: at Tiding Field Farm, Slaithwaite (190), for example, the 1783 building provided a large housebody of traditional use in a house of, originally, only two cells. In larger houses, however, the more common use of the heated kitchen increasingly deprived the housebody of one of its chief functions, and it became more like a parlour. The final stage of the process is seen in houses like

Above: Plate 188 [141] Glenesk Farm, Morton;
fireplace in housebody.

Plate 189 [80] Mould Greave, Haworth, 1742;
fireplace in housebody.

Right: Plate 190 [53] Cherry Tree Farm, Eccleshill, 1754;
fireplace in housebody.

Plate 191 Heaton Royds Farmhouse, Heaton, 1634; the kitchen.

Warren Farm, Swillington (204), and Peckfield House, Garforth (65), where the housebody and parlour, previously so distinct in terms of size and function, had become all but identical reception rooms.

THE KITCHEN

In contemporary terminology the yeoman's 'kitchen' could mean one of two things. The inventories show that up to half of the kitchens listed were not used for cooking, but were instead unheated service rooms used for storage, acting something like a buttery. It is now impossible to distinguish such a room in surviving houses, for it would appear as a featureless area similar to other service rooms. The other type described in the inventories was a kitchen in the modern sense, a heated room used for cooking. These are easy to recognize, for they were usually heated by a large stone stack or firehood. Such kitchens were provided in large houses from the earliest years of the rebuilding: Peel House (228), of 1598, and Lower Old Hall (146), of 1634, are early examples. Slightly later, more modest houses were built with a heated kitchen, as at Mazebrook Farm (73) of 1654, and Fairfield Cottage (21). Other

Plate 192 [95] Hill End House, Horton, 1714; the kitchen.

Plate 193 [230] Greystones, Warley; fireplace and oven in kitchen.

examples are Heaton Royd Farm, Heaton, Hill End House, Horton (95), and Greystones, Warley (230), illustrated in Plates 191–3.

A heated kitchen might share the cooking duties with the housebody or release the latter entirely from the need to serve as a cooking room. The example of Ryecroft (213) has been noted already as a house in which food was prepared in both rooms; another example, this time in a house with a single-storey housebody, is Roebucks, Warley (227), in which the housebody was the main cooking room, equipped with spits and so forth, and the kitchen was used for baking. The best houses, however, had a kitchen which took over all the cooking duties: High Bentley (177) and Lower Old Hall (146) both had heated kitchens, and the effect on the housebody has already been

Fig 48 [118] Old Hall, Liversedge.

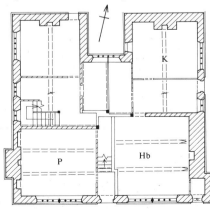

studied. The existence of a heated kitchen used for cooking was a major advance, and, like the minor gentry, the wealthier yeomen clearly sought an improvement which allowed the housebody a more restricted and superior role by removing from it much of the bustle of everyday life.

This motive for the inclusion of a heated kitchen is emphasized by a further feature of the room, its close communication with the outside world, either directly by its own external doorway or indirectly through close proximity with the main doorway serving the housebody. At Mytholme, Wilsden (246), for example, the lobby-entry is sited between housebody and kitchen; by turning one way the visitor could enter the 'living' area of housebody and parlour, and by turning the other way the 'working' part, the kitchen, could be reached. More common was the back door giving an entirely independent entry to the kitchen: examples are Rose Farm, Walton (215), Old Hall, Liversedge (118; Fig. 48) and Hollingthorpe Farm, Crigglestone (45). The provision of this independent entry, a feature of gentry houses too in this period, suggests a desire for functional segregation, for by channelling the traffic associated with the workings of the kitchen along its own route, the better part of the house, especially the housebody, could act more effectively as a private living area. There is, too, an important element of social segregation, just as there was in the gentry household; in the superior yeoman house, the main entry became the preserve of the family and guests, with the rest of the household, specifically the servants and outworkers, using the kitchen doorway. This change has its origin in the 17th century, but was widely accepted by the end of our period, and is expressed clearly in the planning of many later houses, such as Peckfield House, Garforth (65).

Plate 194 [20] Trench Farm, Baildon; the rear kitchen wing, with site of stair shown by raised window in outshut.

There was no single idea of where the kitchen was best sited. It was sometimes placed on the main front, even in some of the biggest houses: Totties Hall (249) and Mytholme (246) are both large houses with a kitchen in this position, and Ryecroft (213) is a slightly smaller example of the plan. More common, however, was a position at the rear of the house, either in a wing (Plates 194–7), as at Trench Farm, Baildon (20), Greystones, Warley (230), and Mazebrook Farm, Gomersal (73), or within the main block, usually behind the housebody, as at New Close Farm, Shipley (180), and Great House, Soyland (199). The close association of kitchen and housebody is very marked. The functions of the two rooms were closely linked, for even if the housebody was not used for any of the cooking processes it was commonly the chief dining room. In 17th-century houses known to have had a dining parlour,

Plate 195 [73] Mazebrook Farm, Gomersal; the rear kitchen wing.

Plate 196 South Bank Road, Nos. 2 and 4, Batley; the rear kitchen wing.

the kitchen appears to have been sited so as to serve that room and the housebody as needs dictated; at Peel House, Gomersal (68), for example, it was close to both. There is little sign that the yeomanry attempted to set the kitchen at a remove, as the gentry contrived through the use of wings to the side and rear; Lands Farm, Gomersal (74), has a kitchen wing to one side (Plate 198), and at Church Street, Nos 10, 12 and 14, Honley (91), a rear wing with a kitchen was built to replace the original kitchen on the main front, but these are the exceptions. Only much later, in houses such as Peckfield House, was the kitchen commonly visually distinct, and in the 17th century the intent of the yeomanry was to incorporate the kitchen into the main block to connect closely with the rooms which it served.

The Parlour

The third of the trio of rooms with closely interconnected functions was the parlour. The inventories show that many yeoman houses had more than one parlour; a third had two, and one in eight had three or more. The use of the parlour varied according to the size and complexity of the dwelling.

Its most common use was as a bedroom, frequently

Plate 197 [230] Greystones, Warley; the rear kitchen wing.

combined with one or more other functions. In small houses, the best parlour might be the principal bedroom and contain furniture showing that it was used for sitting and perhaps even as a dining room, but it was also likely to have been used as a storeroom, while a second parlour was

Plate 198 [74] Lands Farm, Gomersal; kitchen wing to side on left.

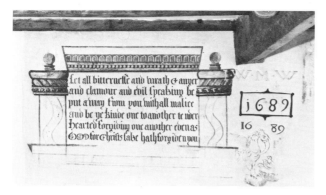

Plate 199 Lane House, Silsden; wall painting in parlour.

generally a minor bedroom and a storeroom for household goods and 'huslement' (a term used by the appraisers of inventories to comprehend the odds and ends deemed unworthy of itemizing). In the house of William Clay of Northowram in 1705, for example, the Sun Parlour was a heated room with the best bed in the house, but it was also used to store household linen and the best tableware, and the Little Parlour had a less expensive bed and a cupboard.[6] Among the poorer yeomen at least, the use of the parlour

as a bedroom continued well into the second half of the 18th century; in 1765, for instance, Matthew Bradley of Almondbury had two beds in his parlour as well as two in the chamber over the housebody.[7] Among poorer yeomen the modern notion of confining the beds to the first floor was, apparently, generally absent in this period. The treatment of the parlour in smaller houses is not likely to have been lavish. At Lane House, Silsden, a wall painting of 1689 survives (Plate 199), but the changes in fashion make it impossible to assess how common such decoration may once have been. In the majority of smaller yeoman houses the parlour was probably a plain room, reflecting its general functions.

In larger yeoman houses the parlour was more developed in its use. The best parlour was frequently heated, even from the earliest years of the rebuilding; in the upper Calder valley houses the parlour at the front of the cross-wing was usually heated by an extruded stack on the side wall, a plan seen at Peel House (228), of 1598, and Roebucks (227), of 1633. Whether these rooms were sophisticated in their use in the early 17th century cannot be established in the absence of inventories of that date, but their size and decoration in some houses certainly suggests that this was the case. An exceptionally fine parlour is that at Lower Old Hall, Norland (146), of 1634: this room is lit by a large window, heated by a well-worked fireplace, and

Plate 200 [146] Lower Old Hall, Norland; the parlour.

Plate 201 [68] Peel House, Gomersal; the parlour.

decorated with a plaster overmantel and a ceiling with moulded beams and joists (Plate 200). Peel House, Gomersal (68; Plate 201), Pyemont House (124), Giles House, Hipperholme with Brighouse, and Headlands Hall (117) all have plaster decoration in the principal parlour, which was clearly more than a simple bedroom. The later inventories show that many middling yeomen used their best parlour as a bedroom, as a sitting room, and sometimes as a dining room as well. George Boyle of Jaque Royd, Shelf, for example, appears to have slept, ate and sat in his Sun Parlour.[8] Yeomen of higher standing went further and excluded the bed from their best parlour, a room used exclusively for sitting and dining. The best parlours at Lower Old Hall and Peel House, for example, were obviously such rooms, and that at Peel House was called the Dining Room in the inventory of 1699. Totties Hall (249) had a Great Dining Room in 1728, and in 1693 the house of Daniel Thorpe of Sharlston had a New Parlour, furnished with twelve chairs and some pictures; it was probably added to act exclusively as a sitting room.[9] Certainly by the end of the 17th century, and, on the evidence of decorative plasterwork, probably long before, the wealthiest yeomen gave specialized and superior functions to the best parlour, and clearly men of this status demanded of their houses some of the comfort and privacy enjoyed by the gentry (Plate 202). They could afford this degree of specialization because in their houses the best parlour was supplemented by one or more lesser parlours

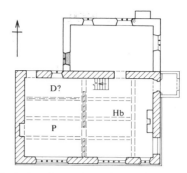

Fig 49 [211] Flailcroft, Todmorden with Walsden.

which continued to be used in the general way characteristic of smaller houses.

The main parlour in the yeoman houses of the 17th and 18th centuries was at the front of the house, next to the housebody, and the second parlour was usually at the rear, either in a wing, as at Hill Top Fold, Slaithwaite (187), or within the main block, sometimes behind the housebody, as at Meltham House, Fulstone (63), where the very small back parlour is distinguished by stop-chamfered joists, and sometimes behind the main parlour, as at Trench Farm, Baildon (20). In the smallest yeoman houses, those of just two cells, the inner cell was subdivided to give a parlour on the main front and a small service room at the rear: such a plan is seen at Flailcroft, Todmorden (211; Fig. 49). In the largest houses the multiplication of parlours created problems of planning that were rarely satisfactorily resolved in the 17th century. At Binroyd (145) and the Old Hall (144), both in Norland, and at Great House, Soyland (199), the need for more living rooms led to the provision of an additional parlour beyond the main one, as well as of further space for lesser parlours at the rear. In 1693 High Bentley (177) was provided with a Sun Parlour and a North Parlour in the cross-wing, and a Kitchen Parlour in the former shop end of the house. Neater solutions were found, however, the best being that adopted by the gentry who utilized the lower end of their house for a parlour, creating in the process a main front lined with the best rooms of the house. Yeomen of high status followed this

Plate 202 [165] Frogden House, North Bierley, 1625; panelled screen with built-in cupboard, facing into parlour.

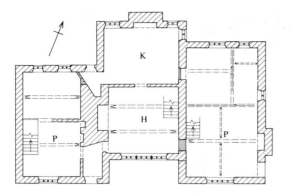

Fig 50 [81] Royds Hall, Heaton.

example, both in houses with cross-wings, such as Royds Hall, Heaton (81; Fig. 50) and Pyemont House (124), and in simple double-pile houses like Peel House, Gomersal (68), and Stoney Royd, Midgley (137).

Service Rooms

Despite the common use of the parlour for storing household goods, more space was needed for the storage and preparation of food and drink. Service rooms abound in the inventories and are given specialist names: the commonest are the buttery, milkhouse, kitchen, back kitchen, dairy and cellar, and there are occasional references to rooms like the oven-house and wash-house. The buttery, as well as being used to store food and drink, could be used to keep the pewter and even as a bedroom: that at Hill Top Fold, Slaithwaite (187), for example, had a bed as well as chests and fifteen pots of butter. The fact that cellars were sometimes used as bedrooms as well as storerooms indicates that they could be ground-floor

rooms rather than being fully subterranean; in 1699 the cellar in John Wilkinson's house in Soyland had two beds in it.[10] The houses confirm the rarity in the 17th century of original sunken cellars, and only in the 18th century were these at all commonly provided. A fine example is that at Longfield House, Heptonstall (84), of c.1730 (Plate 203). A common improvement to earlier houses in the 18th century was the creation of a cellar: at Manor Farm, Denby (49), the house of 1654 was supplemented in the first half of the next century by an outshut which included a sunken cellar, reached through a decorative doorway leading out of the housebody (Plate 204). Cool storage space was more usually provided at the back, generally the north-facing side of the house.

Chambers

The first floor of the yeoman house was made up of a number of chambers used largely for sleeping and storage. Only the most superior yeomen afforded themselves the luxury of a chamber used exclusively as a withdrawing or sitting room, such as could be found in some gentry houses. Henry Jackson of Totties Hall (249) was one such, furnishing his Best Chamber with nine chairs, a looking glass, window hangings and other pieces of furniture. The presence of decoration and of heating in a chamber implies that it was more than just a bedroom; at Lower Old Hall (146), Backhold Hall, Southowram (195), and Prior's Mead, Hipperholme with Brighouse, the heated best chamber is decorated with plasterwork and must have been used either as a combined bedroom and private sitting room or exclusively as a sitting room.[11]

Throughout the 17th century the most common site for the best chamber was over the parlour. The status of the room was reflected in its fenestration, for it often had the largest window on the first floor, as at Frogden House (165), and sometimes the most elaborate, as at Upper Foot

Plate 203 [84] Longfield House, Heptonstall; the cellar.

Plate 204 [49] Manor Farm,
Denby; doorway to cellar steps.

Plate 205 [118] Old Hall, Liversedge; panelling and fireplace in chamber over
housebody.

Farm, Midgley (136), where it is lit by a stepped window. There are, perhaps, two reasons for this siting. In larger houses this chamber was easier to heat than any other, using the stack which heated the parlour below. As long as the housebody was heated by a firehood, there was no means of heating the chamber over it, and this room was invariably undecorated, lit by an inferior window, and used very often simply as a storeroom for crops, taking advantage of the constant warmth from the fire below, or for items of no great value. Furthermore, the planning of the larger 17th-century houses dictated that, wherever the stair was sited, the chamber over the housebody must frequently have been something of a passage from one part of the house to the other, while that over the parlour could be isolated to give privacy. The planning of Lower Saltonstall, Warley (237), shows the importance of this second consideration: built in the early 18th century, the house had a chimney rather than a firehood in the housebody, but the opportunity to provide a fireplace in the chamber over was rejected. Instead it was the smaller chamber over the parlour which was heated, by a small, bolection-moulded fireplace, a choice showing the value attached to the privacy guaranteed by its position at one end, rather than in the middle, of the house.

It was only when the concept of centralized planning was applied to the yeoman house that the chamber over the housebody could be exploited more fully. The change in plan, to be studied in the second part of this chapter, led to a house with two rather than three rooms on the main front. In this the stair could be sited so as to rise into the centre of the first floor, giving access by a landing to the chambers over the parlour and housebody. The latter chamber, therefore, was freed from its role as a channel of communication, and as a result there are signs that by the

early 18th century it was growing in importance (Plate 205). At Old Hall, Eastwood, Stansfield (203), it is the largest chamber and is heated (the housebody below being heated by a stone chimney stack), although the chamber over the parlour has plaster decoration which suggests that it was still the best of the first-floor rooms (Plate 206). By the end of the period it is likely that there was little to choose between the two principal chambers; indeed the fact that the chamber over the housebody was commonly larger than that over the parlour, a relationship determined by the size of the rooms below, indicates that the roles of the two chambers may at last have been reversed.

Plate 206 [203] Old Hall, Eastwood, Stansfield; chamber over parlour.

Plate 207 [16] Kirkbank, Badsworth; top storey lit by two small windows.

Plate 208 Manor Farm, Clayton West.

Plate 209 [193] Common Farm, South Kirkby.

Plate 210 [133] Churchside House, Methley; dormers contribute to symmetry of main front.

ATTICS

Over much of the county attics do not appear to have been widely used. The majority of Pennine houses, for example, make no provision for attics over the chambers, which were probably left open to the roof. In the east of the county, however, there are many houses of the second half of the 17th century which were built either with a full third storey or with an attic (Plates 207–12). Kirkbank, Badsworth (16), and Broad Lane Farm East, South Elmsall (192), both have a full top storey; dormers or windows in the gable walls light an attic at Churchside House, Methley (133), Old Hall, Ackworth (1), and Pear Tree Farm, Wintersett (248). The attics or top storeys were usually poorly lit and unheated, their most likely function being for the storage of crops. This area had an economy dominated by arable husbandry, and a substantial yeoman such as the builder of Broad Lane Farm East may have felt the need to provide safe and dry storage for the valuable produce of his fields. There is a great deal of evidence in the

inventories for the storage of crops within these eastern houses; in 1738 Robert Nottingham of Crofton had chambers full of wheat and beans, and in two inventories the garrets are specifically mentioned as the place where cereals and pulses were stored. Some of the attics and top storeys have lime-ash floors supported on a heavy frame of beams and joists, a method of flooring which may have been designed both to carry a great weight and to prevent the constant seepage of grain and dust through to the chambers below.

Another strong indication that the top floor was used for the storage of crops is the awkwardness or absence of its communication with the rooms below. The main stair at Old Hall and at Churchside House rises to the top floor, but in other houses, for example Home Farm, Oulton (171), and Kirkbank, the means of access is not evident, the top floor having fallen out of use, presumably when they ceased to be the centres of working farms. If used mainly or solely as a farm store, the top floor may not have been

Plate 211 [248] Pear Tree Farm, Wintersett; attic lit by window in gable.

Plate 212 [1] Old Hall, Ackworth; a large attic, probably for storage.

Above: Plate 213 [192] Broad Lane Farm East, South Elmsall; top storey used to store grain taken in through loading door.

provided with a permanent stair, for it would not have been in everyday use as part of the dwelling. The functional connection with the farmyard rather than with the house is seen most clearly at Broad Lane Farm East, where the garrets are reached only by means of a stair rising up the back wall to an external doorway (Plate 213).[12] In some houses attics were used as pigeon lofts. That at the Old Hall, Eastwood, Stansfield (203), is certainly original, but others may be conversions of earlier attics used for crop storage; at Pear Tree Farm, for example, the brickwork making up the nesting boxes appears to be later than the house itself (Plate 214).

THE SHOP AND SHOP CHAMBER

One final element of the house – the shop or workshop – demands special comment, for it has a distinct regional bias in its distribution and is a very important reminder of the source of the wealth which permitted the rebuilding of so many yeoman houses. The shop is unknown in yeoman inventories of the eastern part of the county outside towns, where the term was applied to commercial premises in the modern sense of the word. In the central part of the county only a tenth of the yeoman inventories mention a shop, but in the Pennine west the proportion rises to nearly a third.

Plate 214 [248] Pear Tree Farm, Wintersett; attic converted to pigeon loft.

Here the shop was part of the house rather than a detached structure; the order of rooms in the inventories and the fact that the shop often had a shop chamber over it are proof of this. The shop and its chamber were used for various stages in the production of cloth, or simply for the storage of raw materials or finished pieces, for the inventories commonly show that these rooms were full of looms, presses, wool, yarn, made-up cloth, shears and all sorts of trade tools.

It is no coincidence that the bulk of the inventories listing a shop should come from the upper Calder valley, where, as has been shown, the textile industry was most developed and where the wealth which it produced permitted the construction of so many yeoman houses. The plans of the valley's houses show the way in which the shop was incorporated within the main block. The houses of yeoman-clothiers of any substance almost always have a passage dividing the building into upper and lower parts: above the passage are the main rooms, including the housebody and parlour; below it is a single room. In other parts of the country this lower end might be a service room or rooms, or a byre, but not in the upper Calder valley. Service rooms here were commonly sited above the passage, at the rear of the house in a wing or an outshut; the interpretation of the lower end as a byre is ruled out both by the form of the houses and by the total absence from the inventories of any suggestion of such a use.[13] Nor was the lower end a kitchen, for it was unheated, and the kitchen was usually sited at the rear of the house above the passage. The use of the lower end as a shop is suggested by the inventories and confirmed by the houses themselves. This end received none of the external or internal decoration lavished on that part which lay above the passage, and in very many houses there is a clear contrast in the treatment of the two parts. At Upper Foot Farm (136), for instance, the hood mould with carved stops includes only the entry, the housebody and the parlour, leaving the lower end devoid of elaboration and with an inferior style of window. Many other houses show the same contrast between the window style in the two parts: above the passage the windows lighting the best rooms have recesssed mullions, but below it the mullions are flush with the surface of the wall, a cheaper and more utilitarian form in keeping with the non-domestic use of this part of the house.

The house of the yeoman-clothier was, then, part

dwelling and part manufactory, just as was described by Defoe in the early 18th century when, passing through the valley, he was taken into the house of a master manufacturer (see p. 130 above). The convenience of the most common plan in the area, the hearth-passage arrangement, is immediately apparent: the lower-end shop and shop chamber provided economically for working premises and allowed the yeoman-clothier to exercise close supervision of the work done under his roof and to keep a proprietary eye on the often very valuable stocks of materials and cloth stored there, but at the same time the passage segregated the two parts of the house. There was, it is true, a common entry, but all the industrial functions were restricted to one side of the passage, leaving the dwelling area free of the noise and traffic of the shop. Segregation was a feature of not only the ground floor but, in some houses, of the first floor as well: at both Hartley Royd, Warley (229), and Great House, Midgley (135), the chamber over the shop does not communicate with the adjacent chamber over the housebody (Fig. 51). This lack of communication supposes that the lower end was provided with its own stair and emphasizes the deliberate intent to isolate it from the rest of the house. The importance attached to this segregation is seen in significant changes made to one of the finest of the yeoman-clothiers' houses: when Richard Wade cased the timber-framed High Bentley (177) in stone and enlarged it in the middle of the 17th century, he expanded the dwelling area by turning the former shop into a parlour and eliminating the hearth-passage plan, but was careful to provide a new passage between this parlour and the new shop wing built slightly earlier beyond the lower end of the house (Fig. 52). Despite all the changes at High Bentley, the shop in the post-1661 house enjoyed precisely the same relationship to the dwelling area as had obtained in the house before alterations started.

The houses show other signs of association with the textile industry. A few were provided with an original 'piece door', set at first-floor level in an exterior wall to facilitate the loading in and out of bulky materials like wool and yarn or finished items such as kerseys and shalloons. The presence of such a door in a house as large as Stoney Royd, Midgley (137), demonstrates that, however wealthy a yeoman might become, in this age he felt no shame in the source of his wealth nor felt it below his dignity to assign

Fig 51 [229] Hartley Royd, Warley.

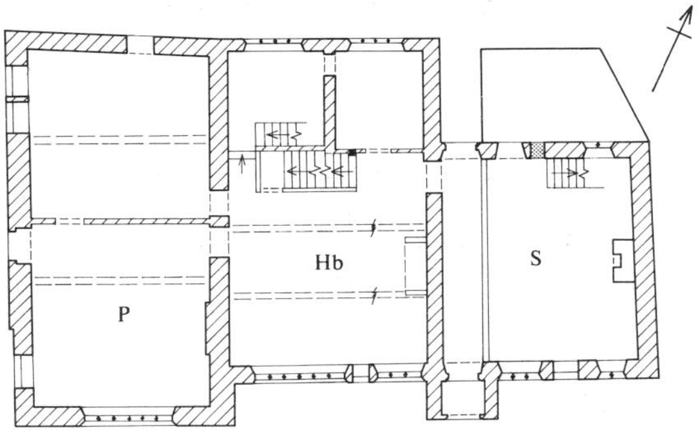

Fig 52 [177] High Bentley, Shelf.

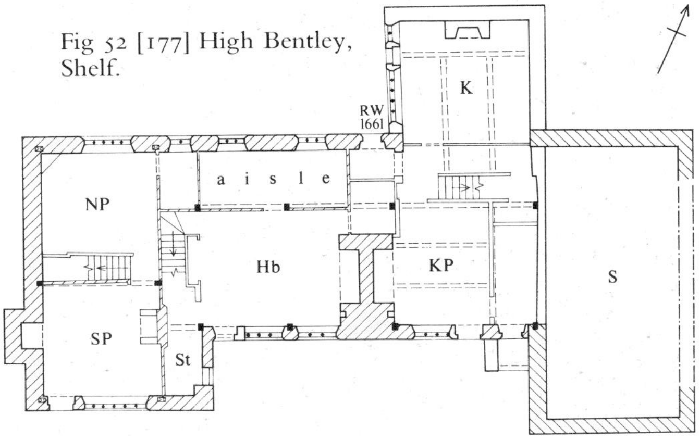

Plate 215 [137] Stoney Royd, Midgley;
'piece door' in rear wall.

Plate 216 [18] Midgley Farm, Baildon; shop added to house
in *c*.1800.

Plate 217 [111] Kilnhurst, Langfield; added wing of 1766,
with first-floor shop.

part of his house to the furtherance of his trade (Plate 215). Most piece doors are not original, being insertions of the second half of the 18th century and of the 19th century, suggesting that this device, while it was convenient for some yeoman-clothiers at an earlier date, was not considered essential by very many others.

Additions to houses sometimes reveal a desire to provide more convenient accommodation for the industrial part of the complex. At Midgley Farm, Baildon (18), outside the upper Calder valley but lying in the textile belt, the house, built in the second half of the 17th century, was expanded in *c*.1800 by the addition of a shop and shop chamber, the latter being lit by windows on three walls and betraying a

Plate 218 [202] Great House Clough Farm, Stansfield; detached shop next to house.

concern with the provision of light which does not appear to have worried earlier builders (Plate 216). The best example of an added shop is that at Kilnhurst, Langfield (111), built in 1766: the wing at the rear of the house provided a kitchen on the ground floor and a shop chamber on the first floor, reached by an external flight of steps (Plate 217). At Great House Clough Farm, Stansfield (202), the shop was a detached building, probably built shortly after the small house of the early 18th century: it provided a shop on the ground floor and a heated shop chamber above (Plate 218).

The upper Calder valley is not unique in having houses which included a shop, for both elsewhere within West Yorkshire and across the Pennines in the textile-producing belt of Lancashire there is evidence that some yeoman houses were built with this special-purpose area.[14] In the upper Calder valley, however, the dual nature of the house is expressed most perfectly in its plan, and is characteristic of most of the largest yeoman houses from the beginning of the rebuilding in the late 16th century until the early years of the 18th century. The proven existence of this shop within the post-medieval houses adds weight to the argument that the late-medieval timber-framed houses of the same area, which show the same hearth-passage plan, were also built with this dual function in mind and were erected out of the profits made from the textile industry.

THE EVOLUTION OF PLAN AND DESIGN

The great variety of yeoman building, in date as well as in form, makes it impossible to outline a simple evolution of the plan and design of the yeoman house that is applicable to all the different building zones within the county. Each area had a different starting point, and although the end of the evolution throughout the county was a single dominant form of house, the roads to that end differed from area to area. There are, however, clear lines of development, and the purpose of the present section is to show how the yeoman house, like the gentry house, underwent an evolution from a plan and design based on medieval ideas to a type of dwelling organized on new principles. The widespread acceptance by the yeomanry of these new ideas signals the decline of the regional diversity which makes the earlier progress of its houses so complex.

In the first half of the 17th century the yeoman house was dominated by the medieval notion of the tripartite division of the dwelling: whether it was of simple linear form, with or without an outshut, or was built with one or even two cross-wings, there were three rooms on the main front, just as in yeoman and gentry houses of the Middle Ages. The idea of a tripartite division persisted well into the 18th century, and houses based on this show a wide variety of plans. The most common, especially in the first half of the 17th century, was the hearth-passage plan, the overwhelmingly dominant form in the upper Calder valley, where early houses are most numerous. There are, perhaps, two reasons for this concentration. This plan had been universally adopted in the late medieval yeoman houses of the same area, and some continuity may be expected in the post-medieval period. Had the plan been inconvenient then, however, it would have been abandoned, and its very frequent use is testimony to its continued utility. The use of the passage as a division between the dwelling and the industrial parts of the house has been outlined above, and the particular convenience of the hearth-passage lay in the way in which the stack providing heating for the housebody backed onto the passage and formed an effective barrier between the two areas.

It need not be maintained that all hearth-passage houses were built by men with an interest in textiles, nor that such men built only hearth-passage houses. The lower-end shop is found, albeit rarely, in other types of house; it will be argued that two lobby-entry houses in Norland – Lower Old Hall and Fallingworth Hall – both had a shop below the entry. Despite these exceptions, the association of the plan with the yeoman-clothiers of the upper Calder valley is very clear. In other parts of the county which are known to have grown wealthy through the textile industry, however, the hearth-passage plan and the lower-end shop are not found. In the central parts of the county, especially in the townships of Gomersal and Liversedge, the large houses of the clothiers display alternative plans with no sign of a shop being included within the main block. Peel House, Gomersal (68), is a large house built by a yeoman-clothier, but the inventory of its builder, Richard Peel, indicates that the shop was a detached building and that the house had a purely residential character. Why there should be this contrast between two areas involved in the textile industry defies easy explanation. The later date of the yeoman rebuilding outside the upper Calder valley, and the lack of a large number of late medieval houses of hearth-passage form inducing a measure of contiuity, possibly contributed to the difference. Outside the upper Calder valley the industry was possibly organized along different lines, with closer control being exercised by a smaller number of large clothiers over a system of production less exclusively centred on the manufacturers' homes than that of the area served by Halifax.

THE LOBBY-ENTRY

Within the period dominated by the hearth-passage plan, three other types of plan were used in houses with three rooms on the main front: the lobby-entry, the entry into the housebody at the opposite end to the fireplace, and the central entry directly into the housebody. The lobby-entry was the first of these forms to appear in some numbers, and the earliest examples include timber-framed houses of the early 17th century from the east of the county, such as Old Malt Kiln, Bramham cum Oglethorpe (33; Fig. 53), and the Old Manor House, Thorner (205), and some dated houses from the upper Calder valley, such as Great Jumps, Erringden, of 1633, and Lower Old Hall, Norland (146), of

Fig 53 [33] Old Malt Kiln, Bramham cum Oglethorpe.

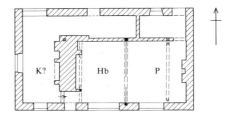

1634. For the rest of the time that tripartite houses were built, the lobby-entry appears commonly over a wide area and is particularly characteristic of the eastern part of the county (Plates 219–21 and Figs. 54–57). The social range covered by it is broad, ranging from hall-and-cross-wings houses like Pyemont House, Lofthouse with Carlton (124), to linear houses, both with an outshut, like Rose Farm, Walton (215), and without, like Hill House Farm, Normanton (164).

The lobby-entry could be sited either between the parlour and the housebody or between the latter and a room of lesser status, a kitchen, a service room, and sometimes a shop. The first position is the most common in the south of England, but not in West Yorkshire. Its convenience was that the parlour, usually heated by the same stack that heated the main room, could be given an independence and privacy not possible in a house where the parlour was reached only by crossing the busy and communal housebody. In some West Yorkshire lobby-entry houses the existence of two parlours, upper and lower, meant that the lobby-entry offered this convenience to the lower parlour. At Pyemont House this is, in fact, the better room (Fig. 56), but in other houses, such as Royds Hall, Heaton (81), the better parlour lay in its traditional position at the upper end and was still reached by crossing the housebody. In these larger houses the housebody is likely to have had a superior use, however, and the lobby-entry, far from being a means of isolating the lower parlour from a communal housebody of general use, served to bring it into more direct contact with the other

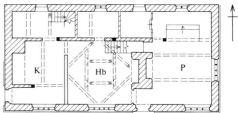

Fig 54 [215] Rose Farm, Walton.

Plate 219 [215] Rose Farm, Walton: a lobby-entry house.

Fig 55 [21] Fairfield Cottage, Bardsey cum Rigton.

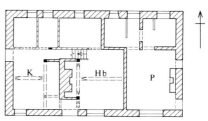

Plate 220 [21] Fairfield Cottage, Bardsey cum Rigton.

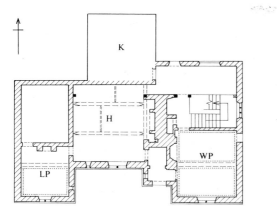

Fig 56 [124] Pyemont House, Lofthouse with Carlton.

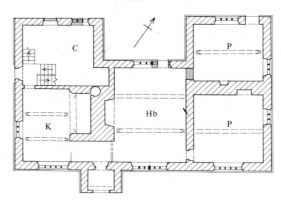

Fig 57 [57] Thorncliffe, Emley.

Plate 221 [57]
Thorncliffe, Emley.

reception rooms than was possible with, for example, the hearth-passage plan. In smaller houses the lobby-entry between housebody and parlour is more clearly the result of a desire to give independent access to the latter, for only one good-quality parlour was provided and the housebody had a more general and communal use. Houses like Rose Farm, Walton, and Church Street, Nos. 10, 12 and 14, Honley (91) are similar in form to the typical lobby-entry house of the south of England (Fig. 54), and the entry provided access on one side to the working area of the house, the housebody and service rooms, and on the other to a private, generally heated, parlour.

The lobby-entry was, therefore, sometimes used to isolate a superior parlour from the general living area of the dwelling. Segregation could, however, work the other way round by isolating a busy, noisy, working part of the house from the better-quality living area. Sited between the housebody and the kitchen, the lobby-entry divided two types of traffic: people seeking the living area turned one way, and those involved in the running of the working part, that is the kitchen, turned the other. This cleared the

housebody from a flow of people coming to and fro between the outside and the kitchen and freed it for superior use, at the same time maintaining the close communication between the kitchen and the rooms which it served (Figs 55, 57). The plan is seen both in large houses like Thorncliffe, Emley (57) and Ryecroft, Tong (213), and in small houses like Kirkbank, Badsworth (16), and Fairfield Cottage, Bardsey-cum-Rigton (21). In none of the smaller houses was the parlour a room of any pretention; that at Kirkbank was heated, but the rest were probably unheated originally. This suggests that the incorporation of the kitchen and the use of the lobby-entry were designed to raise the status of the housebody rather than that of the parlour.

Some yeoman houses have the lobby-entry sited between the housebody and a simple, plain and unheated end cell. In some this end cell probably provided service rooms, and it is not clear why the lobby-entry was chosen in these cases: the advantage of the plan at, for example, Great Slack, Kildwick (108) and Manor Farm, Denby (49), is difficult to see, for the main stack was not utilized to heat

Plate 222 [108] Great Slack, Kildwick, 1674.

Plate 223 [49] Manor Farm, Denby, 1654 : a house with two rooms below entry.

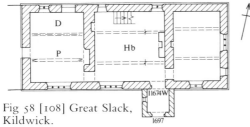

Fig 58 [108] Great Slack, Kildwick.

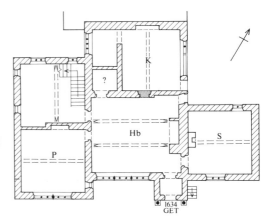

Fig 59 [146] Lower Old Hall, Norland.

Plate 224 [146] Lower Old Hall, Norland; doorway opens against side of stack heating housebody, unheated shop beyond.

159

the end cell, which appears to have been of little importance (Plates 222, 223; Fig. 58). In other houses, however, it
is likely that the end cell was a shop. These are in the upper
Calder valley, where the lower-end shop was standard in
hearth-passage houses. The end cell was treated in the same
inferior way that characterized the lower end in hearth-
passage houses. Fallingworth Hall, Norland (149), Great
Jumps, Erringden, and Lower Clough Foot, Sowerby, all
have small windows lighting the end cell, and at Lower
Old Hall, Norland, this is the only ground-floor room on
the main front not to be lit by a transomed window and the
only one to have poorly finished ceiling beams and joists
(Plate 224; Fig. 59). In none of these houses was the end cell
heated originally.[15] The similarity in the treatment of the
end room in both hearth-passage and lobby-entry houses in
the upper Calder valley indicates that both types could
provide a lower-end shop; the lobby-entry allowed both
parts of the house – dwelling and shop – to function
independently, but the clearer division given by the
hearth-passage plan made this the more common choice.

The incidence of the lobby-entry plan shows its adapta-
bility, for it could meet the needs of yeomen of different
areas and occupations, and of varying degrees of wealth. It
proved as suitable for the wealthy yeoman-clothier of the
upper Calder valley as for the poorer farmer of the east, and
it could be used variously to give privacy to a parlour, to
provide close communication combined with functional
isolation to a kitchen, and to give a distinct lower end in a
house which demanded some accommodation for industrial use. It could separate functions effectively in houses
where this was required, and at the same time make the
house more compact by eliminating the passage where it
was unwanted.

OTHER PLAN TYPES

The two other forms of plan found in tripartite houses – the
entry at the opposite end of the housebody to the fireplace
and the central entry – appear to have been used mainly by
yeomen who did not require a clear functional division
between the rooms on the main front. At two examples of

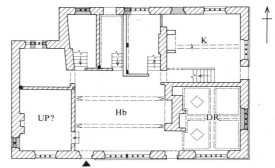

Fig 60 [68] Peel House, Gomersal.

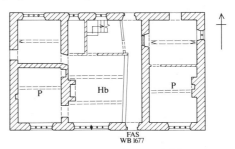

Fig 61 [104] Manor Farm, Utley, Keighley.

the former plan – Peel House, Gomersal (68; Fig. 60), and
Lower Hall, Liversedge (113), – the main front was made
up of the housebody and two parlours, and the same was
the case in smaller houses like Manor Farm, Utley,
Keighley (104; Fig. 61), and Holden Gate, Silsden (182;
Plate 225). In these the entry directly into one end of the
housebody allowed the lower parlour to be reached easily
and made the internal communication between the best
living rooms more immediate and convenient. This was
also the case in some houses with a central entry directly
into the housebody, but two further considerations, those
of external appearance and the housebody's functions, had

Plate 225 [182] Holden
Gate, Silsden.

Plate 226 [137] Stoney Royd, Midgley, 1715.

a strong influence on the design. Totties Hall (249), of 1684, and Stoney Royd (137), of 1715 (Plate 226; Fig. 62), are both large houses, built at a time when the idea of symmetry was gaining universal acceptance among the gentry, and it is no surprise that a wealthy yeoman such as Henry Jackson of Totties should have followed the fashions of the age. That he and others were able to do so implies that they used the principal room more like the entrance and reception hall of the gentry house than the living and working housebody of most yeoman houses. The 1727 inventory of Totties significantly refers to the Hall rather than to the housebody, and although its contents are not listed the sophistication of the domestic arrangements implies that it functioned like the hall in a lesser gentry house. The central entry allowed the rooms on the main

Fig 62 [137] Stoney Royd, Midgley.

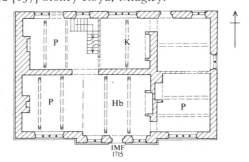

front to be closely linked; at Totties and at a smaller example of the type, Overtown Grange Farm, Walton (216), one of the rooms was the kitchen, but at Stoney Royd the housebody was flanked by parlours.

Many of the houses discussed hitherto, whatever their plan, were large and complex, showing one further feature which distinguishes them from medieval houses. Like the gentry residences of the period before 1680, they had arrived at an informal double-pile plan, with a rear range of rooms behind the main rooms lining the facade. Some houses were double-pile only on plan and only in part of their length: Overtown Grange Farm (216), for example, has a one-and-a-half-storey outshut behind just two of the three rooms (Plate 227), and Greystones (230) has an outshut and a storeyed rear wing above the passage. Neither, therefore, were fully double-pile, for they failed to provide a complete range of full-height chambers. The informal double-pile plan appears in the upper Calder valley from the earliest years of the rebuilding in houses like Peel House (228) and Great House (199; Fig. 63). The existence of the lower-end shop in this area acted as a stimulus to the development of double-pile planning in the dwelling part of the house. It was suggested in Chapter 2 that this pressure probably contributed to the development in the late Middle Ages of the aisled house, and in the post-medieval period solutions to the problem diversified. Deprived of the lower end, the dwelling area could expand either beyond the upper parlour or at the rear or even, in a

Plate 227 [216] Overtown Grange Farm, Walton; outshut along part of rear, with raised window for stair.

few houses, in both directions. At Great House (199), Binroyd (145), and Old Hall (144), the need for multiple parlours and for a kitchen and service rooms led to the elongation of the main front and the inclusion of a rear range of rooms. Other houses, like Lower Old Hall (146) and Roebucks (227), had a kitchen wing at the rear and a cross-wing at the upper end (Fig. 64). In all these houses, therefore, the need to isolate a shop caused the compression of the dwelling part into the area above the passage or

entry, and convenience dictated that the double-pile form be adopted. The living area was two rooms deep on both ground and first floors, and this contrast between an isolated, single-pile lower end and an upper area built as an informal double-pile is repeated in many scores of houses in the upper Calder valley. Progress towards a better-organized block was slow and uneven, but at Westfield, Warley (219), the area above the passage was contained within a roughly rectangular block. In areas where the

Fig 63 [199] Great House, Soyland.

Fig 64 [227] Roebucks, Warley.

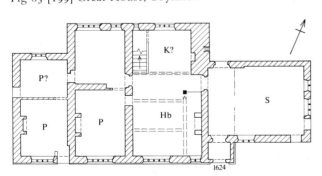

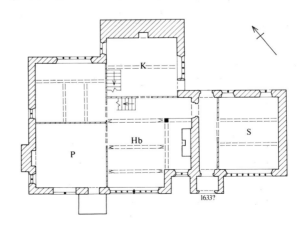

Plate 228 [127] Menston Grange, 1672:
a double-pile house.

Plate 229 [246] Mytholme, Wilsden, 1685.

Plate 230 [247] Hallas Old Hall, Wilsden.

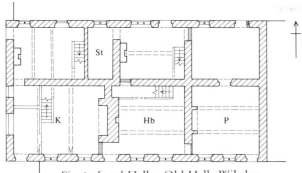

Fig 65 [247] Hallas Old Hall, Wilsden.

lower-end shop was uncommon, some houses were, from the late 17th century, planned as a simple rectangle: Menston Grange (127), of 1672, Mytholme (246), of 1685, and Hallas Old Hall (247) are large examples of the type (Plates 228–30; Fig. 65), and Manor Farm, Utley, Keighley (104), of 1677, is a smaller version. These houses are fully double-pile, in that they contain front and rear ranges of rooms on both ground and first floors.

DOUBLE-FRONTED HOUSES

From the middle decades of the 17th century there began to appear in West Yorkshire a type of house which introduced a new concept into the planning of the dwelling. This had just two rooms on the main front, in contrast to those considered hitherto which all had three or more rooms making up the facade. The earliest reliably dated example is Frogden House, North Bierley (165), of 1625 (Plate 231); an early example lacking a cross-wing is Gill Gate, Cumberworth (47), of 1642 (Fig. 66). The type became increasingly common throughout the rest of the century, and overwhelmingly dominant in the 18th century. The variety of plans within this single type is very great. Those with gable-entry or end-lobby-entry plans may be derived, at least typologically, from the hearth-passage and lobby-entry plans of larger houses: White Birch, Warley (239) and Mazebrook Farm, Gomersal (73), may be considered as houses which lack the passage and lower end of the typical yeoman-clothier house of the upper Calder valley (Fig. 67), and Frogden House or Longdene, Wooldale (250), can be seen as simply lacking the lower room of larger lobby-entry houses (Fig. 68). Haughcroft Head, Elland cum

Plate 231 [165] Frogden House, North Bierley, 1625.

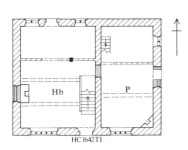

Fig 66 [47] Gill Gate, Cumberworth.

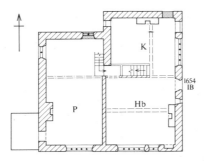

Fig 67 [73] Mazebrook Farm, Gomersal.

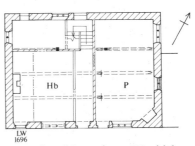

Fig 68 [250] Longdene, Wooldale.

Plate 232 Haughcroft
Head, Elland cum
Greetland, 1705.

Greetland (Plate 232), is one of a small group with an entry into the housebody at the opposite end to the fireplace.

Double-fronted houses vary considerably in size. The smallest had just two cells, with the inner sometimes divided to give a parlour and a small service room: examples are Flailcroft, Todmorden (211), Near Two Laws, Keighley (105), and Gildersber Cottage, Addingham (4; Fig. 69). Perhaps more common than these are houses with an outshut along the rear: White Birch (239) and Longdene (250) are typical examples. The outshut was combined in some houses with a storeyed rear wing, as at South Bank Road, Nos. 2 and 4, Batley, and Woodside Farm, North Bierley (Plate 233). The full double-pile form, that is with front and rear ranges of rooms on the first as well as the ground floor, was not common in the 17th century, but was attained in houses of various degrees of quality. A simple example is Ivy House, Bingley (29), of

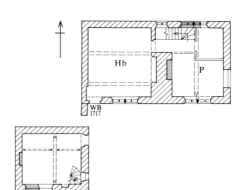

Fig 69 [4] Gildersber Cottage, Addingham.

Plate 233 Woodside Farm, North Bierley; side view, showing kitchen wing behind main range.

Plate 234 [29] Ivy House, Bingley, 1676.

1676 (Plate 234; Fig. 70); slightly more sophisticated in terms of its accommodation is New Close, Shipley (180), probably of much the same date (Fig. 71); and superior versions of the form are Little Horton Hall, Horton (94; Plate 235; Fig. 72), and Towngate, Nos. 18, 19 and 20, Hipperholme with Brighouse (88). Doubtless considerations of economy influenced the choice of a small house for many yeomen, but many of these double-fronted houses, especially those like Little Horton Hall and Towngate with their show of gables and advanced internal plan, were quite the equal in terms of display and living accommodation of the larger upper Calder valley dwellings; in fact, they were only distinguished from them by the lack of the lower-end shop. It is possible therefore, that both within the upper Calder valley and outside it these houses were adopted by yeomen who did not require industrial accommodation within the main block, either because they were not clothiers or because they used a detached shop.

By the late 17th or early 18th century there was no longer a clear contrast between wealthy yeomen building houses planned on a tripartite basis and poorer men building double-fronted houses. Increasingly it was the latter type of house which answered the needs of men of widely differing fortunes. The tripartite house was still built well on into the 18th century, as at Stoney Royd

(137), of 1715, and Mould Greave (80), of 1742, but the majority of men who in the previous century might have built such houses now turned to the double-fronted dwelling. The builders of Trench Farm, Baildon (20), Hill End House, Horton (95), and Longfield House, Heptonstall (84), probably built this type of dwelling from choice

Plate 235 [94] Little Horton Hall, Horton.

Fig 72 [94] Little Horton Hall, Horton.

Fig 70 [29] Ivy House, Bingley.

Fig 71 [180] New Close Farm, Shipley.

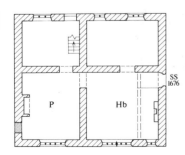

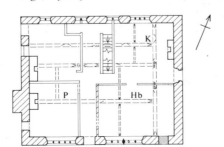

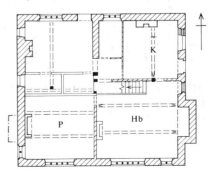

Plate 236 [20] Trench Farm, Baildon, 1697; the main front.

Plate 237 [95] Hill End House, Horton, 1714.

Plate 238 [50] Netherend Farm, Denby.

rather than because they could not afford one with three rooms in the main front (Plates 236–8).

There are a number of reasons why the tripartite form of house with its associated plan forms should have been abandoned. The most important concern the same changes in ideas on planning and aesthetics which had affected the gentry houses in the last part of the 17th century. The tripartite plan had disadvantages, in being wasteful of walling and providing a poor system of internal communication, both on the ground floor, where the house-body was continually crossed by people coming from and going to the outside world and the rooms at the ends of the house, and on the first floor, where the chamber over the housebody acted in much the same way as a passage from one end of the house to the other. The double-pile, double-fronted house improved on both aspects, being more economical in walling materials and allowing each of the main rooms of the dwellng – housebody, parlour and kitchen – to communicate more closely with each other. Furthermore, the invariable pairing of housebody and parlour on the main front opened up possibilities of symmetrical design not available to the majority of builders of tripartite houses. These either had to be of sufficiently high status to use the housebody as an entrance hall and thus to incorporate a central entry, or often needed a type of entry which emphasized the divisions in the main front, rather than its unity; the hearth-passage plan is the commonest of the latter types. Unlike the house with a hearth-passage plan, which was usually divided according to function into upper and lower end, the double-fronted house had the main front lined with the best rooms, and the service rooms and lesser parlours at the rear. This arrangement is, in fact, identical to that of the yeoman-clothier houses of the upper Calder valley, except, of course, for the lower-end shop which there dictated the position and nature of the entry. In the double-fronted house the role of the entry was to unite the main rooms rather than to place a division such as a passage between them, and internal convenience and considerations of external aesthetics made the central doorway the most suitable. From the middle of the 17th century the central entry grew in popularity until it became standard in yeoman houses as it had done in the residences of the gentry. In some houses there was little attempt to exploit the potential for symmetry: at Tudor House, Pudsey (174), Huddersfield Road, Nos. 129 and 131, Shelley (179), and Troydale Farm, Pudsey (Plates 239–41), the entry is off-centre and the fenestration expresses the relative importance of the rooms on the facade. The effect in the best houses, however, could be impressive (Plates 242–5),

Plate 239 [179] Huddersfield Road, Nos. 129 & 131, Shelley.

Plate 242 Manor House Farm, Esholt.

Plate 240 Troydale Farm, Pudsey, 1706.

Plate 243 [141] Glenesk Farm, Morton.

Plate 241 [179] Huddersfield Road, Nos. 129 & 131, Shelley.

Plate 244 [28] Eldwick Hall, Bingley, 1696.

Plate 245 [203] Old Hall, Eastwood, Stansfield.

Plate 246 [45] Hollingthorpe Farm, Crigglestone, 1725.

Plate 247 [118] Old Hall, Liversedge.

as at Glenesk Farm, Morton (141), and Eldwick Hall, Bingley (28). In other houses greater artifice is apparent in the attempt to produce symmetry. Small houses like Churchside House, Methley (133), and larger ones like Hill End House (95) and Hollingthorpe Farm, Crigglestone (45), attain perfect balance on the main elevation (Plate 246), and in others the sense of composition is very strong indeed: at Old Hall, Liversedge (118), the front has balancing gables, and at Trench Farm (20) and Longfield House (84) the symmetry is matched by fine detail (Plates 247–9).

The influence of the new ideas on compact planning brought about the demise of the lower-end shop. Along-side great manufacturers and merchants like Samuel Hill of Soyland, for whom the traditional shop was clearly inadequate, there still flourished in the 18th century smaller manufacturers, the direct successors of the men who in the 17th century had found the lower-end shop so well suited

Plate 248 [84] Longfield House, Heptonstall.

to their needs.[16] The probate inventories show the persistence of this type of modestly prosperous yeoman-clothier, and the very design of the Halifax Piece Hall, built as late as the 1770s to provide facilities for over 300 clothiers, is evidence of the continued, although perhaps by now threatened, importance of the system of production which

Plate 249 [20] Trench Farm, Baildon; the central doorway.

had raised the industry to greatness. Rarely did the yeoman-clothier build in traditional form after 1700, however. The advantages of centralized planning outweighed those of the lower-end shop, and many new houses were built in the 18th century with no sign that the shop formed part of the original accommodation. When one was required, however, it could be incorporated into the new type of house and effectively segregated from the living area, not by siting it at one end and dividing it from the dwelling by a passage, but by putting it at the rear and on the first floor. Two houses show this new disposition. At Stoney Royd (137) a piece door permitted the loading in and out of bulky materials, and at Old Hall, Eastwood, Stansfield (203), the first-floor shop, lit by a long window, functioned entirely independently by means of its own doorway opening onto the slope of the hillside at the rear (Plates 245, 250). This siting of the shop allowed the yeoman-clothier to have the best of both worlds; he still

Plate 250 [203] Old Hall, Eastwood, Stansfield; rear entry to first-floor shop; blocked openings to pigeon loft in gable.

enjoyed the advantage of close supervision over domestic production while living in a house that, externally and internally, incorporated the new ideas on design.

The counterpart to external symmetry, or at least to progress towards that end, was the development of what has been called the 'centralized system of circulation'.[17] We have seen that most 17th-century houses, especially those based on a tripartite division, failed to achieve a close integration of the elements of the dwelling, many because segregation – of a shop or of kitchen traffic – rather than integration was the chief aim. Slow changes in the uses of rooms, studied in the first part of this chapter, acted together with the increasing desire for a degree of symmetry on the main front to produce a re-ordering of the interior of the house. The double-fronted, double-pile design gave a new disposition, with the main rooms on the facade and lesser rooms at the rear, and increasingly, especially in the larger houses, independent entries served the two areas. The central entry on the facade served the principal rooms – housebody and parlour – which in the course of the 18th century were merging in function until both might be called simply reception rooms. As long as the housebody was the dominant room, the entry directly into it, as at Longfield House, Heptonstall (84; Plate 248; Fig. 73), or by means of a lobby, as at Glenesk Farm, Morton (141; Fig. 74), was appropriate, but ultimately the better houses acknowledged the inconvenience of such close communication between entry and living room and incorporated an entrance hall, a device that had been used in gentry houses in the early 18th century. It is not clear when the entrance hall was first incorporated into the

Plate 251 [134] Home Farm, Methley.

Plate 252 [204] Warren House, Swillington.

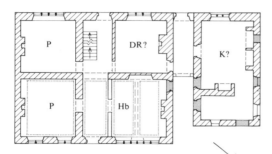

Fig 73 [84] Longfield House, Heptonstall.

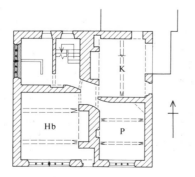

Fig 74 [141] Glenesk Farm, Morton.

design of yeoman houses, but certainly by the end of our period it is present in houses like Warren House, Swillington (204), and Home Farm, Methley (134) (Plates 251, 252; Fig. 75).

The central entry, opening into one corner of the housebody which conventionally occupied half, or slightly more, of the main front, became increasingly closely linked to the stair. The position of the stair in 17th-century houses is not known in very many cases, but in some there was no attempt to link entry and stair closely. At, for example, Mytholme (246; Fig. 76) and Lower Old Hall (146), the

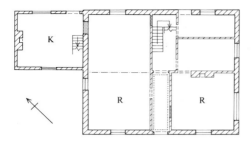

Fig 75 [204] Warren House, Swillington.

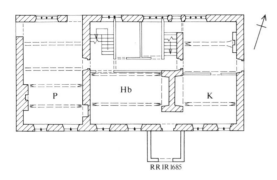

Fig 76 [246] Mytholme, Wilsden.

Plate 253 [117] Headlands Hall, Liversedge; side view showing raised stair window.

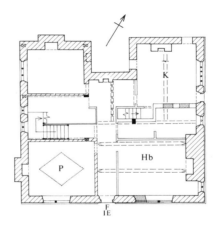

Fig 77 [117] Headlands Hall, Liversedge.

housebody lay between the two, emphasizing its role as the hub of the house. A more direct connection between the entry and the stair improved the system of circulation and raised the status of the housebody. In central-entry houses like Old Hall (118) and Headlands Hall (117), both in Liversedge, the doorway opened directly into the house-body, but people wishing to reach the stair simply crossed one end of the room rather than traversing its length, leaving the main part of the housebody free of traffic (Plate 253; Fig. 77). In many double-fronted houses of 17th-century date the stair was sited behind the parlour and lit by a raised window in either the side wall, as at the two Liversedge houses, or in the rear wall, as at Trench Farm, Baildon (20). In some later houses it was placed behind the parlour but in a rear wing, as at Netherend Farm, Denby (50; Plate 254), but from the late 17th century by far the most common site for the stair was in the centre of the rear range of rooms, lit by a window in the rear wall (Plate 255). This position allowed close connection with the central entry, balancing the doorway on the main front by the stair at the rear. Furthermore, the use of a dog-leg or half-turn stair brought the flight up to a central position in the first-floor plan, and this, together with the creation of a landing, permitted independent access to the main chambers (Plate 256; Fig. 78). This device at last freed the chamber over the housebody from its role as a link between the ends of the house and allowed it to function as one of the best chambers. Because such chambers, in the house of a superior yeoman, might be used as sitting rooms as well as bedrooms, and even, in a few cases, as reception rooms pure and simple, the route to them from the entry was

Plate 254 [50] Netherend Farm, Denby; stair is in rear wing, lit by raised window.

Right: Plate 255 [84] Longfield House, Heptonstall; rear elevation, showing raised window for central stair.

Fig 78 [64] West Royd Farm, Fulstone.

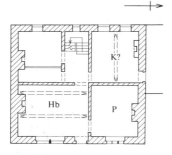

Plate 256 [64] West Royd, Fulstone; the dog-leg stair to a landing.

elaborated, just as it was on a more lavish scale in gentry houses. Fine staircases, rare in yeoman houses of the first half of the 17th century, became more common in the late 17th and early 18th centuries (Plates 257–261), and in some houses the stair hall was decorated with plasterwork: that at Longfield House, Heptonstall (84), is perhaps the finest of its type. Many houses capitalized on the siting of the stair by placing the steps to the cellar, newly important in the early 18th century as a cool storeroom, beneath the main

Plate 257 [117] Headlands Hall, Liversedge; the stair.

Plate 258 [1] Old Hall, Ackworth; the stair.

Plate 260 Lawns Farm, Temple Newsam; the stair.

Plate 259 [84] Longfield House, Heptonstall; the stair hall.

Plate 261 Combs Hall, Thornhill.

Plate 262 Manor House Farm, Esholt; stair hall, with doorway to cellar.

Plate 263 [45] Hollingthorpe Farm, Crigglestone; the stair.

flight; the door to the cellar stair can be seen in the stair hall at Manor House Farm, Esholt (Plate 262) and Hollingthorpe Farm, Crigglestone (Plate 263; Fig. 79).

Between the late 17th century and the end of the 18th century, therefore, the yeoman house underwent a great change. The earlier tripartite planning was abandoned in favour of the double-pile, double-fronted house, and this type itself changed radically between its first appearance at

a relatively modest social level and its all but universal acceptance at all but the poorest levels by the end of our period (Plates 264–7). In a house like Ivy House, Bingley (29), the housebody, entered directly from a doorway on the side wall, was the dominant room, probably with an all-purpose use, and the parlour, smaller than the house-body, was probably still a bedroom as well as a sitting area. At Warren House, Swillington (204), built more than a

Fig 79 [45] Hollingthorpe Farm, Crigglestone.

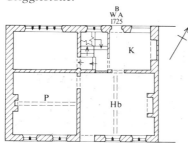

Plate 264 [64] West Royd, Fulstone.

Plate 265 [214] Gregory Farm,
Upper Whitley.

Plate 266 [204] Warren House,
Swillington.

Plate 267 [65] Peckfield House,
Garforth.

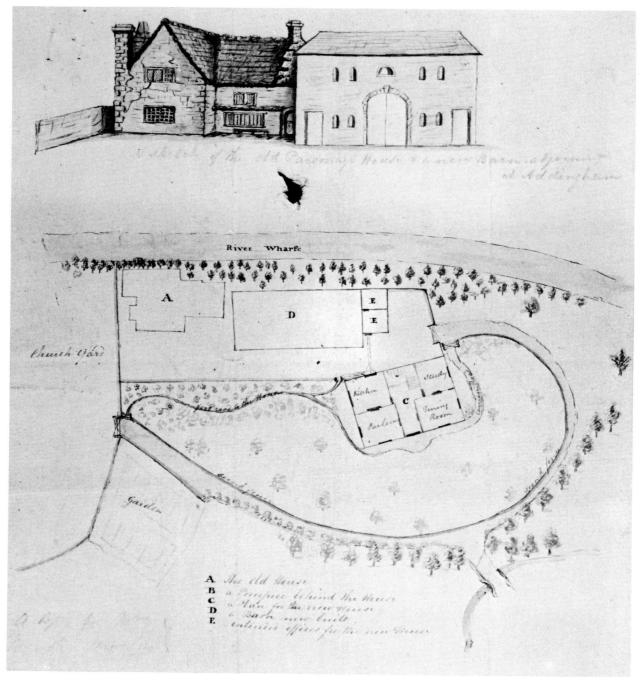

Plate 268 The Parsonage, Addingham: sketch of old house and plan for new house, 1808 (*reproduced by permission of the Borthwick Institute for Historical Research, York*).

century later, there is no longer a housebody, and probably no longer a parlour used as a bedroom (Plate 266). Instead, the main front, disposed according to the now accepted canons of symmetrical design, was made up of two reception rooms, undistinguished from each other by size or elaboration, and an entrance hall, which acted as the link between the entry, these rooms, the lesser rooms at the rear, and the stair. The changes represent both the perfection of the system of centralized planning and the ability of the double-pile house to adapt to the needs of the day.

The evolution of the yeoman house in the post-medieval

period is therefore one from a dwelling based on a medieval plan-type, through many different forms determined by wealth, occupation and date, to a single type able to meet changed requirements. This evolution is summarized graphically by a document of 1808 showing proposals for the rebuilding of the parsonage house at Addingham. The old house was a hall-and-cross-wing building, but the new one was to be a rectangular block giving an entrance hall between Parlour and Dining Room and, at the rear, a stair hall between Study and Kitchen (Plate 268).[18] It may be objected that a parson is not a yeoman, but the similarity between his new house and many yeoman houses emphasizes the fact that the yeomanry lost their special, though always elusive, identity in the course of the 18th century. Their houses had become more and more like those of the gentry and professional classes, and by 1800 not only had local variety of architectural form become the prerogative of lesser members of rural society, but the term 'yeoman' was rapidly ceasing to have any useful meaning.[19] In a new social order there was no yeomanry, and the history of the yeoman house stops with this change in the nature of rural society.

Notes to Chapter 5

[1] For Bean Hole Head, see report in West Yorkshire Metropolitan County Council Archaeology Unit files. For High Hirst, see Stell 1960;, Plate 336.

[2] Other small houses with an open housebody are Little Manor Heptonstall, and Croft, Langfield; see Stell 1960.

[3] For the West Yorkshire single-storey house, see Newton 1976 and Caffyn forthcoming. For the single-storey house or cottage in Wales and Ireland, see Smith 1975, 310–19, and Danaher 1975, 16–36.

[4] BIHR, May 1689.

[5] BIHR, June 1693.

[6] BIHR, May 1705.

[7] BIHR, Oct. 1765. Matthew Bradley is not called 'yeoman', but his wealth (£189) and the description of his house indicate that he was of similar status.

[8] BIHR, Sept. 1693. Jaque Royd still survives and was recorded in the course of this survey. Like Ryecroft, Tong (213), it had an open housebody, but the inventory shows that the kitchen, sited at the lower end and heated by a firehood, was the principal cooking room.

[9] Inventory of Daniel Thorpe, BIHR, Dec. 1693.

[10] BIHR, June 1699.

[11] Other houses with a chamber decorated by plasterwork are noted in Bretton 1967.

[12] Inventory of Robert Nottingham, BIHR, Oct. 1738. The inventories mentioning garrets are those of Michael Craggs of Knottingley,

BIHR, June 1693, and of Thomas Saile of Wentbridge, BIHR, March 1705. See Peters 1969, 195–9, for the use of an upper floor for the storage of grain and of lime plaster for the flooring in Staffordshire farms.

[13] It is not clear how far these upper Calder valley houses with a hearth-passage plan can be seen as 'longhouse derivatives'. It is possible that the longhouse was a common peasant form both in the middle Ages and the post-medieval period, but at much poorer levels of society than are represented by surviving houses, and that the yeomen-clothiers of the late Middle Ages and of the 17th century adapted the type to meet their own specialized requirements. It is equally valid to argue, however, that these houses are closer to the medieval and post-medieval gentry houses built on a hearth-passage plan than to peasant houses of low status.

[14] For the Lancashire houses, see RCHM(E) forthcoming (a).

[15] For Great Jumps and Lower Clough Foot, see Stell 1960.

[16] For the large scale of Samuel Hill's interests, see Atkinson 1956. Dickenson discusses the growing scale of worsted businesses (1974, ch. 4).

[17] Smith 1981, 193.

[18] BIHR, Faculty Plans, Fac 1808/1.

[19] An analysis of Doncaster Nonconformist baptismal registers of the period 1797–1837 showed only two men out of a total of 252 who were called 'yeomen', compared to fifteen who were called 'farmer'; see Unwin 1981, 93.

CHAPTER 6

THE FINAL PHASE OF REGIONAL BUILDING, 1750–1830.

Despite the attention devoted to the yeoman houses in the 17th century, the landscape in many parts of West Yorkshire is dominated not by them but by later houses built by or for men of lesser status. In terms of numbers, the greatest period of house construction, in both rural and urban areas, was after 1750, and gave the first 'permanent' dwellings to a very large proportion of the population. The subject of these later houses is beyond the scope of the present work to explore fully, and this chapter is intended as a summary of the major developments in an age of great change.[1] Developments in industrial organisation make it increasingly difficult to distinguish between 'rural' and 'urban' housing, and there is no hard and fast distinction between the agricultural and the industrial labourer. In spite of the difficulty of definition, the focus of this chapter is the housing of the rural population below the level of the substantial yeomanry, mainly in the 18th and early 19th centuries.

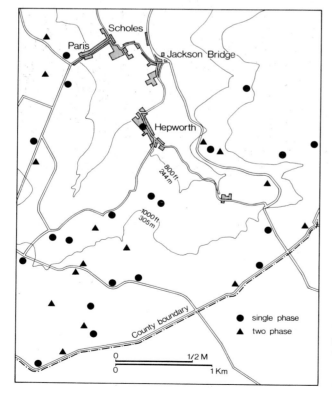

Map 5 Laithe houses in the Hepworth area.

THE LAITHE HOUSE

The laithe house is a building which combines, usually under a single roof and in a simple linear range, a dwelling and a laithe (a dialect word for a combined barn and cowhouse).[2] It is found over a wide area of northern England, but the earliest reliably dated examples come from the Pennine part of West Yorkshire: Bankhouse, Warley (241), is dated 1650 (Plate 269; Fig. 80), and Barrack Fold, Hepworth (85), was built in 1691 (Plate 270). Early laithe houses exist outside the Pennines: a timber-framed example, possibly of the mid 17th century, survives in fragmentary form in the main street of Thorner village. The type did not become common until after 1750; in the second half of the 18th century and the first half of the 19th century many hundreds were built, mainly in the Pennine uplands but also in small numbers in the lowland east.

The laithe house came into its own when the process of parliamentary enclosure, often of marginal land or common, created the need for large numbers of new-built houses serving farms of modest size. Fragmentation of holdings, more practicable in the Pennine part of West Yorkshire than in other parts of the county because of the prevalence there until the middle decades of the 19th century of a system of dual occupation, also created a need for new houses on small farms. Together, enclosure and subdivision gave a pattern of smallholdings over much of upland West Yorkshire. In 1847 the average size of holding

Plate 269
[241] Bankhouse,
Warley, 1650
(*reproduced by permission
of Halifax Antiquarian
Society and Calderdale
District Archives*).

Plate 270 [85] Barrack
Fold, Hepworth, 1691.

in the township of Holme was 25 acres, and when the commons and wastes of Honley were enclosed in 1788 the land was divided into holdings averaging only 14 acres. Doubtless some plots were added to existing farms in the parts of the township already enclosed, but some at least seem to have been established as independent smallholdings with a laithe house as the largest building.[3] Just how common the laithe house became in such regions may be judged from the buildings of an area around Hepworth, an upland township in the south-west of the county. This area was enclosed between 1828 and 1832, and it is likely that many of the isolated farmhouses post-date enclosure. Map 5 shows the existence of twenty-one laithe houses and of a

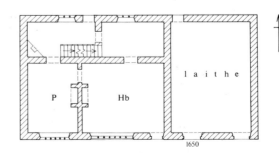

Fig 80 [241] Bankhouse, Warley (after Smith).

Plate 271 [96] Little Horton Green, No. 41, Horton, 1755.

further fifteen houses which were converted to this form. It became not only the smallholder's house *par excellence*, but also the choice for some estate building. The Cragg Hall estate in Erringden provided four identical laithe houses following enclosure in *c*.1836, and it is likely that the two nearly identical laithe houses at Highwood, Kirkburton (109), were built for tenant farmers.[4]

As befits the status of their occupants, most laithe houses are small. There are, it is true, some large and elaborate examples: Bankhouse (241) and Little Horton Green, No. 41, Horton (96) of 1755, both combine a double-pile, double-fronted house with a laithe (Plate 271). Barrack Fold (85) of 1691 had just two main rooms, and very many of the later laithe houses have just a single living room with a service room behind: examples include Upper Hay Hills, Silsden (183), and Fold, Warley (244), of 1831 (Plates 272–4; Fig. 81). The size of the laithe could vary as well; that at Elysium, Cartworth (Plate 275), is much larger than that at, for example, Fold. Some laithes are combined not with a single house but with two or more cottages: at More Pleasant, Longwood (125) of 1851, the builder, a 'woolling manufacturer and farmer', lived nearby and presumably

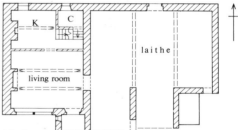

Fig 81 [183] Upper Hay Hills, Silsden.

Plate 272
[53] Cherry
Tree Farm, Eccleshill,
1754.

Plate 273 [183] Upper
Hay Hills, Silsden.

Plate 274 [244] Fold,
Warley, 1831.

Plate 275 [42] Elysium,
Cartworth.

Plate 276 [125] More Pleasant, Longwood, 1851.

had the use of the laithe, using the cottages to house landless tenants (Plate 276).[5]

The popularity of the laithe house was due to its economical form and compact plan. The small farmer, with a few acres of land and a small number of beasts, had no need for, nor could he afford, the detached barns and mistals (cowhouses) built by the wealthier yeomen. His needs were answered perfectly by the laithe house, which represented a saving in walling and roofing, and made the most of the heat from his stock. It was, as we have seen, capable of providing a wide range of accommodation, both

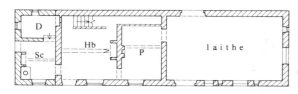

Fig 82 [194] The Longhouse, South Kirkby.

Fig 83 [244] Fold Farm, Warley.

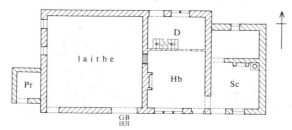

in the dwelling part and in the agricultural area. Furthermore, although in origin designed to serve a predominantly pastoral economy, it could be adapted to meet special agricultural requirements. In the arable-dominated east of the county, for instance, there are examples of the type which lacked a mistal: strictly speaking, The Longhouse, South Kirkby (194), is not a laithe house at all, for the agricultural part was used solely as a barn (Fig. 82). Many laithe houses provide opposed doorways ventilating a threshing floor, and the lack of a doorway in the rear wall of the laithe may be a sign that arable crops were not grown; this is likely to have been the case at Fold (244), high in the moors, where the only crops stored in the laithe would have been the hay mown to feed the livestock (Fig. 83). This specialization was in part forced upon the upland farmers by the poor quality of the land, but in part permitted by improvements in transport in the 19th century which allowed more remote areas to meet the demands of the growing urban centres for dairy produce.

It will be asked whether the laithe house is related to, or derived from, the longhouse. The longhouse has a very long ancestry, having been revealed by excavation on medieval sites, and many surviving examples of 17th-century date exist in various parts of the country, for example on the North Yorkshire moors.[6] The contrast between the North York Moors, where the longhouse was the dominant building type in the post-medieval period, and West Yorkshire, where there are very few indications, either in the documents or in the houses themselves, that the longhouse was ever common, is very marked. The longhouse usually has a hearth-passage plan, a type prevalent in one part of West Yorkshire but used there in a very different sort of special-purpose building, the house of the yeoman-clothier. In West Yorkshire, yeomen of great wealth and those of middling standing provided themselves with detached farm buildings; scores of substantial aisled barns, which were in fact often laithes, as well as many smaller cruck-framed examples, survive in the Pennines. There is as yet no archaeological evidence to suggest that the lesser yeomanry and the poorer levels of rural society built impermanent structures of longhouse form, and when they were able to build permanently, or have permanent houses provided for them, either a simple dwelling detached from farm buildings or a different type of combined dwelling and farm buildings, the laithe house, resulted. This is similar in many respects to the longhouse, but the differences between the two are significant.

The laithe was usually designed both for the storage of crops and the stalling of cattle, but the byre of the longhouse had only the second function.[7] In the longhouse a common entry gives access to both parts of the building, but in the laithe house each part has independent access. Unless archaeological or unequivocal documentary evidence of the nature of peasant building in the medieval and early-modern period in West Yorkshire is one day forthcoming to demonstrate a link between the two types, the laithe house must be seen as a distinct type, designed to meet the needs of a newly emergent class of small farmers in the 17th century and perfectly suited to the circumstances of the 18th and 19th centuries when very many new smallholdings were created. As long as land was being colonized in the Pennines, the laithe house was the most common type of new building over a wide area, but agricultural depression in the late 19th century removed the occasion for further construction. As the tide of colonization receded, many of the upland laithe houses were abandoned and they remain today as derelict monuments to an era which allowed the hill farmer to wrest a living from unfriendly surroundings.

SMALL HOUSES AND COTTAGES

Although some of the smaller 'yeoman' houses considered in Chapter 4 may conceivably have been built by unusually prosperous husbandmen, the housing of the poorer levels of rural society, the numerically dominant classes below the yeomanry, is almost entirely unrepresented in surviving or recognizable structures dating from before 1700. The vast majority of poorer families must have been housed in buildings incapable of standing the test of time or not susceptible of the sort of piecemeal improvement which warranted their retention. The cruck houses of parts of the county may represent the efforts of an upper stratum of this society to build in permanent form, and may be typical of the sort of dwelling inhabited by the poor. Low, single-storey houses are shown on many estate maps of an early date, and there are a very few early survivals of the type: perhaps the best standing example is Sunny Bank, Ovenden (172), which has an attached laithe (Plate 277), and in Middleton, just beyond the county boundary, there

Plate 277 [172] Sunny Bank, Ovenden, 1708.

Plate 278 Red Gables, Middleton, North Yorkshire.

Plate 279 House in Middleton, North Yorkshire.

were two low houses with thatched roofs (Plates 278–9). The single-storey house continued in use in many different forms in West Yorkshire well into the 19th century. Mizpah Cottage, Bardsey-cum-Rigton (23), was probably a squatter's encroachment on the green, while Dove Cottage, Gomersal (76), and a house near Glenesk Farm, Morton (142), were probably the homes of families engaged in farming a small plot of land and in mining or quarrying (Plates 280–3). The single-storey cottage at North Moor House, Kirkburton (110), comprising just a living room and a store room, was probably built for a farm labourer (Fig. 84).

Two-storey small houses built by or for men below the level of the yeomanry began to be common in the 18th century, mainly because the textile industry continued to offer additional income to small landholders. A good example of a house probably built by an independent weaver is Longley, No.177, Almondbury (13; Plate 283), and at Tiding Field, Slaithwaite (190), there is evidence for the long persistence of the system of dual occupation; here

the two-cell house, dated 1783, was later supplemented, first by a workshop, and then by a laithe.

By the late 18th century the system of dual occupation was, however, coming under threat as changes in industrial organization demanded the concentration of the workforce. The landless labourer, almost entirely dependent upon employment in industry for his livelihood, was in no position to build permanent housing on his own account. The provision of housing for this new class is outside the scope of this volume, but many new forms of dwelling

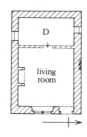

Fig 84 [110] Cottage at North Moor House, Kirkburton.

Plate 280 [23] Mizpah Cottage, Bardsey cum Rigton.

Plate 281 [76] Dove Cottage, Gomersal.

Plate 282 [142] House near Glenesk Farm, Morton.

Plate 283 [13] Longley, No. 177, Almondbury; weaver's house of *c.*1800, with multi-light window for weaving chamber.

Plate 284 Jackson Bridge, Wooldale; terraces of weavers' cottages, *c.*1800.

were developed at this time to meet the needs of the day. This was the age of the terrace and of the back-to-back, provided for the occupants by a number of devices. The landscape of the Pennine part of West Yorkshire is crowded with monuments to the new industrial era; the terraces of weavers' cottages at Jackson Bridge, Wooldale (Plate 284), are typical of the sort of small-scale development which characterized this phase of industrial expansion.[9]

Below the level of the landless labourer were the destitute, the aged, and the infirm. When work was scarce, he might join their ranks, swelling dangerously the number of people dependent on relief. These bottom levels of rural society never engaged in lasting building activity, but a very few benefited from the philanthropy of the rich. Almshouses were established at Methley by the Saviles, at Ledsham Sir John Lewis built almshouses and Lady Betty Hastings an orphanage, and in Ackworth Mary Lowther provided a hospital of six tenements. Perhaps the most unusual charitable foundation is Frieston's Hospital, Warmfield-cum-Heath (245). Built in 1595 by John Frieston to accommodate seven poor men, it takes the form of seven cells grouped around three sides of a top-lit, central open hall which had the only heating and was used for communal living (Plates 285–6; Fig. 85). However, the problem of the poor was immeasurably greater than could be solved by a few almshouses, and the scale of the crisis is finally evident in the institutionalization of the destitute in the draconian workhouses of evil reputation.

The provision of permanent shelter for the poorer members of society ushered in a new age in the history of domestic building. The social upheaval which attended the creation of an urban industrial economy in the 19th century brought new opportunities and new problems. The scale of operations needed to solve the housing demands of the new middle and working classes was unprecedented and the forces underlying the provision of mass housing were radically different from those prevailing in the pre-industrial era. Speculative investment, philanthropy, government legislation and co-operation all played a significant part where before they had been of little or no importance. The end of a predominantly rural society and of the independent evolution of gentry and yeoman houses, as well as the slow dissolution of a recognizable yeomanry, mark the limits of this volume. The houses of the dominant classes of rural society in West Yorkshire continued to change in the 19th century, but henceforth they differed little from houses in many other parts of the country. The acceptance of national ideas on architectural fashion by non-gentry society, represented by the adoption of a standardized form of house, signalled the end of a long process of evolution stretching back to the late Middle Ages.

Plate 285 [245] Frieston's Hospital, Warmfield cum Heath; the outshuts contain cells grouped around the top-lit central hall.

Fig 85 [245] Frieston's Hospital,
Warmfield cum Heath;
isometric view.

Plate 286 [245] Frieston's Hospital; the hall.

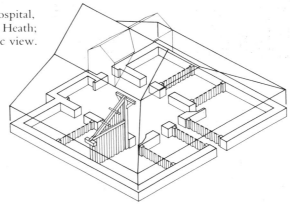

Notes to Chapter 6

[1] The subject of workers' housing in West Yorkshire has been studied by Lucy Caffyn, whose findings will be published in Caffyn forthcoming.

[2] These definitions of laithe and laithe house have been taken from Stell 1960, 100.

[3] For these see WYAS, Headquarters, Tithe Awards, T.10 (Holme) and Enclosure Awards, B.17, 1 (Honley).

[4] For Erringden, see Stell 1960, 109.

[5] 1861 Census Returns RG9/3272, Longwood township, District 14, 115 (held in microfilm form at WYAS, Wakefield Office).

[6] For a review of the longhouse, see Mercer 1975, 34–44. For the North Yorkshire evidence, see Harrison and Hutton 1984, 43, and RCHM(E) forthcoming.

[7] The lower end of the Breton longhouse could have many uses, however; see Meirion-Jones 1982, ch. 10.

[8] One – Red Gables – still survives and is cruck-built. Some early single-storey houses were subsequently heightened by the addition of a second storey.

[9] Many early industrial monuments are illustrated in Thornes 1981.

INVENTORY

This inventory gives brief details of houses recorded in the course of the survey or known from other sources. The number (251) is less than half of those recorded. The complete record may be consulted either at the West Yorkshire Metropolitan County Council's Archaeology Unit, in the Sites and Monuments Record office at 14 St. John's North, Wakefield, on application to the County Archaeologist, or at the National Monuments Record, 23 Savile Row, London W1. Because the two institutions use different territorial units in their record systems, this inventory is designed to provide the information needed to use both archives. It is arranged alphabetically by ancient townships, the boundaries of which were recorded on the First Edition of the Ordnance Survey 6 inch maps. The system of filing records by township was adopted by the Archaeology Unit, and the buildings records can be found there under the township names. The National Monuments Record files according to civil parishes, using the boundaries adopted on 1 April 1974. Some townships lie in a civil parish of the same name, others in a differently named civil parish: Bramley, for example, is in the modern civil parish of Leeds. In these cases, the name of the civil parish is given in parentheses after that of the township. Many townships lie in two or more civil parishes; Warley, for example, is split between Halifax and Sowerby Bridge. In these cases, the names of the civil parishes are indicated as before, and the location of each individual monument is shown by an initial or initials after its name. Thus, in Warley, Peel House (H) lies in Halifax and Roebucks (S/B) in Sowerby Bridge. Each house is identified by a six figure map reference; the exceptions lie in densely built urban areas or have been demolished and their sites are no longer known. All houses are of stone and of two storeys unless the contrary is stated.

ACKWORTH
(1) OLD HALL (SE 438180).
Second half of 17th cent. T-plan, two-and-a-half storeys. Main range contained housebody and parlour with rear range for stair and kitchen (Pls 165, 212, 258; Fig. 86). Entry at rear, opening into housebody alongside gable stack. Secondary entry gives independent access to kitchen. Rebuilt range to N may have provided service rooms. Good quality stair gives access to first-floor chambers and to attic. Attic provides large room in main range, smaller in rear range, possibly used for storage.

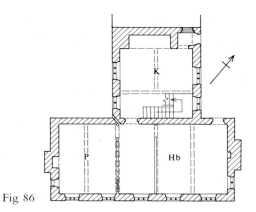

Fig 86

ADDINGHAM

(2) FARFIELD HALL (SE 076515).

1728. Large gentleman's residence, seat of Myers family (Pl. 106, 120, 131; Figs 42, 87). Seven-bay front with pediment over projecting central bays. Three-bay entrance hall flanked by parlours. Transverse corridor between front and rear allows independent access to all rooms and, via stair, to first floor. Service wing at NW angle, connecting with transverse corridor. Main stair rises to landing; first floor also has transverse corridor. Secondary stair from basement to second-floor chambers, contrived only at rear of house. Many later alterations and additions, including ballroom. Hodgson 1933; Pevsner 1967, 195.

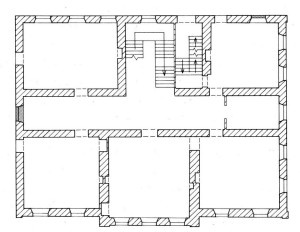

Fig 87 [2] Farfield Hall, Addingham; first-floor plan.

(3) MANOR HOUSE (SE 076498).

Second half 17th cent. Three-cell linear plan. Details of plan obscured by later alterations. Housebody originally heated by firehood, replaced in late 17th cent. by large fireplace. W cell subdivided to give heated parlour to front and service room to N. E cell converted to kitchen in 18th cent. Outshut has datestone 1774.

(4) GILDERSBER COTTAGE (SE 069489).

1717. Two-cell house (Pl. 155; Fig. 69). Entry into main room, inner cell subdivided to give parlour to front and service room and stair to rear. Detached single-cell build possibly labourer's cottage.

(5) CRAGG HOUSE (SE 082476).

1695. Double-pile, double-fronted house. Off-centre entry against wall dividing parlour from housebody. Housebody heated by large fireplace on gable wall. Service rooms and stair at rear.

(6) OVERGATE CROFT (SE 083480).

Second half 17th cent. Similar to (5), but with gable entry.

(7) HIGH HOUSE MOORSIDE (SE 070481).

1697?. Double-pile, double-fronted house with central lobby-entry (Pl. 154). Housebody heated by large fireplace. Service rooms and stair at rear; stair lit by raised window. Refronted in 18th cent.

(8) BROCKA BANK (SE 071485).

1728. Similar in plan to (7) (Fig. 88). Main stack heats

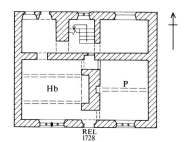

Fig 88

housebody and parlour. Unheated service rooms and stair at rear.

(9) HOUSE AT SMALL BANKS (SE 077486).

1785. Later example of double-pile type, with stacks on gable walls. Off-centre entry into living room. Kitchen at rear? Stair sited centrally, lit by raised window in rear wall.

(10) SMALL BANKS (SE 077486).

1740. Linear plan of three cells. Lobby entry against stack heating housebody and kitchen. Heated parlour. Kitchen has own external doorway. Outshut behind housebody gives sunken pantry.

Houses showing 17th century work.

GHYLL HOUSE (SE 076477); STREET HOUSE FARM (SE 067496); LUMB BECK FARM (SE 077477), 1670 (see Mercer 1975, 219); FIR COTTAGE (approx. SE 082496), 1677; UPPER GATE CROFT (SE 078476); SCHOOL WOOD FARM (SE 071480); FELL EDGE (SE 073478).

Houses with datestones.

LOW HOUSE, 1663, 1675; LOW SANFITT, 1671; OLD SCHOOL, 1669; PARKINSON FOLD, 1677; FRIENDS' MEETING HOUSE, 1689; RAILWAY VIEW, 1730; WINEBECK FARM, 1733; LOWER GATECROFT, 1743; THE GREEN, 1746. (I am grateful to Mrs Kate Mason for much of this information. Precise location of houses not known.)

ADEL CUM ECCUP (Leeds)

(11) CRAG HOUSE (SE 245412).

Timber-framed house, mid 16th cent. (Pl. 180; Fig. 89). Single bay survives in part, showing existence of low open housebody. Outshut form of building after stone casing of mid 17th cent. suggests that timber-framed house may have been aisled. Mid 17th cent. rebuilding of original lower end to give principal block containing housebody and parlour to front and service rooms in outshut at rear.

Fig 89

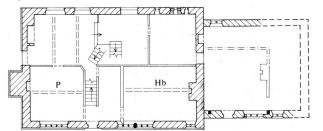

Off-centre entry on main front. Surviving part of timber-framed range possibly turned to service use, later cased in stone as low range of one storey with loft; provision of independent entry suggests continued use as kitchen. Main block retains 'lant stone' and spout for collection of urine used in scouring processes in textile industry.

ALLERTON (Bradford)

(12) SHUTTLEWORTH HALL (demolished, approx site SE 131336).

Second quarter 17th cent. Hall-and-cross-wings, hearth-passage plan, with hall open through two storeys (Fig. 33). Two departures from medieval type of house: lower wing contained heated parlour on main front and rear wing gave kitchen. Best parlour and chamber in upper wing, lit by transomed windows. Sunderland family, engaged in trade in London. Cudworth 1888, 11–12; NMR, Threatened Buildings Records. (I am grateful to Mr. William Walker for permission to redraw plans made in 1955.)

ALMONDBURY (Huddersfield)

(13) LONGLEY, No. 177 (SE 154150).

c.1800. Two main rooms – living room and parlour – on ground floor (Pl. 283; Fig. 90), and possibly one large chamber for weaving on first floor, lit by fourteen-light window. Single-storey scullery added to E; cottage added to W.

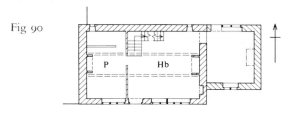

Fig 90

ALVERTHORPE WITH THORNES (Wakefield)

(14) LUPSET HALL (SE 315189).

Built of brick with stone dressings in 1716. Seven bays by five, with wings projecting slightly on entrance and garden fronts. Central area occupied by entrance hall and large stair hall, with reception rooms in wings (Pls 105, 121; Fig. 91). Main stair, possibly later in date, rises to landing giving access to chambers. Service rooms in attached block

to N; this block partly demolished and much altered, but Buck sketch of c.1720 shows probably earlier hall-and-cross-wings house in this position. Hall 1979, 148–9.

AUSTHORPE

(15) AUSTHORPE HALL (SE 369343).

Brick house, 1694, seven bays by three (Pls 103, 116, 128, 129; Fig. 38). Symmetrical facade with projecting central bay with miniature pediment. Three-bay entrance hall flanked by best parlours. Parlours are heated and have good decorative plasterwork and panelling. Main stair and secondary stair to rear. Low kitchen wing, stone-built, at rear. Ambler 1913, 94.

BADSWORTH

(16) KIRKBANK (SE 462149).

Late 17th cent. Linear plan of three cells (Pl. 207; Fig. 92) and three storeys. Lobby-entry against stack heating housebody and kitchen. Parlour to S heated originally. Poorly lit second floor probably used for storage.

Fig 92

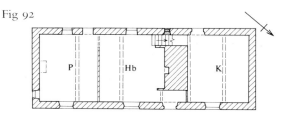

BAILDON

(17) BAILDON HALL (SE 155393).

Timber-framed and stone house (Pls 10, 56, 69, 89; Fig. 93). Timber-framing, probably of late 15th-cent. date, survives in S cross-wing of three bays, apparently built to provide expanded solar and service accommodation; its connection with a pre-existing house is demonstrated by its incorporation on the ground floor of an earlier partition with three grouped doorways. Outer doorways gave access from hall to service rooms or possibly parlours, central doorway opened into passage leading through wing, probably to detached block (kitchen?); mortices in ceiling beams show position of stud walls defining passage. First floor of wing has main chamber (solar?) of two bays and single-bay chamber. Early hall range replaced in

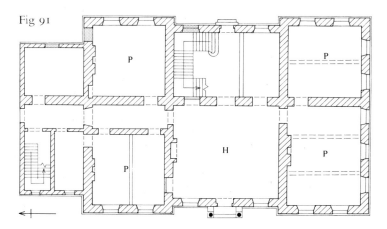

Fig 91

early-mid 17th cent. by present two-and-a-half storey block, giving hall, heated by lateral stack, stair turret, and upper wing. Wing includes heated parlour, with decorative plaster ceiling, and rear parlour raised above half-sunk cellar. S wing cased in stone mid 17th cent. Baildon family.

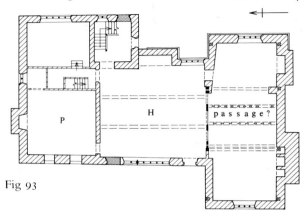

Fig 93

(18) MIDGLEY FARM (SE 143385).
Late 17th cent. Two cells plus outshut. Shop and shop chamber added to W gable c.1800; chamber lit by windows in front, rear and side walls, and has piece door (now blocked) to give easy access for bulky goods into and out of first-floor working area. (Pl. 216)

(19) COTTAGE at Bracken Hall (demolished, SE 131390).
W. P. Baildon noted a cruck-built thatched cottage
> of singularly primitive construction. The rock, which is here covered very thinly with soil, had been bared and levelled, and in it were sunk four holes, one at each corner of a square. Four massive oak timbers, shaped something like a boomerang, or a ship's rib inverted, were inserted into the holes, two and two, so that each pair met at the top. These carried the roof tree, which in turn supported the rafters. A wall has been built round, and a fireplace and chimney in the middle completed the cottage. I saw this picturesque and interesting building in 1884; it was pulled down shortly afterwards

Baildon 1913, 46; a sketch opposite 48 and 49 has been redrawn as Fig. 20.

(20) TRENCH FARM (SE 132386).
1697. Informal double-pile plan with main range supplemented by storeyed rear wing and outshut (Pls 194, 236,

Fig 94

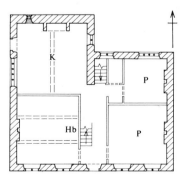

249; Fig. 94). Main front of high quality with symmetrical design and good decorative detail. Doorway opened originally into W room, the housebody. Rear wing provides kitchen with independent entry. Outshut has back parlour and site of original stair, shown by position of raised window in rear wall. Steps below stair led down to cellar. 19th-cent. alterations to plan.

BARDSEY CUM RIGTON
(21) FAIRFIELD COTTAGE (SE 373438).
Second half 17th cent. Three-cell linear plan with continuous outshut (Pl. 220; Fig. 55). Lobby entry between housebody and kitchen; back-to-back firehoods heat both rooms. Parlour probably unheated originally. Timber arcade between main span and outshut.

(22) OAK TREE COTTAGE (SE 363430).
Timber-framed house, second half 16th cent? Three bays of once larger house survive, with two long bays divided by short bay (Pl. 34). Original plan and extent unclear, but remains suggest narrow central bay contained a firehood heating floored-over housebody. Other main bay apparently unheated and possibly open to roof, suggesting use as service room or unheated kitchen. Inferior framing, with light scantling and poor finish to timbers.

(23) MIZPAH COTTAGE (SE 372438).
Single-storey cottage, early 19th cent. (Pl. 280; Fig. 95). Main room heated, second room unheated. Possibly open to roof originally. Position just off green may indicate origin as squatter's cottage.

Fig 95

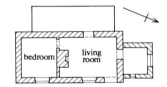

BARKISLAND (Ripponden)
(24) BARKISLAND HALL (SE 060199).
1638. Large double-pile three-storey block with gabled front and projecting upper wing (Pl. 42). Direct entry into single-storey hall. Heated parlours in wings, service rooms at rear. Large number of flues (chimney stack in upper wing has cluster of eight) suggests that many rooms on upper floors also heated (Pl. 61). Gledhill family. Ambler, 1913, 77.

(25) HOWROYD (SE 058194).
1642. Hall-and-cross-wings, hearth-passage plan (Pls 44, 48, 49, 92; Fig. 30). Hall open through two storeys; decoration – fireplace and plaster overmantel, plaster ceiling, gallery, painted glass – shows hall functioned as impressive reception area. 1655 inventory shows *Dineing Parlour, litle Parlour, Maids Parlour* in E wing, *Lower parlour* and *Shopp* in W wing, *Kitchin* and *Buttery* at rear. Kitchen had independent entry, blocked when room converted to dining room. Shop and Shop Chamber used for storage of wood rather than for weaving. Horton family. Inventory of goods of William Horton, Jan. 1655, WYAS, Bradford, Horton MSS, D225; Ambler 1913, 80.

BARWICK IN ELMET

(26) KIDDAL HALL (demolished, SE 394393).
Stone house, early 15th cent., with timber-framed additions of late 15th cent. (Pls. 3, 14). Early part gave low open hall and through passage. Hall had decorative roof with 'fluted rafters gracefully springing from embattled hammer heads, or beams terminating with pendants' (Waddington 1891, 55). Unclear how hall heated originally; probably lateral stack, replaced in early 19th cent. (Kitson 1913). Original house had linear plan, but both ends replaced by timber-framed cross-wings in late 15th cent. Oriel bay added in stone to hall in 1501. Massive stack added to lower wing to give heated kitchen, possibly in late medieval period. House expanded by addition of heated room in outer E wing, late 16th cent. Ellis family. Ambler 1913, 48; Faull and Moorhouse 1981, vol. 3, pl. XB.

BINGLEY

(27) ST. IVES (now Harden Grange, SE 096382).
House designed by James Paine (Pls 132, 137). Main block of five bays, with central three rising to three storeys and crowned by pediment. Principal floor raised above service basement. Entrance hall leads through to semi-circular staircase hall, with reception rooms grouped around. Main stair rises only from ground to first floor, but secondary stair, sited at rear of main block, descends to basement. Kitchen and service rooms removed to separate block at rear of house, linked by short, single-storey corridor. Unclear whether house ever built; present house shows little trace of building of this form. Paine 1767, Pls 63–7.

(28) ELDWICK HALL (SE 126412).
Double-pile, double-fronted house with lobby-entry sited off-centre 1696. Good detail on main front, but not perfectly symmetrical. Housebody and heated parlour to front, back parlour, service room and kitchen at rear; kitchen has independent entry in E gable. Stair rises between front and rear parlours, lit by raised window in W gable; steps to vaulted cellar below. (Pl. 244).

(29) IVY HOUSE (SE 083377).
1676. Double-pile, double-fronted house, with gable entry into housebody (Pl 234; Fig 70). Housebody heated by firehood. Full height range of chambers gives true double-pile.

BOWLING (Bradford)

(30) NEW HALL (SE 170302).
1672. Hall-and-cross-wings, lobby-entry plan (Pl. 46; Fig. 31). Inventory of 1699 shows *Hall* used for sitting and possibly dining. Wings contained heated parlours: *Dineing Roome* in E wing, *Sun Parlour* and *Little Parlour* (both bedrooms) in W wing. *Kitching* at rear of E wing with independent entry (now blocked); kitchen originally heated by firehood. First floor provided many of best private rooms in 1699: *best Chamber*, *Buttery Chamber* and *Sun Chamber* were all heated and furnished as sitting rooms as well as bedrooms. *Garden House* furnished with table, buffetts and chairs. Richardson family. Inventory of Richard Richardson, gent., BIHR, Sept. 1699.

BRAMHAM CUM OGLETHORPE

(31) BRAMHAM PARK (SE 408417).
Country house, built 1700–1710. Eleven-bay main block with low projecting wings on main front and kitchen and chapel wings linked by colonnades (Pl. 93). Principal apartments on piano nobile, grouped around hall (a 30-foot cube) and saloon. Two main staircases. Service rooms confined to basement. Campbell 1717, Pls 81–2; Lees-Milne 1970, 201–5.

(32) MANOR HOUSE (SE 428428).
Early 18th cent. L-plan, with two-storey main range of four bays and two rooms, and rear range of two-and-a-half storeys (Pl. 159; Fig. 96). Entry into side wall at junction of ranges; doorway opens into kitchen. Housebody and parlour at front of house. Outshut behind parlour gives stair area. Later subdivision.

Fig 96

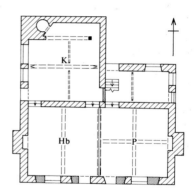

(33) OLD MALT KILN (SE 428429).
Timber-framed house, early 17th cent. Three-and-a-half bays, linear plan with continuous outshut along rear (Pl. 160; Fig. 53). Outshut divided from main span by screen on line of arcade structure. Existence of mid-rail between posts of arcade structure, and height of chambers, suggests that house always floored throughout. Lobby-entry plan probably original. Fragments of firehood survive in roof, which is of common rafter form; timbers of slight scantling. Stone casing of early-mid 18th cent.

(34) HEYGATE FARM (SE 427428).
1682. Three-cell linear plan with lobby-entry (Pl. 161; Fig. 97). Not clear whether stack heating end cell is original; if it is addition, doorway originally opened into end cell rather than into lobby.

Fig 97

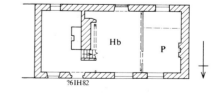

(35) HILLSIDE (SE 426429).
Possibly timber-framed, early 17th cent., cased in stone late 17th cent. Stone house gives long linear range of one-and-a-half storeys (Pl. 162; Fig. 98). Lobby-entry. Lengthened lower end. Access to chambers necessitated

cutting of tie-beams; this and suggestion of posts buried in walls indicates existence of earlier, single-storeyed timber-framed house.

Fig 98

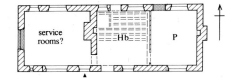

(36) LAUREL FARMHOUSE (SE 427428).
1675. Linear three-cell plan, much altered.

(37) GREENHILL FARM (SE 426428).
Late 17th-cent house of two cells, end lobby-entry. Fragments of timber framing suggest that stone walls have replaced timber.

(38) ASHDOWN COTTAGE (SE 426429).
Early-mid 18th-cent. house of two small cells with central entry into larger (Fig. 99). Smaller cell divided to give two rooms.

Fig 99

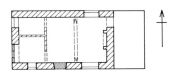

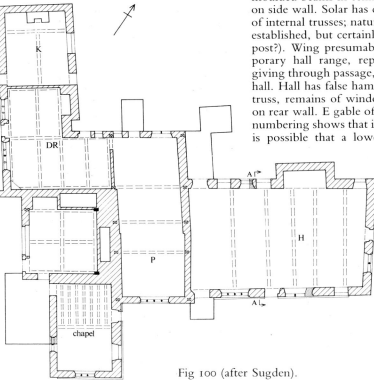

Fig 100 (after Sugden).

BRAMLEY (Leeds)
(39) TOWN STREET, NO. 112.
Timber-framed aisled house, first half 16th cent. Linear plan with hearth-passage entry originally. Only two bays survive, comprising upper end and part of housebody. Upper-bay ground-floor room ceiled with heavy laid-on joists. Later flooring in housebody, together with evidence for fully-framed wall, with no space for a door, at first-floor level between the bays, indicate that housebody was originally open to roof. Aisle survives in area of housebody, but removed in upper bay. Two bays of house demolished: these would have provided firehood for housebody, passage, and lower end. Collar rafter roof with raked queen posts. Later stone casing, partial demolition, and conversion to lobby-entry plan.

BURLEY IN WHARFEDALE (Ilkley)
(40) BURLEY HOUSE (SE 170461).
1783. Gentleman's residence. Five-bay entrance front with three-bay pediment (Pls 101, 124). Entry into single-bay hall leading to stair hall at right angles. Main rooms line garden front: *Dining Room* in centre with canted bay, flanked by *Drawing Room* and *Breakfast Parlour?*. Also on ground floor was *Study*. Detached offices. WYAS, Bradford, Hailstone Collection, Deed Box 1, Case 5, Item 50: 1788 description, with advertisement of house to be let.

CALVERLEY WITH FARSLEY (Pudsey)
(41) CALVERLEY HALL (SE 208369).
Stone and timber-framed house of many periods (Pls 1, 16; Figs 7, 100, 101). Earliest phase to survive is timber-framed solar wing of four bays, *c.*1400, giving parlour, with moulded beams in ceiling, and solar over, heated by stack on side wall. Solar has carved knee-braces up to tie-beams of internal trusses; nature of roof above tie-beam level not established, but certainly of common rafter form (crown-post?). Wing presumably built against earlier or contemporary hall range, replaced *c.*1485 by stone hall block giving through passage, next to solar wing, and large open hall. Hall has false hammer-beam roof, evidence for spere truss, remains of windows with tracery, and lateral stack on rear wall. E gable of hall rebuilt in 17th cent., but truss numbering shows that its roof continued no further to E; it is possible that a lower linear end or cross-wing gave

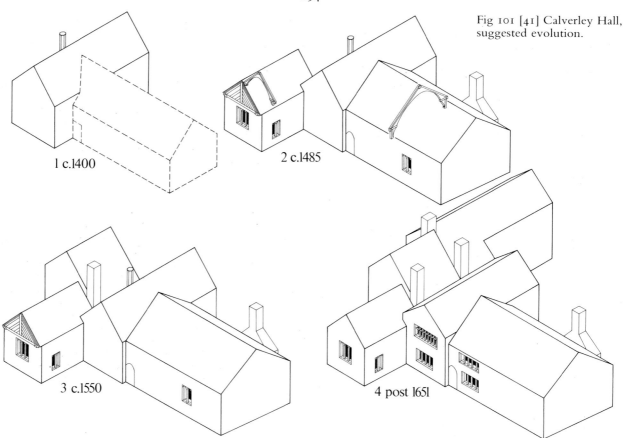

Fig 101 [41] Calverley Hall, suggested evolution.

1 c.1400

2 c.1485

3 c.1550

4 post 1651

rooms at this end, but perhaps more likely that Calverley had end-hall plan. Contemporary with hall is chapel, built to communicate with solar wing and runing S from its SW corner. Chapel open to roof in S bay, but floored over in N bay to give private pew and closet opening out of solar. Chapel roof a smaller version of that in hall; dendrochronological testing suggests that chapel built 1485–95. Later additions include single-cell timber-framed block in angle between solar and chapel (16th cent.), and 17th-cent. stone-built block giving dining room and kitchen, heated respectively by a stone stack and by a firehood. These additions probably post-date 1651, when inventory of goods of Henry Calverley mentions kitchen and buttery in a way suggesting that they lay at E end of hall, possibly in lean-to structure. Likely that work of second half of 17th cent. represents updating, resiting and enlarging of kitchens and dining area. Further 17th-cent. work includes

partial flooring-over of hall, and new chamber lit by mullioned window. House ceased to be seat of Calverley family when Esholt Hall (59) built 1706–10; house subdivided, floor inserted through hall range. Inventory of Henry Calverley, *Bradford Antiq (old series)* 1 (1888), 172. Dendrochronology report by Jennifer Hillam, University of Sheffield, in record file for Calverley Hall, NMR and Archaeology Unit. Photographs of chapel wing in Faull and Moorhouse 1981, vol. 3, Pls XIIA, B.

CARTWORTH (Holmfirth)

(42) ELYSIUM (SE 133054).
Laithe house, *c.*1845. Built after Cartworth Enclosure Award of 1832 on moorland at 1100 feet above sea level. Dwelling gave living room to S and parlour to N (Pl. 275; Fig. 102). Large laithe has mistal at E end, entered through

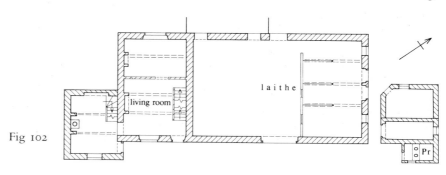

Fig 102

doorways in gable wall, and extensive area for storage. Outbuildings include privy, added cottage or scullery, and later attached cowshed.

CRIGGLESTONE (Crigglestone and Wakefield)
(43) KETTLETHORPE HALL (W) (SE 332166).
1727. Gentleman's residence, with five-bay main block flanked by single-storey wings (Pl. 100; Fig. 103). Entry into single-bay hall leading to stair hall at rear and to reception rooms on either side. Extent of 1727 build not clear due to later rebuilding at rear. Norton family.

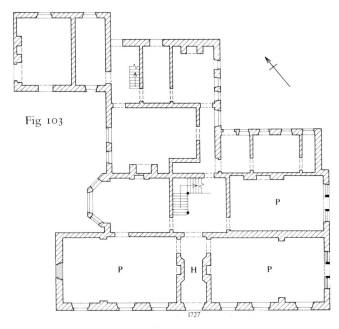

Fig 103

(44) STONEY LANE, NOS. 2, 4 (C) (SE 322155).
Stone and timber-framed house, 16th cent. Linear plan, two bays survive (Fig. 22). Low walls suggest either open housebody with one-and-a-half storey ends, or completely storeyed house with low chambers throughout. Evidence of early plan form (hearth-passage) strengthens case for open housebody. Housebody heated by firehood. Hipped roof at upper end. Lower end rebuilt in first half 17th cent. as two-storey stone cross-wing with heated parlour; rebuilding involved destruction of original passage area, with new doorway provided in wing on line of earlier entry. W wing added in 19th cent. Hall range cased in stone.

(45) HOLLINGTHORPE FARM (C) (SE 312151).
1725. Double-pile, double-fronted house (Pls 246, 263; Fig. 79). Symmetrical elevation, with central doorway opening directly into housebody. Rear rooms include kitchen, with back door, and half-sunk cellar at NW corner. Stair sited centrally at rear; closed string, moulded handrail, turned balusters. Attic storey lit by window in gable wall.

(46) PUG COTTAGE (C) (SE 328160).
Late 17th cent. Two-cell house, entry into housebody at end of front wall. Housebody heated by extruded stack on gable wall; parlour unheated. Later rear extension reuses plaster panel reading 'NSA 1683', possibly recording date of main build.

CUMBERWORTH
(47) GILL GATE (SE 232106).
1642. Two-cell with rear outshut (Fig. 66). Off-centre doorway opened originally into lobby against firehood heating housebody. Unheated parlour to E, service rooms in outshut. 19th-cent. alterations include removal of firehood; site occupied by present stair. Added fireplaces in housebody and parlour.

DALTON (Huddersfield)
(48) RAWTHORPE OLD HALL (SE 162176).
Timber-framed house, early 16th cent. built on hall-and-cross-wings plan with central open hall, hearth-passage entry (Pl. 5; Fig. 104). Hall and fire-area of two full bays, with passage in half-bay to E. Upper (W) wing gave parlour to S on ground floor, two-bay solar or chamber on first floor; central truss of solar has short king-post on collar. Stair bay in angle between upper wing and hall range at front of house. Lower (E) wing probably gave service rooms and possibly lower parlour on ground floor. First floor has chambers, single-bay to N, two-bay to S; central truss of larger has principal rafters rising from stub tie-beams; principal rafters rise to support ridge and are linked by a collar at apex. Later underbuilding shows that E wing jettied on S gable (Pl. 23). Piecemeal casing of house in 17th cent. and later.

Fig 104

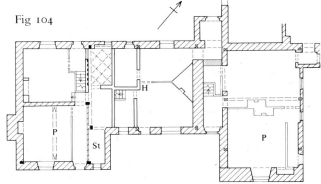

DENBY (Denby Dale)
(49) MANOR FARM (SE 226073).
1654. Hall-and-cross-wing plan (Pls 204, 223; Fig. 105). Main range, unusually, of three cells, with lobby-entry

Fig 105

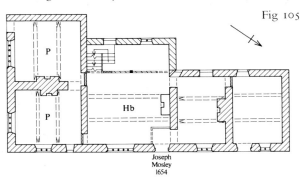

Joseph
Mosley
1654

into housebody. Outer rooms, both unheated originally, perhaps for service and dairying. Cross-wing provides two parlours. Outshut behind housebody added in early 18th cent. to provide service room, stair and cellar.

(50) NETHEREND FARM (SE 246078).
c.1725. Main block of four bays with off-centre doorway into housebody, parlour to E (Pls 238, 254; Fig. 106). Fashionable detail of main front contrasts with traditional features of rear range, which has outshut along W side, mullioned windows with decorative hood-mould and elaborate doorway. Inferior detail reflects function: range gives kitchen and service rooms, with stair in angle with main block. Outbuildings include cruck-built barn (for a report on this, see West Yorks Archaeology Unit Sites and Monuments Record).

Fig 106

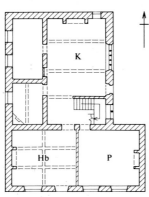

DRIGHLINGTON (Morley)
(51) LUMB HALL (SE 227293).
Mid 17th cent. U-plan, with three-gabled elevation (Pls 55, 62, 63, 73, 88; Fig. 28). Lobby-entry between hall and kitchen, with parlour at upper end. Hall, parlour and best chambers heated by decorative fireplaces; some decorative plasterwork. Main stair rises out of NW corner of hall; steps to cellar below. Stair and service room give double-pile plan. Kitchen, heated by large fireplace, has secondary stair rising to undecorated chamber. Brooke family. Ambler 1913, 78.

EAST ARDSLEY (Morley)
(52) OLD HALL (SE 305252).
1622, 1652 and later (Figs 26, 36). W wing of 1622, providing large parlour and chamber, probably added to earlier hall. Latter replaced in 1652 by existing hall range, designed to give nearly symmetrical elevation. Gabled porch shelters entry into middle of hall. Hall, originally decorated by plaster overmantel, has character of entrance area giving access to best parlours and, via stair, to best chambers. Bolection-moulded panelling survives in chamber over E parlour. Central rear wing built second half 17th cent., probably to provide kitchen. Shaw family. Ambler 1913, 72–3; Batty 1889.

ECCLESHILL
(53) CHERRY TREE FARM (SE 189352).
1754. Laithe house (Pls. 190, 272; Fig. 107). Dwelling part

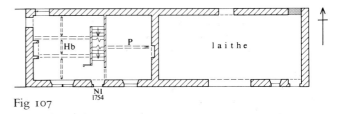

Fig 107

of two cells, with central entry. Housebody heated by fireplace on gable wall. Unclear whether parlour heated originally. Steps below stair to cellar under parlour. Laithe larger than dwelling, with main area for storage of crops and mistal at E end.

ELLAND CUM GREETLAND (Elland)
(54) NEW HALL (SE 119209).
Timber-framed house, built c.1490 by Nicholas Savile. Hall-and-cross-wings, hearth-passage plan (Pls 4, 19; Fig. 3). Hall range of two bays, giving open hall of one-and-a-half bays, heated by firehood, and passage. Hall had dais canopy: remains of embattled rail forming its springing survives at upper end. Upper (W) wing had parlour to S, rooms to N, with chambers over. Extruded stack on W wall heated parlour and chamber originally, for framing reportedly left gap for original stack. E wing has room (lower parlour?) to S, heated by large fireplace in stack certainly older than 17th-cent. stone casing and maybe original. Stair of late medieval house in bay at rear between upper wing and hall range. 16th-cent. work includes reflooring of wings to give compartmented ceilings in parlours. House cased in stone in various stages in 17th cent. Open hall retained, firehood replaced by stone chimney stack with decorative plaster overmantel, gallery inserted. Giles 1981.

(55) CRAWSTONE HALL (SE 072211).
1631. Double-pile house with three main rooms to front (Pl. 87). Three gables to front and rear. Entry in rear wall. Fenestration (mullioned windows on ground floor, mullioned and transomed windows on first floor) suggests best rooms on first floor. New parlour wing added c.1700. Ambler 1913, 76; Pacey 1964, 4.05–6, 4.21.

(56) FLEECE INN (SE 105210).
Early 17th cent. Hall-and-cross-wings, hearth-passage plan. Housebody and parlours make up main front, service rooms and kitchen wing at rear.

EMLEY
(57) THORNCLIFFE (SE 250134).
Mid 17th cent. U-plan (Pl. 221; Fig. 57). Flat elevation with three gables and single-storey porch. Lobby-entry between housebody and kitchen; housebody heated by fireplace, kitchen by firehood. Heated parlour at front of E wing. Rear of W wing has half-sunk cellar, lit by window at mezzanine level; window above, also at half-storey level, possibly designed to light stair landing.

ERRINGDEN (Erringden and Hebden Royd)
(58) FROST HOLE (H/R) (SE 000249).
First half 17th cent. Two cells survive from this date: housebody (open to roof) and storeyed end cell giving

parlour and service room on ground floor. Extent of original house masked by later rebuilding and additions. Stell 1960, 79–80 (I am grateful to Mr. Stell for permission to publish, in redrawn form, his section as Fig. 47).

ESHOLT (Idle)
(59) ESHOLT HALL (SE 188396).
Gentleman's residence, built by Sir Walter Calverley 1706–10 (Pl. 104). Seven bays by seven, with small inner court. Later alterations obscure details of original plan, but likely that best rooms lined S and E fronts. Large windows on first floor suggest that chambers had superior use. References to construction in Sir Walter's diary: e.g., in 1706 'in the first week in May we laid the foundation of my new house at Esholt, having made preparation for the work in the winter before, and Joseph Pape was the chief mason'. Margerison 1886.

FARNLEY TYAS (Kirkburton)
(60) WOODSOME HALL (SE 180144).
Timber-framed house, first half 16th cent. Hall-and-cross-wings, hearth-passage plan (Pls 7, 17, 70; Figs 4, 8). Hall range of six short bays, with passage occupying one bay and open hall five. Hall heated by firehood. Decorative central truss with arch-braces to collar, meeting at plain boss. Roof of principal rafter and collar form, with two tiers of windbraces (now removed); unusually these extend over passage area. Cross-wings have king-post trusses. Wings provided parlours on ground floor: Low, Dining and Upper parlours mentioned in Kaye Commonplace Book. Outer N wing, projecting from NE corner of upper wing, may have been chapel originally, converted to two parlours 'for lakk of Rowme' in late 16th cent. Stone casing of hall range and wings in 17th cent. Present courtyard plan may be early creation. N range of mid 17th cent perhaps added to provide lodgings for visiting households: extruded stacks on N wall show existence of six fireplaces; remains of decorative plasterwork on ground and first floors. Ambler 1913, 59 (plan and elevations pl. LXIII); Redmonds 1982, 7–10 (I am grateful to Mr. Redmonds for allowing me to use his work on the Kaye Commonplace Book, a microfilm copy of which is kept at Huddersfield Central Library).

FOULBY (Huntwick with Foulby and Nostell)
(61) NOSTELL PRIORY (SE 404175).
Country house, seat of the Winn family, built 1733–50 to designs by James Paine. Thirteen-bay main block with, in the original scheme, four pavilions linked by quadrant colonnades. Similar to Bramham in having principal rooms on piano nobile, with apartments and common rooms grouped around hall and saloon. Two main staircases and two service stairs. Rusticated basement contained servants' rooms: *Stewards Parlour, Servants' Hall, Butler's Pantry, Common Eating Room, Housekeeper's Room,* bedrooms. Kitchen in only one of pavilions to be built. Alterations and additions by Adam, 1765–85. Hussey 1955, 187–94; Woolfe and Gandon 1767, Pls 70–73.

FULSTONE (Holmfirth)
(62) BUTTERLEY HALL (SE 166081).
1742. Small, L-shaped, minor gentleman's residence. Three-bay front made up of hall and parlour, with central entry directly into housebody (Pl. 110; Fig. 39). Service rooms and, probably, further parlours, in rear range. Lack of ground-floor reception rooms compensated for by use of chamber for dining: visiting in 1744, Arthur Jessop 'went up into the room to dinner'. Two-and-a-half storeys. Minor branch of Kaye family. Whiting 1952, 94.

(63) MELTHAM HOUSE (SE 168076).
Late 17th cent. Two cells with outshut. Rebuilding of front wall in 19th cent. and additions to W gable removed evidence for original entry position. Housebody heated by firehood on W gable, parlour by extruded stack on E gable. Outshut lacks original divisions, but grooves in soffits of beams reveal positions of timber screens. Small back parlour behind housebody, with stop-chamfered joists. Stair sited centrally in outshut, rising into chamber over housebody.

(64) WEST ROYD FARM (SE 174093).
c.1800. Double-pile, double-fronted house (Pls 256, 264; Fig. 78). Off-centre doorway into living room, smaller parlour to N. Rear rooms include kitchen to NW with independent entry, probably unheated originally. Stair central at rear: plain stair with simple newels and rails rising to first-floor landing. Steps to cellar below.

GARFORTH
(65) PECKFIELD HOUSE (SE 429317).
c.1825. Brick house, double-pile, with original service wing set back from main front (Pl. 267). Near-symmetrical elevation, with central entry into entrance hall lit by fanlight. Main reception rooms to front. Stair hall sited centrally at rear. Wing contains kitchen, has independent entry and staircase to chamber for servants.

GOMERSAL (Batley and Gomersal)
(66) OAKWELL HALL (B) (SE 217271).
Stone house, 1583, built by Batt family on standard medieval plan of hall-and-cross-wings with hearth-passage entry (Pls 43, 51, 52, 68, 91; Fig. 32), but with innovations of single-storey hall, kitchen within house at rear of lower wing. 1611 inventory describes house: *hall* for reception; upper wing with heated *Great Parlore* for dining, heated *Little Parlore* for sleeping, *Maydes Parlore, Buttrie, Inner Buttrie* and *Mylkhouse*; lower wing with *Tavourne, Kitchine* and *New Parlor*. First floor includes *Hall Chambor*, showing hall was then single-storeyed. Structural breaks in upper wing and mention of New Parlor suggest prolonged building activity. Significant remodelling of house c.1630–40, when single-storey hall replaced by hall open through two storeys; front wall of hall rebuilt to provide large window, firehood backing onto passage replaced by lateral stack; gallery, stair, elaborate screen and plaster ceiling inserted to make hall an impressive entrance area. Plaster ceiling inserted into Great Parlour. Inventory of goods of Robert Batt, 1611, in Foster 1954; Ambler 1913, 55; Woledge 1978.

(67) POLLARD HALL (G) (SE 208261).
Timber-framed house, late medieval. Cased in stone 1659, retaining hall open through two storeys. Hall has gallery and plaster ceiling. Ambler 1913, 84.

(68) PEEL HOUSE (G) (SE 206267)
Timber-framed house, cased in stone and remodelled, probably in 1651 (date formerly on plasterwork). Stone house has irregular double-pile plan with outshuts and rear wings (Pls 151, 178, 201; Fig. 60). Three-gabled facade. Entry into housebody at opposite end to fireplace; housebody has richly carved overmantel. *Dining Room* to E, heated and with plaster ceiling and wooden overmantel. *Kitchin* behind, formerly heated by firehood and with independent entry. 1699 inventory suggests use of housebody as reception and sitting room, with SW room (*Upper Parlour?*) as bedroom. Rear rooms include head of household's *Lodging Room, Maid Servants' Lodging roome, Pantry,* cellars. Some chambers well-furnished for superior use, others for servants (*Men Servants' Lodging room*) and storage. Outhouses include back kitchen (for brewing and baking), *Madder House, shopp* and *shopp chambers*, the contents of which show substantial involvement in textiles. Dual occupation shown by list of agricultural goods and crops, with £25 worth of corn in the ground. Cadman 1930, 40; inventory of goods of Richard Peel, BIHR, Nov. 1699; sketches by John Dixon, Thoresby Soc. Library.

(69) HIGHFIELD FARM (B) (SE 222266).
Mid 17th cent., large and similar in form to (68). Double-pile, with rear wings and outshut. Three-gabled facade, entry into housebody at opposite end to firehood. Housebody and parlour lit by mullioned and transomed windows, other rooms by mullioned windows.

(70) OLD HALL (B) (SE 223264).
1700. Double-pile, double-fronted house. Central entry direct into housebody. Housebody and parlour heated by fireplaces in stacks on spine wall dividing front rooms from rear. Rear rooms unheated, suggesting cooking in housebody. Stair sited centrally at rear: good quality woodwork, with open splat balusters, moulded handrail, square newels, ball finials. NMR Threatened Buildings Records.

(71) SIGSDEN HOUSE (G) (SE 207265).
Three-cell linear plan with outshut along rear. Position of original entry unknown. Doorway in rear wall has datestone '1634 N K', but lack of detail of this date suggests reuse, perhaps *c.*1700.

(72) LANESIDE HOUSE (B) (SE 212258).
Late 17th cent. Three-cell linear plan, with outshut and rear wings.

(73) MAZEBROOK FARM (G) (SE 193267).
1654. L-plan, with two rooms – housebody and parlour – in main range, kitchen behind housebody and outshut behind parlour (Pl. 195; Fig. 67). Gable entry into housebody. Housebody and kitchen heated by firehoods originally.

(74) LANDS FARM (G) (SE 194263).
House of two builds (Pl. 198; Fig. 108). Earlier, possibly mid-late 17th cent., gives low two-storey block comprising kitchen, heated by firehood on gable wall and with independent entry, and chamber. Main block, dated 1693, built at slight angle; provides main rooms to front and service rooms in outshut to rear; central entry.

(75) EGYPT FARM (G) (SE 194261).
Late 17th-cent. house of two main cells and rear outshut.

Fig 108

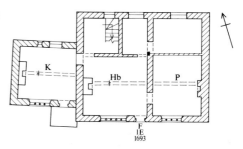

Central entry into housebody. Housebody probably heated by firehood against gable wall. Parlour unheated originally. Timber arcade and screens between front rooms and rear.

Houses with evidence of 17th and early 18th-cent. work.
THE RYDINGS (SE 222258); LITTLE COURT (SE 202252), similar in plan to (72); RICHMOND GRANGE (SE 206269); HOUSE AT LITTLE GOMERSAL (SE 205252); CROSS HOUSE (SE 207265); UPPER LANE HOUSE, dated 1626 (site unknown; Cadman 1930, 108).

(76) DOVE COTTAGE (G) (SE 198253).
Single-storey house, early 19th cent. (Pl. 281; Fig. 109). Two rooms; doorway, now window, opened into main room. Later addition in brick.

Fig 109

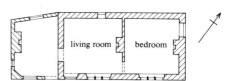

GUISELEY (Aireborough)
(77) THE RECTORY (SE 194420).
1601. Main front of four rooms, permitting central entry into passage. Facade not perfectly symmetrical, but gables at ends of elevation and central porch show concern for design (Pl. 84). Outshut and wing at rear. Ambler 1913, 58.

HAVERCROFT WITH COLD HIENDLEY
(78) NEWSTEAD HALL (demolished, site SE 401148).
1708. Gentleman's residence. Double-pile plan with service wing at rear (Pls 98, 122, 138; Fig. 110). Central entry, originally opening into single-bay entrance hall leading through to stair hall. Heated reception rooms in three corners of main block, backstairs and service rooms in fourth corner adjacent to service wing. NMR, Threatened Buildings Records.

HAWKSWORTH (Aireborough)
(79) HAWKSWORTH HALL (SE 169416).
Late 16th or early 17th cent. Hall-and-cross-wings plan (Pls 59, 77, 127). Single-storey *Hall* and *Great Chamber* over, both heated by lateral stack. Great Chamber decorated by segmental vaulted plaster ceiling of 1611; on structural grounds this may be an addition, for joists holding it are tenoned into roof trusses at one end only, their other end being halved over the arch-braces of the trusses (of short king-post on collar form). Lack of elaboration of roof,

Fig 110

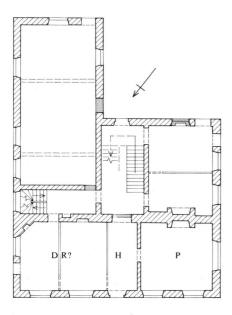

D|R?   H   P

however, suggests ceiling intended from inception. 1657 inventory shows wealth of family and complexity of domestic arrangements. Rooms include many private apartments (*Mr. Bayldon Chamber, Sir Richard Chamber, Young Mr. Chamber, Mr. Parkinson Chamber*), two nurseries, servants' rooms (*Maids Chamber, Cooke Lodging*), and long list of service rooms (*Butterry, Kitchinge, Deary, pastry, Backha house, Booting house, Larder, Low Seller, Storehouse, Brewhouse*). 1664 additions to E provided more parlours and a kitchen, producing elongated plan. Alterations in second half 18th cent. converted original E cross-wing into roughly central entrance and staircase hall. Inventory of goods of Sir Richard Hawksworth, 1657, Sheffield City Libraries, Bright Papers, 89a/1; Cliffe 1969, 371–2; Ambler 1913, 62; WYAS, Yorks Archaeol Soc., DD161.

HAWORTH (Keighley)
(80) MOULD GREAVE (SE 024355).
1742. Linear three-cell plan with outshut behind housebody (Pl. 189; Fig. 111). Hearth-passage entry. Housebody heated by fireplace which, in absence of kitchen, must have been used for cooking. Heated upper and lower parlours. Later alterations include expansion of outshut along rear, blocking of passage by insertion of stair, and construction of large warehouse, now demolished, against W gable.

Fig 111

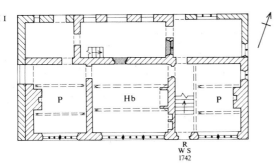

P   Hb   P

R
W S
1742

HEATON (Bradford)
(81) ROYDS HALL (SE 136361).
Hall-and-cross wings house of two builds (Fig. 50). E wing probably mid 17th cent., giving large parlour, heated by extruded stack, and service rooms; wing added to earlier timber-framed house? House assumed present form in second half 17th cent. Hall range, W wing and rear wing replace timber-framed house. Lobby-entry in W wing against stack heating housebody and parlour. Rear wing gives kitchen, entered independently by original rear door. Service rooms at rear of cross-wings. Built by Rhodes family, maltsters. Inventory of goods of Timothy Rhodes, BIHR, July 1722 (I am grateful to Mr. George Sheeran for bringing this and related documents to my attention).

HECKMONDWIKE
(82) OLD HALL (SE 214239).
Late medieval, timber-framed, aisled house. Hall-and-cross-wing, hearth-passage plan (Pls 172, 173; Fig. 46). Open housebody heated by firehood, dais canopy originally present over upper end, springing from side wall of cross-wing. Wing gave two rooms on both floors. Linear lower end. Evidence in wing that ground-floor walls were of stone, with timber-framing above a mid-rail. Alterations of first half 17th cent.: hall range cased in stone, retaining open housebody but inserting plaster ceiling at tie-beam level. Addition of kitchen wing suggests cooking removed from housebody at this time. Cross-wing cased in stone in various stages; extruded stack provides fireplaces for parlour and chamber over. 19th-cent. alterations include subdivision into cottages and loss of much of lower end at construction of railway line.

HEPTONSTALL
(83) GREENWOOD LEE (SD 970295).
Hall-and-cross-wing house with central rear wing (Pl. 169). Date of 1712 on porch but unclear if this refers to construction of house. Hearth-passage plan. Inventory of 1718 lists well-furnished *Hall body* (for sitting, reception, dining); *Great parlour* (for sitting and possibly dining); *Little parlour* (for sleeping); *Kitchin* (for cooking); *back kitchen* and various service rooms. Clearly within the house, probably below the passage, was *Shop*, full of cloth presses, plates, papers, shears. Sutcliffe had stock of 86 White Kerseys and a stake in agriculture (shown also by the large barn adjacent to house); the value of all his goods amounted to £670. Inventory of goods of Robert Sutcliffe, BIHR, July 1718; Stell 1960, 45–6.

(84) LONGFIELD HOUSE (SD 987280).
*c.*1730. Double-pile, double-fronted house (Pls 203, 248, 255, 259; Fig. 73). Originally symmetrical main front with central entry, cross-windows. Doorway probably opened directly into housebody. Rear has two parlours and stair hall; stair, lit by raised window in rear wall, rises to first-floor landing. Stair hall decorated with plaster ceiling. Steps beneath stair give access to vaulted cellar. Detached single-storey block to W probably provided kitchen. Number of flues in gable stacks suggests four chambers heated. Attic lit by windows in gable walls.

HEPWORTH (Holmfirth)

(85) BARRACK FOLD (SE 163066).

1691. Laithe house, with dwelling area of two cells (Pls 186, 270; Fig. 112). Lobby-entry against heck of firehood heating housebody. Parlour and service room to W. Laithe has large doorway in central area and small doorway to mistal at E end.

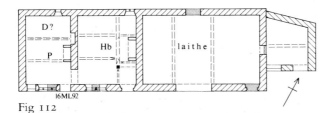

Fig 112

HIPPERHOLME WITH BRIGHOUSE (Brighouse)

(86) COLEY HALL (SE 128269).

17th-cent. house, form and extent unclear, but possibly with detached kitchen; block of two cells at rear has large chimney stack, no sign of kitchen within main block (Pls 74, 112). Remodelling of c.1730 gave symmetrical nine-bay facade. Entry directly into hall, with new stair hall to rear.

(87) SMITH HOUSE (SE 124426).

Timber-framed house, late medieval, cased in stone 1672. Early house of single-aisled form, with open aisled housebody, cross-wing at upper end (Fig. 113). Stone casing retains open housebody, but with new stack and lobby-entry. Lower end of stone house in form of cross-wing, with *Dineing room* to front and *kitchine* to rear. Upper wing provided *Sun parlor* and *North parlor*. Firehood heating kitchen replaced in 1726 by stone stack. Further additions at rear. Inventory of goods of John Brooke of Smith House, BIHR, March 1689.

Fig 113

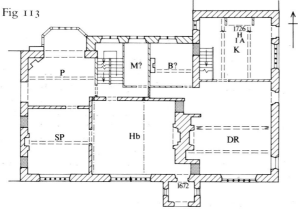

(88) TOWNGATE, NOS 18, 19, 20 (SE 122257).

Formerly dated 1693? Double-pile, double-fronted house with display facade; two gables, stepped windows to chambers, oval windows in gables. Entry into bay projecting from W wall, giving gable-entry form (Fig. 114). Housebody originally heated by firehood and decorated with plaster frieze. Heated parlour next to housebody. Rear range provides heated back parlour and kitchen.

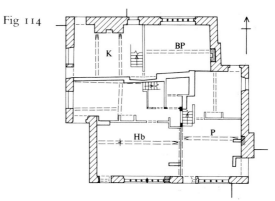

Fig 114

HONLEY (Holmfirth)

(89) UPPER OLDFIELD (SE 133101).

Cruck-built house, mid 16th cent., cased in stone and enlarged mid 17th cent. Early house had linear plan, probably four bays long, with hearth-passage entry (Pl. 28; Figs 16, 115). Central area gave open housebody of one-and-a-half bays, the half-bay largely occupied by firehood backing onto passage. End-bays replaced, but probably provided open or one-and-a-half storey parlour and service ends. 17th-cent. alterations include rebuilding of upper end in cross-wing form, with heated parlour, and casing of main range in stone, retaining open housebody. 18th-cent. rebuilding of lower end in two-storey form; unfinished walling of upper storey indicates intention to provide chamber over housebody. This never effected, leading to survival of cruck trusses. Low chamber created over housebody only in 19th cent. Cruck barn existed to W of house. Walton 1948, 64.

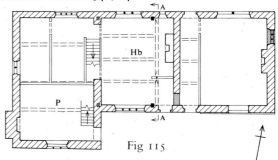

Fig 115

(90) HOUSE opposite Upper Oldfield (SE 133101).

Cruck-built dwelling, second half 16th cent? Originally timber-framed, with linear plan of unknown length; two bays survive, with two cruck trusses (one buried in later stone gable wall). Stone casing, c.1700, creating single-storey dwelling with end-lobby entry against firehood heating housebody (Pl. 29). Clarke and Lunn 1964.

(91) CHURCH STREET, NOS 10, 12, 14 (SE 138120).

1692. L-plan, with three rooms in main range and one in wing to rear (Fig. 116). Lobby-entry between housebody and parlour. Kitchen to N, heated by firehood against N gable originally. Rear wing also heated, probably providing back parlour. Early 18th-cent. addition at rear, giving two-cell block, each cell with independent entry. Outer room, heated originally by firehood, linked to main block by passage, and may have been back kitchen; inner room and first floor possibly for agricultural use.

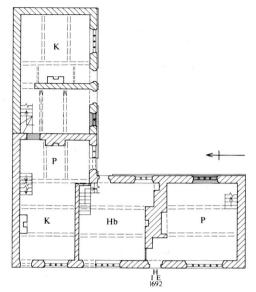

Fig 116

HORBURY

(92) HORBURY HALL (SE 295183).

Stone and timber-framed house, with later brick casing. Remains comprise three-bay block (Figs 1, 6, 10); dendrochronology indicates a post-1478 date for construction. This block built to replace earlier hall range up against pre-existing wing of perhaps five bays, a size suggesting combined service and solar functions. Through passage divided wing from hall block. Open hall, of two bays, with evidence for spere truss, lateral stack, dais canopy; decorative roof, with king-post trusses (with carved central tie-beam) and arch-braced intermediate trusses and cusped windbraces (Pl. 11). Single-bay W end has heavy joists showing position of stair; small size of this bay and absence from it of any decoration suggests that E wing continued to provide superior private rooms. Hall block front wall of stone on ground floor and timber-framed above. Later work includes addition of wing to W, probably in 16th cent., conversion of main block to lobby-entry, two-storey house in early 18th cent., and demolition of both early E wing and W wing. Documentary evidence for use of detached kitchen in 16th cent. Michelmore and Sugden 1980; dendrochronological work by Jennifer Hillam, University of Sheffield; WYAS, Yorkshire Archaeol Soc. MD225/1572,m.1 (ref. in Wakefield Manor Court Roll to detached kitchen).

HORTON (Bradford)

(93) HORTON HALL (demolished, SE 157321).

1675–80. Gentleman's residence, seat of Sharp family (Fig. 35). Near symmetrical elevation given by central entry in main range, which was of two rooms (hall, open through two storeys, and parlour) and flanked by cross-wings. Entry into lobby against stack heating hall and parlour. Rear of main range had entrance hall, with plaster ceiling, and two staircases, both with steps to cellars below. Service

rooms in rear wings. E wing rebuilt in 19th cent. to give modern suite of reception rooms. Ambler 1913, 87; RCHM(E) 1963, 67; NMR, Threatened Buildings Records.

(94) LITTLE HORTON HALL (SE 155320).

Second half 17th cent. Double-pile, double-fronted house, entry at side into housebody (Pl. 235; Fig. 72). Two-gabled elevation. Housebody heated by large fireplace, parlour originally heated by fireplace in extruded stack. Rear rooms include kitchen at NE corner, heated by firehood. Original internal walls were of timber. Roof trusses with short king-posts on collars.

(95) HILL END HOUSE (SE 132311).

1714. Two cells plus outshut along rear (Pls 192, 237). Symmetrical elevation with central doorway. Plan altered but probably housebody and parlour to front, kitchen and service rooms to rear; kitchen heated by large fireplace.

(96) LITTLE HORTON GREEN NO. 41 (SE 154321).

1755. Laithe house. Dwelling area is double-pile, double-fronted house, with housebody and parlour at front, kitchen, back parlour or service room at rear (Pl. 271; Fig. 117). Stair sited centrally at rear, lit by raised stair window. Kitchen/scullery added to E gable in 19th cent. Laithe, slightly larger than dwelling, altered recently.

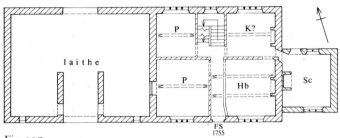

Fig 117

HUDDERSFIELD

(97) NEWHOUSE HALL (SE 155197).

House with early 17th-cent. wing and late 17th-cent. hall range (Pls 114, 123). Early wing probably built against pre-existing hall range to provide new main parlour and chamber; both rooms heated by good fireplaces. Hall range replaced c.1690 by existing build, which has direct entry into hall. Hall heated by lateral stack and decorated by plaster ceiling. Stair rises out of one corner of hall; stair well has contemporary plaster ceiling. 19th-cent. wing to E replaces 17th-cent. work. Brooke family.

HUNSWORTH (Cleckheaton)

(98) WEST ROYD FARM (SE 188271).

Timber-framed and stone house, hall-and-cross-wing plan. Timber-framing survives in W wing of two bays; central truss has emphatically-curved braces up from posts to cambered tie-beam; roof with heavy squat crown-post, which suggests date in first half 15th cent. Wing may have been larger originaly. 17th-cent. work includes casing of wing in stone and rebuilding of hall range to give end-lobby entrance. Lowering of roof pitch of wing involved conversion of crown-posts to king-posts. Modest size of house in 17th cent. suggests yeoman status, but early date and crown-post roof of wing indicate early gentry status, family not known.

ILKLEY
(99) MANOR HOUSE (SE 116478).
Stone house, early 15th cent., remodelled late 16th and 17th cents (Pls 9, 66; Fig. 5). Early house survives in area of through passage; two-centred outer doorways and pair of doorways with shouldered lintels leading from passage to lower end. Lower end originally linear; straight joint at N end of passage shows line of earlier wall ('x' on plan). Well-worked nature of doorways to lower end suggests that they were intended to be seen from hall, which was therefore heated by lateral stack. Late 16th-cent. rebuilding of house above passage gives single-storey hall heated by lateral stack, stair turret, and large parlour on ground floor; on first floor, chamber over hall and, in wing, large heated chamber with garderobe. Lower end rebuilt mid 17th cent. as two-and-a-half storey wing. Family not known.

KEIGHLEY
(100) LAVEROCK HALL (SE 014381).
1641. Hall-and-cross-wings house (Pl. 152; Fig. 118). Through-passage plan with lateral firehood heating housebody. Wings have parlours to S, service rooms to N.

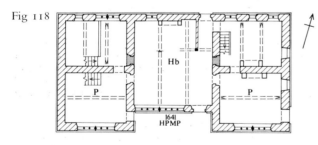

Fig 118

(101) DEANFIELD (SD 993375).
Late 17th cent. Four-cell linear plan (Fig. 119). Lobby-entry into housebody. Functions of rooms unclear. Added cell to W, possibly of similar date to main build, reuses datestone of 1697. Added porch dated 1722.

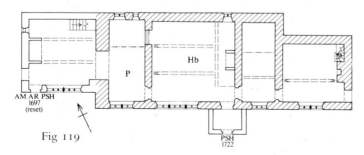

Fig 119

(102) INGROW LANE, NO. 124 (demolished, site not known).
1663. Hall-and-cross-wing house, lobby-entry. Photograph in NMR.

(103) MANOR FARM, Braithwaite (SE 039414).
1648. Three-cell linear plan, hearth-passage. Housebody heated by firehood, parlour by extruded stack. Outshut behind housebody and parlour, but not behind lower end, which may have been shop originally.

(104) MANOR FARM, High Utley (SE 054426).
1677. Double-pile plan with three rooms on main front (Pl. 153; Fig. 61). Through passage at opposite end of housebody to fireplace; passage probably not screened from housebody originally. Heated parlours flank housebody. Service rooms at rear.

Some other three-cell houses recorded in the course of the survey are: UTLEY HOUSE, UTLEY (SE 054429); CHURCH FARM, NEWSHOLME (SE 020398); MAIN STREET, LAYCOCK (SE 032410).

(105) NEAR TWO LAWS (SD 981381).
Late 17th cent. Two-cell, end-lobby entry plan (Fig. 120). Housebody heated by firehood originally. Inner cell divided to give unheated parlour and small service room. Single-cell, two-storey addition to E gable, *c.*1800; long windows suggest use as weaving shop. Laithe added to W gable.

Fig 120

(106) NEAR SLIPPERY FORD (SE 002405).
Late 17th cent. Two-cell, gable-entry plan (Fig. 121). Housebody originally heated by firehood. Inner cell divided to give parlour and service room. Doorway leading out of parlour to W may be later insertion on addition of cell at this end, or may indicate that 17th-cent. house had a third cell here, possibly laithe.

Fig 121

Other two-cell houses: MIDDLE DEANFIELD (SD 991376); HOLME HOUSE FARM (SE 028402); FAR SLIPPERY FORD (SE 001408); CLOUGH HOUSE, OAKWORTH (SE 031386); BIRCHWOOD ROAD, NO. 9, UTLEY (SE 054428).

KILDWICK
(107) KILDWICK HALL (SE 011462).
1663? Hall-and-cross-wings plan, three storeys plus basement (Pls 41, 75). Direct entry to hall at opposite end to fireplace. Wings have parlours to S. Stair opens out of hall and occupies rear of W wing; plaster decoration on landings. Rich plaster decoration in main chamber of E

wing. Rainwater head gives date 1663, but not certain that it relates to construction of house; plaster in chamber suggests a date nearer 1650. Detached kitchen block, dated 1673, probably replaced earlier impermanent kitchen. Later buildings now link kitchen to main block and make unclear extent of service rooms at rear. 'Justice Room' and garden house in grounds. Ambler 1913, 85–7 (includes plan).

(108) GREAT SLACK (SE 019470).
1674. Three-cell, linear plan, with lobby-entry between housebody and unheated parlour or service room (Pl. 222; Fig. 58). Housebody originally heated by firehood. W cell divided to give heated parlour to front, service room to rear. Porch added 1697.

KIRKBURTON
(109) LAITHE HOUSE AT HIGHWOOD (SE 206124).
One of a pair of almost identical laithe houses, this one dated 1825. Dwelling area of two rooms. Similarity of houses suggests estate building for tenant farmers.

KIRKHEATON (Kirkburton)
(110) COTTAGE AT NORTH MOOR HOUSE (SE 186190).
Single-storey cottage, early or mid 19th cent. (Fig. 84). Main room heated, used as general living and sleeping room. Rear outshut provides storeroom. Built to house labourer by adjacent farm?

LANGFIELD (Todmorden)
(111) KILNHURST (SD 945239).
Late 17th-cent. house of three cells, lobby-entry plan (Pl. 183). Problems of interpretation include nature of heating in housebody and relationship of house to contiguous house at SE angle. W wall of housebody of well-finished stone with projecting cornice; two elaborate doorways show end cell subdivided to give parlour and service room. Rear wing added 1766 to provide kitchen on ground floor and shop chamber over, reached by external stair. (Pl. 217)

LIVERSEDGE
(112) LIVERSEDGE HALL (SE 204230).
Parts of early building survive, but largely 19th cent. Original hall, seat of Nevile family, described as 'a hall house, with a centre and two wings, about the time of Henry VII. The hall, which in late times has been cut asunder horizontally by a floor, has a deep bay window to the south yet entire except the battlement. The roof has light flying principals, and, as is usual in halls of that age and rank, a wall-plate with embattled carving. The chapel is said to have been in the west wing' (Whitaker 1816, 249).

(113) LOWER HALL (demolished, site SE 198239).
Very large house, built by Greene family, probably mid 17th cent. Double-pile plan, multi-gabled elevations. Three rooms and storeyed porch on main front; doorway opened into housebody at opposite end to fireplace. Decoration included plasterwork and panelling. Ambler 1913, 84; Sumner 1978, 19.

(114) HAIGH HALL (SE 198238).
Large, three-gabled house, mid 17th cent. Main rooms – housebody and two parlours – on S front, with service rooms at rear in wings. Presence of arcade structure

between front and rear rooms suggests that wings may replace earlier and lower outshut.

(115) MIDDLE HALL (SE 196248).
Timber-framed house, first half 16th cent., enlarged and cased in stone in 17th cent. (Fig. 122). Two bays survive of timber-framed house of aisled form. Arcade-plate had close-studded wall beneath it in W (parlour?) bay, suggesting that this bay was floored to give chamber, but had no division beneath it in E (housebody?) bay, indicating that main room was open to roof. Storeyed cross-wing of early 17th cent. replaces original linear E end. Main range cased in stone, floor inserted into housebody, in late 17th or early 18th cent.

Fig 122

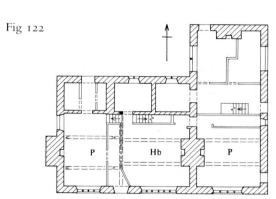

(116) NOAH'S ARK (demolished, approx. site SE 197238).
Old photograph shows hall-and-cross-wings house. One wing probably timber-framed, with projecting gable truss. Rest of house in stone, giving housebody lit by mullioned and transomed window, lobby-entry, upper wing. Sumner 1978, 20.

(117) HEADLANDS HALL (SE 201233).
Late 17th cent., incorporating remains of timber-framed cross-wing, early 16th cent. (Pls 253, 257; Fig. 77). Wing of three bays, with roof hipped to N. Stone casing involved destruction of early hall range. Late 17th-cent. house of U-plan, with two rooms – housebody and parlour – on main front, and wings to rear on either side of central area beneath outshut. Central entry directly into housebody. Parlour with decorative plasterwork. Stair sited behind parlour, lit by raised window in W wall. Kitchen, with independent entry, at N end of E wing, other service rooms at rear.

(118) OLD HALL (SE 198229).
Late 17th cent. Double-pile, double-fronted house with two-gabled elevation (Pls 205, 247; Fig. 48). Wings run back from main range on either side of narrow central area housed in outshut extension of main roof, giving U-plan. Central entry into housebody, which has small closet, lit by two-light window, in SE corner. Stair behind parlour, lit by raised window. Service rooms at rear; kitchen at NE corner, with independent entry. Good quality work on first floor includes SE chamber with bolection-moulded fireplace and panelling (like housebody below, this chamber has closet); records suggest existence of decorative plasterwork in SW chamber. Peel 1893, 165.

(119) POGG MYERS (SE 195229).
1638? Linear plan of three cells, with outshut along rear. Probably lobby-entry plan originally, but 19th-cent. conversion gives central doorway, reusing datestone.

(120) SYKE FOLD (demolished, site SE 190250).
Mid 17th cent, possibly incorporating remains of earlier timber-frame. 17th-cent. house of hall-and-cross-wing form with lower end gabled to give impression of second wing. Lobby-entry. Kitson family. Inventory of 1694 lists *house Body* (for cooking, sitting, dining), *kitching, Buttry, Sun Parlour* (heated, used for sitting and sleeping), *Lesser Parlour* and *North Parlour* (both bedrooms) on the ground floor and chambers over. A *Shopp* with a broad loom and presses was probably an outbuilding. Bulk of value of £194 made up of stock and crops. Inventory of goods of John Kitson, BIHR, May 1694; Sumner 1978, 23.

(121) ATACK FARM (SE 194238).
Mid 17th cent. Two cells plus outshut (Fig. 123). Original central entry? Housebody and parlour on main front, service rooms in outshut.

Fig 123

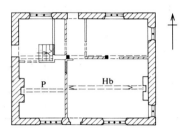

(122) THE CROFT (SE 190239).
Mid 17th cent. Two cells plus outshut (Fig. 124). Gable entry into housebody. Housebody probably heated by firehood originally.

Fig 124

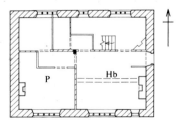

Other houses with 17th-cent. work: LOWER BLACUP (SE 185247); BULLACE TREES (SE 191232); DUXBURY HALL (SE 201231): UPPER HALL, said to have been one of houses of prosperous Greene family (demolished; Sumner 1978, 16, 21).

LOFTHOUSE WITH CARLTON (Lofthouse)
(123) LEEDS ROAD, No. 176 (SE 333258).
Timber-framed house, early 17th cent. Hall-and-cross-wing plan, with outshut behind main range (Fig. 125). Uniform height of two ranges shows that housebody always floored over. Original entry possibly into narrow bay at junction of ranges; this bay gave firehood heating housebody. Internal divisions on ground floor and under

arcade-plate on first floor are of unpegged studs. Roof trusses of king-post and 'V' brace form: internal trusses have single 'V' brace, gable trusses have five (hall range) or seven (wing); similar to front range of Nook Inn, Oulton with Woodlesford, dated 1611. Stone and brick casing of 18th and 19th cent., with alterations to original plan.

Fig 125

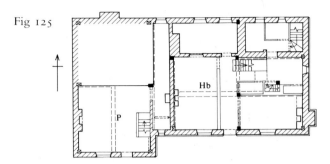

(124) PYEMONT HOUSE (SE 333261).
Brick house, mid 17th cent. Hall-and-cross-wings plan with lobby-entry between main range and E wing (Pls 163, 177; Fig. 56). Single-storey porch sheltering doorway has eroded lintel with initials of John Pyemont and arms of chevron between three miners' picks and three bunches of grapes. Outshut behind housebody and E wing contrived through use of timber arcade structure within the brick house; post at E end stands next to brick wall, but no proof that this indicates existence of earlier timber-framed structure. Inventory of 1723 aids interpretation. Central room, '*Hall*', included area of outshut, for beams and joists of ceiling designed to take in area N of arcade posts. Hall used for sitting and dining; heated *White Parlour* for sleeping; *litle parlour* as bedroom; *Dining room* had none of usual furniture and seems to have been purely a bedroom at the time of the inventory. Plaster decoration survives in the parlours. *Kitching* (used for cooking) probably in wing at rear. List of goods outside house shows Pyemont to have been a substantial farmer and coal miner. Status of family unclear: house shows many gentry features (Hall, Dining room, arms over doorway), and gravestone reported to describe John Pyemont as 'gentleman', but burial register and inventory both describe him as 'yeoman'. Inventory of goods of John Pyemont, BIHR, Jan. 1723; Banks 1871, 162–4.

LONGWOOD (Huddersfield)
(125) MORE PLEASANT (SE 078174).
Terrace of three cottages with laithe at one end, built in 1851 by J and H Brooke (Pl. 276). In 1861 a John Brooke, 'wooling Manufacturer and Farmer', is recorded at nearby Spring Head, and he was possibly responsible for the construction of the terrace, perhaps designed both to house his workforce and serve his farm. 1861 Census Returns, RG9/3272, Longwood Township Enumeration District 14 (microfilm copy held at WYAS, Wakefield).

MARSDEN (Colne Valley)
(126) GREEN TOP (SE 042108).
1671. Two cells plus outshut, with end-lobby entry plan (Pl. 158; Fig. 126). Housebody heated by fireplace in

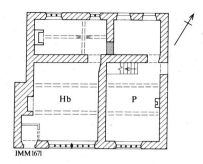

Fig 126

IMM 1671

extruded stack. Parlour unheated originally. Service rooms in outshut. Later subdivision.

MENSTON (Aireborough and Ilkley)

(127) MENSTON GRANGE (I) (SE 166441).
1672. Double-pile house with four rooms on main front and service rooms at rear (Pl. 228; Fig. 127). Slightly off-centre gabled porch shelters entry into lobby against main stack. Functions of rooms not entirely clear. House-body, heated by fireplace, to W of entry, kitchen, heated by firehood, to E; outer rooms probably parlours, of which E heated by fireplace in extruded stack, W parlour by fireplace, of 17th-cent. form, in thickness of gable wall but probably reused from elsewhere. Attic lit by windows in gables.

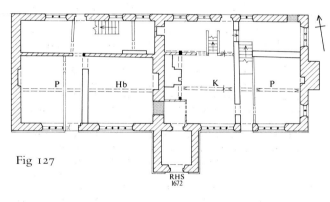

Fig 127

RHS
1672

METHLEY (Rothwell)

(128) METHLEY HALL (demolished, site SE 376265).
Great house, built of stone by Waterton family in first half 15th cent. Later rebuilding by Savile family masked nature of early plan, but clear that house had large open hall, heated by lateral stack and with screens passage. Vaulted porch opened into passage; grouped doorways with moulded surrounds in lower wall of passage. Late 16th and early 17th-cent. remodelling gave lofty great hall with elaborately carved screen, chamber over hall, and expanded upper wing with new entrance front, suite of private rooms and long gallery. Inventory of 1657 shows complexity of domestic planning among great gentry, with hall, great and little dining rooms, chapel, a number of private chambers, many service rooms and accommodation for servants (baker, bailiff, butler, glazier, porter, schoolmaster). Crump 1945; Ambler 1913, 57; inventory of goods of John Savile, Esquire, 1657, WYAS, Leeds, Mexborough

Papers, MS358 (I am grateful to Lord Mexborough for permission to use this).

(129) SHANN HOUSE (SE 388273).
Early 18th-cent. gentleman's residence, incorporating remains of earlier timber-framed structure (Pls 115, 119, 134). Fragments of a storeyed timber-framed range survive at rear. Main range of seven bays with perfect symmetry of facade precluded by existence of earlier work to E. Central doorway opens directly into hall, with parlour to W and service room to E. Hall opens at rear into stair hall; stair sited in angle between main block and rear wing. Hall and hall chamber retain early decoration, although hall received further embellishment later. Shann family. Hall 1979, 216.

(130) OLD RECTORY, Mickletown (SE 400273).
Brick house, c.1700. Small residence, built by Gilbert Atkinson, rector 1685–1709. Two storeys and attics (Pls 99, 118; Fig. 40). Five-bay facade, with central entry into entrance hall. Main reception rooms at front of house. Kitchen in NW corner, with back stairs down to cellar and up to first floor and attics. Best stair sited centrally at rear, rising to first-floor landing giving access to chambers. Three chambers have plaster mouldings round beams. Darbyshire and Lumb 1937, 55–6.

(131) LANES FARM (SE 371254).
Timber-framed house, second half 16th cent.? Original house of at least three bays, but only one survives. Low walls suggest that house may have been single-storey or lofted throughout. Internal divisions of unpegged studs. Roof of common-rafter form, similar to that of (175). 17th-cent. work includes addition of large stack, probably for kitchen.

(132) MAIN STREET, Nos 8 AND 10, Mickletown (SE 398272).
Timber-framed house, second half 16th cent.? Hall-and-cross-wing plan, with low main range and higher storeyed wing; discrepancy suggests that main range provided low open housebody. Details of plan unclear.

(133) CHURCHSIDE HOUSE Methley (SE 390266).
Second half 17th cent. Double-pile, double-fronted house (Pl. 210). Central entry into housebody; symmetry of facade emphasized by use of balancing dormers above eaves, gable stacks, disposition of windows. Double-pitched roof over two-and-a-half storey front range and two-storey rear range. 19th-cent. alterations at rear.

(134) HOME FARM (SE 378261).
Brick house, second half 18th cent. (Pl. 251). T-plan, with three-bay main range and wing projecting from centre at rear. Hipped roof. Central entry into entrance/staircase hall. Reception rooms on main front, small service rooms to rear, with rear wing providing sunken keeping cellar. Kitchen in 19th-cent. wing to W, possibly replacing earlier kitchen on same site.

MIDGLEY (Hebden Royd, Sowerby Bridge, Wadsworth)

(135) GREAT HOUSE (S/B) (SE 030263).
Mid 17th cent. Hall-and-cross-wing with rear service wing. Hearth-passage plan. Good remains of firehood surround – heck post, bresummer – in housebody. Heated

parlour in cross-wing, kitchen in rear wing. Lower end of house, unheated originally, has inferior detail and no communication on first floor between it and main part of house. Evidence suggests lower end segregated to give shop and shop chamber.

(136) UPPER FOOT FARM (S/B) (SE 033255).
1659. Hall-and-cross-wing plan, the wing not projecting at front but having a gable (Pl. 143). Lobby-entry against stack heating housebody. Kitchen wing at rear, heated by stack on gable wall. Best decorative stonework on main front confined to housebody and parlour. Lower end had windows with flush mullions, no hood moulds, indicating use as shop, entered separately through doorway in rear. Sutcliffe. 1928, 114–27.

(137) STONEY ROYD (H/R) (SE 021266).
1715. Double-pile house with three rooms on main front (Pls 215, 226; Fig. 62). Elaborate facade, with projecting central bays with pediment. Central entry into housebody, with heated parlours completing front range. Kitchen, back parlour and service rooms at rear, with stair area lit by raised window. First floor includes room used for industrial purposes, reached by original piece door in rear wall.

MIRFIELD

(138) LILEY HALL (SE 206173).
Timber-framed house, early 16th cent. Hall range of two-and-a-half bays, giving passage to E and two-bay open hall (Pl. 12; Fig. 9). Hall heated by firehood backing onto passage and decorated by central truss with deep arch-braces rising to saddle and with moulding continuing around braces to stop against carved boss on soffit of collar. Other trusses of plain king-post form. Original plan probably gave upper and lower cross-wings, but both replaced by later work. E wing of stone and of mid 17th-cent. date, providing large heated parlour and kitchen heated by firehood. W wing rebuilt 19th cent. Thurgoland family: John Thurgarland of 'le Lyley, gent.' is recorded as holding the capital messuage before his death in 1546. Ellis 1882, 418, esp. n. 35.

(139) CHADWICK HALL (demolished, site SE 198194).
Stone house with timber-framed gables, mid 16th cent. Hall-and-cross-wings, hearth-passage plan. Hall range of two bays giving open hall and passage; hall heated by firehood contained within half-bay screened from body of hall by stud wall rising from bressumer to tie-beam of central truss. Parlour and best chamber, both heated, in upper wing; lower wing probably gave service room and possibly parlour. Stair in bay in angle between upper wing and hall at rear of house. Possibly house originally had gallery along back wall of open hall; framing shows space for doorway leading from chamber over passage area to gallery over hall. Internal trusses of plain king-post form, but timber-framed trusses employed in gables to give decorative effect with herringbone struts. House has many features of post-medieval minor gentry house, but is dated to mid 16th cent. partly on evidence of combined stone and timber-framed character, partly because it lacks some improvements associated with later houses, especially kitchen giving double-pile plan.

MORTON (Keighley)

(140) EAST RIDDLESDEN HALL (SE 078420).
Stone house, evolution complex. Present house comprises hall in central block, 1648 block to SW, 1692 block to NE (Pls 53, 57, 58, 64, 65, 67, 72, 90; Fig. 128). Suggested evolution:
i. Late medieval house of standard hall-and-cross-wings plan, timber-framed; nothing survives apart from reused timbers. Paslew family in late Middle Ages.
ii. 1648 replacement of lower end and passage by large dwelling block, giving new passage on site of old and rooms identified with help of inventory of 1662. Rooms with plaster ceilings probably *Dineinge Parlour* and John Murgatroyd's *owne Parlour*. *Kichen* unusually sited, for best rooms could only be reached by crossing it. Many chambers heated, even small porch chamber. Attics provided rooms, some heated, for servants. Large decorative fireplace heating hall also belongs to this

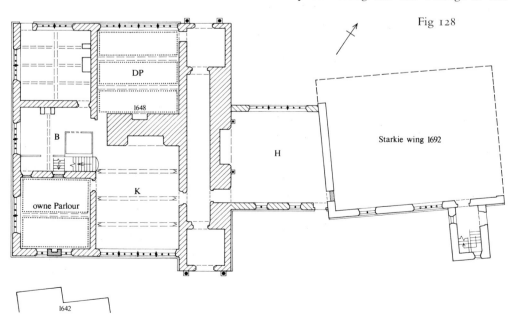

Fig 128

phase. Fireplace above this shows plan to rebuild early open hall as floored-over room with heated chamber, but shortly after 1648 the hall range was rebuilt giving room open to roof. In 1662 the original upper end, probably still in medieval form of timber-framed cross-wing, provided *old buttery, old sqire parler*, and *Old Mistrs p(ar)ler*, presumably indicating that a new buttery and parlours for the owner and his wife were now provided in the 1648 block.

iii. 1692 replacement of upper wing by expanded block providing up-to-date chambers for family or possibly as lodgings for visiting households. Best rooms on first floor. Starkie family.

Outbuildings include 1642 block close to house, probably providing estate workshop and *servants parler* (decorated by plaster frieze) and two large aisled barns. Inventory of John Murgatroyd, gentleman, 1662, WYAS, Calderdale, HAS/B; 13/42; Ambler 1913, 79; Hussey 1943; National Trust 1977.

(141) GLENESK FARM (SE 089427).
Late 17th cent. Double-pile, double-fronted house with central lobby-entry plan (Pls 188, 243; Fig. 74). Housebody heated by very large fireplace and probably shared cooking with kitchen; latter at NE corner, has independent entry in E gable. 18th-cent. alterations in stair area.

(142) COTTAGE near Glenesk Farm (SE 090429).
Single-storey cottage, mid 18th cent.? (Pl. 282). Two-room plan; main room heated by firehood, cap of which, with diamond-set chimney flue, survives. Further room added.

NORLAND (Sowerby Bridge)
(143) TOWN HOUSE (SE 069229).
Timber-framed aisled house, mid 16th cent., cased in stone and enlarged at various dates in 17th cent. (Pls 25, 149; Figs 14, 15, 129). Aisled house was of hall-and-cross-wing plan with hearth-passage entry. Housebody certainly aisled to N and probably also to S; evidence of peg-holes in plate inconsistent with fully-framed external wall. Open housebody probably had dais canopy over upper end: evidence for footings of ribs springing from side wall of cross-wing. Housebody has collar-rafter roof with raked queen-posts clasping purlins. W cross-wing appears to be original; end truss of main range was open and shows no evidence for a linear continuation of the range. Wing, however, has

king-post roof with central truss having single 'V' braces. Lower (E) end of house of linear plan originally. 17th-cent. alterations and additions include construction of range of rooms to S of housebody, occupying area of former front aisle, necessitating creation of main entry and new front to N; casing in stone in this area, possibly dated 1677 by a scratched date over doorway, provided transomed window lighting housebody and small window lighting fire-area of new large stone stack. Due to loss of front aisle, housebody, still open at least through two storeys in this phase, was smaller than in late medieval period, and stack built partly in main span of room and partly in area of N aisle; arcade posts of former rear aisle removed. Upper cross-wing cased in stone and given outshut form by extension of roof down to single-storey height along W wall. Lower end rebuilt in cross-wing form.

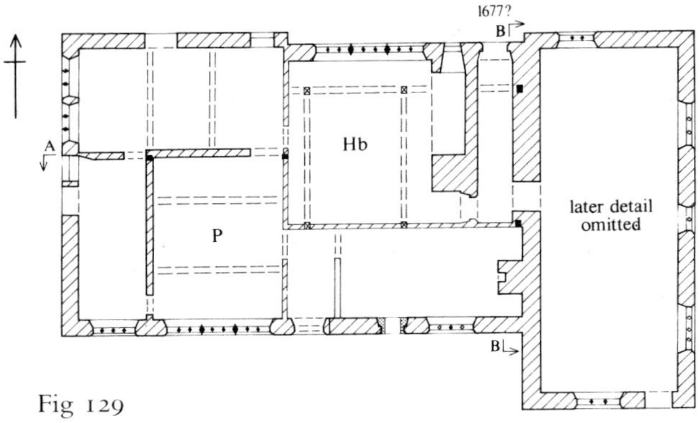

(144) NORLAND HALL (demolished, site approx. SE 069229).
Stone house, 1672, encasing earlier timber-framed structure. Timber-framed house on linear plan, probably with hearth-passage entry (Fig. 130). Prosperous Taylor family here by mid 17th cent.; 1672 casing and additions by John Taylor, retaining open housebody but with addition of dated fireplace, gallery and decorative plasterwork. Heated parlour in upper wing, unheated outer parlour with decorative plasterwork. Kitchen wing at rear. Lower end rebuilt in form of cross-wing. Kendall 1905, 101–3; Kendall 1911; Ambler 1913, 85; WYAS, Calderdale, HAS/E:D/24, 26–47, 49–50.

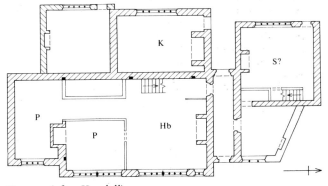

Fig 130 (after Kendall).

(145) BINROYD (SE 076227).
Large stone house of 17th cent., encasing earlier timber-framed structure (Pl. 148). Form of medieval house not known. Casing in stone in a number of phases produced hall-and-cross-wings house with hearth-passage plan. Open housebody retained, lavishly decorated with plaster-work and gallery. Expansion of dwelling area above passage led to addition of outer wing and of kitchen wing at rear. Wing below passage unheated originally and had plain window details, suggesting use as shop. House demolished in early 20th cent. and rebuilt on site in new form, reusing materials. Plasterwork removed to Bankfield Museum, Halifax. Kendall 1913; Ambler 1913, 59; WYAS, Calderdale, HAS/E:C/37–50; D/1–6.

Fig 129

(146) LOWER OLD HALL (SE 069229).
1634. Hall-and-cross-wing plan with rear kitchen wing (Pls 150, 176, 200, 224; Fig. 59). Impressive facade with three gables, storeyed gabled porch, large transomed windows. Porch doorway lintel shows date, initials of George Taylor, and arms of dyers' guild. Lobby-entry into housebody, an elaborate room with decorative fireplace, plaster overmantel and plaster frieze. Cross-wing has heated parlour with plaster overmantel. Further plaster-work in chambers. Kitchen wing behind housebody heated by gable stack; presence of ornamental fireplace in house-body demonstrates that kitchen was part of original design, although junction of ranges not effected neatly. Contrast between lower (E) end and rest of house: it is single plain cell with poor detail, its ground-floor window only one on facade not to have transom and only one to have splayed rather than cyma-moulded mullions. Evidence suggests lower end was shop or storeroom connected with builder's trade. External steps to original cellar under shop. Kendall 1905, 105; Ambler 1913, 77–8.

(147) LOWER WAT ING (SE 073231).
17th cent. and later. Present form of house explicable by piecemeal replacement of timber-framed structure? Hall-and-cross-wing plan, with central rear wing (Pl. 168; Fig. 131). Cross-wing projects far to S, possibly because originally built against timber-framed double-aisled range; when main range rebuilt in stone, aisled form abandoned and loss of front aisle left cross-wing with unusually long projection. Re-set datestone (IMM 1664) possibly dates rebuilding of main range as two-storey block with hearth-passage plan. Housebody heated by fireplace. Pre-existing kitchen wing causes passage to turn corner at N end; N doorway of passage thus in E wall of kitchen wing. Kitchen is heated by large fireplace and divided from housebody by plank screen. Lower end of house gives single cell. Adjacent to house at lower end is five-bay, single-aisled barn of 17th-cent. date.

(148) UPPER WAT ING (SE 072230).
Stone house, various phases of 17th. cent., encasing remains of timber-framed wing. Wing survives internally with remains of close-studded side wall. Rebuilding in stone commenced 1638, the date worked into label stops of E wing windows and repeated on fireplace heating housebody. Later work dated 1668 by reused datestone. 19th-cent. alterations obscure original plan, but clear that house had three rooms on triple-gabled main front with further rooms at rear. Kendall 1905, 98–9.

(149) FALLINGWORTH HALL (SE 067228).
1642. Linear plan of three cells with central rear wing (Fig. 132). Lobby-entry sheltered by storeyed gabled porch. Housebody heated by decorative fireplace, indicating that kitchen wing part of original design. Plain treatment of lower end suggests use as shop; this end lit by mullioned window, all other rooms on main front by transomed windows. 19th-cent. alterations include insertion of door-way into main front (reused from Fields Farm) and extension of rear to give warehouse above kitchen wing.

Fig 132

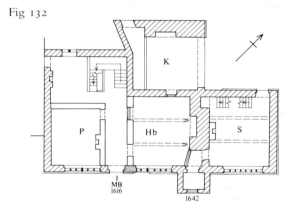

Fig 131

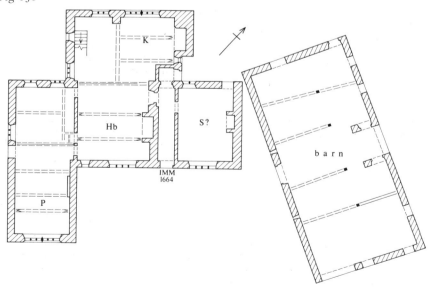

(150) HULLEN EDGE (SE 055226).
1677. Linear plan of three cells with outshut and kitchen wing at rear (Fig. 133). Hearth-passage plan, with housebody and parlour above passage. Housebody heated by large fireplace, parlour by fireplace in extruded stack. Outshut behind parlour provided service rooms. Kitchen wing heated by large fireplace; report of former existence of oven. Original lower end rebuilt in enlarged form in 19th cent.

Fig 133

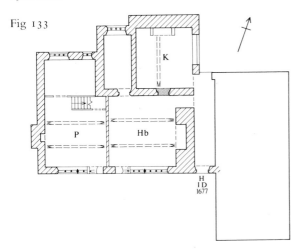

(151) HARPER ROYD (SE 060226).
1677. Subdivision has obscured plan, but likely that house of conventional hearth-passage type, with three rooms on main front and outshut along part of rear. Possible original kitchen wing at rear behind housebody. Kendall 1913a.

(152) LANE ENDS FARM (SE 061230).
17th cent. Hall-and-cross-wing form. Earliest phase is S part of main range, probably dated to 1628 by doorway in rear wall. Cross-wing of first half 17th cent. Later alterations include conversion of main range into double-pile block through additions along rear.

(153) FIELDS FARM (demolished, site approx. SE 067230).
1616. Three-cell plan with gable over upper end for wing projecting at rear? Hearth-passage entry. Known only from photograph. Kendall 1913b; WYAS, Calderdale, HAS/E:D/13.

(154) BUTTERWORTH END (SE 051213).
1656? Much rebuilt, but probably of linear hearth-passage plan originally. Housebody heated by large fireplace with carved date. Rear wings behind housebody and parlour, both 17th-cent. but of different dates, one possibly contemporary with main range and designed as kitchen wing. Lower end gives single cell, unheated. Added porch, c.1700, protects rear doorway of passage. Kendall 1905, 107–111.

(155) UPPER HALL (SE 069233).
Early 17th cent. and 1690. Early build gives wing with parlour and rear room, presumably added to pre-existing timber-framed house. 1690 build by John Taylor replaced early main range by range roofed parallel to earlier wing, giving double-pile, double-gabled block. Main front has porch, central doorway opening into housebody. Housebody and parlour at front of house, service rooms at rear. Ambler 1913, 90; Kendall 1905, 101; Pacey 1964, 4. 10.

(156) HOLLAS FARM (demolished, site approx. SE 074227).
Second half 17th cent. Square, double-pile plan roofed in two parallel ranges giving double-gabled facade. Entry on side wall into housebody. Housebody and parlour heated by stacks in wall dividing front rooms from rear. WYAS, Calderdale, HAS/E:D/14–17.

(157) UPPER BUTTERWORTH (SE 053213).
1663? Two cells plus outshut (Fig. 134). Gable entry, doorway lintel reportedly dated 1663, now painted over. Doorway opened into housebody alongside firehood. Service rooms in outshut. Laithe to S, possibly contemporary, contains early detail of windows.

Fig 134

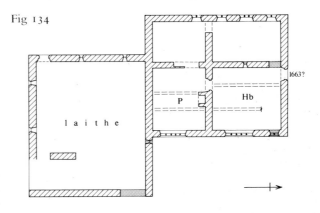

(158) SUN LONGLEY (SE 057222).
Laithe house, dated 1661. House of two main rooms with entry into housebody at junction of dwelling and laithe. Early laithe doorway replaced by larger opening in 19th cent. Modern restoration has obscured original plan and removed original details. Pacey 1964, 8.03–4.

(159) SOWERBY CROFT (SE 062229).
c.1700, altered and enlarged in 19th cent. Double-pile, double-fronted plan, with entry possibly in gable, opening into housebody alongside firehood. Yeoman-clothier family; house became centre of manufacturing hamlet in 18th and 19th cent. Kendall 1913c.

(160) LOWER HARPER ROYD (demolished, site SE 059227).
Represented on map as stone house, probably hall-and-cross-wing plan, possibly with housebody open through two storeys. Demolished 1876. Kendall 1913a, plan facing 159.

(161) NETHER LONGLEY (SE 052223).
Second half 17th cent. Originally two-cell with outshut along rear. Later additions include added cell and laithe.

(162) LONGLEY FARM (SE 049219).
Two-cell house dated 1735. Earlier window surrounds reused in outbuildings. Double-aisled barn suggests existence of substantial house on site pre-1735.

Houses with remains of 17th or early 18th-cent. work BANK HOUSE (SE 052226); EAST LONGLEY (SE 053222); HOLLINGWELL (SE 049219), datestone 1660; PICKWOOD HOUSE (SE 072226), datestone 1664; SHAW (SE 062224); LOWER SPARK HOUSE (SE 066233), datestone 1677; BLUE BALL INN (SE 068229); UPPER HARPER ROYD, datestone 1637 reused at (150).

NORMANTON
(163) HANSON HOUSE (SE 388224).
Timber-framed house, mid 16th cent. Good quality framing and scantling. Two bays of once larger linear range survive; later stone house replaces W end of original building (Fig. 23). Unusual form, with E end bay open to roof, possibly providing unheated kitchen or service room. W bay ceiled with heavy joists; chamber lit by window beneath eaves, in contrast to open E bay which has window set well below wall-plate. Original plan not clear.

(164) HILL HOUSE FARM (SE 382217).
Timber-framed house, mid or late 16th cent. (Fig. 135). Linear plan of three cells and four bays, originally with outshut along NW side. Stack in narrow bay heated housebody and possibly also NE room (kitchen?). Probably storeyed throughout. Gable roof trusses have king-post and five 'V' braces. Partial stone casing of late 17th cent. involved removal of outshut and creation of lobby entry on NW front. Room beyond parlour at SW end added later.

Fig 135

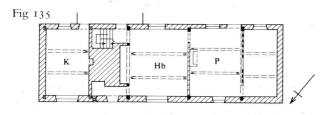

NORTH BIERLEY
(165) FROGDEN HOUSE, Nos 439, 441, 443, Shetcliffe Lane (SE 177294).
1625. Hall-and-cross-wing plan but without conventional lower room ((Pls. 202, 231; Fig. 136). Hall range double-pile on plan with end-lobby entry in rear wall. Housebody heated by firehood against gable wall. Cross-wing has heated parlour to front. Re-used in parlour is panelled partition with decorative frieze and roundels and built-in cupboard; this may originally have faced into housebody.

Fig 136

IH 1625 EH

Fig 137

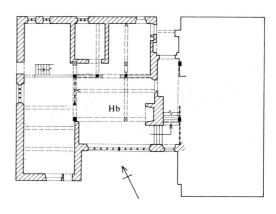

NORTHOWRAM (Halifax and Queensbury and Shelf)
(166) DAM HEAD (H) (SE 100274).
Timber-framed aisled house, early 16th cent. (Pl. 24; Fig. 137). Originally linear plan, hearth-passage entry. Open housebody with front and rear aisles? Replacement of S arcade-plate removes proof of original nature of front aisle, and peg-holes in N arcade-plate indicate that rear aisle may have been screened from housebody. Dais with plank screen, mortices for dais bench. Surviving herringbone framing visible in housebody may be part of side wall of bay added to upper end as expansion of superior part of house, converting linear bay to cross-wing form. 17th-cent. casing in stone, retaining open housebody; existence of front aisle in this phase is strong evidence for its earlier presence. Central rear wing and expanded upper wing built in late 17th cent. Lower wing mainly 19th cent. in detail and appears to replace original lower bay of end-aisle form; tie-beam of truss of lower side of passage has angled sockets to take rafters of roof, indicating single-storey form. Pearson 1906, 157–64.

(167) MARSH HALL (H) (SE 108278).
1626. Seat of minor gentry Otes family. Hall-and-cross-wings plan with direct entry into hall (Pls 71, 78–83; Figs 29, 34). Hall open through two storeys, probably had gallery and decorative plaster ceiling originally. Both wings have heated parlour and chamber on main front, all with decorative plasterwork. Outshut behind hall gives kitchen, heated by firehood on W wall, and service room. James Otes, the builder, was first-generation gentleman risen from ranks of yeoman-clothiers. Pearson 1898, 225–7; Ambler 1913, 72–3.

(168) SCOUT HALL (H) (SE 094277).
1681, built by John Mitchell, first-generation gentleman risen from local yeoman-clothier family. Simple rectangular double-pile block of three storeys, with near-symmetrical facade (Pls 96, 97; Figs 37, 138). Hall flanked by heated parlours; rear rooms include kitchen. Cellars at rear. Site of stair not known. Trigg 1946.

OULTON WITH WOODLESFORD (Rothwell)
(169) CHEESECAKE HALL (demolished, site SE 360269).
Small timber-framed aisled house, second half 16th cent.? Linear plan with unaisled end-bays and double-aisled

Fig 138 [168] Scout Hall, Northowram; frieze over doorway.

housebody open to roof. Entry position unclear. Service bay rebuilt and extended. Hutton 1974; Michelmore forthcoming (this will contain evidence of aisled construction not apparent when building recorded as standing structure by Mr. Hutton).

(170) MANOR FARM (SE 362283).
Timber-framed house, second half 16th cent. Linear plan of four bays of unequal length, with continuous outshut along rear. Likely that house was two-storeyed throughout, for no evidence of open housebody. Arcade structure visible in storeyed W bay; lack of evidence for framed wall beneath arcade-plate suggests original divisions were applied to plate rather than jointed into it. Short wings added to front of house in 17th cent.

(171) HOME FARM (SE 361273).
Second half 17th cent. Four-cell linear plan with central lobby-entry (Fig. 139). Three storeys. Main stack comprises back-to-back firehoods heating two central rooms, probably housebody and kitchen. Outer rooms now heated, but not clear that gable stacks original; possibly at least one of these rooms was unheated service area. Top storey poorly lit, probably used for storage of crops.

Fig 139

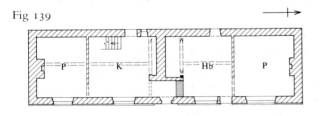

OVENDEN (Halifax)
(172) SUNNY BANK FARM (SE 060274).
Single-storey house, dated 1708 by datestone on porch (Pl. 277). Two-cell, central entry plan. Laithe built at right angles soon after construction of house.

POTTER NEWTON (Leeds)
(173) GLEDHOW HALL (SE 315370).
Built c.1766 by John Carr. Rectangular block with canted bay-windows at ends of main front and at centre of garden front. Three-bay entrance hall leading to top-lit staircase hall. Main floor has four reception rooms and kitchen. Dixon family. Kitson 1910, 253; Colvin 1978, 194.

PUDSEY
(174) TUDOR HOUSE (SE 219329).
Mid 17th cent. Two cells plus outshut (Fig. 140). Off-centre doorway into housebody, heated originally by firehood against gable wall. Heated parlour. Timber arcade structure between main span and outshut.

Fig 140

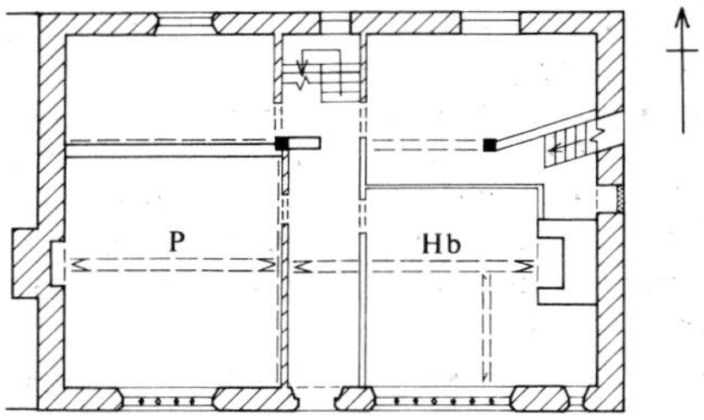

ROTHWELL
(175) HAZELWOOD COTTAGES (SE 348281).
Timber-framed house, late 16th or early 17th cent.? Four-bay linear plan, one-and-a-half storeys (Pl. 33; Fig. 21). Poor quality framing, with unpegged studs and light scantling. Ceiling in housebody later than that in parlour; probable that parlour was originally floored to give chamber, but that housebody was open to roof or simply lofted-over. Roof with raked queen-posts clasping purlins against common rafters.

SHARLSTON

(176) SHARLSTON HALL (SE 396188).

Timber-framed house of many periods (Pl. 2; Figs 2, 141, 142). Earliest part is hall range of first half 15th cent., giving open hall and hearth-passage plan. Hall originally heated by firehood. Crown-post roof appears to have continued to both E and W to give linear plan, but W end replaced *c.*1450 by three-bay cross-wing and E end in late 15th cent. by two-bay cross-wing. W wing of two storeys with solar on first floor; crown-post roof. Wing built to allow narrow bay between it and hall, possibly for stair. E wing has collar-rafter roof, reusing timbers from earlier roof of similar form. Early 16th-cent. addition of outer E wing, timber-framed; construction of massive stack to heat this suggests use as kitchen. Further additions, of stone, to E, probably late 16th or 17th cent. Low timber-framed wing added against S gable of solar wing has king-post roof, and siting suggests use as chapel. Addition of porch with decorative framing; dated 1574 by inscription (see Chapter 1, n. 54). House cased in stone in post-medieval period, hall floored over in early 18th cent. to give chamber. Fleming family in Middle Ages, then Stringer family. Hunter 1851, 73–7.

Fig 141

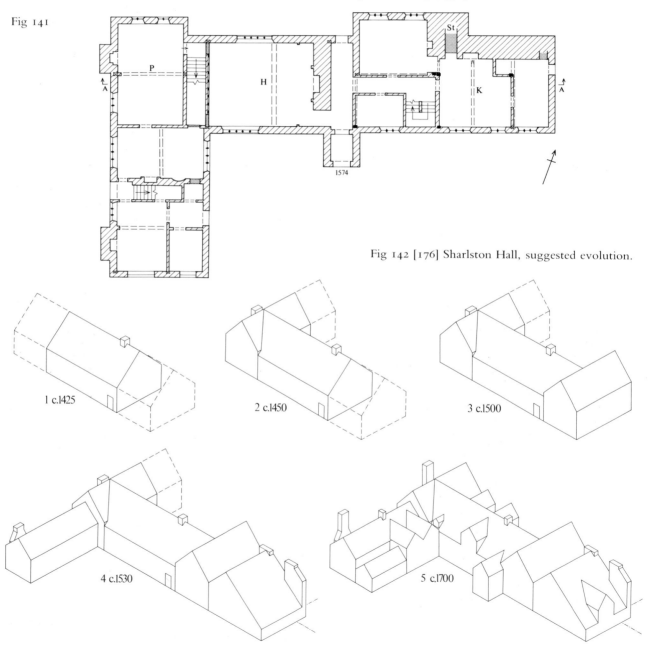

Fig 142 [176] Sharlston Hall, suggested evolution.

1 c.1425

2 c.1450

3 c.1500

4 c.1530

5 c.1700

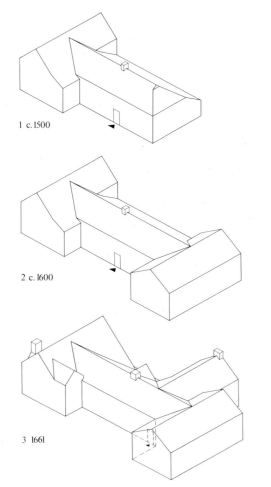

1 c.1500

2 c.1600

3 1661

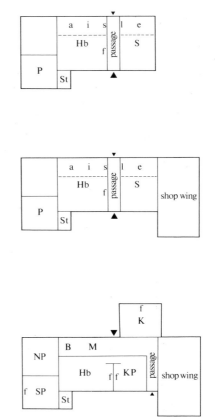

Fig 143 [177] High Bentley, Shelf; suggested evolution.

SHELF (Queensbury and Shelf)
(177) HIGH BENTLEY (SE 131285).
Timber-framed aisled house, late medieval. Hall-and-cross-wing, hearth-passage plan (Pl. 171; Figs. 52, 143). Aisle undivided from open housebody. Cross-wing gave parlours on ground floor, chambers over. Stair in angle between housebody and wing at front of house. Lower end, isolated from rest of house by passage, gave single large room, probably shop, on ground floor and chamber over. House built by Benteley family? First addition was stone wing at lower end, probably an expansion of working area. House occupied by yeoman-clothier Wade family in 17th cent. Richard Wade remodelled it, altering plan and making significant improvements. Stone casing of 1661, the date over N doorway; house now entered from rear, through newly contrived lobby-entry. Stack set in area of former passage, replacing firehood in housebody. Addition of kitchen wing released housebody from cooking duties: it rose in status, ceiled at tie-beam level and decorated by plaster overmantel and gallery. Main stack also heated new *Kitching Parlor*, in area of original shop. *Sun parlour* and chamber over in cross-wing heated by extruded stack. Service rooms created in area of aisle, now screened off from housebody. Wade's improvements added greatly to extent and comfort of living area, and show sophisticated division of functions. Significantly, however, shop wing retained as vital part of house; although shop end of original house converted to kitchen parlour, newly created passage between this and shop wing maintained same segregation of dwelling and working parts; passage gives secondary entry on S front.

Inventory of 1693 shows functions of rooms. *Housebody* used for sitting and dining; *Sun parlour* was best bedroom, used also for sitting and possibly dining; *north parlour* for storage; *Kitchinge Parlor* for sleeping, with bed of high value; *Kitchinge* for cooking. *Chamber over Shopp* and *Shopp chamber* mentioned, with trade tools, large stocks of made-up cloth, one cloth in loom. Large sums of money owed to Wade for cloth in London. Stock and crops show interest in agriculture. Inventory valued £782. Inventory of goods of Samuel Wade, yeoman, BIHR, May 1693; Atkinson and McDowall 1967, 81–5; Lister 1903, 241–4.

(178) LOWER FIELD FARM (SE 124273).
Timber-framed aisled house, mid 16th cent. Hall-and-cross-wing, hearth-passage plan. Wing and main range framed together. Stone casing in 17th cent.; front wall of housebody brought forward flush with cross-wing, housebody ceiled to give chamber over, but firehood retained with addition of decorative plaster panels to fire area.

SHELLEY (Kirkburton)

(179) HUDDERSFIELD ROAD, NOS 129, 131 (SE 205111). 1703. Double-pile, double-fronted house with off-centre lobby-entry (Pls 239, 241; Fig. 144). Housebody and parlour to front, service rooms to rear. Double-pitch roof with narrower, lower rear range.

Fig 144

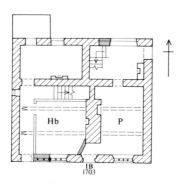

SHIPLEY

(180) NEW CLOSE FARM (SE 123369).
Second half 17th cent. Double-pile, double-fronted plan with gable entry into housebody (Fig. 71). Housebody and kitchen to N heated by firehoods against gable wall, supported by bressumer beam spanning entire depth of house. Parlour heated by extruded stack on W gable.

SHITLINGTON (Sitlington)

(181) NETHERTON HALL (SE 280168).
c.1775. Minor gentleman's residence, with three-bay, three-storey main block and two-storey flanking wings (Pls 108, 117, 136; Fig. 41). Giant pediment over main block on entrance front, which has balancing bay windows. Single-bay entrance hall leads through to staircase hall; transverse corridor links service rooms in wings with reception rooms. Wings have doorway only on main front but windows overlooking rear. System of segregation by status contrived through use of servants' stairs in wings, leaving main stair for use by family. Built by Perkins family, with clerical background (information from John Goodchild).

SILSDEN

(182) HOLDEN GATE (SE 066442).
Second half 17th cent. Three-cell linear plan with entry directly into housebody at opposite end of room to firehood (Pl. 225). Housebody flanked by upper and lower parlours, with small service rooms at rear. Curved wall in NW corner of housebody indicates site of original stair. Added porch re-uses datestone of 1619. Large aisled barn, dated 1641, among outbuildings.

(183) UPPER HAY HILLS (SE 034478).
Laithe house, early 19th cent. (Pl. 273; Fig. 81). Dwelling with living room to front and kitchen and sunken pantry to rear. Laithe has aisle projecting to give porch sheltering doorway to house.

SKIRCOAT (Halifax and Sowerby Bridge)

(184) BANKHOUSE (H) (SE 095225).
Timber-framed aisled house, late medieval. Linear hearth-passage plan (Pls 26, 27; Figs 12, 13). Open housebody with dais canopy of planks nailed to ribs and firehood. Upper bay of house of end-aisle form; tie-beam at upper end of housebody has no evidence for king-post truss, and shows angled sockets for rafters of end-aisle roof, rising to hip over housebody. Casing in stone and expansion of house in 17th cent. Open housebody retained, but upper end converted to cross-wing form, giving parlour and rear room on ground floor and chambers over. Lower end expanded to give two cells with rear outshut. 19th-cent. subdivision and loss of part of rear when railway line constructed. Kendall 1914.

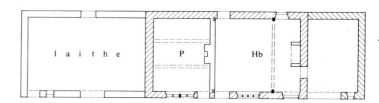

Fig 145

SLAITHWAITE (Colne Valley)

(185) BIRKS (SE 058145).
Cruck house, probably timber-framed and of mid/late 16th cent., cased in stone second half 17th cent. and later. Original house probably of four bays, with linear hearth-passage passage plan (Pls 30, 31; Fig. 145). Open housebody of one-and-a-half bays, heated by firehood. Low side walls suggest that end bays gave ground-floor rooms either open to roof or lofted over. Piecemeal stone casing, first of housebody and parlour, retaining single-storey form but converting to lobby-entry plan. 19th-cent. rebuilding of lower end and addition of second storey to parlour end. Laithe added later in 19th cent.

(186) OLD HALL (SE 055129).
Cruck house, late 16th cent.? Single cruck truss survives in area of open housebody; truss of heavy scantling but of poor workmanship. Early house probably had linear plan of three cells, with open or lofted end-bays. Stone casing and replacement of original linear upper end by storeyed cross-wing. Later rebuilding of lower end. Ahier 1933, 1–9.

(187) HILL TOP FOLD, NOS 13–16 (SE 079142).
Stone house, first half 17th cent. and 1685, with evidence for earlier phase, probably timber-framed and possibly cruck-built (Fig. 146). Roof-line of single-storey main range survives on side wall of cross-wing, suggesting that wing added to pre-existing house to provide storeyed accommodation. Form of house at this stage illuminated by inventory of goods of Edmund Bothomley, 1668. *Housebody*, used for cooking, sitting, dining, still open to roof; wing gave *great Parlor*, a heated room used as best bedroom and possibly as sitting room, *litle Parlor*, a bedroom and storeroom, and *Buttry*, apparently used for sleeping as well as storage, although bed may belong to unlisted chamber

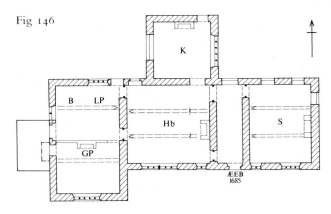

Fig 146

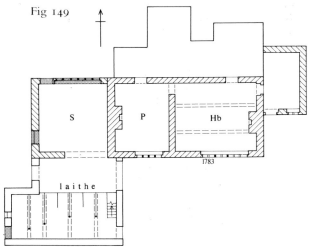

Fig 149

floor. On decline of domestic weaving, shop taken into laithe for additional crop storage.

over great Parlor. Lower end of house gave *Shope below the entry joyneing to the house*, stocked with goods showing that Bothomley was a dyer. In 1685 earlier main range replaced by two-storeyed stone range on similar plan, with hearth-passage dividing housebody from shop. Kitchen wing at rear added either at this stage or slightly later. Inventory in Brears 1972, 134–8.

(188) WOOLROYD (SE 060147).
Second half 17th cent., single-storey house of two or three cells (Pl. 179; Fig. 147). Open housebody heated by firehood. Nature of original plan unclear. Lower end rebuilt in 19th cent. as two-storey cottage.

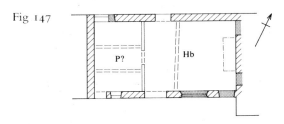

Fig 147

(189) HOUSE NEXT TO BIRKS (SE 058145).
Laithe house of two builds (Fig. 148). Single-cell dwelling of two storeys, early 18th cent., probably added to pre-existing structure which provided entry. 1736 addition of laithe on site of earlier build, giving entry to dwelling.

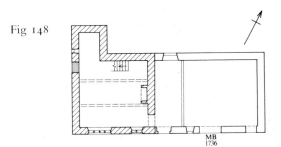

Fig 148

(190) TIDING FIELD FARM (SE 068148).
Two-cell house, 1783? (Fig. 149). Addition of three-storey cell at W end, *c*.1800; long windows in N wall suggest use as shop for weaving. Laithe added early/mid 19th cent., with stalls for cattle, storage for crops over, and threshing

SOUTH CROSLAND, DETACHED (Huddersfield)
(191) MANOR HOUSE FARM (SE 117148).
Timber-framed aisled house, late medieval. Hall-and-cross-wing, hearth-passage plan. Casing in stone and enlargement of house in mid 17th cent. Housebody ceiled at tie-beam level but, uniquely, large chamber set over it. Earlier roof of main range replaced by new roof with arch-braced collars, short king-posts, cusped braces from king-posts to ridge. Later additions at lower end and demolition of upper wing.

SOUTH ELMSALL
(192) BROAD LANE FARM EAST (SE 456097).
Large house, late 17th cent. Three storeys, L-plan (Pls 164, 213; Fig. 150). Main range of three cells; heated parlour to W, housebody and heated kitchen. Behind housebody and parlour are narrow rooms for storage. Rear wing behind kitchen possibly gave back kitchen, heated by firehood on N gable. First floor has chamber with plaster moulding around beams and acanthus leaves in angles. Poorly lit second floor gave storage area, probably for crops, with heavy lime-ash floor; access to this level through doorway in rear wall, reached by external steps.

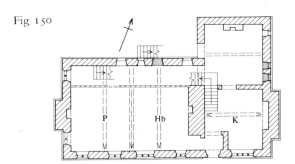

Fig 150

SOUTH KIRKBY
(193) COMMON FARM (SE 436102).
Early/mid 18th cent. Two cells plus outshut, three storeys (Pl. 209; Fig. 151). Central entry, opening against stair, which has splat balusters. Housebody heated by large fireplace. Service rooms in outshut.

Fig 151

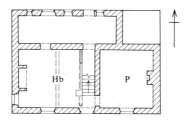

(194) THE LONGHOUSE (SE 449109).
Laithe house, second half 18th cent. Dwelling of two cells, enlarged by added cell at N end of range (Fig. 82). Laithe probably functioned as barn only rather than as combined barn and mistal; separate doorways for cattle absent.

SOUTHOWRAM (Brighouse and Halifax)
(195) BACKHOLD HALL (H) (SE 101230).
1668. Large house; long facade has gables over passage area, housebody and parlour end. Hearth-passage plan (Fig. 152). Dwelling has large housebody with decorative fireplace, heated parlour, kitchen with large fireplace, further rooms behind parlour. Stair opens out of corner of housebody. Chamber over parlour decorated with plaster ceiling. Lower end of house has plain details, suggesting use as shop.

Fig 152

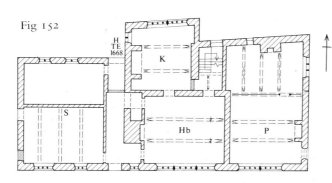

SOWERBY (Hebden Royd and Sowerby Bridge)
(196) WOOD LANE HALL (S/B) (SE 043236).
1649. Double-pile plan with projecting upper wing (Frontispiece and Pls 47, 50, 54; Fig. 27). Hearth-passage form, but passage only so long as to give access to hall beyond fireplace. Hall open through two storeys, richly decorated with plasterwork, panelling, fireplace, gallery. Gallery emphasizes role of hall as channel of communication on first as well as ground floor. 1696 inventory names five parlours. Kitchen behind hall with independent entry.

Dearden family; John Dearden, the builder, was first-generation gentleman risen from yeoman-clothier family. Kendall 1906; Ambler 1913, 81; inventory of goods of Joshua Dearden, gentleman, BIHR, Nov. 1696.

(197) WHITE WINDOWS (S/B) (SE 053232).
Built 1767–8, possibly to designs by John Carr, for prosperous Priestley family, merchants (Pls 125, 139, 140; Fig. 153). Rectangular block, seven bays by five, three storeys plus basement. Entry into single-bay entrance hall giving access to main reception rooms at front and to transverse corridor and stair hall at rear. Kitchen probably in low attached block at rear. Secondary stair sited to communicate with transverse corridor and with kitchen wing. Kendall 1906a; Colvin 1978, 193.

Fig 153

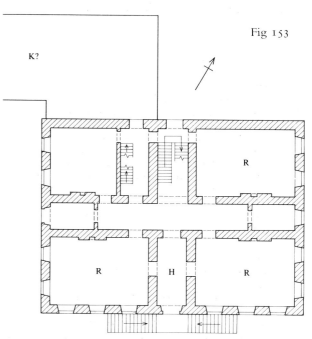

(198) HAUGH END (S/B) (SE 053231).
Third quarter 18th cent. Five-bay, double-pile block, with central entry into single-bay entrance hall (Pl. 102). Stair hall sited at centre of rear. Reception rooms occupy most of ground floor, with service rooms in long attached range at NW angle. Lea family, Kendall 1910, 165.

SOYLAND (Ripponden)
(199) GREAT HOUSE (SE 024192).
1624. Hearth-passage plan, but with marked imbalance between areas above and below passage (Pl. 144; Fig. 63). Above passage is large double-pile block with three-gabled facade. Housebody, originally heated by firehood, and two heated parlours on main front, smaller rooms (lesser parlours and service rooms) and kitchen at rear; thick E wall of kitchen probably contains large fireplace. Below passage, house rebuilt in modern times, but earlier photo-

graph shows that lower end comprised single cell with inferior details of masonry and windows, indicating use as shop. Unclear whether this end dated from 1624 or from late 17th-cent. rebuilding of earlier, probably timber-framed, structure.

(200) GREAT GREAVE (SE 017206).
First half 17th cent. (Pl. 181). Earliest part is hall and W cross-wing, probably built up against timber-framed structure to E; this latter replaced by E cross-wing to give hall-and-cross-wings plan. Hearth-passage entry. House-body originally heated by firehood. W wing has outshut along W side, probably to provide service rooms; main part of wing has heated parlour to S, lesser parlour and stair to N. E wing contains passage and probably provided small service rooms, lit by two-light windows in front and rear walls.

STANLEY CUM WRENTHORPE (Stanley and Wakefield)
(201) CLARK HALL (W) (SE 341221).
Brick house, completed c.1680. Near-symmetrical facade with central entry and balancing bay windows (Pls 95, 113, 130, 135). Not a double-pile house. 1680 plan gave entry directly into hall, with kitchen to E and dining room and dairy to W. Hall acted as entrance area, living room, and hub of house; decorated with plasterwork over fireplace. Dining room decorated by rich plaster ceiling. Heated chambers. House had attic storey originally. Wing added c.1700 to give heated parlour and chamber. Clarke family. Brears 1978.

STANSFIELD (Blackshaw, Hebden Royd and Todmorden)
(202) GREAT HOUSE CLOUGH FARM (T) (SD 953257).
Early 18th-cent., double-pile, double-fronted house with gable entry (Pl. 215; Fig. 154). Housebody heated by fireplace rather than firehood. Heated parlour. Stair sited centrally at rear, lit by small raised window. Early-mid 18th-cent. addition of detached single-cell build giving unheated ground-floor room and heated chamber, probably used for weaving.

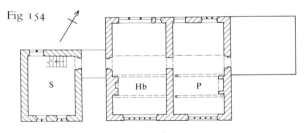

Fig 154

(203) OL HALL, Eastwood (T) (SD 961258).
c.1740, double-pile, double-fronted house. Near-central entry opening directly into housebody (Pls 206, 245, 250; Fig. 155). Rear rooms include kitchen and dairy, the latter

backing into hillside on N and therefore lit by window in W wall. Simple decorative plaster ceilings in parlour and chamber over. First floor includes weaving chamber, lit by long window and entered from ground level at rear by external doorway in N wall. Single-pitch roof gives attic, partly used as pigeon loft; W gable has flight-holes in apex (now blocked). Laithe added to E gable in 1767. Newell 1916.

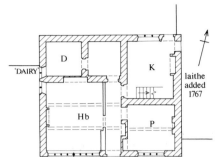

Fig 155

SWILLINGTON
(204) WARREN HOUSE (SE 380330).
Brick house, early 19th cent. double-pile main block, with central entry into entrance hall flanked by reception rooms (Pls 252, 266; Fig. 75). Stair hall sited centrally at rear. Rear rooms possibly included a back parlour or dining room. Lower service wing projecting from NW corner provided kitchen, with independent entry and stair to chamber for servants' accommodation.

THORNER
(205) OLD MANOR HOUSE (SE 377403).
Timber-framed house, late 16th/early 17th cent. Linear plan of four bays of unequal length, continuous outshut along rear (Fig. 156). Back-to-back firehoods heat house-body and kitchen; firehood bressumers have pyramid stops, suggesting early date. Spine beam of housebody stop-chamfered against firehood, indicating that house-body always ceiled to give chamber over. Heavy inferior joists in kitchen. Arcade-plate visible in area of housebody and kitchen; no evidence for framed wall beneath it, but chamber over housebody screened from outshut by remains of stud and plank partition nailed to, rather than jointed into, plate; this is likely to be original means of division. Early plan lost on 18th-cent. casing in stone, but siting of firehood suggests lobby-entry.

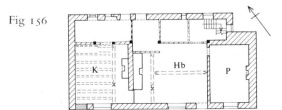

Fig 156

218

(206) CHURCH FARM (SE 379405).
1707. Three-cell linear house, with entry at opposite end of
housebody to fireplace (Fig. 157). Not clear whether end
rooms heated originally, but fenestration suggests that N
room was parlour and S room was service area.

Fig 157

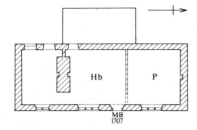

Fig 158

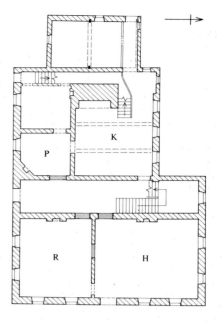

THORNHILL (Dewsbury)
(207) LEES HALL (SE 233199).
Timber-framed house, early 16th cent. Built on hall-and-
cross-wings, hearth-passage plan (Pls 6, 8, 13, 60). Open
hall of one-and-a-half bays, with dais canopy over upper
end. Upper wing of two bays, with two rooms on ground
floor and large solar on first floor. Parlour and solar heated
by fireplaces in extruded stack on side wall; absence of
evidence for framing in this area suggests that stack is
original. Stair bay at rear in angle between upper wing and
hall. Lower wing demolished. Early 17th-cent. work
includes insertion of rich plaster ceiling into solar, and
construction of outer W wing in stone to provide kitchen
(heated by large fireplace) and parlour on ground floor,
large dining chamber above. Nettleton family. Timber-
framed outbuilding survives, function unclear. Manby
1972; Walton 1955, 56–7; Empsall 1895.

THORPE (Lofthouse)
(208) THORPE HALL (SE 316270).
Brick house of 1735 incorporating remains of late medieval
timber-framed wing (Pl. 133; Fig. 158). Main block of five
bays by five and of three storeys. E front made up of hall
and parlour, with central entry opening directly into hall.
Long corridor behind gives side door to S, stair to N, and
divides best rooms from service rooms to rear. Stair rises
to first floor only. Chambers on E front are richly decorated and were clearly impressive rooms. Proctor family.
Whitaker 1816a, pl. opposite 161.

THURSTONLAND (Holmfirth and Kirkburton)
(209) UPPER FOLD FARM (K) (SE 164104).
House and farm buildings, late 17th cent. Large house, of
four-cell, double-pile plan. Two large barns, both using
aisled construction. Single-storey outbuilding, stone-built
but with two cruck trusses of poor finish (Pl. 32; Fig. 17).
Unclear whether stone walls, which retain some late
17th-cent. features, are contemporary with crucks or
replaced earlier, less substantial walls. Function of building
uncertain: possibly workshop or shelter for animals.

TODMORDEN AND WALSDEN (Todmorden)
(210) INCHFIELD HOUSE (SD 933219).
Stone and timber-framed cruck-built house, possibly 17th
cent. (Figs 18, 19). Cruck building survives as one-and-a-
half storey range of three bays, with four trusses. Lower
walls always of stone; one early mullioned window
survives at rear. Masonry of upper walls in different style;
this has replaced large timber-framed panels, surviving
from which are posts at intermediate points in each bay.
Surviving wall-plates show that these posts were pegged to
plate but that infill must have been of sprung staves. E
gable wall probably always of stone. E cruck truss shows
no evidence of halvings for windbraces continuing to E and
no evidence of having been an external wall; truss,
therefore, probably always designed to sit inside stone
gable wall. W truss similarly shows no evidence for
continuation of range to W nor of being external wall;
stone cell to W is possibly, therefore, part of original
scheme, designed to provide superior, fully storeyed end.
Cruck range, therefore, probably provided open range,
with one-and-a-half bay housebody, heated by firehood,
and single-bay lower (E) end of unknown function.
Position of entry unclear. Crucks of heavy scantling but
poor finish. Truss IIII has evidence for original nature of
timber-framed infill: cruck blades, collar and tie-beam have
holes for staves forming framework of lathe and plaster
panels. Later alterations give low upper floor throughout
range.

(211) FLAILCROFT (SD 923248).
Second half 17th cent; reused datestone in barn, 'IMC
1708', seems too late to have come from house. Two-cell,
gable-entry plan (Pl. 141; Fig. 49). Housebody heated by
firehood originally. Dividing wall between cells of single
thickness of dressed stone, with projecting cornice. Inner
cell originally subdivided to give parlour to S and service
room to N. Outshut added in 18th cent.

TONG

(212) TONG HALL (SE 218307).
1702. Gentleman's residence built of brick with stone dressings (Pl. 109). Seven-bay block, originally with wings of two storeys and central range of three storeys crowned by a pediment. Raised ground floor provided principal reception rooms and entrance and stair halls. Basement has kitchen, servants' rooms, storage area. Backstairs rise around newel from basement to first floor. House remodelled in late 18th cent. to give three storeys throughout: new main stair inserted, new secondary stair contrived, rising from basements to second floor. Bay windows added to N front. Tempest family. Linstrum 1978, 59 shows early view by Knyff.

(213) RYECROFT (SE 201306).
1669, built by Christopher Nettleton. Linear plan of three cells with outshut along part of rear (Pls 174, 175; Fig. 159). Entry into lobby against side of firehood heating open housebody. Inventory of 1693 shows *housebody* used for sitting, dining, some cooking. Main cooking hearth in *kitchinge* to E, heated by firehood and with own external doorway. Heated *great Parlor* for sitting. *Little parlor, Buttery, Milkhouse, Wash house* and *Cellar* at rear. Inventory of goods of Christopher Nettleton, yeoman, BIHR, Jan. 1694; Robertshaw 1936.

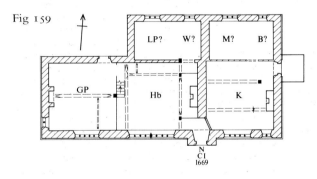

Fig 159

LP? W? M? B?
GP Hb K
N C1 1669

UPPER WHITLEY (Kirkburton)

(214) GREGORY FARM (SE 203170).
c. 1800. Double-pile, double-fronted house. Off-centre entry into housebody, parlour to W (Pl. 265; Fig. 160). Smaller rear rooms with stair sited centrally; steps down to cellar.

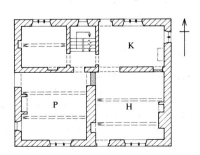

Fig 160

K
P H

WALTON

(215) ROSE FARM (SE 355164).
Mid 17th cent. Linear three-cell plan with continuous outshut along rear (Pls 182, 219; Fig. 54). Lobby-entry against stack heating housebody and parlour. Unusual pattern of ceiling beams in housebody. Kitchen has fireplace and original doorway in gable wall. Arcade structure between main span and outshut. Roof timbers of massive scantling, with trusses of king-post and 'V'-brace form.

(216) OVERTOWN GRANGE FARM (SE 355165).
Late 17th cent. Three-cell linear plan with outshut behind central and S cells (Pl. 227; Fig. 161). Two storeys plus attics. Original plan had central entry directly into housebody. Kitchen at S end, heated by original large fireplace and with independent entry. Outshut contained stair, lit by raised window in rear wall, and service rooms. Attics lit by window in gable wall.

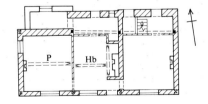

Fig 161

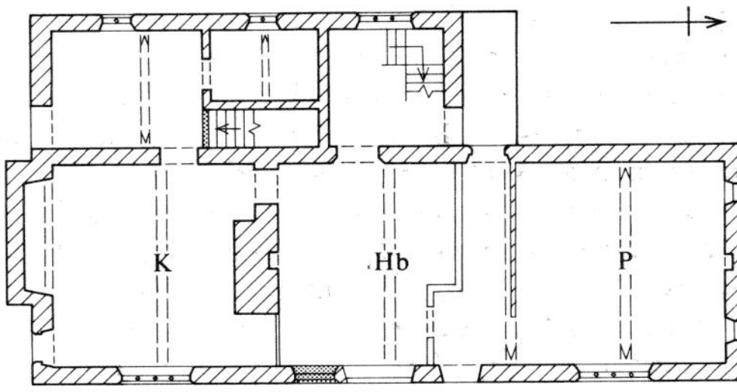

K Hb P
M M

WALTON IN AINSTY (Walton)

(217) CROFT HOLDING (SE 442477).
Timber-framed house, first half 17th cent. Three-bay, three-cell linear plan with outshut along rear (Fig. 162). Lobby-entry. Probably floored throughout originally. Arcade-plate visible in central and E bays; no evidence for original framed wall beneath plate, indicating that applied screen in E bay is original method of dividing chambers from open outshut. Late stone casing.

Fig 162

P Hb

WARLEY (Halifax and Sowerby Bridge)

(218) LOWER HOLLINS, NOS. 43, 45, 47, HOLLINS LANE (S/B) (SE 057238).
Timber-framed aisled house, late medieval. Linear, hearth-passage plan with open housebody heated by firehood and with dais canopy. Hipped roof over upper end of range. Expansion of upper end by addition of two-bay timber-framed wing projecting at front, mid 16th cent. Firehood replaced by stone stack with decorative fireplace, dated 1688 (Fig. 45). 19th-cent. casing in stone and subdivision into cottages; floor inserted over housebody.

(219) WESTFIELD (S/B) (SE 047246).
Timber-framed house, late medieval. Unaisled, hall-and-cross-wing plan. Stone casing and additions, 17th cent. (Pl. 147; Fig. 163). Housebody enlarged to give front wall flush with that of cross-wing and ceiled to give chamber over. Housebody and kitchen heated by firehoods. Cross-wing heated by stack on side wall; this appears to be combined with outshut projection, possibly designed to give garde-robe serving chamber. Dwelling area, forming large double-pile block, divided from lower end by passage. Lower end rebuilt in expanded form c.1800.

Fig 163

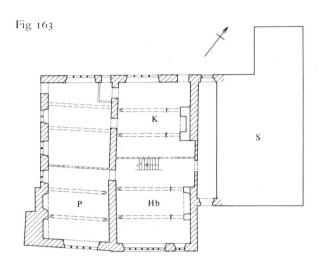

(220) THROSTLE NEST (S/B) (SE 046243).
Timber-framed house, late medieval. Unaisled, with hall-and-cross-wing, hearth-passage plan. Stone casing in 17th cent. with remodelling of 19th cent. Gilks 1972.

(221) MARE HILL (H) (SE 049272).
Stone house, 17th cent. and later, incorporating remains of earlier aisled house. Two bays of aisled range survive, with single post supporting arcade-plate. Mortice in post for bressumer of firehood.

(222) SOUTH IVES HOUSE (H) (SE 044257).
Stone house, 17th and 19th cent., incorporating remains of timber-framed house of late medieval date. Early house survives as single unaisled bay, with evidence for close-studded walls and window openings. Earliest stonework is cross-wing; main range cased at later date, taking form of linear range with outshut at rear; part of arcade structure between main span and outshut survives. 19th-cent. alterations include conversion to cottages.

(223) THE HOLLINS alias Murgatroyd (H), (SE 047257).
19th cent., but incorporating fireplace, dated 1632, from house of gentry Murgatroyd family. By 1695 house in possession of Oates family; inventory of goods of James Oates describes sophisticated style of life, with Withdraw-ing Room and Dining Room (BIHR, Nov. 1695).

(224) HOYLE HOUSE (S/B) (SE 053244).
Early 17th cent., commenced by John Ramsden; will of 1617 includes provision 'to my son John, all the timber prepared towards the building of the Hoyle House, and £60 towards paying £40 I owe to the daughters of John Denton and towards the furnishing of the house at Hoyle House, which I new built'. House survives only in part, with three-gabled facade. Lower end rebuilt 1885 after collapse, destroying evidence for original entry position. House was probably very large, with lower end giving entry and service/shop area, housebody in W of surviving cells, inner and outer parlours in projecting double-gabled block at E end. Sutcliffe 1918, 35.

(225) UPPER SALTONSTALL (H) (SE 035284).
Stone house, early 17th cent., incorporating remains of earlier timber-framed structure. Early house, probably of late medieval date, of hall-and-cross-wing form; close-studded side wall of wing remained intact until recently. Housebody open to roof even after casing in stone. Stone house had unusual plan, with entry directly into housebody next to cross-wing and at opposite end to fireplace. Addition of kitchen wing at rear. Later additions and alterations to lower end of house. Ruinous. WYAS, Calderdale, HAS/E; K/7–19; Sutcliffe 1903, 1921.

(226) LOWER HALL, Upper Saltonstall (H) (SE 034284).
Mid 17th cent.? Three-cell, double-pile plan, with main rooms to front and smaller rooms to rear. Hearth-passage entry. Doorway inscribed faintly: variously reported to read '1605' or '1633–5'., but plan and details suggest that first date might refer to earlier building phase, of which there are some remains in W gable wall. Sutcliffe, 1903, 1921.

(227) ROEBUCKS (S/B) (SE 053252).
1633. Hall-and-cross-wing, hearth-passage plan (Pl. 187; Fig. 64). Housebody heated by firehood originally; bres-sumer of fire-area still survives. Inventory of 1689 lists Housebody (used for cooking and dining), great parlor (a bedroom and sitting room), little parlor (a bedroom), Kitchen (used for baking and dairying), Buttery and Milk-house. Best room on first floor was Parlour Chamber, used as good quality bedroom and contrasting with house chamber, used to store meal, a riddle, a saddle and other items of small value. Lower end of house not listed in inventory, but inferior detail of windows suggests use as shop. Inventory of goods of Phebe Tattersall, BIHR, April 1689; Sutcliffe 1914.

(228) PEEL HOUSE (H) (SE 044268).
1598. Hall-and-cross-wing, hearth-passage plan (Pl. 146; Fig. 164). Very similar to (227) and probably functioned in same way. Best masonry is on facade, but restricted to area above passage; lower end of house has inferior details of masonry and windows. Parlour originally heated by stack on side wall; stack combined with outshut projection at SW corner, possibly designed to provide garderobe or stair. Housebody and kitchen both heated by firehoods; that in housebody replaced in 1691 by dated chimney stack. Sutcliffe 1920.

Fig 164

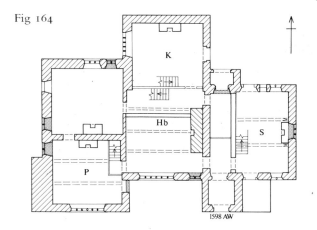

1598 AW

(229) HARTLEY ROYD (H) (SE 044262).
First half 17th cent. Hall-and-cross-wing, hearth-passage plan (Fig. 51). Outshut behind housebody, providing service rooms. Inferior details of masonry and windows in lower end suggests use as shop. No original access from suggested shop chamber to rest of first-floor rooms. Cross-wing largely rebuilt in 19th cent.

(230) GREYSTONES (S/B) (SE 043250).
Second half 17th cent. Probably linear plan originally, with storeyed kitchen wing behind housebody and outshut behind parlour (Pls 193, 197; Fig. 165). Hearth-passage entry. Kitchen stack provides fireplace and oven. Slightly raised window in rear wall of outshut probably indicates site of stair. Timber arcade structure between main span and rear rooms; some timbers reused from earlier framed structure. Lower end rebuilt in 18th cent. as cottages.

Fig 165

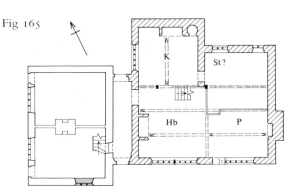

(231) OLDFIELD (H) (SE 049270).
1683. Linear plan with storeyed kitchen wing behind housebody and outshut behind end cells. Hearth-passage entry. Parlour possibly unheated originally. Kitchen heated by stack on gable wall.

(232) HAIGH HOUSE (H) (SE 050257).
1631. Three-cell linear plan with continuous outshut along rear (Pl. 145; Fig. 166). Hearth-passage entry. Better windows lighting housebody and parlour. Arcade structure between main span and outshut.

Fig 166

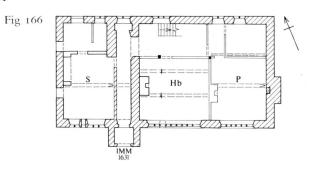

IMM
1631

(233) LITTLETOWN (H) (SE 051260).
Mid 17th cent. Similar to (232) but without porch (Fig. 167).

Fig 167

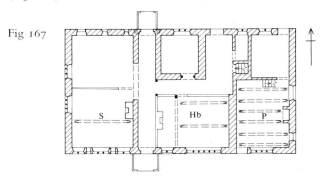

Similar houses are: OLD RIDING (H) (SE 046271); LOWER POPPLEWELLS (H) (SE 049252), of 1666 and lacking an outshut at the lower end; and BOOTHSTEADS (H) (SE 050263), a house with late 18th or early 19th-cent. masonry and windows, but with earlier plan form and many reused timbers.

(234) THE GRANGE (H) (SE 057247).
Second half 17th cent. Linear plan of three cells with continuous outshut along rear (Fig. 168). Hearth-passage entry. Long lower end with very large window, possibly unheated originally and probably used as shop, converted to parlour through addition of gable stack. Firehood in housebody replaced in 1711 by stack with dated fireplace. Later wing at rear.

Fig 168

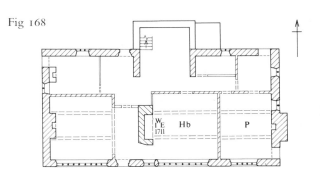

(235) 'GREENHILL', Lower Saltonstall (H) (SE 040283). 1711. Three-cell double-pile plan; hearth-passage entry (Fig. 169). Main rooms to front and smaller rooms to rear. Masonry in gable walls and existence of 19th-cent. windows lighting rear chambers suggest that house originally had continuous outshut, raised later to give two full storeys.

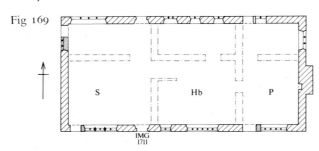

Fig 169

(236) WEST ROYD (S/B) (SE 045251). 1624?. Linear plan of three cells; hearth-passage entry (Fig. 170). Function of long lower room unclear; possibly shop or parlour. Inserted doorway in main front reuses datestone 'M M 1624'; its original position unknown. Plasterwork internally, said to date from 1630s, repeats initials of Martin Milnes, who paid 2s. copyhold rent in 1608 and grave rents in 1624 for West Royd. Bretton 1967, 122; WYAS, Calderdale, SH6/WM1.

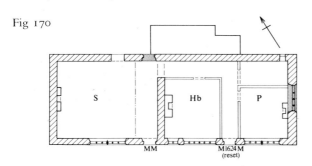

Fig 170

(237) LOWER SALTONSTALL (H) (SE 039283). Late 17th/early 18th cent. Linear plan of three cells with entry into housebody at opposite end to fireplace (Fig. 171). Fireplace is large and has spandrels carved with foliage motif. E room was probably heated parlour, with fireplace enlarged on modern conversion to kitchen. W room, lit by long window, probably shop originally, converted to kitchen in mid 18th cent. by addition of large

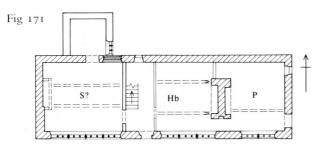

Fig 171

fireplace. First floor included unheated chamber over housebody and heated chamber over parlour; fireplace has bolection-moulded surround. Late additions include rear wing giving cellar on ground floor and chamber with taking-in door; wing probably added when shop converted to kitchen, and designed to provide a service room for kitchen and new 'industrial' area on first floor.

(238) SOUTH CLOUGH HEAD (H) (SE 053254). Second half 17th cent. Original house of two cells with outshut along rear (Fig. 172). Gable entry into housebody alongside firehood, unheated parlour to W. Timber arcade structure between main span and outshut. Added cell of late 17th cent. converted house to hearth-passage plan and provided kitchen heated by large stack on gable wall.

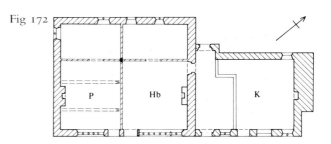

Fig 172

(239) WHITE BIRCH (H) (SE 044258). 1654. Two cells plus outshut (Fig. 173). Gable entry. Housebody heated by firehood; bressumer and heck-post survive. LOWER HEIGHTS (H) (SE 028292) has similar plan (Fig. 174).

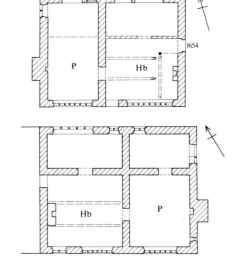

Fig 173

Fig 174

(240) LOWER GREEN EDGE (H) (SE 035285). c.1700. Two-cell plan, with gable entry alongside firehood heating housebody (Fig. 175). Parlour cell subdivided to give parlour to front and small service room to rear. 1731 addition of outshut, dated by inscription over doorways leading out of housebody. Passage divides house from

Fig 175

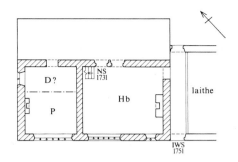

laithe of 19th-cent. date, but earlier roof line in gable wall of dwelling demonstrates existence of earlier building on site of laithe; evolution of house and laithe, therefore, recalls that of many longhouses.

(241) BANKHOUSE (H) (SE 040279).
1650. Earliest known standing laithe house (Pl. 269; Fig. 80). Dwelling part double-pile on plan, with housebody and parlour to front and smaller rooms to rear. Laithe has main doorway to threshing floor and smaller doorway to mistal. Smith 1963, 431–3 (I am grateful to Peter Smith for permission to redraw his plan which first appeared there); Sutcliffe 1913.

(242) LONG RIGGING (H) (SE 043276).
Late 17th/early 18th cent. Laithe house. Long linear range with continuous outshut along rear, giving aisle in area of laithe and service rooms in dwelling (Fig. 176). Timber arcade structure defines range of four-and-a-half bays. Gable entry to dwelling alongside firehood sited in half-bay at end of range. Disturbed masonry shows many alterations to original building.

Fig 176

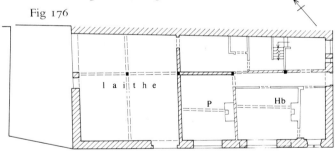

(243) BULLACE TREES (H) (SE 042276).
Stone house of 1851, built up against part of earlier lower range with single surviving cruck truss. Function of cruck building unclear. Masonry details suggest late 17th-cent. date, possibly representing casing of timber-framed structure.

Other houses showing 17th or early 18th-cent. work
YEW TREES (S/B) (SE 061244); NEWLANDS (H) (SE 053252); BLACKWALL (S/B) (SE 056242); UPPER LONG-BOTTOM (S/B) (SE 043243), with reset datestone '1641'; UPPER STUBBINS (H) (SE 046262); UPPER HEYS (H) (SE 029289), with datestones '1674' and '1716'; PEACE COTE (H) (SE 043280); SLODE (H) (SE 047281), with datestone '1662'; LOWER SHAW BOOTH (H) (SE 047276); MOOR-COCK INN (H) (SE 045291); WARLEY EDGE FARM (H) (SE

059252), with datestone '1633'; WARLEY EDGE CLOSE (H) (SE 058252); LITTLE HOLME HOUSE (H) (SE 040277); COOPER HOUSE (S/B) (SE 041245); WARLEY WOOD (S/B) (SE 048242); UPPER REAP HIRST (H) (SE 051275); CAUSEWAY FARM (H) (SE 048260); MAGSON HOUSE (S/B) (SE 040248); CLIFFE HILL (H) (SE 057246), with reset datestone '1704'; STOCK LANE HOUSE (H) (SE 063251), with storeyed porch dated 1633; BENNS (H) (SE 040269), with reset datestone '1692' and adjacent double-aisled barn; LITTLE PEEL HOUSE (H) (SE 044269); STONE FARM (H) (SE 047288).

Demolished houses of 17th or early 18th-cent. date.
DAISY BANK (S/B) (SE 044241), 1647 (WYAS, Calderdale, HAS/E: J/23–4); EAVES HOUSE (H) (SE 046266) (R C Cross / W J Smith collection, 91/1957); HIGH STREET, NO. 51, LUDDENDEN (H) (SE 041261), 1653 (NMR, Threatened Buildings Records) OLD HALL (site unknown; WYAS, Calderdale, HAS/E: J/43); Old Marsh (S/B) (approx site SE 058241); BACHE and a house in TUEL LANE (S/B), noted but now demolished (Kendall 1913b). The existence of two further houses may be inferred from the survival of substantial aisled barns and documentary references to yeoman occupiers of the sites. A five-bay, double aisled barn survives at HIGHER OLDFIELD (S/B) (SE 044245), and James Oldfield was recorded as paying rent for High Oldfield in 1624 (WYAS, Calderdale, SH4:T.Sy, 1624). At STEPS (062242) there exists a large double-aisled barn and, reset in a nearby barn, a datestone 'I D 1661', recording building activity by John Dearden (Tordoff 1979, 57).

(244) FOLD FARM (H) (SE 024295).
1831. Laithe house. Dwelling has single large living room and storage room at rear (Pl. 274; Fig. 83). Laithe lacks rear doorway, suggesting that threshing floor not required for this upland dairy or livestock farm. Mid 19th-cent. addition of wash house/scullery.

WARMFIELD CUM HEATH
(245) FRIESTON'S HOSPITAL (SE 360208).
1595. Built to provide accommodation for seven poor men. Rectangular building, aisled on three sides (Pls 285, 286; Fig. 85). Aisles or outshuts, with timber-framed dividing walls and arcade structure, divided to give seven cells, grouped around the core of the building, a lofty top-lit hall, the only heated room and the area used for communal living.

WILSDEN (Bingley)
(246) MYTHOLME (SE 089376).
Datestone of 1685 reset in rebuilt porch probably refers to construction of house. Tripartite, double-pile plan, with lobby-entry against stack heating housebody and kitchen (Pls 184, 229; Fig. 76). Parlour heated by fireplace in stack with blank arcaded panels on cap. Rear gave service rooms, possibly lesser parlours. Stair area lit by raised window in rear wall; present stair occupies only part of original stair area. Stair rose to landing on first floor, with doorways giving independent access to chambers.

(247) HALLAS OLD HALL (SE 075365).
Late 17th cent. Tripartite, double-pile plan, with lobby-entry against stack heating housebody and kitchen (Pl. 230; Fig. 65). Kitchen and parlour have independent doorways to exterior; style of doorways suggest that they are original. Smaller rooms at rear, with raised window in rear wall showing position of stair. Jefferys' map of 1775 shows 'Hallowes Hall' within Denholme Park, suggesting that by this date, and possibly originally, it was a gentleman's seat.

WINTERSETT
(248) PEAR TREE FARM (SE 384158).
Second half 17th cent. Two-and-a-half storeys, two-cell central lobby-entry plan (Pls 211, 214; Fig. 177). Outshut at rear has stair to first floor and steps down to cellar. Arcade structure of heavy scantling, reversed assembly. Top storey with lime-ash floor converted to pigeon loft in 18th cent. Wing added in late 18th cent. to provide kitchen.

Fig 177

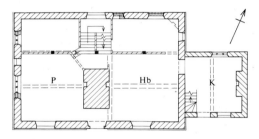

WOOLDALE (Holmfirth)
(249) TOTTIES HALL (SE 157082).
Reset '1684' datestone probably records date of construction. Hall-and-cross-wings plan, symmetrical facade (Pl. 156; Fig. 178). Central entry directly into hall. Inventory of 1728 aids interpretation. W wing probably provided *fore kitching* to S (for cooking, sitting and possibly dining), *back kitchin* and *kitching parlour* to N. *Great dining Room* and *Pantry* probably made up E wing. Stair in outshut projection behind hall. *Best Chamber*, probably over Great dining Room, was used as a superior first-floor sitting room. Other chambers for sleeping; *Garrett* used for sleeping and storage of crops. Jackson family; inventory shows that Henry Jackson was a substantial farmer, with no interest in textiles (BIRH, Feb. 1728).

Fig 178

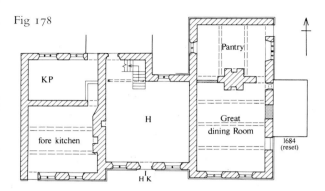

(250) LONGDENE, 43 Main Street (SE 152089).
1696. Two cells plus outshut, with end-lobby entry (Pl. 157; Fig. 68). Housebody heated by firehood originally. Parlour heated by original fireplace, sited in corner to allow windows on front and side walls. Joists in parlour have reed-mouldings on soffits. Timber arcade structure between main span and outshut.

WYKE
(251) HIGH FEARNLEY (SE 149247).
1698. Built as three-gabled house with off-centre doorway; original appearance recorded by Samuel Buck, *c.*1720. Inventory of 1727 shows sophisticated way of life, with comfortable *Drawing Room*, heated chambers used as bedrooms and private sitting rooms, heated *Masters Clossett*. Impressive stair area, decorated with '1 Mapp & 54 Black and White Cutts'. Mention of *kitchen staires*, showing divisions within household. Inventory of goods of Thomas Ramsden Esq., BIHR, Oct. 1727; Hall 1979, 157.

BIBLIOGRAPHY

AHIER, P., 1933, *The halls in the Colne valley* (Huddersfield).

AIRS, M., 1978, 'The designing of five East Anglian country houses, 1505–1637', *Architectural History* 21, 58–67.

ALCOCK, N.W., 1981, *Cruck Construction, an introduction and catalogue*, CBA Research Report 42.

AMBLER, L., 1913, *The old halls and manor houses of Yorkshire, with some examples of other houses built before the year 1700* (London).

ANDREWS, D.D. and MILNE, G. (eds), 1979, 'Domestic Settlement, 1; Areas 10 and 6' in Hurst, J.G. (ed), *Wharram: a study of settlement on the Yorkshire Wolds*, Soc Medieval Archaeol, Monograph Series 8.

ANON., 1902, *Index of wills in the York Registry, A.D. 1620–1627*, Yorkshire Archaeol Soc, Record Series 32.

ANON., 1905, *Index of wills in the York Registry, 1627–1636*, Yorkshire Archaeol Soc, Record Series 35.

ATKINSON, F. (ed), 1956, *Some aspects of the eighteenth century woollen and worsted trade in Halifax* (Halifax).

ATKINSON, F. and McDOWALL, R.W., 1967, 'Aisled Houses in the Halifax Area', *Antiq J* 47, 77–94.

BAILDON, W.P. and MARGERISON, S. (ed), 1904, 'The Calverley Charters . . . .', I, *Publ Thoresby Soc* 6.

BAINES, E., 1822, *A Directory of the County of York* (Leeds).

BANKS, W.S., 1871, *Walks in Yorkshire: Wakefield And Its Neighbourhood* (London and Wakefield).

BARBER, F., 1870, 'On the Book of Rates for the West Riding of the County of York', *Yorkshire Archaeol J* 1, 153–68.

BARLEY, M.W., 1961, *The English Farmhouse and Cottage* (London).

BARLEY, N.W., 1963, 'A glossary of names for rooms in houses of the sixteenth and seventeenth centuries' in Foster, I.Ll. and Alcock, L. (eds), *Culture and Environment, essays in honour of Sir Cyril Fox* (London), 479–501.

BARLEY, M.W., 1967, 'Rural housing in England' in Thirsk, J. (ed), *The Agrarian History of England and Wales, Volume IV, 1500–1640* (Cambridge), 696–766.

BARLEY, M.W., 1979, 'The Double Pile House', *Archaeol J* 136, 253–64.

BATTY, J., 1889, 'The Old Hall at East Ardsley' in Smith, W. (ed), *Old Yorkshire*, New Series 1, 16–18.

BAUMBER, M.L., 1977?, *A Pennine Community on the eve of The Industrial Revolution: Keighley and Haworth between 1660 and 1740* (Keighley).

BLACK, D.W., 1968, 'Harewood Castle (319457)', *Archaeol J* 125, 339–41.

BOWDEN, P.J., 1962, *The Wool Trade in Tudor and Stuart England*

BREARS, P.C.D., 1967, Excavations at Potovens, near Wakefield', *Post-Medieval Archaeol* 1, 3–43.

BREARS, P.C.D. (ed), 1972, *Yorkshire Probate Inventories 1542–1689*, Yorkshire Archaeol Soc, Record Series 134.

BREARS, P.C.D., 1978, 'Clarke Hall, Wakefield: Architectural innovations in 17th century West Yorkshire', *Post-Medieval Archaeol* 12, 86–100.

BREARS, P.C.D., 1982, 'Shibden Hall: the early development of an important Halifax house', *Old West Riding* 3, 15–21.

BRETTON, R., 1942, 'Ashday in Southowram', *Trans Halifax Antiq Soc*, 1942, 75–94.

BRETTON, R., 1967, 'Seventeenth Century Plasterwork', *Trans Halifax Antiq Soc*, 115–22.

BROWN, W. (ed), 1909, *Yorkshire Deeds I*, Yorkshire Archaeol Soc, Record Series 39.

BROWN, W. (ed), 1922, *Yorkshire Deeds III*, Yorkshire Archaeol Soc, Record Series 63.

BRUNSKILL, R.W., 1971, *Illustrated Handbook of Vernacular Architecture* (London).

CADMAN, H.A., 1930, *Gomersal Past and Present* (Leeds).

CAFFYN, L., forthcoming, *Workers' housing in West Yorkshire, 1750–1920*.

CAMDEN, W., 1610, *Britain, newly translated into English by Philemon Holland* (London).

CAMPBELL, C., 1715–25, *Vitruvius Britannicus* Vols I–III (London).

CAMPBELL, M., 1967, *The English Yeoman under Elizabeth and the early Stuarts* (New Haven).

CARUS-WILSON, E.M., 1929, 'The Aulnage Accounts: a criticism', *Econ Hist Rev* 2, 114–23.

CHADWICK, S.J., 1911, 'The Dewsbury Moot Hall', *Yorkshire Archaeol J* 21, 345–51.

CHARLESWORTH, J. (ed), 1939, *Wakefield Manor Book, 1709*, Yorkshire Archaeol Soc, Record Series 101.

CITY OF BRADFORD ART GALLERIES AND MUSEUMS, 1978, *A Guide to Bolling Hall* (4th ed., Bradford).

CLARKE, D. and LUNN, N., 1964, 'The small barn at Upper Oldfield', *Huddersfield Dist Archaeol Soc Bull* 11.

CLAY, J.W. (ed), 1890, *Abstracts of Yorkshire Wills in the time of the Commonwealth, at Somerset House, London, chiefly illustrative of Sir William Dugdale's visitation of Yorkshire in 1665–6*, Yorkshire Archaeol Soc, Record Series 9.

CLAY, J.W. and LISTER, J., 1900, 'Autobiography of Sir John Savile of Methley, Knight, Baron of the Exchequer, 1546–1607', *Yorkshire Archaeol J* 15, 420–27.

CLIFFE, J.T., 1969, *The Yorkshire Gentry from the Reformation to the Civil War* (London).

COLVIN, H., 1978, *A Biographical Dictionary of British Architects 1600–1840* (London).

CROSSLEY, E.W. (ed), 1920, *Wills in the York Registry, 1666–1672*, Yorkshire Archaeol Soc, Record Series 60.

CROSSLEY, E.W., 1920a, 'A Templenewsam inventory, 1565', *Yorkshire Archaeol J* 25, 91–100.

CRUMP, W.B., 1945, 'Methley Hall and its builders', *Publ Thoresby Soc* 37, 313–32.

CUDWORTH, W., 1888, 'The Thornton Valley', *Bradford Antiq* 1, 10–16.

DANAHER, K., 1975, *Ireland's vernacular architecture* (Cork).

DARBYSHIRE, H.S. and LUMB, G.D., 1937, 'The History of Methley', *Publ Thoresby Soc* 35 (for 1934).

DEFOE, D., 1971, *A Tour through the Whole Island of Great Britain*, Rogers P. (ed), (Harmondsworth).

DICKENSON, M., 1974, 'The West Riding woollen and worsted industries, 1689–1770, an analysis of probate inventories and insurance policies' (unpublished Ph D dissertation, University of Nottingham).

ELLIS, A.S. (ed), 1882, 'Dodsworth's Yorkshire Notes (Agbrigg)', *Yorkshire Archaeol J* 7, 119–41, 259–83, 401–28.

ELLIS, M.J., 1962, 'A Study in the manorial history of Halifax parish in the sixteenth and early seventeenth centuries', *Yorkshire Archaeol J* 40, 250–64, 420–42.

EMPSALL, T.T., 1895, 'Lees Hall, Thornhill', *Bradford Antiq* 2, 95–6.

EVERITT, A., 1967, 'Farm Labourers' in Thirsk J. (ed), *The Agrarian History of England and Wales, Volume IV, 1500–1640* (Cambridge), 396–465.

EVERITT, A., 1969, *The Local Community and the Great Rebellion*, Historical Assoc Pamphlet G.70 (London).

FAULKNER, P.A., 1958, 'Domestic planning from the twelfth to the fourteenth centuries', *Archaeol J* 115, 150–83.

FAULL, M.L. and MOORHOUSE, S.A. (eds), 1981, *West Yorkshire: an archaeological survey to A.D. 1500*, 4 vols (Wakefield).

FAWCETT, R., 1972, 'The early Tudor house in the light of recent excavations', *Leeds Art Calendar* 70, 5–12.

FORSTER, G.C.F., 1967, 'From the foundation of the borough to the eve of the Industrial Revolution' in Beresford, M.W. and Jones, G.R.J. (eds), *Leeds and its Region* (Leeds), 131–45.

FORSTER, G.C.F., 1973, *The East Riding Justices of the Peace in the seventeenth century*, East Yorks Local History Series 30 (York).

FORSTER, G.C.F., 1975, 'The North Riding Justices and their Sessions, 1603–1625', *Northern Hist* 10, 102–25.

FORSTER, G.C.F., 1976, 'Faction and county government in early-Stuart Yorkshire', *Northern Hist* 11, 70–86.

FORSTER, G.C.F., 1976a, 'County government in Yorkshire during the Interregnum', *Northern Hist* 12, 84–104.

FOSTER, A., 1954, 'Oakwell Hall, Birstall, inventory of goods 1611', *Publ Thoresby Soc*, Miscellany 12, 114–16.

GILBERT, C.G., 1963, 'Light on Sir Arthur Ingram's reconstruction of Temple Newsam, 1622–1638', *Leeds Arts Calendar* 61, 6–12.

GILES, C.P., 1981, 'New Hall, Elland; The Story of a Pennine gentry house from c.1490 to the Mid 19th century', *Old West Riding* 1, no. 2, 1–11.

GILKS, J.A., 1971, 'Halifax W.R., SE 083268' [White Hall, Ovenden], *Yorkshire Archaeol J* 43, 196.

GILKS, J.A., 1972a, 'Triangle, W.R. (SE 049229)', *Yorkshire Archaeol J* 44, 223.

GILKS, J.A., 1972b, 'Halifax, W.R. (SE 047243)', [Throstle Nest], *Yorkshire Archaeol J* 44, 222.

GILKS, J.A., 1972c, [Lower High Sunderland], *Post-Medieval Archaeol* 6, 216–17.

GILKS, J.A., 1974, 'Boothtown Hall: a fifteenth-century house in the Parish of Halifax', *Yorkshire Archaeol J* 46, 53–81.

GILKS, J.A., 1974a, 'Yorkshire, West Riding: Halifax, Ovenden Wood (SE 068264)' [Long Can], *Medieval Archaeol* 17, 178.

GILKS, J.A., 1977, 'Northowram (SE 103263)', *Yorkshire Archaeol J* 49, 16.

GIROUARD, M. 1966, *Robert Smythson and the Architecture of the Elizabethan Era* (London).

GIROUARD, M., 1978, *Life in the English country house: a social and architectural history* (London).

GOODER, A. (ed), 1938, *Parliamentary Representation of Yorkshire, 2*, Yorkshire Archaeol Soc, Record Series 96.

GUNTHER, R.T., 1928, *The architecture of Sir Roger Pratt . . . . from his Note-books* (Oxford).

HALL, I. (ed), 1979, *Samuel Buck's Yorkshire Sketchbook* (Wakefield).

HALL, I., forthcoming, *John Carr, a study of a northern practice*.

HALL, I. and HALL, E., 1975, *Heath: an architectural description* (Heath).

HANSON, T.W., 1934, *A Short History of Shibden Hall* (Halifax).

HARRISON, B.J.D. and HUTTON, B., 1984, *Vernacular houses in North Yorkshire and Cleveland* (Edinburgh).

HEAPE, R., 1926, *Inscribed and dated stones and sundials in and adjoining the ancient parish of Rochdale* (Cambridge).

HEATON, H., 1920, *The Yorkshire woollen and worsted industries* (Oxford).

HODGSON, H.R., 1933, 'Quaker Sketches', *Bradford Antiq* 7 (New Series 5), 249–55.

HUNTER, J., 1851, *Antiquarian Notices of Lupset, The Heath, Sharlston and Ackton*.

HUSSEY, C., 1943, 'East Riddlesden Hall, Yorkshire', *Country Life* 93, 440–43.

HUSSEY, C., 1955, *English Country Houses: Early Georgian, 1715–1760* (London).

HUSSEY, C., 1957, *English Country Houses open to the public* (3rd edition, London).

HUTTON, B., 1973, 'Timber-framed houses in the Vale of York', *Medieval Archaeol* 17, 87–99.

HUTTON, B., 1977, 'Rebuilding in Yorkshire: the evidence of inscribed dates', *Vernacular Architect* 8, 819–24.

HUTTON, K., 1974, 'Cheesecake Hall, Oulton, West Riding', *Yorkshire Archaeol J* 46, 82–6.

JARRETT, M.G. and WRATHMELL, S., 1977, 'Sixteenth and Seventeenth Century farmsteads: West Whelpington, Northumberland', *Agr Hist Review* 25, 108–19.

JENNINGS, B., forthcoming, *Pennine Valley: a history of Upper Calderdale*

JONES, S.R., 1974, 'Ancient domestic buildings and their roofs', *Archaeol J* 131, 309–13.

KENDALL, H.P., 1905, 'Ancient Halls of Norland', *Trans Halifax Antiq Soc*, 93–111.

KENDALL, H.P., 1906, 'Wood Lane Hall', *Trans Halifax Antiq Soc*, 124–34.

KENDALL, H.P., 1906a, 'Famous Sowerby Mansions, White Windows', *Trans Halifax Antiq Soc*, 105–15.

KENDALL, H.P., 1911, 'Norland Hall', *Trans Halifax Antiq Soc*, 1–35.

KENDALL, H.P., 1912, Copy of Extracts from Halifax Wills in York Minster made by Edward Johnson Walker of Halifax, WYAS, Yorkshire Archaeol Soc MS 624.

KENDALL, H.P., 1913, 'Binroyd in Norland', *Trans Halifax Antiq Soc*, 179–92.

KENDALL, H.P., 1913a, 'The Harper Royds', *Trans Halifax Antiq Soc*, 159–66.

KENDALL, H.P., 1913b, 'Fields', *Trans Halifax Antiq Soc*, 133–7.

KENDALL, H.P., 1913c, 'Sowerby Croft', *Trans Halifax Antiq Soc*, 141–55.

KENDALL, H.P., 1914, 'Bankhouse in Skircoat', *Trans Halifax Antiq Soc*, 99–109.

KENDALL, H.P., 1925, 'Some old Skircoat homesteads', *Trans Halifax Antiq Soc*, 1–56.

KITSON, S.D., 1910, 'Carr of York', *J Roy Inst British Architects*, 17, 241–61.

KITSON, S., 1913, 'A lesser country house of the fourteenth century, Kiddal Hall, Barwick-in-Elmet, Yorkshire', *Country Life* 63.

KITSON, S.D. and PAWSON, E.D., 1927, *Temple Newsam Guide* (Leeds).

LEACH, P., forthcoming, *James Paine*.

LEES-MILNE, J., 1970, *English Country Houses: Baroque, 1685–1715* (London).

LINSTRUM, D., 1978, *West Yorkshire, Architects and Architecture* (London).

LISTER, J., 1888, 'Musters, West Riding of York, Temp xiii and xviii, Hen 8 (Chapter House Books A2/23)', *Bradford Antiq* 1, 218–24.

LISTER, J., 1895, 'Chapter House Records', *Bradford Antiq* 2, 140.

LISTER, J., 1905, 'Excursion to Shelf', *Trans Halifax Antique Soc*, 231–49.

LISTER, J., 1907, 'High Sunderland', *Trans Halifax Antiq Soc*, 113–38.

LISTER, J., 1926, 'History of Shibden Hall', *Trans Halifax Antiq Soc*, 1–11.

LISTER, J. and BROWN, W., 1902, 'Seventeenth-Century Builders' Contracts', *Yorkshire Archaeol J* 16, 108–10.

MACHIN, R., 1977, 'The Great Rebuilding: a Re-assessment', *Past and Present* 77, 33–56.

MACHIN, R., 1978, *The Houses of Yetminster* (London).

MANBY, T.G., 1964, 'Fletcher House, Almondbury: A late-medieval timber-framed building near Huddersfield', *Yorkshire Archaeol J* 41, 297–305.

MANBY, T.G., 1972, 'Lees Hall, Thornhill, a medieval timber-framed building in the West Riding of Yorkshire', *Yorkshire Archaeol J* 43, 112–27.

MARGERISON, S. (ed), 1886, 'Memorandum Book of Sir Walter Calverley, bart., A.D. 1663–1748', *Publ Surtees Soc* 77.

MARKHAM, G., 1979, *Woolley Hall: the historical development of a country house* (Wakefield Historical Publ 3, Wakefield).

MAYES, P. and BUTLER, L.A.S., 1983, *Sandal Castle Excavations 1963–1973 – a detailed archaeological report* (Wakefield).

MEADS, D.M. (ed), 1930, *Diary of Lady Margaret Hoby, 1599–1605* (London).

MERCER, E., 1954, 'The Houses of the Gentry', *Past and Present* 54, 11–32.

MERCER, E., 1975, *English Vernacular Houses: a study of traditional farmhouses and cottages* (London).

MERCER, E., 1980, Review of Machin 1978, *Antiq J* 60, 408–9.

MEIRION-JONES, G.I., 1982, *The Vernacular Architecture of Brittany* (Edinburgh).

MICHELMORE, D.J.H., 1977, ' Elland Hall (SE 106214)' *Medieval Archaeol* 22, 182–4.

MICHELMORE, D.J.H., 1978, 'Hepworth, Dean Head Farm (SE 15750600)', *Yorkshire Archaeol J* 50, 17.

MICHELMORE, D.J.H., 1981, 'Township Gazetteer' in Faull and Moorhouse 1981, 294–579.

MICHELMORE, D.J.H., 1981a, 'Township and Tenure' in Faull and Moorhouse 1981, 231–64.

MICHELMORE, D.J.H., 1983, 'Interpretation of the buildings of the timber phase' in Mayes and Butler 1983, 73–5.

MICHELMORE, D.J.H., 1983a, 'The collar from the outer moat' in Mayes and Butler 1983, 303–4.

MICHELMORE, D.J.H. and SUGDEN, J., 1980, 'Horbury Hall, West Yorkshire', *Archaeol J* 131, 40–43.

MOORHOUSE, S.A., 1981, 'Rural Houses' in Faull and Moorhouse 1981, 802–21.

MOORHOUSE, S.A., 1981a, 'Settlements' in Faull and Moorhouse 1981, 585–613.

MOORHOUSE, S.A., 1981b, 'Field Systems' in Faull and Moorhouse 1981, 656–80.

MOORHOUSE, S.A., 1983, 'A semi-circular firecover from the Tyler Hill Kilns, Canterbury', *Medieval Ceramics* 7, 101–7.

MOREHOUSE, H.J., 1861, *History of the Parish of Kirkheaton* (Huddersfield).

MOREHOUSE, H.J., 1874, *Extracts from the diary of the Reverend Robert Meeke* (Huddersfield).

NEALE, J.P., 1818–23, *Views of the seats of noblemen and gentlemen in England, Wales, Scotland and Ireland, from drawings by J.P. Neale*, 6 vols (London) [esp vol 5, which includes Yorkshire].

NEWELL, A., 1916, 'Eastwood and the Eastwood family', *Trans Halifax Antiq Soc*, 145–67.

NEWTON, G.D., 1976, 'Single-storey cottages in West Yorkshire', *Folk Life* 14, 65–74.

NUTTALL, B., 1963, *A History of Thornhill* (Ossett).

OGDEN, J.H., 1903, 'Three Old Homesteads: Broadbottom, Follingroyd and Mayroyd', *Trans Halifax Antiq Soc*. [no pagination].

OGDEN J.H., 1905, 'Antiquarians at Ovenden', *Trans Halifax Antiq Soc*, 213–30.

OSWALD, A., 1938, 'Ledston Hall', *Country Life* 84, 556–61, 580–85.

PACEY, A.J., 1964, 'Elland buildings; notes on a survey of vernacular architecture in the urban district of Elland' (unpublished).

PAINE, J., 1967, *Plans, elevations and sections of noblemen's and gentlemen's houses* (2 vols in one, Gregg Press reprint of original edition in 2 vols, London, 1767, 1783).

PARSONS, D. (ed), 1836, *The Diary of Sir Henry Slingsby of Scriven, Bart.* (London).

PEARSON, M., 1898, *Northowram, its history and antiquities* (Halifax).

PEARSON, M., 1906, 'Ancient Shibden Mansions', *Trans Halifax Antiq Soc*, 141–64.

PEEL, F., 1893, *Spen Valley past and present* (Heckmondwike).

PETERS, J.E.C., 1969, *The development of farm buildings in Western Lowland Staffordshire up to 1880* (Manchester).

PEVSNER, N., 1966, *The Buildings of England: Yorkshire, The North Riding* (Harmondsworth).

PEVSNER, N., 1967, *The Buildings of England: Yorkshire, The West Riding*, 2nd ed. (Harmondsworth).

PEVSNER, N., 1969, *The Buildings of England: Lancashire, the industrial and commercial south* (Harmondsworth).

PEVSNER, N., 1972, *The Buildings of England: Yorkshire, York and the East Riding* (Harmondsworth).

PICKLES, M.F., 1981, 'Agrarian Society and Wealth in mid-Wharfedale, 1664–1743', *Yorkshire Archaeol J* 53, 63–78.

PLATT, G.M. and MORKILL, J.W., 1892, *Records of the parish of Whitkirk* (Leeds).

PRESTON, W.E. (ed), 1929, *Wills proved in the Court of the Manor of Crossley, Bingley, Cottingley, and Pudsey in Co. York, with Inventories and Abstracts of Bonds* (Bradford).

PRESTON, W.E., 1935, 'A Sixteenth-Century Account Roll of the Building of a House at Chevet', *Yorkshire Archaeol J* 32, 326–30.

PURDY, J.D., 1975, 'The Hearth Tax Returns from Yorkshire' (unpublished M.Phil thesis, University of Leeds).

RCHM(E), 1910, *An inventory of the historical monuments in Hertfordshire* (London).

RCHM(E), 1936, *An inventory of the historical monuments in Westmorland* (London).

RCHM(E), 1963, *Monuments threatened or destroyed: a select list* (London).

RCHM(E), 1968, *An inventory of the historical monuments in the County of Cambridge, Volume I, West Cambridgeshire* (London).

RCHM(E), 1972, *An inventory of the historical monuments in the City of York, Volume III, South-West of the Ouse* (London).

RCHM(E), 1981, *An inventory of the historical monuments in the City of York, Volume V, The Central Area* (London).

RCHM(E), forthcoming (a), *Rural Houses of the Lancashire Pennines*.

RCHM(E), forthcoming (b), *The houses of the North York Moors*.

RCHM(Wales), 1981, *An inventory of the Ancient Monuments in Glamorgan, Volume IV, Domestic Architecture from the Reformation to the Industrial Revolution, Part I: The Greater Houses* (Cardiff).

REDMONDS, G., 1982, *The heirs of Woodsome* (Huddersfield).

ROBERTS, D.L., 1974, 'The vernacular building of Lincolnshire', *Archaeol J* 131, 298–308.

ROBERTSHAW, W., 1936, 'The Settlement of Ryecroft, in Tong', *Bradford Antiq* 8, 141–58.

ROEBUCK, P., 1980, *Yorkshire Baronets 1640–1760: families, estates, and fortunes* (Oxford).

RYDER, P.F., 1979, *Timber-framed buildings in South Yorkshire* (Barnsley).

RYDER, P.F., 1980, 'Vernacular buildings in South Yorkshire', *Archaeol J* 137, 377–85.

RYDER, P.F., 1982, *Medieval Buildings of Yorkshire* (Ashbourne).

SELLERS, M., 1912, 'Textile Industries' in Page, W. (ed), *Victoria County History of Yorkshire* 2, 406–29.

SENIOR, A., 1950, 'Fold Farm, Illingworth', *Trans Halifax Antiq Soc*, 81–3.

SHEERAN, G., forthcoming, *Good houses, built of stone* (Hebden Bridge).

SMITH, J.T., 1974, 'The early development of timber buildings, the passing-brace and reversed assembly', *Archaeol J* 131, 238–63.

SMITH, J.T., 1975, 'Cruck distributions: an interpretation of some recent maps', *Vernacular Architect* 6, 3–18.

SMITH, P., 1963, 'The long-house and the laithe-house: a study of the house-and-byre homestead in Wales and the West Riding' in Foster, I.Ll. and Alcock, L. (ed), *Culture and Environment: essays in honour of Sir Cyril Fox* (London), 415–37.

SMITH, P., 1975, *Houses of the Welsh Countryside: a study in historical geography* (London).

SMITH, P., 1981, 'Some reflections on the development of the centrally-planned house' in Detsicas, A. (ed), *Collectanea Historica: Essays in Memory of Stuart Rigold* (Maidstone), 182–212.

SMITH, P., 1984, 'Hall, Tower and Church; some themes and sites reconsidered' in Davies, R.R., et al. (eds), *Welsh Society and Nationhood; Historical essays presented to Glanmore Williams*, (Cardiff), 122–60.

SMITH, R.B., 1962, 'A Study of landed income and social structure in the West Riding of Yorkshire, 1535–1546' (unpublished PhD thesis, University of Leeds).

SMITH R.B., 1970, *Land and politics in the England of Henry VIII: the West Riding of Yorkshire 1530–46* (Oxford).

STELL, C.F., 1960, 'Vernacular architecture in a Pennine community' (Unpublished MA thesis, Univesity of Liverpool).

STELL, C.F., 1965, 'Pennine houses: an introduction', *Folk Life* 3, 5–24.

STONE, L. and STONE, J.C.F., 1972, 'Country Houses and their owners in Hertfordshire, 1540–1879' in Aydelotte, W.O. (ed), *The dimensions of quantitative research in History* (London), 56–123.

STONE, L., 1979, *The family, sex and marriage in England, 1500–1800* (London).

SUMMERSON, J., 1977, *Architecture in Britain, 1530 to 1830*, 6th ed. (Harmondsworth).

SUMNER, C., 1978, *A History of Hightown for its people* (Cleckheaton).

SUTCLIFFE, T., 1903, 'Saltonstall, Warley', *Trans Halifax Antiq Soc*, May [no pagination].

SUTCLIFFE, T., 1913, 'Bankhouse and the Brooksbanks', *Trans Halifax Antiq Soc*, 243–54.

SUTCLIFFE, T., 1914, 'Old Warley Houses, The Roebucks', *Trans Halifax Antiq Soc*, 225–36.

SUTCLIFFE, T., 1918, 'Some old Warley houses', *Trans Halifax Antiq Soc*, 33–67.

SUTCLIFFE, T., 1920, 'Peel House in Warley', *Trans Halifax Antiq Soc*, 53–62.

SUTCLIFFE, T., 1921, 'Saltonstall in Warley', *Trans Halifax Antiq Soc*, 109–28.

SUTCLIFFE, T., 1928, 'A tour in Midgley', *Trans Halifax Antiq Soc*, 113–57.

THIRSK, J., 1961, 'Industries in the Countryside' in Fisher, F.J. (ed), *Essays in the economic and social history of Tudor and Stuart England.* (Cambridge).

THORNES, R., 1981, *West Yorkshire: 'a noble scene of industry'. The development of the county 1500–1830* (Wakefield).

TIPPING, H.A., 1937, *English Homes: medieval and early-Tudor 1066–1558* (London).

TORDOFF, C.H., 1979, 'The Warley Story' (unpublished; copy in Reference Library, Calderdale Central Library, Halifax).

TRIGG, W.B., 1942, 'Holdsworth House', *Trans Halifax Antiq Soc*, 29–44.

TRIGG, W.B., 1946, 'Scout Hall', *Trans Halifax Antiq Soc*, 37–47.

TURNER, J.H., 1881–5, *The Reverend Oliver Heywood, B.A., 1630–1702: his autobiography, diaries, anecdotes and event books* (4 vols, Brighouse).

UNWIN, R.W., 1981, 'Tradition and transition: market towns of the Vale of York, 1660–1830', *Northern Hist* 17, 72–116.

UPTON, A.F., 1961, *Sir Arthur Ingram, c.1565–1642: A study of the origins of an English landed family* (London).

WADDINGTON, G.W., 1891, 'The Ellis family, and description of their manor hall at Kiddal, parish of Barwick-in-Elmet, County of York', *Publ Thoresby Soc* 2, 55–61.

WALKER, J.W., 1939, *Wakefield; its history and people*, 2nd ed., 2 vols (Wakefield).

WALTON, J., 1948, 'Cruck-framed buildings in Yorkshire', *Yorkshire Archaeol J* 37, 49–66.

WALTON, J., 1955, *Early timbered buildings of the Huddersfield district* (Huddersfield).

WATSON, J., 1775, *The history of antiquities of the parish of Halifax* (reprinted, Manchester 1973).

WEAVER, O.J., 1977, 'Heath Old Hall, Yorkshire' in Apted, M.R., Gilyard-Beer, R. and Saunders, A.D. (eds), *Ancient Monuments and their interpretation* (London), 285–301.

WESTERDALE, W., 1983, 'The houses of Shibden Dale' (unpublished MA thesis, University of Manchester School of Architecture and Planning).

WHITAKER, T.D., 1816, *Loidis and Elmete* (Leeds).

WHITAKER, T.D. (ed), 1816a, *Thoresby, R., Ducatus Leodiensis*, 2nd ed. (Leeds).

WHITING, C.E. (ed), 1951, 'The Diary of Arthur Jessop (1682–1751)' in *Two Yorkshire Diaries*, Yorkshire Archaeol Soc, Record Series 117.

WILSON, R.G., 1971, *Gentlemen Merchants, The Merchant Community in Leeds, 1700–1830* (Manchester).

WOLEDGE, G., 1978, *Oakwell Hall* (Huddersfield).

WOOD, B., 1923, *Official Handbook of the Bolling Hall Museum*, 4th ed. (Bradford).

WOOD, M., 1965, *The English Medieval House* (London).

WOODFIELD, P., 1981, 'The larger medieval houses of Northamptonshire', *Northamptonshire Archaeology* 16, 153–95.

WOOD-JONES, R.B., 1961, 'Notes and Communications', *Ancient Monuments Soc Trans*, New Series 9, 7–14.

WOOD-JONES, R.B., 1963, *Traditional Domestic Architecture of the Banbury Region* (Manchester).

WOOLFE, J., and GANDON, J., 1767, *Vitruvius Britannicus* IV.

WRATHMELL, S., 1972, 'Earlsheaton Hall: A Sixteenth Century timber-framed building near Dewsbury', *Yorkshire Archaeol J* 44, 173–7.

WRIGHT, T. (ed), 1842, *The autobiography of Joseph Lister*.

YARWOOD, R.E., 1981, 'The distribution of wealth' in Faull and Moorhouse 1981, 290–3.

YARWOOD, R.E., 1981a, 'Temple Newsam, Colton (SE 365325)', *Yorkshire Archaeol J* 53, 141–2.

SUBJECT INDEX

INDEX OF PERSONS AND PLACES

Map 6 West Yorkshire; townships

The grid references indicate the approximate centre of each township. All are in 100 km square SE except those beginning with the figure 9, which are in square SD. The stippled areas show the centres of the five principal towns.

Aberford 4238
Ackton 4123
Ackworth 4517
Addingham 0749
Adel cum Eccup 2640
Allerton 1134
Allerton Bywater 4128
Almondbury 1514
Altofts 3723
Alverthorpe with Thornes 3120
Alwoodley 2940
Armley 2633
Arthington 2745
Austhorpe 3734
Austonley 1007
Badsworth 4515
Baildon 0539
Bardsey cum Rigton 3643
Barkisland 0619
Barwick in Elmet 3937
Batley 2324
Beeston 2830
Bingley 1039
Bolton 1635
Bowling 1731
Bradford 1733
Bramham cum Oglethorpe 4242
Bramhope 2443
Bramley 2435
Burley in Wharfedale 1545
Calverley with Farsley 2036
Carleton 4620
Carlton 2243
Cartworth 1306
Castleford 4225
Chapel Allerton 3038
Chevet 3415
Churwell 2729

Clayton 1131
Clayton West 2610
Cleckheaton 1726
Clifford cum Boston 4245
Clifton 1623
Cliviger 9026
Collingham 3845
Crigglestone 3116
Crofton 3718
Cumberworth 2109
Cumberworth Half 2310
Dalton 1617
Darrington 4820
Denby 2308
Dewsbury 2321
Drighlington 2228
Dunkeswick 3047
East Ardsley 3025
East Hardwick 4618
East Keswick 3545
Eccleshill 1836
Elland cum Greetland 0921
Emley 2413
Erringden 9823
Esholt 1840
Farnley 2531
Farnley Tyas 1613
Featherstone 4321
Ferry Fryston 4625
Fixby 1219
Flockton 2314
Foulby 4017
Fulstone 1708
Garforth 4033
Gildersome 2428
Glass Houghton 4324
Golcar 0915
Gomersal 2126

Great and Little Preston 3929
Guiseley 1942
Halifax 0825
Harewood 3245
Hartshead 1822
Havercroft with Cold Hiendley 3713
Hawksworth 1542
Haworth 0235
Headingley cum Burley 2736
Heaton 1335
Heckmondwike 2124
Hemsworth 4214
Heptonstall 9430
Hepworth 1606
Hessle 4217
Hill Top 4218
Hipperholme with Brighouse 1325
Holbeck 2932
Holme 1006
Honley 1310
Horbury 2919
Horsforth 2338
Horton 1431
Huddersfield 1519
Hunslet 3031
Hunsworth 1928
Idle 1738
Ilkley 1147
Keighley 0240
Kildwick 0146
Kippax 4130
Kirkburton 2013
Kirkheaton 1818
Knottingley 5023
Langfield 9523
Ledsham 4529
Ledston 4329
Leeds 3034